Hello! HTML5 & CSS3

D0912286

Hello! HTML5 & CSS3

A user-friendly reference guide

Rob Crowther

MANNING

SHELTER ISLAND

Manning Publications Co.
20 Baldwin Road
PO Box 261
Shelter Island, NY 11964

Development editor: Cynthia Kane
Copyeditor: Tiffany Taylor
Technical proofreader: Adam London
Typesetter: Marija Tudor
Cover designer: Marija Tudor

ISBN: 9781935182894

Printed in the United States of America
1 2 3 4 5 6 7 8 9 10 – MAL – 17 16 15 14 13 12

brief contents

contents

preface

I first saw the web in my final year of university in 1993-94. All the cool kids (bear in mind, this was a Computer Science department) were playing with a strange bit of software called Mosaic on their Sun 4 workstations. I had some fun with it and created my first web page (a guide to Edinburgh pubs), but it didn't strike me as anything more than a curiosity and it certainly didn't measure up to "proper" document preparation formats like LaTeX. It's not the first time I've been completely wrong about technology—and it won't be the last!

I went back to experimenting with websites in 1997, a full-on blinking, scrolling plethora of tacky animated gifs which is thankfully long lost. As I learned more about the web I stopped seeing it as a poor-quality typesetting system and started seeing it as a great equalizer. Not only was *visiting* a web page something anyone could do, *making* a web page was also something anyone could do. Since then I've been on a mission, not only to learn as much as I can about making web pages, but to help others learn how to make them, and this book is a natural extension of that mission.

HTML5 and CSS3 are fascinating to me not only because of their technical features, but because they represent growth in the web platform after several years of stagnation. The more the web can do, the more content can be shared across the world by ordinary people like you and me.

acknowledgments

I'd like to thank my Mum for inspiring my lifelong love of books, my Dad for inspiring my lifelong love of computers, and my brother for under-writing my move to London and giving me a chance to get a full-time web development job. Also sincere thanks to the rest of my family for being there for me over the years.

A big thank you to Boyd Gilchrist who, while we were both at university, patiently answered such questions as "What's this web browser thing, then?" and "HTML, what the fudge is that?" among many others I couldn't be bothered to research on my own in the pre-Google era. Also, thanks to my other friends at university, especially Graham Barr who not only put up with living with me for several years but also managed to keep in touch long enough to read drafts of several chapters in this book.

I'd like to thank everyone at Net Resources, especially my tutor John Ayscough; Richard O'Connor for giving me the subsequent placement which was my first commercial web development experience; and Esther Kuperij for talking him into it. My adventures in web standards have been greatly aided by the vibrant London web developer community, particu-larly the London Web Standards and London Web Meetup groups.

Troy Mott at Manning is the person who originally got me involved with this book project, though at times I'm not sure whether to blame him or thank him for that! But Troy and all the other people I've worked with at Manning have been massively supportive throughout the writing and production processes. I'd especially like to thank Katharine Osborne, Candace Gillhoolley, Cynthia Kane, Bert Bates, Katie Tennant, Tiffany

Taylor, Martin Murtonen, Janet Vail, Mary Piergies, and of course Marjan Bace, for making this book what it is.

Many people reviewed the manuscript at various stages of its development, and I would like to thank all the MEAP readers who provided comments in the forum as well as the following peer reviewers for their invaluable feedback: 'Anil' Radhakrishna, Braj Panda, Brian R. Bondy, Curtis Miller, Dave Nicolette, Dave Pawson, David McWhirter, Diane C. Leeper, Edward Welker, Eric Pascarello, Gary Rasmussen, Greg Donald, Greg Vaughn, James Hatheway, Jason Jung, Jason Kaczor, John Griffin, Keith Kim, Kieran Mathieson, Lester Lobo, Lisa Morgan, Mike Greenhalgh, Nikolaos Kaintantzis, Rudy Pena, Sarah Forst, Stuart Caborn, Tijs Rademakers, and Yvonne Adams. Special thanks to Adam London for his careful technical review of the final manuscript and for testing the code.

Finally, I'd like to acknowledge J. D. "Illiad" Fraser of *User Friendly* for letting Manning use the *User Friendly* cartoon characters in the *Hello!* series and for allowing me to put my own words in the characters' mouths.

about this book

You should read this book if you're interested in learning about the new features in HTML5 and CSS3 available to web developers and enjoy an example-driven, visual approach to learning. Readers in any of the following categories should find this book useful:

- Experienced web developers
- Novice web developers
- App developers (iPhone, Android, Windows 8 Metro)
- Interactive media designers
- Web designers

Different readers will find different parts of the book interesting. Please see the later section "Book structure and suggested reading order" for further guidelines on how to navigate the book.

Extra content for beginners

This book focuses on the new features of HTML5 and CSS3; as such it expects the reader to have a little experience with their predecessors. But we will take things slowly, especially in the early chapters, and each feature discussed will come with example code you can try yourself. If you know what *tags* are and what a *CSS rule* looks like, then you should have few problems. If you're new to web development, then you'll benefit from the short introduction to HTML and CSS in appendixes B and C.

To use many of the new features in HTML5, it is helpful to have some knowledge of JavaScript. If you are a complete beginner, then you will still find this book useful as it mostly uses small examples which are easy to experiment with. Appendix D is provided to get you started in JavaScript.

Book structure and suggested reading order

This book is split into two sections: part 1 concentrates on HTML5 and part 2 on CSS3. The HTML5 section has chapters on the new markup features of HTML5, forms and form validation, HTML5's new dynamic graphics capabilities, using video and audio, new JavaScript APIs for client-side development, and new APIs related to networking. As a rough guideline, the early chapters require little-to-no knowledge of JavaScript, with each successive chapter building your knowledge base. The second section starts with a couple of chapters on the nuts and bolts of CSS3 and selectors, followed by chapters on layout, motion and color, borders and backgrounds, and fonts and text formatting.

Most of the chapters are self-contained, although there are a few dependencies. The following chapter diagrams show a

⟶ RECOMMENDED ORDER

┈┈▶ OPTIONAL STEP

few suggested reading orders, based on your role and what you expect to get out of the book. Each diagram consists of chapter numbers in boxes as well as the recommended and optional steps, which are indicated by two types of arrows as shown in the key above.

If you are a ...	Read chapters in this order
WEB DEVELOPER If you're a web developer looking to get up to speed, then you should have no problem reading the chapters in numerical order. The CSS used in chapters 2 through 6 should be easy for you to follow. If you're interested in the history of HTML and the standards process, then you can read appendix A before you dive in. It's likely that appendixes B through D are not going to tell you anything you don't already know, so there's no need to bother with them.	

If you are a ...	Read chapters in this order

NOVICE WEB DEVELOPER

If you're a novice web developer, then a slightly different approach is recommended. Again, read appendix A only if you're interested in history, but do read appendixes B, C, and D if you have little-to-no experience with HTML, CSS, and JavaScript. Read appendix C and chapter 7 right after chapter 1 to build your familiarity with CSS so that the limited amount of CSS used in chapters 2 through 6 doesn't hold you back.

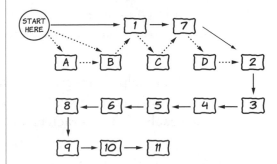

APP DEVELOPER

If your goal is to be an app developer, either targeting mobile devices or Windows 8 Metro style apps, then the key chapters for you are 1 through 6 which concentrate on the markup and programming platform provided by HTML5. Include appendixes B and D plus chapter 7 if you're coming to HTML5 from another platform. Chapter 8 discusses CSS layout, which will be useful for apps. This diagram assumes a graphic designer will handle the detailed design work, so chapters 9 through 11 are not shown.

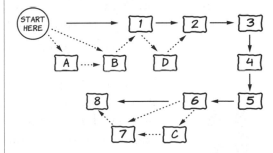

INTERACTIVE MEDIA DESIGNER

If you're an interactive media designer who is a heavy user of Flash for media, animation, or interactive content, then you can safely skip chapters 2, 5, and 6. Chapter 3 deals with dynamic graphics and 4 with audio and video, and chapters 9 and 10 deal with the more visual-impact aspects of CSS3. Chapter 8 on layout will be of less interest to you, but chapter 11 covers using custom fonts, so you may want to read that section.

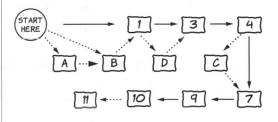

WEB DESIGNER

If you're a pure web designer with no interest in JavaScript, then you can read the book while avoiding most of the code. Any snippets of JavaScript you'll come across in chapters 1 and 7 through 11 can be ignored unless you want to try replicating CSS3 effects in JavaScript for backwards compatibility.

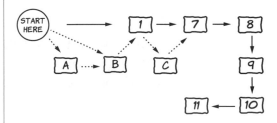

Characters and conventions

This book uses many graphic elements and typographical conventions to guide you and help you learn about HTML5 and CSS3. This section summarizes what you can expect to see.

CHARACTERS

You'll be helped along by the characters from the popular *User Friendly* cartoons. In case you're not familiar with this web comic, let me introduce each of the characters and explain their roles in this book.

A.J. is the Columbia Internet Web Developer. He loves computer games, nifty art, and has a big-brother relationship with the Dust Puppy. He'll be your main guide through HTML5 and CSS3, pointing out gotchas and giving you extra tips.

The Dust Puppy was born inside of a network server, a result of the combination of dust, lint, and quantum events. He is wide-eyed and innocent, with no real grasp of reality, but he's pretty cute and people love him. In this book, Dust Puppy's main role will be to help you move from one topic to the next, summarizing what you've just learned and letting you know what's coming next.

Erwin is a highly advanced Artificial Intelligence (AI) that resides somewhere on the network. He was created overnight by the Dust Puppy, who was feeling kind of bored. Erwin will help out whenever something needs looking up on the internet or when you need to think like a computer.

Miranda is a trained Systems Technologist and an experienced UNIX sysadmin. A.J. is her boyfriend and she'll be helping him out throughout the book.

Greg is in charge of Technical Support at the company. He has broad technical knowledge but no expertise in web development. A.J. is helping him learn about web development, and he'll ask questions when A.J. isn't being clear.

Stef works as the Corporate Sales Manager. He can't understand the way techies think, so he doesn't get very far with them. Although he admires the power of Microsoft's marketing muscle, he has a problem with Microsoft salesmen, probably because they make much more money than he does.

Mike works as a System Administrator, and is responsible for the smooth running of the network at the office. He will help us out whenever we need to understand some details of server-side setup.

Sid is a self-described "lichen of the tech-forest floor," a long-lived, deeply experienced and acerbic observer of the geek gestalt. His history in computing involved vacuum tubes and, later, punch cards. He carries with him an air of compassion mixed with disdain for the younger geeks around him.

Pitr works with Mike as a System Administrator. For some reason he always wears dark glasses and has adopted a guttural Eastern European accent. Pitr will take some time out from his plans for world domination to keep A.J. in his place and to demonstrate that attention to minor technical details that makes geeks so well loved.

Crud Puppy is Dust Puppy's evil twin and nemesis, born from the crud in Stef's keyboard. Whenever we need an antagonist, Crud Puppy will be happy to oblige.

CARTOONS & DIAGRAMS

There are many cartoons and diagrams in this book. The cartoons are based on the actual *User Friendly* comic strips. Their intent is humorous rather than educational as they poke fun at various aspects of web development. A sample cartoon is shown below.

Diagrams are part of the text; they present information that's easier to understand in pictorial form. An example diagram follows.

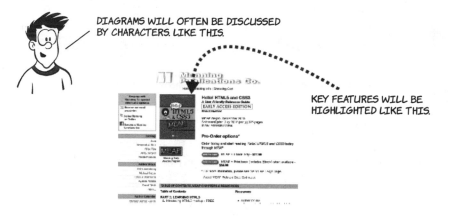

CODE LISTINGS & SNIPPETS

Code listings and snippets and any occurrence of code in the text will appear in the LucidaMonoEF font. Here is a typical code snippet:

```
<body>
    <p>HTML5 and CSS3</p>
</body>
```

Longer listings will look like this:

LISTINGS WILL ALSO BE DISCUSSED BY CHARACTERS. HERE IS A SIMPLE WEB PAGE.

```
<!DOCTYPE html>
<html>
<head>
    <title>Hello!</title>
</head>
<body>
    <p>HTML5 and CSS3</p>
</body>
</html>
```

MORE DETAILED LISTINGS HAVE ANNOTATIONS JUST LIKE DIAGRAMS. THIS ONE POINTS OUT THE EARLIER SNIPPET.

Code downloads

Up-to-date downloadable code samples and other news about the book are available from the publisher's website at www.manning.com/ HelloHTML5andCSS3.

Author Online

Purchase of *Hello! HTML5 & CSS3* includes free access to a private web forum run by Manning Publications where you can make comments about the book, ask technical questions, and receive help from the author and from other users. To access the forum and subscribe to it, go to www.manning.com/HelloHTML5andCSS3. This page provides information on how to get on the forum once you're registered, what kind of help is available, and the rules of conduct on the forum.

Manning's commitment to our readers is to provide a venue where a meaningful dialogue between individual readers and between readers and the author can take place. It's not a commitment to any specific amount of participation on the part of the author, whose contribution to the book's forum remains voluntary (and unpaid). We suggest you try asking the author some challenging questions, lest his interest stray!

The Author Online forum and the archives of previous discussions will be accessible from the publisher's website as long as the book is in print.

About the author

Rob Crowther is a web developer and blogger based in London, UK. Currently he works for a small software company building web applications for corporate clients such as BNP Paribas, BNY Mellon, Honeywell, and Young & Co.'s Brewery.

Part 1

Learning HTML5

This part of the book focuses on HTML5. Chapter 1 introduces you to new and updated markup features in HTML5, chapter 2 discusses forms and form validation, chapter 3 explores HTML5's new dynamic graphics capabilities, chapter 4 talks about how to use video and audio on your web pages, and chapters 5 and 6 look at the new APIs you can use for client-side development and networking.

Introducing HTML5 markup

This chapter covers

- *New semantic elements in HTML5*
- *Updated HTML4 elements*
- *New global attributes*
- *The HTML5 content model*
- *Getting new elements to work in old browsers*

This chapter assumes you have some knowledge of previous versions of HTML. If you're new to HTML, check out appendix B—it should give you enough information to understand this chapter.

We'll start with some background on how and why the particular set of new elements in HTML5 was chosen. Then we'll examine new elements for the overall structure of web pages before moving on to elements, both new and redefined, intended for particular bits of content. You'll then learn about the new attributes in HTML5. Next, we'll spend a few pages considering the more conceptual issue of the new approach to element categorization in HTML5. Finally, you'll go back to practicalities and learn how to make sure your new HTML5 content will work in old browsers.

Why do we need new elements?

This section looks at some of the research that went into understanding the document structures that web authors were trying to describe semantically with HTML; this information was used to decide which new elements should be added in HTML5. We'll then look at each of the new elements in turn.

What does *semantic* mean?

At heart, HTML is a way of describing hyperlinked documents: documents that are linked together as part of a network of knowledge. The elements of HTML are meant to *mean something*, and that meaning is what we refer to as the *semantics*. Because HTML describes documents, the semantics are along the lines of "this content is a paragraph," "this content is a level-one heading," and "this content is an unordered list."

Being able to describe the structure of a document this way is valuable because it lets you keep the details of how to best display content separate from the content itself. The result is that the same web page, if well structured, can easily be read on a desktop computer, a mobile phone, and a text-to-speech converter. Compare this to a document format like PDF, where the layout and content are deeply interlinked because the fidelity of the eventual printed output is the primary goal. It's usually awkward to read an A4 PDF on a mobile device because there's no option other than to view it at A4 size.

HTML4 has two built-in methods for extending the semantics of elements: the id and class attributes. The id attribute is a unique identifier, but, rather than a random string, the identifier can be a meaningful word—in other words, it can have semantic value. The class isn't unique, but multiple classes can be applied to a single element like tagging in popular social network tools. Some examples are shown in the following table.

Markup	Suggested meaning
<p>	A paragraph
<p id="author">	A paragraph that represents a particular author
<p class="bio">	A paragraph that represents a biography
<p class="author bio">	A paragraph that represents an author biography

No definitive standard sets down which values mean what,[1] so one site could use *writer* for the same thing another site uses *author* for, or two sites could use *author* to mean something completely different. This isn't a huge issue, because HTML isn't intended to describe real-world things like authors, so the meaning behind those values is likely to be site-specific anyway. But id and class attributes can also be used to describe document features; for instance, a nav class would probably indicate an element that contains navigation. If you were looking for ideas for new elements to add to HTML to improve its ability to describe documents, a survey of the sorts of values used in id and class attributes would be a good place to start.

With this in mind, in 2005 several studies were done that attempted to analyze how authors were using id and class values in markup on the web. Two of these are of particular interest to us:

- In November 2005, a study of 1,315 websites counted how often different values for the id attribute were used.
- In December 2005, a study of slightly over a billion web pages analyzed, among other things, how often particular class names appeared.

---

[1] Although some have attempted it. See the discussion of microformats later in this chapter.

The diagram that follows shows the top 20 results in each category down each side and the corresponding new HTML5 elements along with the IDs and classes that inspired them in the middle.

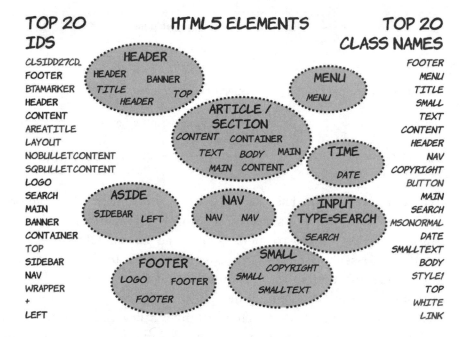

MANY OF THE TOP IDS, LIKE btamarker AND nobulletcontent, ARE AUTOMATICALLY GENERATED BY SOFTWARE SUCH AS MICROSOFT FRONTPAGE AND OTHER OFFICE PRODUCTS. THEIR POPULARITY IS THEREFORE MORE AN INDICATION OF THE MARKET PENETRATION OF THE PRODUCTS THAN AUTHOR REQUIREMENTS OR INTENTIONS.

In the next section, you'll learn about some of the new elements that have been added to HTML5 as a result of this research.

New elements for page structure

By *page structure* we mean the top-level items: the header, the footer, the navigation, the main content, and so on. Let's join A.J. and Greg, who are discussing the research results from the previous section.

Sectioning content

It's common for web pages to have many distinct sections. A blog homepage usually has several blog posts, each a section in itself, and each blog post may have a comments section or a related-posts section. HTML4 offers only one type of element for this common need: <div>. HTML5 adds two new elements: <section> and <article>.

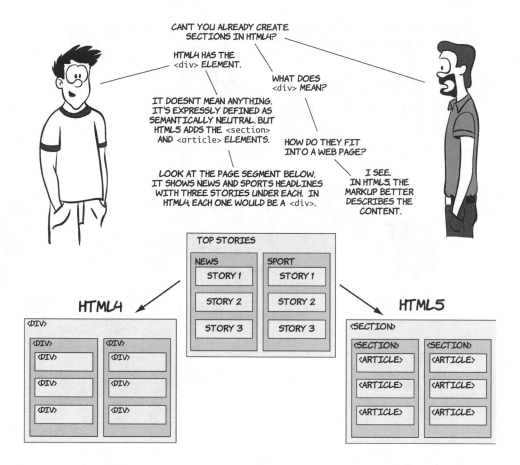

The <section> and <article> elements are conceptually similar. Articles and sections can be interchangeable—articles can exist happily within sections, but articles can also be broken down into sections, and there's been a lot of discussion about whether HTML5 really needs both of them. For now, though, we have both, and you're probably asking yourself how to decide which one to use. The key parts of the spec to focus on when choosing one or the other are as follows:

- An *article* is intended to be independently distributable or reusable.
- A *section* is a thematic grouping of content.

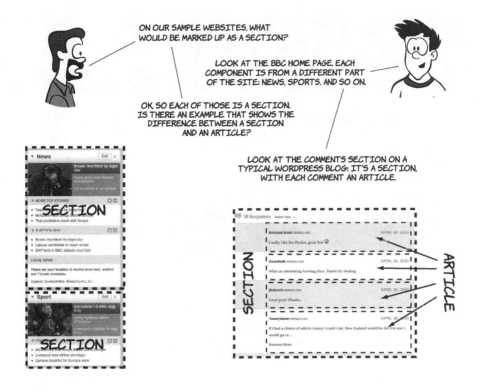

Headings, headers, and the outlining algorithm

Heading elements provide an implicit structure for documents. A *heading* indicates the start of a new section and briefly describes the topic of the text that follows. The level of a heading (levels 1 through 6 in HTML) indicates an implicit hierarchy. This implicit structure is useful for the automatic generation of a table of contents. Some websites, such as Wikipedia, generate a table of contents for each page; screen readers and other accessibility tools use the table of contents to allow users to navigate the page more easily. HTML5 formalizes this implicit structure with the outlining algorithm. In this section, you'll learn about this algorithm as well as how it interacts with the two new heading elements, <header> and <hgroup>.

A <header> element appears near the top of a document, a section, or an article and usually contains the main heading and often some navigation and search tools. Here's an example from the BBC website.

Here's how that might be marked up in HTML5:

```
<header>
  <h1>BBC</h1>
  <nav>
    <ul>
      <li><a href="/options">Display Options</a></li>
      <li><a href="/access">Accessibility Help</a></li>
      <li><a href="/mobile">Mobiles</a></li>
    </ul>
  </nav>
  <form target="/search">
    <input name="q" type="search">
    <input type="submit">
  </form>
</header>
```

YOU'LL LEARN MORE ABOUT THE `<nav>` ELEMENT LATER IN THIS CHAPTER. HTML5'S NEW FORM ELEMENTS WILL BE COVERED IN DEPTH IN CHAPTER 2.

The `<hgroup>` element should be used where you want a main heading with one or more subheadings. For an example, let's look at the HTML5 spec:

```
<hgroup>
  <h1>HTML5
    (including next generation
    additions still in
development)
  </h1>
  <h2>Draft Standard &mdash;
    12 May 2010</h2>
</hgroup>
```

HTML5 (including next generation additions still in development)
Draft Standard — 12 May 2010

The `<header>` element can contain any content, but the `<hgroup>` element can only contain other headers—that is, `<h1>` to `<h6>`, plus `<hgroup>` itself. The following diagram demonstrates the differences.

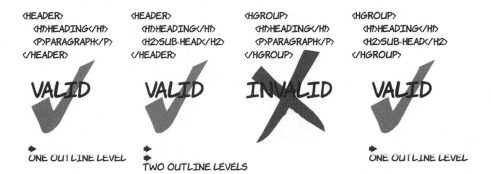

The outlining algorithm generates a table of contents for your document based on the section and heading markup you've used. In HTML4, the overall structure of a document was left up to individual browsers to decide; in HTML5, it's part of the spec. This benefits you because any user agents that need an outline, often for accessibility purposes,[2] will generate the same outline for any given document. To help you get the idea, let's look at several sample documents. Erwin will generate the document outline according to the HTML5 spec. You'll see how the outline is impacted both by headings and heading groups as well as the articles and sections we discussed in the previous section.

---

[2]   The W3C's User Agent Accessibility Guidelines recommend that browsers generate a document outline in guideline 1.10.2: www.w3.org/TR/UAAG20/#gl-alternative-views.

```
<body>
    <h1>Main heading</h1>
    <p>Some text</p>
    <h2>Level 2 heading</h2>
    <p>Some more text</p>
    <h3>Level 3 heading</h3>
    <p>A bit more text</p>
    <h2>Another level 2 heading</h2>
    <p>The last bit of text</p>
</body>
```

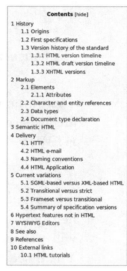

In a plain document with no other sectioning content, the outline will match the heading levels. This is similar to the way a table of contents in Wikipedia is generated (right). Headings can also be grouped using the `<hgroup>` element. Let's see how they affect the document outline:

```
<hgroup>
    <h1>Main heading</h1>
    <h2>
      Subheading to main heading
    </h2>
</hgroup>
<p>Some text</p>
<h2>Level 2 heading</h2>
<p>Some more text</p>
<h3>Level 3 heading</h3>
<p>A bit more text</p>
<hgroup>
    <h2>Another level 2 heading</h2>
    <h3>
      Subheading to level 2 heading
    </h3>
</hgroup>
<p>The last bit of text</p>
```

The outline will only show the highest level heading from any <hgroup>: you can see the headings "Subheading to main heading" and "Subheading to level 2 heading" don't appear in the outline. The <hgroup> element can contain any number of subheadings, but it can only contain other heading elements.

Next, let's look at how sections affect the outline:

```
<h1>Sections</h1>
<section>
    <h1>Main heading</h1>
    <p>Some text</p>
    <h2>Level 2 heading</h2>
    <p>Some more text</p>
    <h3>Level 3 heading</h3>
    <p>A bit more text</p>
    <h2>Another level 2 heading</h2>
    <p>The last bit of text</p>
</section>
<section>
    <h1>Main heading</h1>
    <p>Some text</p>
    <h2>Level 2 heading</h2>
    <p>Some more text</p>
    <h3>Level 3 heading</h3>
    <p>A bit more text</p>
    <h2>Another level 2 heading</h2>
    <p>The last bit of text</p>
</section>
```

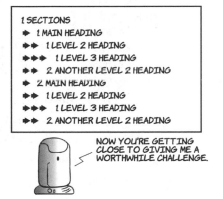

As you can see, there are now multiple <h1> elements in the document, but they don't all sit at the same level of the document outline. In fact, you can do without any heading element other than <h1>. Let's look at another example.

```
<h1>Main heading</h1>
<p>Some text</p>
<section>
    <h1>Level 2 heading</h1>
    <p>Some more text</p>
    <article>
        <h1>Level 3 heading</h1>
        <p>A bit more text</p>
    </article>
</section>
<section>
    <h1>Another level 2 heading</h1>
    <p>The last bit of text</p>
</section>
```

We have achieved the exact same outline as the original example but using only level-one headings. Earlier, we discussed the similarity between <section> and <article>. If we replace one with the other in the previous listing, you can see how similar they are:

```
<h1>Articles</h1>
<article>
    <h1>Main heading</h1>
    <p>Some text</p>
    <h2>Level 2 heading</h2>
    <p>Some more text</p>
    <h3>Level 3 heading</h3>
    <p>A bit more text</p>
    <h2>Another level 2 heading</h2>
    <p>The last bit of text</p>
</article>
<article>
    <h1>Main heading</h1>
    <p>Some text</p>
    <h2>Level 2 heading</h2>
    <p>Some more text</p>
    <h3>Level 3 heading</h3>
    <p>A bit more text</p>
    <h2>Another level 2 heading</h2>
    <p>The last bit of text</p>
</article>
```

Now let's consider the <header> element. It represents the header of a document, a section, or an article, typically containing headings and other metadata about the section. You'll frequently have content that you don't want to be part of the heading element itself but that doesn't fit in with the following content. Examples would be subheadings, author bylines, and publishing date information:

```
<h1>Articles</h1>
<article>
    <header>
        <h1>Main heading</h1>
        <p>Some text</p>
    </header>
    <h2>Level 2 heading</h2>
    <p>Some more text</p>
    <h3>Level 3 heading</h3>
    <p>A bit more text</p>
    <h2>Another level 2 heading</h2>
    <p>The last bit of text</p>
</article>
<article>
    <header>
        <h1>Main heading</h1>
        <p>Some text</p>
    </header>
    <h2>Level 2 heading</h2>
    <p>Some more text</p>
    <h3>Level 3 heading</h3>
    <p>A bit more text</p>
    <h2>Another level 2 heading</h2>
    <p>The last bit of text</p>
</article>
```

```
1 ARTICLES
    ➡ 1 MAIN HEADING
    ➡➡ 1 LEVEL 2 HEADING
    ➡➡➡ 1 LEVEL 3 HEADING
    ➡➡ 2 ANOTHER LEVEL 2 HEADING
    ➡ 2 MAIN HEADING
    ➡➡ 1 LEVEL 2 HEADING
    ➡➡➡ 1 LEVEL 3 HEADING
    ➡➡ 2 ANOTHER LEVEL 2 HEADING
```

THE <header> ELEMENT DOES NOT HAVE ANY IMPACT ON THE DOCUMENT OUTLINE. IT'S AS IF IT'S NOT THERE.

Common page elements

There are more new elements than <article>, <section>, <header>, and <hgroup>. Let's look at some more pages from our set of typical websites.

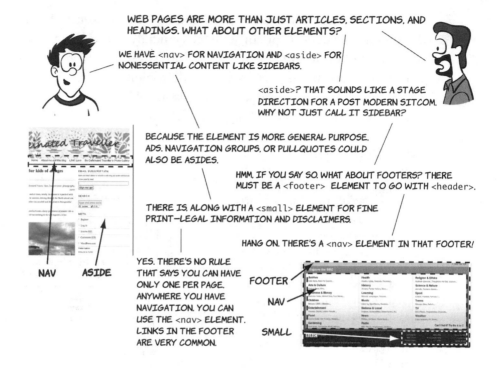

The <aside> element is intended for content that isn't part of the flow of the text in which it appears but is still related in some way. In many books, including this one, you'll see sidebars for things such as terminology definitions and historical background, like the one that follows—these would be marked up as <aside> if the book was HTML5. Sidebars are also common in website design, although the meaning is slightly different: often they contain navigation or related links.

Sidebar
This is an example sidebar. If this were an HTML5 document, it would be marked up with the <aside> element.

The <nav> element is intended for navigation, both within the page itself, as in the Wikipedia table of contents, and through the rest of the website. You can have any number of <nav> elements on a page. On large sites, it's common to have global navigation across the top (in the <header>) and local navigation in a sidebar (in an <aside> element).

The <footer> element generally appears at the end of a document, a section, or an article. As with the <header> element, its content is generally metainformation—author details, legal information, or links to related information. But it's valid to include <section> elements within a footer—for example, when marking up appendixes.

The <small> element often appears within a <footer> or <aside> element—it contains copyright information, legal disclaimers, and other fine print. Note that it's *not* intended to make text smaller. You may choose to style its contents smaller than your main text, but, as with other elements, its role is to describe its contents, not prescribe presentation.

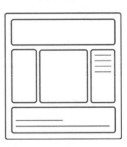

The HTML DOCTYPE

The DOCTYPE declaration optionally appears at the start of an HTML document. It comes from the Standard Generalized Markup Language (SGML) that was used to define previous versions of HTML in terms of the language syntax. The DOCTYPE serves two practical functions:

- It's used by HTML validation services to determine which version the document uses.
- Browsers use the DOCTYPE to determine which rendering mode to use.

The rendering modes are Standards, Almost Standards, and Quirks mode. These modes represent various stages in the history of browser development and allow modern browsers to display old web pages the way they were intended. See appendix C for a discussion of these factors—the short version is, Standards mode is what you want.

HTML5 is defined in terms of its DOM representation after parsing, so it doesn't need a DOCTYPE for validation, but we still want legacy browsers to render pages in standards-compliant mode. With this in mind, the authors of the HTML5 spec worked out the minimal amount of markup required to trigger Standards mode in browsers:

```
<!DOCTYPE html>
```

Compare this with similar declarations for HTML4 and XHTML1:

```
<!DOCTYPE HTML PUBLIC "-//W3C//DTD HTML 4.01//EN"
          "http://www.w3.org/TR/html4/strict.dtd">
```

```
<!DOCTYPE html PUBLIC "-//W3C//DTD XHTML 1.0 Strict//EN"
        "http://www.w3.org/TR/xhtml1/DTD/xhtml1-strict.dtd">
```

You can see that the HTML5 DOCTYPE is much shorter, easier to type, and easier to remember.

New elements for content

There are several other new or redefined elements in HTML5, and in this section you'll learn about some of them. HTML5 includes dedicated elements for dates as well as figures and captions, all common elements of modern web pages. It also rehabilitates the <b> and <i> elements that were deprecated in HTML4. This section looks at each of these in turn.

Time

The <time> element allows an unambiguous ISO 8601 date to be attached to a human-readable version of that date. This is useful if you want some other website or service to look at your web pages and extract information. A common use case for this is that you're advertising an event on your website and you'd like it to appear in search results for queries such as "events in London next week." Alternatively, you might decide to write a program to build a timeline of the English monarchy by crawling Wikipedia; being able to parse all the dates in a straightforward way would make this much easier. Following are three examples of these sorts of pages:

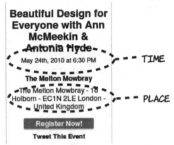

This WordPress blog is advertising an upcoming event. You can see the key components are all present here:

- An event title
- A time
- A place

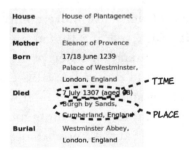

The BBC website has a page for each program, and this contains information about when the program will next be broadcast. Although the title isn't shown here, you can see the key components: a time and a place (although in this case the "place" is more abstract).

Finally, Wikipedia has events on many pages—in this example, the "event" is the death of Edward I. You may not consider this the same sort of thing as the previous two examples, but it shares the same basic characteristics. This pattern is so common that the microformats movement established a standard way of marking it up called hCalendar.

In the previous examples, it should have been fairly easy for you to pick out the key bits of information even without the big dotted circles, but computers need a more structured form of data. One approach to this is microformats.

> **Microformats**
>
> *Microformats* are an effort to extend the expressive power of standard HTML by using certain attributes, mostly the `class` attribute, in a standardized way. Popular microformats include hCard, for describing contact information, adr for addresses, and hCalendar for describing events. Similar technologies include the more formal RDFa and HTML5's own microdata (see section 2.5.3).

The main goal of microformats is to render common information like events easily parseable by computers without affecting the end-user presentation.

MICROFORMATS ENABLE A NUMBER OF USEFUL APPLICATIONS: SEARCH ENGINES THAT CAN TELL YOU ABOUT NEARBY UPCOMING EVENTS AND BROWSERS THAT CAN AUTOMATICALLY ADD THE EVENTS TO YOUR CALENDAR.

Addresses, being naturally plain text information with some internal structure (house number, street name, city, and so on) are relatively easy to deal with, as long as there's some way to demarcate the components. Microformats manage this by adding a class of location to the containing element, or alternatively using another microformat, adr, to describe the address in detail. Dates and times are more complicated. Take the simple example 1/6/2011. If you're reading this in the United States, you probably interpret that as January 6, whereas in the UK the date is 1st June. Or have another look at the earlier BBC example: the date is "today." I took that screenshot some time ago—how useful is "today" now? You may think this is no more or less ambiguous than the addresses, but the frustrating thing is that we know that an absolute date and time underlie the more ambiguous human expression that we see more commonly.

COMPUTERS LIKE DATES AND TIMES IN AN UNAMBIGUOUS FORMAT. PEOPLE OFTEN FIND THE UNAMBIGUOUS FORMAT HARD TO DIGEST BUT CAN EASILY UNDERSTAND AMBIGUOUS DATES FROM THE CONTEXT. TO SERVE BOTH, WEB PAGES NEED TO PROVIDE DATES IN TWO FORMATS.

HTML5 solves this problem by providing a `<time>` element. Let's look at an example:

```
<time datetime="2011-06-01">today</time>
```

We can be more specific:

```
<time datetime="2011-06-01T18:00:00+01:00">6 o'clock on 1/6/2011</time>
```

Humans get a readable time that they can disambiguate through the context in the normal way, and computers can read the ISO 6801 date and see the date, time, and time zone.

Time and data

Originally the `<time>` element had a pubdate attribute to allow for its use in marking up blog posts and other articles. Early in 2012, the entire `<time>` element was removed from the WHATWG version of the spec because it didn't appear to be getting used for that purpose. There was something of an uproar within the community, and the `<time>` element was reinstated shortly after, along with a new element, `<data>`, for more general-purpose association of human-readable text with data for computers. At the time of writing, this new element has not yet made it into the W3C version of the spec, so it isn't covered here.

Images and diagrams with `<figure>` and `<figcaption>`

Putting an image in a web page is easy enough: the `<img>` element has existed since the early days of the web. It was somewhat controversial at the time, and several alternatives were put forward; but the most popular browser (Mosaic) implemented it, so it became a de facto standard. The ability to add images was one of the main things that catapulted the web from being an academic document-sharing network into a worldwide phenomenon in the mid 1990s, but since that early take-up not much has changed.

The `<img>` tag is limited from a semantic standpoint—there's no visible way to associate explanatory text with the image. It's possible to use the `alt` and `longdesc` attributes, but because neither is visible by default, both have been somewhat ignored or misused in the real world. The `<figure>` element offers an alternative—it groups the figure with its caption.

This is what the markup for the following screenshot looks like:

```
<figure>
    <img src="scenery.jpg" alt="Picture of the Irish south coast">
    <figcaption>Looking out into the Atlantic Ocean
     from south west Ireland</figcaption>
</figure>
```

Note that `<figure>` doesn't have to contain an `<img>` element. It might instead contain an SVG drawing or a `<canvas>` element, or even ASCII art in a `<pre>` element. Whatever type of graphic it contains, the `<figure>` element links the graphic to the caption.

Looking out into the Atlantic Ocean from south west Ireland

Emphasizing words and phrases

The `<b>` and `<i>` elements have a long history in HTML. They were listed, along with the `<em>` and `<strong>` elements, in the character-highlighting section of the 1993 IETF draft proposal for HTML. The `<b>` and `<i>` elements are listed in the subsection "Physical Styles" (along with `<tt>`)—that is, their purpose was entirely presentational. Meanwhile, `<em>` and `<strong>` (along with several others) are in the subsection "Logical Styles"—elements with semantic meaning. This early distinction highlights the problem `<b>` and `<i>` would later run into.

You saw at the start of this chapter that separation of concerns is the Holy Grail of web authoring—HTML for content, CSS for presentation, and JavaScript for behavior. Because `<b>` and `<i>` are entirely presentational, their use has long been frowned on, and there have been several serious proposals to remove them from HTML. Meanwhile, `<strong>` and `<em>` have always had a semantic definition while appearing identical to `<b>` and `<i>`, respectively, in most browsers.

EVER PRAGMATIC, THE HTML5 SPEC RECOGNIZES THAT, WITH MILLIONS OF PAGES OF LEGACY CONTENT OUT THERE, BROWSERS AREN'T GOING TO BE DROPPING SUPPORT FOR `<b>` AND `<i>` ANY TIME SOON. ON THE OTHER HAND, BLINDLY USING `<em>` INSTEAD OF `<i>` AND `<strong>` INSTEAD OF `<b>`, OR USING A `<span>` ELEMENT TO APPLY A BOLD OR ITALIC STYLE TO A WORD ISN'T GOOD PRACTICE SEMANTICALLY.

So, instead of removing either <b> or <i>, HTML5 redefines and rehabilitates them.

Element	HTML4 definition	HTML5 definition (taken from the spec on May 12, 2010)
<i>	Renders as italic text style	"The i element represents a span of text in an alternate voice or mood, or otherwise offset from the normal prose, such as a taxonomic designation, a technical term, an idiomatic phrase from another language, a thought, a ship name, or some other prose whose typical typographic presentation is italicized."
<b>	Renders as bold text style	"The b element represents a span of text to be stylistically offset from the normal prose without conveying any extra importance, such as key words in a document abstract, product names in a review, or other spans of text whose typical typographic presentation is boldened."

As you can see, the HTML4 definition is entirely presentational, whereas the HTML5 definition goes to great lengths to give a semantic meaning while remaining compatible with the purely presentational uses of the two elements for backward compatibility.

HTML5's new global attributes

An attribute is *global* if it can be applied to all elements. The two most obvious global attributes in HTML4 are id and class, which, as you saw in the section "Why do we need new elements?" can be used to add extra semantic information to elements. In this section, you'll learn about new HTML5 global attributes from three major categories:

- Accessibility for Rich Internet Applications (ARIA), for providing extra data to accessibility tools
- Data-* attributes, for providing extra data for scripts on your page
- Microdata attributes, for providing extra data to browsers and scripts on other sites

Accessibility with ARIA

ARIA is a standard developed at the W3C in response to the generally poor accessibility of early AJAX-based web applications.

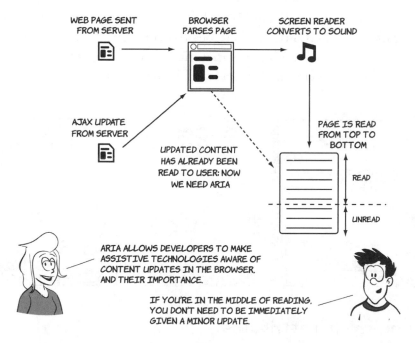

Notifying users of AJAX updates isn't the only benefit ARIA can provide. ARIA consists of a set of attributes and values that can describe to assistive technology the roles of various page elements and their status. In other words, they add semantic value to HTML elements so you can say "this element is a header," "this element is navigation," "this element is a toolbar," and so on. Let's look at an example:

```
<body role="document">
  <div role="note" aria-live="polite"
   aria-relevant="additions removals">
    An update added by JavaScript
  </div>
  <div role="banner">
    <h1 role="heading" aria-level="1">The heading</h1>
  </div>
  <div role="navigation">
    <a role="link" href="/home">Home Page</a>
    <a role="link" href="/inbox">Inbox</a>
  </div>
  <div role="main">
    A very interesting article goes here.
  </div>
  <div role="footer">
    All rights reserved.
  </div>
</body>
```

This should all sound a little familiar to you. What HTML5 aims to accomplish through additions such as the `<header>` and `<nav>` elements is similar to what ARIA tries to accomplish in providing better semantics to assistive technology. But it's still worth bothering with ARIA because it has a wider and more far-reaching vocabulary than HTML5 for describing the components of web applications. Plus it already has wide support among vendors of browsers, operating systems, and assistive technology.

The HTML5 spec has a long list of elements to which user agents should automatically assign particular ARIA roles. These elements are said to have *strong native semantics*, so if you use HTML5 correctly you'll get a certain amount of accessibility for free compared to what HTML4 offered once the browsers and assistive technologies implement support. The HTML5 spec also explicitly lists the allowed ARIA roles for those elements where there's a risk the ARIA role will be in conflict with the HTML5 semantics—these are *implied native semantics*. Validation tools can then flag inappropriate combinations.

Using HTML5, you can cut down on the amount of markup required to provide an accessible user experience. This listing updates the previous one but takes advantage of the strong and implied native semantics in place of several of the ARIA attributes:

```html
<body>
  <aside aria-live="polite" aria-relevant="additions removals">
    An update added by JavaScript
  </aside>
  <header role="banner">
    <h1>The heading</h1>
  </header>
  <nav>
    <a href="/home">Home Page</a>
    <a href="/inbox">Inbox</a>
  </nav>
  <article role="main">
    A very interesting article goes here.
  </article>
  <footer>
    All rights reserved.
  </footer>
</body>
```

ALTHOUGH YOU DON'T HAVE TO USE THE IMPLIED ARIA ROLES ON ELEMENTS WITH STRONG SEMANTICS, SUCH AS `<link>` AND `<nav>`, AT PRESENT NO ASSISTIVE TECHNOLOGIES RECOGNIZE THE HTML5 ELEMENTS. YOU SHOULD SPECIFY BOTH FOR BACKWARD COMPATIBILITY.

Extending HTML with custom attributes

Custom data attributes allow authors to add arbitrary data to elements for their own private use. The idea is that some data isn't directly relevant to the user but does have meaning to the JavaScript on the page that can't be expressed in HTML semantics. It's a standardization of an approach taken by several JavaScript widget libraries, such as Dijit (the Dojo toolkit). These libraries, like HTML5, set out to enhance and extend the application abilities of HTML4—adding things such as combo boxes and date pickers, which HTML5 also provides, but also more complex UI elements such as tree views, drop-down menus, and tabbed containers. Using one of these libraries, you declare an element to be a tab control like this:

```
<div dojoType="dijit.layout.TabContainer">
    <div dojoType="dijit.layout.ContentPane" title="My first tab">
        Lorem ipsum and all around...
    </div>
    <div dojoType="dijit.layout.ContentPane" title="My second tab">
        Lorem ipsum and all around - second...
    </div>
    <div dojoType="dijit.layout.ContentPane" title="My last tab">
        Lorem ipsum and all around - last...
    </div>
</div>
```

A browser, as with HTML elements, will parse the attribute, even though it doesn't recognize it, and add it to the DOM. The Dijit library will run when the page has loaded, search for these attributes, and run the appropriate JavaScript to enable the advanced control.

It may seem as though everyone has been getting along fine with creating their own attributes, so why add support for custom attributes to HTML5? Well, for one thing, creating your own will stop your markup from validating.

Failing validation may not bother you too much, but if you're looking for that one unintended mistake, having to sift through many intended ones should be unnecessary. Plus there's a risk that the attribute names chosen by the widget libraries will be used in future versions of HTML— after all, one of the goals of the spec is to codify existing common uses.

The HTML5 solution to both the validation and potential name-clash issues is the data-* attribute collection. The * is a wildcard—that is, it can be whatever you want it to be. But anything starting with data- will be allowed through the validator, and you're guaranteed that no data-* attributes will be made part of HTML.

THE data-* ATTRIBUTES ALLOW YOU TO ADD INFORMATION TO YOUR PAGE FOR YOUR OWN PERSONAL USE. IF YOUR GOAL IS TO SHARE INFORMATION WITH OTHER WEBSITES, YOU SHOULD INSTEAD USE MICRODATA.

Expressing more than just document semantics with microdata

Microdata extends the expressive power of HTML to cover things that aren't strictly markup. You can use microdata to designate a portion of your page as describing contact information, a calendar event, or licensing information.

Microdata uses three global attributes: item, itemtype, and itemprop. All three can be seen in action in this short example that describes contact information:

```
<section id="rob" itemscope
  itemtype="http://microformats.org/profile/hcard">
  <h1 itemprop="fn">Rob Crowther</h1>
  <p itemprop="n" itemscope>Full name:
    <span itemprop="given-name">Robert</span>
    <span itemprop="additional-name">John</span>
    <span itemprop="family-name">Crowther</span>
  </p>
  <p itemprop="org" itemscope>
    <span itemprop="organization-name">Manning Publications Co.</span>
    (<span itemprop="organization-unit">Hello! Series</span>)
  </p>
</section>
```

This code, because of the itemtype attribute on the parent element referencing the hCard vocabulary, describes a person—me! The itemprop attributes are extracted as a set of name-value pairs into a tree-like data structure following the markup, like this:

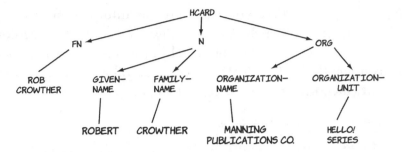

This information could then be recovered from the page in a usable format by a web browser or a search engine. Of course, you may not want the information to be more easily usable by computers; normal rules of internet publishing apply.

YOU'LL LEARN MORE ABOUT MICRODATA IN CHAPTER 5 WHEN WE LOOK AT THE MICRODATA API, A CONVENIENT METHOD FOR EXTRACTING THE DATA FROM A DOCUMENT. THE NEXT SECTION LOOKS AT HOW YOU CAN PRODUCE A VALID HTML5 DOCUMENT BY LEARNING ABOUT THE CONTENT MODEL.

The HTML5 content model

The content model is somewhat theoretical, but it's important because it's the main way of determining whether it's valid to use a certain element at a particular place in your document. In HTML5, elements are split into categories. One element can be a member of several categories; it can also be a member of a category only in particular circumstances, such as when an attribute is given a certain value. In this section, you'll learn where you can find this information in the spec, what elements fit into which content categories, and what the content categories are. The categories of which an element is a member are stated prominently in the HTML5 spec. The following diagram shows the content categories of the <hgroup> element.

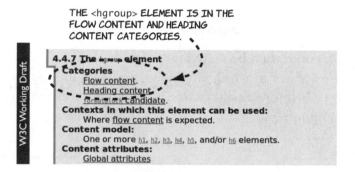

The spec is good if you have a question about a particular element, but it's cumbersome if you want a quick overview. Rather than trawl through the entire spec, the content categories can be summarized in a table.

Element	Metadata content	Flow content	Phrasing content	Interactive content	Embedded content	Heading content	Sectioning content
<a>, <button>, <input>, <keygen>, <label>, <select>, <textarea>		•	•	•			
<abbr>, <area>, <b>, <bdo>, , <cite>, <code>, <datalist>, <del>, <dfn>, <em>, <i>, <ins>, <kbd>, <map>, <mark>, <meter>, <output>, <progress>, <q>, <ruby>, <samp>, <small>, <span>, <strong>, <sub>, <sup>, <time>, <var>, <wbr>		•	•				
<address>, <blockquote>, <div>, <dl>, <fieldset>, <figure>, <footer>, <form>, <header>, <hr>, <ol>, <p>, <pre>, <table>, <ul>, <Text>		•					
<article>, <aside>, <nav>, <section>		•					•

Element	Metadata content	Flow content	Phrasing content	Interactive content	Embedded content	Heading content	Sectioning content
`<audio>`, `<embed>`, `<iframe>`, `<img*>`, `<object>`, `<video>`		●	●	●	●		
`<base>`, `<title>`	●						
`<canvas>`, `<math>`, `<svg>`		●	●		●		
`<command>`, `<link>`, `<meta>`, `<noscript>`, `<script>`	●	●	●				
`<details>`, `<menu>`		●		●			
`<h1>`, `<h2>`, `<h3>`, `<h4>`, `<h5>`, `<h6>`, `<hgroup>`		●				●	
`<style>`	●	●					

Now you know which content models apply to which elements, but that's only part of the story. You also need to know what content categories are allowed as children of any given element. The following diagram shows a couple of other excerpts from the HTML5 spec to illustrate where you can find this information.

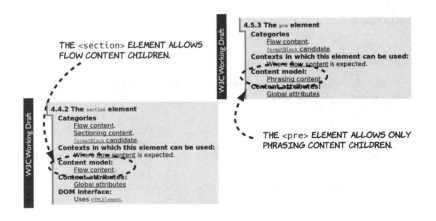

The different content types aren't applied arbitrarily; each has a distinct meaning. The following table summarizes the different types.

Flow content	Most elements are categorized as flow content. It's the default content type for elements visible on the page.
Sectioning content	Sectioning content defines the scope of headers and footers and feeds into the document outline.
Heading content	Heading content, as you might expect, is just for headings and `<hgroup>`.
Phrasing content	Phrasing content is mostly used to describe the text of a document. In most cases, phrasing content can only contain other phrasing content.
Embedded content	Embedded content is used to put an external resource into the web page—for example, an image or video.
Interactive content	Interactive content is elements that are specifically intended for user interaction—mostly form controls. Note that other elements can be made responsive to user input through the use of JavaScript, but elements categorized as interactive content have default functionality in the browser.
Metadata content	Metadata content sets up the presentation or behavior of the rest of the content, or sets up the relationship of the document with other documents, or conveys other out-of-band information.

Now that you know all about the content model, you'll be able to use the HTML5 spec to write valid HTML5 documents. That's more than enough theory for now. The next section gets back to practicalities and considers whether your users' browsers will support HTML5 and what to do about it if they don't.

Browser support

Do the new elements we've discussed in this chapter work in today's browsers? The short answer is, yes (with a couple of exceptions); the

FOR A TEXT ELEMENT LIKE `<p>`, WHICH ISN'T REQUIRED TO DO MUCH EXCEPT APPEAR ON THE PAGE, THERE ARE TWO PRINCIPAL REQUIREMENTS:

- IT SHOWS UP IN THE DOM WITH AT LEAST A STANDARD SET OF ELEMENT PROPERTIES.
- IT SHOWS UP IN THE USER'S BROWSER WITH SOME SORT OF DEFAULT PRESENTATION.

long answer is a little more complex. Consider this question: what does it mean to say that a browser supports the <p> element?

It turns out that the first requirement is easy to satisfy—as long as you follow simple tag-naming rules, you can put any tags in your HTML, and all browsers will put the tags in the DOM with a default set of properties.

Where problems arise is with regard to the second requirement: having a default presentation. Browsers have only recently started providing any default presentation for the new elements in HTML5; for instance, Firefox 3.6 doesn't, but Firefox 4.0 does. But this isn't much of a problem. As you know, we web authors define our content in HTML and our presentation in CSS—and browsers work exactly the same way. The default presentation for the supported elements is defined in CSS. If you use Firefox, you can even find this file on your hard drive—it's called html.css.

USING THESE NEW ELEMENTS IS A MATTER OF TAKING ON THE RESPONSIBILITY OF PROVIDING SOME DEFAULT CSS RULES FOR THEM. IN MOST CASES YOU'LL WANT TO WRITE CSS FOR THESE ELEMENTS ANYWAY, SO THIS DOESN'T SEEM LIKE TOO MUCH EFFORT. LET'S SEE HOW IT WORKS WITH AN EXAMPLE.

Here's a simple HTML5 document to experiment with:

```
<header>
  <hgroup>
    <h1>Hello! HTML 5</h1>
    <h2>An example page by Rob Crowther</h2>
  </hgroup>
</header>
<nav>
  <ul>
    <li><a href="#">Link 1</a></li>
    <li><a href="#">Link 2</a></li>
    <li><a href="#">Link 3</a></li>
  </ul>
</nav>
<section>
  <article>The first article.</article>
  <article>The second article.</article>
</section>
```

Starting with the following basic styles, this screenshot shows what the page looks like in a browser that doesn't have any default HTML5 styles:

```
header, nav, section, article
  {padding: 4px; margin: 4px;}
header
  { background: #000; color: #999; }
nav
  { border: 4px solid #000; }
section
  { border: 4px dashed #000; }
article
  { border: 2px dotted #000; }
```

By making a single change to that CSS, you can make the page work in most older browsers. See if you can spot it:

```
header, nav, section, article
  { padding: 4px; margin: 4px;
    display: block; }
header
  { background: #000; color: #999; }
nav
  { border: 4px solid #000; }
section
  { border: 4px dashed #000; }
article
  { border: 2px dotted #000; }
```

If you specify that the block-level HTML5 elements <header>, <nav>, <section>, and <article> should be display: block, everything works as you want.

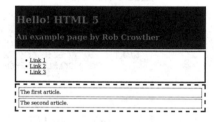

Most of the major browsers work identically in this regard. Unfortunately, there are two exceptions, one minor and one major. The minor one is Firefox 2.0; Firefox users tend to upgrade regularly, so this version is now used by a very small number of people and we won't worry about it. The larger problem is Internet Explorer 8 and earlier, which is still one of the most commonly used browsers on the web.

Supporting Internet Explorer

Internet Explorer won't apply CSS rules to any elements it doesn't recognize. Here's what the sample page looks like in IE7.

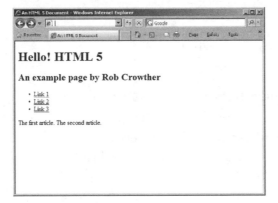

But all is not lost. You can trick IE into recognizing elements with a bit of JavaScript. This code will persuade IE that the `<section>` element exists and should have styles applied to it:

```
document.createElement("section");
```

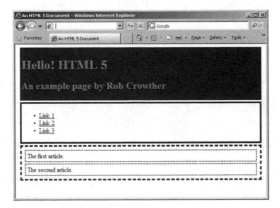

Here's the final listing, with each element we want to use enabled in IE:

```
<script>
  document.createElement("header");
  document.createElement("nav");
  document.createElement("article");
  document.createElement("section");
</script>

<style>
  header, nav, section, article {
   padding: 4px; margin: 4px; display: block; }
  header { background: #000; color: #999; }
  nav { border: 4px solid #000; }
  section { border: 4px dashed #000; }
  article { border: 2px dotted #000; }
</style>
```

Enabling HTML5 support in Internet Explorer with html5.js

Rather than work out for yourself what elements you need to fix in Internet Explorer, you can use one of the freely available compatibility scripts. A simple one with a good following is html5.js, available at http://code.google.com/p/html5shiv/.

Of course, the main drawback of these approaches is that they won't work if JavaScript is disabled in the browser or if something blocks your JavaScript from being downloaded, such as a corporate content filter or a personal firewall. Although this is likely to be a small percentage of users for most sites, you should do some analysis of your existing site visitors before embarking on an HTML5 redesign.

Summary

In this chapter, you've learned about the new markup elements in HTML5 and the formal structure provided for them, and the elements inherited from HTML4, provided by the outlining algorithm and the content model. You've looked at several popular websites and seen how the content they display fits naturally into the new semantic elements of HTML5, reducing the need for content authors to add semantic meaning to neutral <div> and <span> tags through the id and class attributes. You've also seen how the new global attributes in HTML5 allow you to extend the expressive power and accessibility of HTML documents.

NOW THAT YOU'VE LEARNED HOW HTML5 IMPROVES MATTERS FOR THOSE WRITING TRADITIONAL HTML DOCUMENTS, IT'S TIME TO MOVE ON TO THE MAIN FOCUS OF HTML5: MARKUP FOR APPLICATIONS. WE'LL START IN THE NEXT CHAPTER WITH A LOOK AT THE ENHANCED SUPPORT FOR FORMS.

HTML5 forms

- *New input types in HTML5*
- *HTML5 form features for improved user experience*
- *Automatic client-side form validation*

Forms are fundamental components of web applications. This chapter starts with a quick review of the limited options offered in HTML4 and then moves on to the new form controls HTML5 adds. We'll investigate the built-in validation features offered in HTML5 and then look at more new field types that take advantage of that functionality. After that, we'll examine some other new features in HTML5 forms, such as placeholder

USER FRIENDLY by J.D. "Illiad" Frazer

I NEED A FORM ON OUR WEBSITE SO PEOPLE CAN TELL ME THEIR EMAIL ADDRESSES.

WHAT MAKES YOU THINK PEOPLE WILL WANT TO?

THERE'S A PRIZE.

IT'S WIN-WIN. I GET RID OF MY OLD IPOD, AND THEY GET TO RECEIVE TARGETED MARKETING EMAILS BASED ON THEIR INFO.

OK IT'LL TAKE ME A DAY TO CODE UP THE VALIDATION.

DON'T WASTE TIME WITH THAT. JUST SLAP IT TOGETHER TIME IS MONEY!

text and autofocus, before taking a look at the current state of browser support and learning how you can take advantage of these new features without leaving older browsers behind.

The limitations of HTML4 forms

HTML4 has a paltry selection of input types: three ways of entering text and three ways of selecting from a predefined list of options. Let's review what's available in HTML4 before you learn about the new features available in HTML5:

The text input is the workhorse of HTML4 forms:

```
<input type="text" value="abc">
```

Usually, when you can't predict what the user will want to enter but know it will be fairly short, you have to use an input of type text. This includes usernames, dates and times, search terms, email addresses, URLs, telephone numbers, currency, credit card numbers, and any simple numeric values.

If the user needs to choose from a limited number of possible values, you can use a <select> element. A <textarea> element is for larger amounts of free text, when you expect paragraphs rather than a few words:

```
<select>
    <option selected>Option 1
    </option>
    <option>Option 2</option>
    <option>Option 3</option>
</select>
```

The <select> element allows the user to select from predefined options. It's normally a drop-down list (top), but you can also use the size attribute so that more than one option shows (bottom):

```
<select size="3">
    <option selected>Option 1
    </option>
    <option>Option 2</option>
    <option>Option 3</option>
</select>
<textarea>abc</textarea>
```

An alternative to the <select> element is the use of radio buttons. These are another type of <input> element, but, in normal circumstances, there's more than one in a set. They're linked by having the same value for their name attribute:

```
<label for="exradio1">Radio 1: </label>
<input type="radio" id="exradio1"
 name="exradio">
<label for="exradio2">Radio 2: </label>
<input type="radio" id="exradio2"
 name="exradio">
<label for="exradio3">Radio 3: </label>
<input type="radio" id="exradio3"
 name="exradio" selected>
```

Within a set of radio buttons, only one can be selected at a time. If you want the user to be able to select multiple items, you can use either the <select> element or a set of check boxes:

```
<label for="excheckbox1">
  Checkbox 1:
</label>
<input type="checkbox"
```

```
  name="checkbox1" id="excheckbox1">
<label for="excheckbox2">
  Checkbox 2:
</label>
<input type="checkbox"
  name="checkbox1" id="excheckbox2">
```

Finally, this example shows the <field-set> element with its <legend>, a file-upload input, and a submit input:

```
<fieldset title="Other form elements">
  <legend>Example</legend>
  <label>
    Upload file
    <input type="file" name="name">
  </label>
</fieldset>
<input type="submit">
```

The <fieldset> and <legend> elements are useful for grouping sets of controls together in long forms. When used correctly, they're also good

COLUMBIA INTERNET CUSTOMER SURVEY

HI, I'M STEF MURKY OF COLUMBIA INTERNET. SIGN UP FOR OUR FREE NEWSLETTER BY FILLING IN THIS FORM. ALL COMPLETED SURVEYS WILL BE ENTERED INTO A PRIZE DRAW TO WIN AN IPOD.*

*TERMS AND CONDITIONS AVAILABLE ON REQUEST

for accessibility. The file control is a way to transfer files to the server, and the Submit button is the most obvious way for the user to send the entire form back to the server. This set of controls has existed mostly unchanged since before forms were first added to the standard in 1996. You can build Stef's sign-up form out of these rudimentary controls.

The figure shows Stef's form implemented using HTML4 form controls. The full source code is available for download from www.manning .com/crowther/. If you're in the United States and wondering what a postal code is, it's similar to a ZIP code—remember that Columbia Internet is a Canadian ISP.

A LOT OF THE IDEAS FOR HTML5 FORMS WERE TAKEN FROM THE XFORMS 2 PROPOSAL, A PARTNER STANDARD IN WHAT WAS TO BE THE XML-BASED FUTURE OF THE WEB WITH XHTML2 (SEE APPENDIX A FOR MORE DETAILS).

But the HTML4 forms solution requires a number of compromises. It uses text inputs for purposes such as numbers and email addresses. For the rest of this chapter, you'll learn about the new form controls provided by HTML5, which are more appropriate for such input.

Numbers, ranges, dates, and times

HTML5 introduces several new form controls that didn't exist in HTML4; they give you more precise control over how you gather user input. In HTML4, all text inputs were just that: text. HTML5 significantly expands the range of controls available, not least by providing two ways of entering numbers and multiple controls for dates and times. We'll look at these new controls for numbers, dates, and times in this section.

Form submission

For a form to be useful in this scenario, there needs to be some server-side processing to deal with the form values the browser sends when the user clicks Submit Query. We don't want to get bogged down in backend issues in this book, so

(continued)

we assume that one of the techies—Mike, Miranda, or Pitr—will take care of that. If you want to test your own forms to see what values they're sending to the server, you can create a simple PHP file:

```php
<?php
foreach ($_POST as $field_name => $field_value) {
    print "Field $field_name : $field_value <br />\n";
}
?>
```

At the top of your HTML form you'll then have some code like this:

```html
<form action="collector.php" method="post">
```

A prebuilt collector.php is available for download from the book's website at www.manning.com/crowther/.

Browser support quick check		Number	Range	Datetime
	Chrome	5	4	20
	Firefox	~	~	~
	Internet Explorer	10	10	~
	Opera	9	9	9
	Safari	5	4	~

MOST OF THE SCREENSHOTS IN THE FOLLOWING SECTIONS WERE TAKEN IN OPERA 11.60 AND 12 BECAUSE THAT WAS THE FIRST BROWSER TO ADD FULL SUPPORT FOR THE NEW CONTROLS. EXCEPTIONS ARE MENTIONED IN THE TEXT.

The basic number input provides a spinbox:

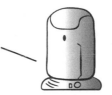

```html
<input type="number" value="4">
```

Normally the arrows increment or decrement by 1, but you can adjust this by using the step attribute. This example increments in steps of 2:

```html
<input type="number" value="4" step="2">
```

If an exact number isn't necessary, you can use a range control. In the browser, this renders as a slider:

```
<input type="range" min="1"
  max="10" value="2">
```

As you can see, the exact value of the range input isn't clearly visible. In practice, you might use it for large numbers where accuracy isn't important. As with the number control, you can specify a step value:

```
<input type="range" min="0" max="1000" value="20" step="20">
```

IF YOU WANT TO USE RANGE FOR A NUMERIC INPUT, THE BEST APPROACH IS TO EITHER LABEL THE HIGH AND LOW VALUES IN YOUR HTML OR PROVIDE SOME OTHER USER FEEDBACK WHEN THE CONTROL IS ADJUSTED—PERHAPS WITH AN <output> ELEMENT (SEE THE SECTION "ELEMENTS FOR USER FEEDBACK"). IN THE MEANTIME, LET'S MOVE ON TO DATES AND TIMES.

Create a simple date input like this:

```
<input type="date">
```

In its unexpanded state (top), it looks similar to a <select> element. But if you activate the control, a date picker pops up (bottom).

The value returned from the date control, and any default value you want to set, are in the format *yyyy-mm-∂∂*. Using this standard ordering prevents any confusion relating to date formats in different countries.

WHAT THE DATE PICKER LOOKS LIKE IS LEFT UP TO THE BROWSER. CURRENTLY THERE'S NO WAY TO STYLE IT THROUGH CSS.

Next, the time input:

```
<input type="time" value="10:30">
```

Again, styling is determined by the browser.

If you want the user's local time, use `datetime-local`:

```
<input type="datetime-local"
 value="2010-05-31T21:00">
```

This looks the same as the `datetime` control but without the UTC annotation. In this example, you can see how to specify a default value for the `datetime` and `datetime-local` input types: `yyyy-mm-ddThh:mm`.

As well as full dates, you can have months or weeks:

```
<input type="month"
 value="2010-05">
```

```
<input type="week">
```

In Opera, these look identical to the full date picker, but some browsers may choose to implement a custom UI.

Validation

Validation is often a crucial issue on the web, both for security and for general smooth operation of apps, but it's something that content authors frequently get wrong. HTML5 has built-in form-validation features. In this section, we'll look at how you can specify that filling in certain fields is required, delimit numeric inputs with maximum and minimum values, and define arbitrary format requirements for any other text field with regular expressions. We'll then examine how these features interact with CSS and JavaScript to allow you to give useful feedback to your users.

		Required	Min/Max	Pattern
Browser support quick check		5	5	5
		4	4	4
		10	10	10
		9	9	9
		5	5	5

If you're accepting input from users through forms, there should always be validation going on at the server. But it provides a better experience to let users know they've made mistakes immediately rather than to let them fill out the whole form, submit, wait for a response, and only then find out they made a mistake.

The required attribute

The simplest form of validation is to mark a field as required. In HTML5 this is done by adding the `required` attribute. If an input is marked as required, the browser shouldn't allow the form to be submitted until the user has provided a value.

This image shows what happens when a text input is marked as required and the user tries to submit the form without entering a value:

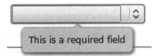

```
<input type="text" required
  name="myrequiredfield">
```

You can add the `required` attribute to any type of input:

```
<input type="date" required
  name="myrequireddate">
```

As the image shows, the results of not entering a value are the same in both examples.

NOTE THAT A `name` ATTRIBUTE IS INCLUDED IN THE EXAMPLE; THIS WILL LABEL THE FIELD'S VALUE WHEN IT'S SENT TO THE SERVER. THE AUTOMATIC VALIDATION OCCURS WHEN THE FORM IS SUBMITTED, SO YOU NEED A SUBMITTABLE FORM FOR THESE EXAMPLES TO WORK.

The min, max, and pattern attributes

The only native validation built into HTML4 for the text input is the `maxlength` attribute. It allows you to specify the maximum number of characters the user is allowed to enter. This is somewhat useful for things like dates and phone numbers that have a well-defined length, but it's not much use for anything else.

In HTML5, you can use the `min` and `max` attributes on the number input type. You already saw these attributes on the range control, where they specify the limits of the slider. On the number control, they trigger an error when the user tries to submit the form:

```
<input type="number" max="10"
  name="exnumber">
```

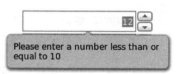

The `min` attribute works exactly the same way:

```
<input type="number" min="4"
name="exnumber">
```

There's also help if the format you require is somewhat more exotic. You can use the `pattern` attribute to supply a regular expression that is then used to validate the field. This example is taken from the HTML5 spec:

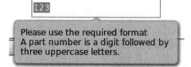

```
<input type="text" name="partno"
 pattern="[0-9][A-Z]{3}"
 title="A part number is a digit
 followed by three uppercase
 letters.">
```

If the validation fails, the browser displays the value of the `title` attribute, so you should include some information there that will help the user in filling out the form.

Taking advantage of validation with CSS

In addition to the visible support in the browser for validation (the messages you've seen in the earlier screenshots), HTML5 provides behind-the-scenes hooks for CSS and JavaScript. These let you provide immediate visual feedback. CSS has two pseudo-classes that allow you to provide different styles based on whether they're currently valid or invalid.

Here's a simple pair of CSS rules to put a green outline around valid controls and a dotted red outline around invalid controls:

```
input:valid {
    outline: 5px solid green;
}

input:invalid {
    outline: 5px dashed red;
}
```

The images show the result of applying this CSS to these three number controls:

```
<input type="number" required>
<input type="number" min="4"
  value="4">
<input type="number" min="4"  value="3">
```

IN REAL LIFE, OF COURSE, YOU WOULDN'T SPECIFY SOMETHING INVALID AS THE DEFAULT VALUE! NOTE THAT THE VALIDITY STATE APPLIES EVEN IF THE FORM ISN'T SUBMITTABLE.

The same CSS works equally well with text controls using the pattern attribute. The three images shown here are based on the example from the section "The min, max, and pattern attributes":

```
<input type="text"
 pattern="[0-9][A-Z]{3}">
<input type="text"
 pattern="[0-9][A-Z]{3}"
 value="1abc">
<input type="text"
 pattern="[0-9][A-Z]{3}"
 value="1ABC">
```

There's also CSS support for styling required controls differently through pseudo-classes:

```
input:required {
    outline: 5px dashed blue;
}
input:optional {
    outline: 5px solid green;
}
```

The images show the result of this CSS applied to these two inputs:

```
<input type="number" required>
<input type="number">
```

Turning off validation

Sometimes you want the user to be able to submit the form without triggering validation. For example, if a form is long and has many sections, you might want to let the user save their progress and come back and complete the form later. To do this, HTML5 provides two new attributes: novalidate and formnovalidate.

The novalidate attribute can be applied to the <form> element itself, whereas the formnovalidate attribute affects the enter form but should be applied only to a Submit button:

```
<input type="submit" value="Save for Later" formnovalidate>
```

Email and URLs

Now that you've seen the validation features, let's consider two further new input types: email and url. We didn't look at them until now because, without HTML5's validation features, they look and behave identical to HTML4 text inputs.

ON THE WEB, THERE ARE PROBABLY MORE FORMS WHERE YOU NEED TO ENTER AN EMAIL ADDRESS THAN FORMS WHERE YOU DON'T.

		email	url
Browser support quick check		5	4
		4	4
		10	10
		9	9
		5	4

Email addresses

Having seen the pattern attribute, you're probably thinking it would be straightforward to either write your own regular expression or find one on the web and then implement your own email field. The problem is, you'd probably get it wrong. Email had reached the popular consciousness even before the web was born, and despite some confusion, most people can recognize an email address. Let's have one of our resident experts do a quick test to see if you really know what an email address looks like.

PITR'S EMAIL VALIDITY TEST FOR ASPIRING EVIL GENIUSES

WE WILL BE SEEINK IF YOU HALF AS SMART AS YOU THINKINK YOU ARE

VALID?

1. ROB+CROWTHER@DOMAIN.COM ☐
2. ROB!CROWTHER@DOMAIN.COM ☐
3. ROB@CROWTHER@DOMAIN.COM ☐
4. ROB.CROWTHER@DOMAIN.COM ☐ ← THAT'S A COMMA
5. ROB-CROWTHER@DOMAIN.COM ☐
6. ROB_CROWTHER@DOMAIN.COM ☐
7. ROB CROWTHER@DOMAIN.COM ☐
8. "ROBCROWTHER"@DOMAIN.COM ☐
9. 'ROB CROWTHER'@DOMAIN.COM ☐
10. 'ROBCROWTHER'@DOMAIN.COM ☐

Easy? Half of them are valid and half of them invalid; Pitr will tell you which ones are which at the end of the section. Note that by *valid* we mean they're constructed correctly, not that you'll be able to send email to them successfully. The reason you'd be almost certainly wrong if you implemented an email field yourself is that even the experts can't agree on what a valid email address looks like. The HTML5 spec itself is "willfully violating" the standard:

A valid e-mail address is a string that matches the ABNF production 1*(atext / ".") "@" ldh-str 1*("." ldh-str) *where* atext *is defined in RFC 5322 section 3.2.3, and* ldh-str *is defined in RFC 1034 section 3.5.*

This requirement is a willful violation of RFC 5322, which defines a syntax for e-mail addresses that is simultaneously too strict (before the "@" character), too vague (after the "@" character), and too lax (allowing comments, whitespace characters, and quoted strings in manners unfamiliar to most users) to be of practical use here.

Here's the code for this email input:

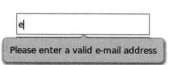

```
<input type="email">
```

Visually it looks the same as a normal text input.

If you type in an invalid email address and submit the form, you'll get an error message similar to the one shown here.

IN HTML5, THE INVALID EMAILS ADDRESSES ARE BEINK 3, 4, 7, 8, AND 9. 1, 2, 5, 6, AND 10 ARE BEINK VALID.

Web addresses

Forms in which you enter a URL are also common. Think about the last time you posted a comment on a blog; it's likely the form included a URL field. Like email addresses, valid URLs have some esoteric rules, but HTML5 means you don't need to worry about what they are.

Creating a URL control is as easy as changing the type:

```
<input type="url">
```

Again, there's no visual indication that a URL is required. But when you attempt to submit an invalid URL, you get a similar message.

> u
>
> Please enter a valid web address

Elements for user feedback

Sometimes you may want to show the user a result—something calculated from the values on the rest of the form. Think of a shopping cart that shows the running total of the user's expenditures. In HTML4, you could use JavaScript to insert the value into a read-only field, or you might have written the value into the HTML content, but there was no way to indicate that the field or the value had any sort of relationship to the form values or even was part of the form at all. HTML5 changes all that with its three built-in form controls for user feedback: output, progress, and meter.

Browser support quick check	Output	Progress	Meter
	13	8	8
	4	6	6
	10	10	~
	9	11	11
	5	~	~

The <output> element

The <output> element allows you to declare a relationship between one or more <input> elements and its own value. The value of the <output> element can be anything you'd have been happy to put in an <input> element in HTML4, such as text, numbers, and dates.

To see <output> in action, first create a couple of numeric form inputs in a <fieldset>:

```
<fieldset>
    <legend>Output example</legend>
    <label for="one">Number: </label>
    <input type="number" name="one">
    <label for="two">Range: </label>
    <input type="range" name="two" min="0" max="10">
</fieldset>
```

Now add an <output> element just before the closing </fieldset>:

```
<label for="out">Output: </label>
<output id="out" for="one two">
    0
</output>
```

Number:	6
Range:	
Output:	11

The value goes between the tags rather than in an attribute as with an <input> element. The for attribute indicates the fields with which the <output> is associated.

Finally, you need some script to update the <output> element when there is input. You do this on the parent <fieldset> element:

```
<fieldset oninput="out.value = one.valueAsNumber + two.valueAsNumber;">
```

THE EXACT RELATIONSHIP BETWEEN THE <input> ELEMENTS LISTED IN THE for ATTRIBUTE AND THE <output> VALUE HAS TO BE DEFINED IN CODE. HTML5 DOESN'T ATTEMPT TO GUESS WHETHER YOU WANT TO ADD, SUBTRACT, MULTIPLY, OR CALCULATE INTEREST. WE'LL DISCUSS THE oninput EVENT LATER IN THIS CHAPTER.

The `<progress>` element

You often see complex processes broken into several steps. Buying a book at Amazon, for instance, usually proceeds through pages for entering your personal information, entering your credit card details, and entering the delivery details, among others, before finally confirming your purchase. If you make a purchase at Amazon you'll notice, at the top of the screen, a progress indicator.

This follows user interface design best practice: when you're putting a user through a multistep process, always give them an indication of how far along they are. This is such a common requirement that HTML5 adds a special element to support it:

```
<progress value="5" min="0" max="9">5 out of 9</progress>
```

WebKit has an initial implementa-   Progress
tion in its nightly builds.

The max attribute gives the value that represents completion and the value that indicates how close to completion you are. The `<progress>` element can contain phrasing content—text, inline markup, and images—but no other `<progress>` elements. You could represent Amazon's progress bar like this:

```
<progress max="7" value="2">
    <img src="order-progress-step-2.png" alt="Step 2 of 7">
</progress>
```

The `<progress>` element can also be used in applications to give feedback on long-running operations like file uploads.

THE `<progress>` ELEMENT HAS STRONG NATIVE SEMANTICS FOR THE PURPOSES OF ARIA. IT SHOULD BE REPORTED AUTOMATICALLY AS BEING IN THE ARIA progressbar ROLE BY SUPPORTING AGENTS. AS WE DISCUSSED IN CHAPTER 1, THIS IMPROVES THE ACCESSIBILITY OF YOUR WEB APPS WITH NO EXTRA EFFORT ON YOUR PART.

The <meter> element

The <meter> element is similar to <progress> but more general-purpose in its semantic value. It should be used to indicate a scalar measurement within known bounds—for example, disk-space usage, progress through an audio track, or share of a popular vote.

Chrome has support for the <meter> element in version 6:

Meter

```
<label for="exmeter">Meter</label>
<meter id="exmeter"
 value="3" min="1" max="6"
 high="5" low="2" optimum="3">
    3 out of 6
</meter>
```

Note the high and low attributes—if the value encroaches into them, it has a visible effect:

Meter

```
<label for="exmeter">Meter</label>
<meter id="exmeter"
 value="5" min="1" max="6"
 high="5" low="2" optimum="3">
    5 out of 6
</meter>
```

As with the <progress> element, browsers that don't support the <meter> element display the fallback content between the opening and closing tags. Although we use text here, you can include an image or even some SVG that more closely resembles the rendering of the browsers that do support <meter>.

Meter   5 out of 6

Less-common form controls

Numbers, dates, times, email addresses, and URLs—these are all fields you're likely to need in nearly every form, but HTML5 doesn't stop there. There are some additional form controls that you'll need either less regularly or when you're building particular types of web applications. These controls so far lack implementations or common use cases, but they may see more uptake in the future as HTML is used for more desktop-style (or mobile) applications.

Browser support quick check		Tel	Color	<keygen>
		4	20	1
		4	~	1
		10	~	~
		9	11	3
		4	~	1.2

Telephone numbers

You don't often need telephone numbers in a web app, but they're a common requirement for things like credit card forms, so HTML5 has an input type for them:

```
<input type="tel">
```

But the format for a telephone number is unpredictable. Phones tend to deal in strings of digits, but people break them into international dialing codes, area codes, and local numbers with spaces, brackets, and dashes.

WHAT VALUE CAN THESE FORM FIELDS HAVE? THE tel TYPE SEEMS PARTICULARLY USELESS—IT DOESN'T EVEN OFFER VALIDATION.

SURELY THERE'S MORE TO IT THAN THAT.

MY BROWSER SEEMS TO DO PRETTY WELL WITH THAT ALREADY.

IT'S AN ACCESSIBILITY WIN—YOU CAN TELL USERS WHAT TYPE OF INFORMATION THE FIELD EXPECTS EVEN IF THE PAGE CONTENT DOESN'T MAKE IT CLEAR.

IT'S ALSO HELPFUL IN FORM AUTOFILL FUNCTIONALITY. THE BROWSER CAN OFFER ONLY EMAIL ADDRESSES YOU'VE PREVIOUSLY USED FOR EMAIL FIELDS AND PHONE NUMBERS FOR TELEPHONE FIELDS. MOBILE BROWSERS CAN AUTOMATICALLY INSERT YOUR OWN PHONE NUMBER.

BUT IT'S BASED ON GUESSING AND HEURISTICS. THE EXTRA INFORMATION MAKES IT MORE ACCURATE.

The HTML5 spec therefore doesn't specify a format; the tel type is basically the same as a text input other than in its semantic content. If you want to enforce a particular format on the tel field, you'll have to use the pattern attribute discussed in the section "The min, max, and pattern attributes."

Color pickers

Color isn't widespread in today's web forms. But because one of the key focuses of HTML5 is to enable HTML applications, color pickers are likely to be a more common requirement in the future. The first implementation of the color input type is in Opera 11.

The HTML5 markup for a color picker is

```
<input type="color">
```

The default value is #000000. Selected values are always in #rrggbb hexadecimal shorthand.

When the user expands the control, a selection of common colors is presented. Currently there's no way to configure this set of colors, but clicking the Other button brings up the full color picker.

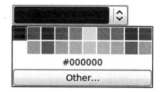

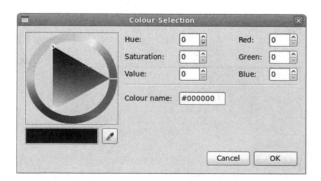

<keygen>

THE PURPOSE OF <keygen> IS TO PROVIDE AN API INTO YOUR OPERATING SYSTEM'S CRYPTOGRAPHY STORE. IT ALLOWS PUBLIC/PRIVATE KEY EXCHANGE TO TAKE PLACE BETWEEN YOU AND THE SERVER. IF THAT DOESN'T MAKE ANY SENSE TO YOU, IT'S SAFE TO SKIP AHEAD TO THE NEXT SECTION.

<keygen> originated as a proprietary feature in Netscape Navigator. It was then reverse-engineered by Opera and WebKit. As long as the element is useful, the HTML5 way is to document existing behavior so that everyone can implement in an interoperable manner. We won't use <keygen> in this book, because it depends on relatively complex server-side code to be useful, but it's mentioned here for completeness.

YOU'VE NOW LEARNED ABOUT THE MANY NEW INPUT TYPES AND ELEMENTS AVAILABLE IN HTML5 FORMS, BUT IT DOESN'T STOP THERE. THE NEXT SECTION INVESTIGATES NEW FORM FEATURES THAT AREN'T TIED TO SPECIFIC ELEMENTS.

New attributes for the <input> element

Browser support quick check		placeholder	autofocus	autocomplete
		10	6	17
		4	4	4
		10	10	10
		11	11	10
		5	5	5

In addition to the new form controls in HTML5, existing HTML4 form controls have been extended with new attributes. You've already seen some of these in the section on validation, "The required attribute," where we covered attributes such as required and pattern, but several others can be applied to most <input> elements: placeholder, autofocus, and autocomplete.

Placeholder text

A popular technique in recent years has been to put a suggestion for a field's required user input in the field by default. This is called *placeholder text*. Here are two examples of placeholder text on the Firefox search bar and on the WordPress login.

THIS APPROACH IS POPULAR WITH DESIGNERS BECAUSE USING FIELD NAMES AS PLACEHOLDERS DOESN'T TAKE UP ANY EXTRA SPACE, BUT PROVIDES THE USER WITH USEFUL INFORMATION ABOUT THE EXPECTED INPUT. IT'S ALSO A COMPACT WAY OF INDICATING THE DESIRED INPUT FORMAT.

There are several common approaches to achieving this look with JavaScript. They mostly boil down to two alternatives:

- Make the input transparent, and place the label element behind it.
- Hide the label element, but copy the text of the label into the input.

You then have to add JavaScript to remove the placeholder text when a user clicks the control and put it back if the user leaves the control without entering a value. But a number of issues can occur:

1 Errors in the JavaScript can stop the placeholder text from being removed when a user clicks into the element. If users have JavaScript disabled, the text won't work properly or at all.

2 The placeholder can interfere with browser form-fill functionality that remembers values for frequently used forms.

3 Assistive technology has no way of distinguishing between placeholder text and valid input.

HTML5 HAS SUPPORT FOR PLACEHOLDERS BUILT IN THANKS TO THE NEW placeholder ATTRIBUTE. ADD THIS ATTRIBUTE TO THE <input> ELEMENT WITH THE VALUE YOU WANT TO USE.

```
<input type="email"
 placeholder="email@example.com">
```

You're protected from JavaScript errors causing issues because the functionality no longer depends on your (or indeed, any) JavaScript. Browsers can handle the interaction with native functionality better because everything is now under their control; and for the same reason, browsers can keep assistive technology better informed of what's going on.

Form autofocus

As a convenience, many web forms use JavaScript to put the focus on the first <input> element when the page loads. For instance, if you visit the Google homepage and start typing, the text will appear in the search field in the middle of the page. Rather than have everyone write their own JavaScript routine to achieve this, HTML5 adds support directly to HTML:

```
<input type="text" autofocus>
```

Protecting private information with the autocomplete attribute

The autocomplete attribute allows you to provide a hint to the browser that the values entered into a field shouldn't be remembered for future use by the browser's auto-form-filling functionality. This could be because the field accepts information that's supposed to be secret (for instance, a PIN number) or because the field expects a one-off value where past values entered are likely to be irrelevant (such as a password-reset code):

```
<label>Account: <input type="text" name="ac" autocomplete="off"></label>
<label>PIN: <input type="password" name="pin" autocomplete="off"></label>
```

Extending forms with JavaScript

THERE ARE SEVERAL OTHER ENHANCEMENTS TO FORMS IN HTML5 OVER AND ABOVE THE NEW CONTROLS. THESE INCLUDE WAYS TO ACCESS VALIDITY INFORMATION THROUGH JAVASCRIPT AS WELL AS CONVENIENCE FEATURES THAT EITHER COMPLETELY REPLACE THE JAVASCRIPT YOU WOULD COMMONLY WRITE FOR EVERY FORM TODAY OR MAKE VARIOUS SCRIPTING OPERATIONS MUCH EASIER.

Customizing the validation messages

The default validation messages are a little bland. And although the `pattern` attribute allows you to include a custom message in the `title` attribute, there's no attribute you can use to provide a custom message to the other input types. But you can supply a custom message in script.

Use the `setCustomValidity` property of the `<input>` element in the DOM:

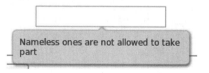

```
var fldName =
document.getElementById('fullname');
fldName.oninvalid =
 function () {
  fldName.setCustomValidity("");
  if (!fldName.validity.valid) {
    fldName.setCustomValidity(
      "Nameless ones are not " +
      "allowed to take part"
    );
  }
};
```

As you can see, your message is displayed if the field fails the `validity` check. In this case the required attribute was set on the text field like this:

```
<input id="fullname" type="text" required>
```

Also, for the `oninvalid` event to fire, the form must be submitted; see more on this in the section "Triggering validation with JavaScript."

NOTE THAT THE FIRST STEP IN THE FUNCTION IN THE PRECEDING CODE SNIPPET RESETS THE CUSTOM VALIDITY MESSAGE TO AN EMPTY STRING. THIS IS BECAUSE SETTING THE CUSTOM VALIDITY MESSAGE FORCES THE VALID STATUS TO BE FALSE. IT WILL BE IMPOSSIBLE TO SUBMIT THE FORM AFTER THE ERROR IF THE MESSAGE ISN'T RESET.

Overriding the `invalid` event on the form element in question lets you take more complete control of the user experience while still taking advantage of built-in validation.

Check the validity property in the DOM, and add your own code to report the validity status:

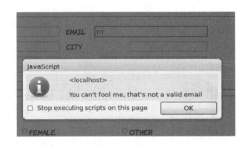

```
var fldEmail =
document.getElementById('email');
fldEmail.addEventListener(
  'invalid',
  function(event) {
    alert(
    "You can't fool me, " +
    "that's not a valid email"
    );
    event.preventDefault();
  }
  ,false);
```

This code assumes you have a submittable form with an input like this:

```
<input id="email" type="email">
```

The browser will fire the invalid event when the form is submitted and there is text which is not a valid email address in the field. Note that the event handler function cancels the default event processing (with event.preventDefault()) in order to prevent the message from the browser from also appearing.

Triggering validation with JavaScript

A browser will only trigger form validation when the form is submitted. This is sensible: having error messages pop up repeatedly while the user's trying to fill in the form would be distracting.

 THERE MAY BE OCCASIONS WHEN YOU WANT TO TRIGGER VALIDATION WITHOUT SUBMITTING THE FORM—POSSIBLY THE ALLOWED VALUES FOR A LATER FIELD ON THE FORM DEPEND ON THE USER ALREADY HAVING ENTERED A VALID EMAIL ADDRESS, OR MAYBE THE INPUT ISN'T PART OF A FORM AT ALL.

Suppose you have an email input in your HTML, like this:

```
<input id="email" type="email">
```

You can trigger validation by calling the checkValidity() method:

```
document.getElementById('email').checkValidity();
```

 IN OPERA, THE FIELD WILL BE VALIDATED AS IT WOULD BE WHEN THE FORM IS SUBMITTED. THUS IF THE EMAIL ADDRESS IS INVALID, THE NORMAL MESSAGE WILL POP UP, ALTHOUGH THIS ISN'T REQUIRED BY THE SPEC. THE METHOD ALSO WORKS IN FIREFOX 4 AND RECENT CHROME AND SAFARI RELEASES, RETURNING false IF THE EMAIL ADDRESS IS INVALID. YOU CAN USE THE RETURN VALUE TO IMPLEMENT YOUR OWN NOTIFICATIONS.

Responding to any changes in value

Before HTML5, when you had to write your own form-validation code, it was a common technique to attach the JavaScript validation to the onchange event handler. But in HTML4, onchange was only a valid attribute on <input>, <select>, and <textarea>, and it was fired only when the form control that changed lost focus.

 AN *EVENT HANDLER* IS A HOOK HTML PROVIDES TO JAVASCRIPT TO LET YOU RUN CODE WHEN PARTICULAR THINGS HAPPEN. YOU MIGHT WANT TO KNOW WHEN THE PAGE FINISHES LOADING (onload), OR WHEN THE USER CLICKS SOMETHING (onclick), OR, AS IN THIS CASE, WHEN THE USER LEAVES AN INPUT FIELD IN WHICH THE VALUE HAS CHANGED (onchange). WHEN THE EVENT HAPPENS, IT IS SAID TO *FIRE*. CHECK APPENDIX D FOR MORE ON EVENT HANDLERS.

HTML5 provides a new event—oninput—which is fired by any form element when the value changes, as the value changes, and allows all event-handling attributes to be specified on any element. You've already seen this feature in action when we discussed the <output> element. Let's compare the code that powered the <output> element earlier (on the left) with a version that relies on attaching to the event handler of each field (on the right):

```
<fieldset oninput="value =
    one.valueAsNumber +
    two.valueAsNumber">
  <label for="one">Number: </label>
  <input type="number" name="one">

  <label for="two">Range: </label>
  <input type="range" name="two"
    min="0" max="10">

  <label for="out">Output: </label>
  <output id="out" for="one two">
    0
  </output>
</fieldset>
```

```
<fieldset>
  <label for="one">Number: </label>
  <input type="number" name="one"
    onchange="out.value =
      one.valueAsNumber +
      two.valueAsNumber">

  <label for="two">Range: </label>
  <input type="range" name="two"
    onchange="exoutput1.value =
      one.valueAsNumber +
      two.valueAsNumber">

  <label for="out">Output: </label>
  <output id="out"
    for="one two">6</output>
</fieldset>
```

HAVING TO HANDLE CHANGES ON EACH <input> ELEMENT INDIVIDUALLY CAN LEAD TO EXTRA CODE, BUT THERE'S A MORE IMPORTANT ADVANTAGE: THE onchange EVENT ONLY FIRES AFTER THE USER LEAVES THE FIELD BY TABBING OUT OF IT OR CLICKING ELSEWHERE ON THE PAGE. THE oninput EVENT FIRES FOR ANY CHANGE.

Creating combo boxes with <datalist>

One type of form control that's common in desktop applications but not available in HTML4 is the *combo box*, so named because it's a combination of a text box and a select list—the user can select from a list or free-type a value that isn't on the list. When AJAX was becoming popular, one of the most common features of the early JavaScript libraries was support for creating combo-box-like features.

HTML5 adds support for this directly into the markup with the <datalist> element. A *datalist* is a named list of options, similar to the list of options in a <select> element, which can then be associated with one or more <input> elements using the list attribute.

In this example, with a screenshot taken in Firefox, the input has been associated with a <datalist> with the id value "browsers". When a user selects the input, the list of options pops up. The user can pick one of the options using the cursor keys or type their own:

```
<input type="text" name="browser"
 list="browsers">
<datalist id="browsers">
    <option
     value="Internet Explorer">
    <option value="Firefox">
    <option value="Safari">
    <option value="Chrome">
    <option value="Opera">
</datalist>
```

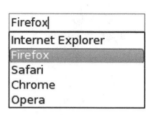

At the time of writing, Opera is the only browser to implement the color input type and allow the <datalist> element to be attached to that. This sets the default colors available on the initial drop-down:

```
<input type="color"
       list="greyscale">

<datalist id="greyscale">
    <option value="#000000">
    <option value="#333333">
    <option value="#666666">
    <option value="#999999">
    <option value="#cccccc">
</datalist>

<input type="color"
       list="rainbow">

<datalist id="rainbow">
    <option value="#FF0000">
    <option value="#FFA500">
```

Color:

Color:

```
      <option value="#FFFF00">
      <option value="#008000">
      <option value="#0000FF">
      <option value="#4B0082">
      <option value="#EE82EE">
</datalist>
```

Easy ways to work with form values in JavaScript

This is another feature you've already seen in action. When you're dealing with forms in JavaScript, the value is always a string, even if it represents a date or a number. Because JavaScript automatically converts the types of any value involved in an expression, this can easily lead to errors that are hard to spot.

This code looks similar to the code you saw in the section "The <output> element," but it doesn't have the results you might expect:

Number: 5

Range:

Output: 53

```
<label for="one">Number: </label>
<input type="number"
 value="5" name="one">

<label for="two">Range: </label>
<input type="range" name="two"
 min="0" max="10" value="3">

<label for="out">Output: </label>
<output id="out" for="one two"
 onforminput="value =
  one.value +
  two.value">0</output>
```

Can you spot the difference?
Compare the last two lines with the code used earlier (on the right):

```
  one.value +
  two.value">0</output>
```

```
one.valueAsNumber +
two.valueAsNumber">0</output>
```

YOU MIGHT EXPECT 5 + 3 TO BE 8, BUT BECAUSE THE FORM VALUES ARE STRINGS, YOU AREN'T PERFORMING ADDITION—YOU'RE PERFORMING CONCATENATION. IT'S RELATIVELY STRAIGHTFORWARD TO WORK AROUND THE ISSUE IN HTML4, BUT WHY SHOULD YOU HAVE TO? HTML5 PROVIDES THE PROPERTIES valueAsDate AND valueAsNumber SO THAT YOU CAN GET DIRECTLY AT THE VALUES YOU NEED.

Browser support and detecting HTML5 features

Unlike the structural elements we looked at in chapter 1, the new form elements have more complex associated behavior and APIs. The structural elements merely had to exist; these form elements have to do something for you to be able to say a browser supports them. With these more complex requirements, it's not surprising that support isn't yet as far advanced as it might be. The following table shows the level of support in the current and, where known, upcoming versions of all the major browsers.

	12	14	4	6	8	9	10	11.1	11.5	5	5.1
Input types	●	●	●	●			●	●	●	●	●
Validation API	●	●	●	●			●	●	●	●	●
Placeholder	●	●	●	●			●	●	●	●	●
Autofocus	●	●	●	●			●	●	●	●	●
Input UI								●	●		
Range	●	●						●	●	●	●
Meter	●	●						●	●		
Progress	●	●		●				●	●		
Output		●	●	●			●	●	●		●

Key:
- ● Complete or nearly complete support
- ○ Incomplete or alternative support
-   Little or no support

Browser inconsistencies

WebKit was one of the first browsers to support the new input types, enabling keyboards tuned to the required input type on the iPhone. The latest versions support the validation API, but you need to write your own code to take advantage of it. Support for the <output> element was only added in recent versions, but you can always access the value with innerHTML instead.

Firefox 4 has support for HTML5 forms in the beta release, including <datalist>. Current versions of Firefox support everything but the new input types that require some UI (dates and times, numbers). Firefox 4 also added default styling for the :invalid pseudo-class; if you want to turn that off, use the following in your CSS:

```
:invalid { box-shadow: none; }
```

Firefox also has an experimental attribute, x-moz-errormessage, to allow you to customize the error message:

```
<input type="email" name="email" x-moz-errormessage="Email please!">
```

Detecting supported features

As mentioned, if a browser has no support for one of the new form input types, it will convert it to an input of type text. This makes it easy to detect whether an input type is supported in JavaScript—just create an element of the desired type and then immediately look to see if it's a text input:

```
var el = document.createElement("input");
el.setAttribute("type", "date");
if (el.type == "text") {
    implementDateValidation();
}
```

THE PREVIOUS SNIPPET CREATES A date INPUT AND THEN CHECKS TO SEE WHAT TYPE THE BROWSER THINKS IT IS. IF IT'S text, YOU CALL A FUNCTION implementDateValidation TO DEAL WITH BROWSERS THAT DON'T SUPPORT THE date INPUT TYPE.

For date inputs you have to go one step further. If you remember, WebKit implements the date input type but doesn't provide any UI for it. To detect if a UI is provided, set a value on the date element that isn't a date:

```
var el = document.createElement("input");
el.setAttribute("type", "date");
el.value = "text";
if (el. value == "text") {
    implementDateUI();
}
```

IF THE BROWSER IMPLEMENTS THE DATE UI COMPONENTS, THEN IT WILL BE IMPOSSIBLE TO SET THE VALUE OF THE INPUT TO THE STRING "TEXT". THEREFORE, IF THE ELEMENT REPORTS ITS VALUE AS "TEXT" AFTER YOU'VE SET IT, THE UI ISN'T IMPLEMENTED BY THE BROWSER AND YOU SHOULD PROVIDE YOUR OWN. YOU MIGHT ALSO CONSIDER SETTING AN APPROPRIATE pattern ATTRIBUTE AT THIS POINT.

You may also want to check whether the user's browser supports one of the new form attributes, such as autofocus or placeholder. Here's some code to do this:

```
var el = document.createElement("input");
if (!!('placeholder' in el)) {
    window.alert('Placeholder supported');
} else {
    window.alert('Placeholder not supported');
}
```

THE EASIEST APPROACH IS TO LOOP THROUGH THE AVAILABLE PROPERTIES ON AN ELEMENT AND SEE IF ONE OF THEM IS THE ATTRIBUTE YOU'RE LOOKING FOR. THIS SAME APPROACH CAN BE USED FOR ANY OF THE OTHER NEW HTML5 ATTRIBUTES, NOT JUST FORM ELEMENTS.

The final thing you might want to check is whether the browser supports a particular event, such as the oninvalid event we discussed earlier:

```
var eventName = "oninvalid";
var isSupported = !!(eventName in el);
```

```
if (!isSupported && el.setAttribute) {
    el.setAttribute(eventName, 'return;');
    isSupported = typeof el[eventName] == 'function';
}
if (isSupported) {
    window.alert('oninvalid supported');
}
```

THE PREVIOUS CODE TRIES TWO DIFFERENT APPROACHES. FIRST IT LOOKS TO SEE IF THE oninvalid EVENT EXISTS IN THE ELEMENT PROPERTIES. IF THAT FAILS, IT TRIES TO SET THE EVENT ON THE ELEMENT AND, SIMILAR TO THE EARLIER INPUT-TYPE DETECTION, LOOKS TO SEE IF THE TYPE OF THE ATTRIBUTE IS A FUNCTION.

YOU DON'T HAVE TO WRITE ALL THIS DETECTION CODE YOURSELF—THERE'S ALREADY A LIBRARY THAT WILL DO THE WORK FOR YOU. CHECK OUT THE MODERNIZR LIBRARY AT WWW.MODERNIZR.COM. IF YOU DON'T FANCY WRITING ANY OF YOUR OWN FORM-VALIDATION CODE, YOU CAN TRY A DIFFERENT LIBRARY THAT ENABLES HTML5 FORMS SUPPORT IN ALL BROWSERS: HTML5-NOW.

The html5-now library

Html5-now is an open source project started by Dean Edwards. Dean is famous for writing several drop-in scripts for old versions of Internet Explorer, which made them behave in a standards-compliant manner. The aim of html5-now.js is to provide a drop-in solution that patches the browser's holes in HTML5 support. It's currently in alpha, but it already provides a lot of support for HTML5 form controls. Download it from http://code.google.com/p/html5-now/, and then include it in your page like this:

```
<script src="html5-now/html5-now.js"></script>
```

The result of adding the script to a form can be seen in the screenshots that follow. On the left is a screenshot of our HTML5 form in Firefox 3.6; all the HTML5 controls render as text. On the right, after html5-now.js is added, the number and date controls work.

COLUMBIA INTERNET CUSTON

    YOUR DETAILS
    NAME   EM/
    ADDRESS   CI1
    POSTAL CODE   PRC
    TELEPHONE

    PERSONAL INFORMATION

    GENDER:

    ○ MALE   ○ FEMALE
    DATE OF BIRTH

    SURVEY
    AVERAGE NUMBER OF HOURS SPENT BROWSING PER
    DAY: WH

    WHAT IS YOUR FAVORITE WEBSITE?:

    Submit Query

COLUMBIA INTERNET CUSTON

    YOUR DETAILS
    NAME   EM/
    ADDRESS   CI1
    POSTAL CODE   PRC
    TELEPHONE

    PERSONAL INFORMATION

    GENDER:

    ○ MALE   ○ FEMALE
    DATE OF BIRTH   1971-09-20

                September 1971
                M T W T F S S
                30 31 1 2 3 4 5
                 6 7 8 9 10 11 12
                13 14 15 16 17 18 19
                20 21 22 23 24 25 26
                27 28 29 30 1 2 3

    SURVEY
    AVERAGE NUMBER   ING PER
    DAY: WH

    WHAT IS YOUR FA

    Submit Query

HTML5-NOW IS SMART ENOUGH TO FIGURE OUT WHETHER THE BROWSER ALREADY HAS SUPPORT FOR PARTICULAR HTML5 FEATURES; IT WON'T INTERFERE IF THAT'S THE CASE, SO IT'S SAFE TO USE ACROSS ALL BROWSERS. BUT IT'S A HEAVYWEIGHT SCRIPT, SO IF YOU'RE ONLY INTENDING TO USE A SMALL NUMBER OF HTML5 FEATURES YOU'LL BE BETTER OFF DETECTING THEM DIRECTLY, AS DISCUSSED IN THE SECTION "DETECTING SUPPORTED FEATURES."

Summary

In this chapter you've learned about the following:

☺ How the new form input types available in HTML5 greatly increase the range of options you had in HTML4

☺ How you can reduce the amount of JavaScript you have to write to validate input

☺ Other new features, such as autofocus and placeholder text

☺ Support available in web browsers right now, and how to detect what support is provided by your users' browsers

You should now be ready to take your forms to the next level with HTML5!

IN THE LAST TWO CHAPTERS, YOU'VE LEARNED ABOUT HTML5 FEATURES THAT ARE EXTENSIONS OF COMMON USAGES OF HTML4 MARKUP. IN THE NEXT FEW CHAPTERS, YOU'LL LEARN ABOUT SOME OF THE COMPLETELY NEW FUNCTIONALITY IN HTML5 FOR DEALING WITH MEDIA AND DYNAMIC GRAPHICS. WE'LL START IN CHAPTER 3 WITH A LOOK AT CANVAS AND SVG, THE TWO HTML5 TECHNOLOGIES FOR DRAWING GRAPHICS IN THE BROWSER.

3

Dynamic graphics

This chapter covers

- *Using the* <canvas> *element to draw shapes, text, and images*
- *Transforming existing images with* <canvas>
- *Using Scalable Vector Graphics (SVG) in your web pages*
- *The strengths and weaknesses of* <canvas> *and SVG*
- *Cross-browser support*

In this chapter, you'll learn about HTML5's facilities for dynamic graphics—graphics that can change in response to user input, data, or simply time passing. This could include charts representing network activity or the location of people on a map.

 THIS CHAPTER, ESPECIALLY THE PARTS TO DO WITH THE <canvas> ELEMENT, WILL MAKE A LOT OF USE OF JAVASCRIPT. IF YOU'RE NOT FAMILIAR WITH JAVASCRIPT, YOU SHOULD CHECK OUT APPENDIX D BEFORE PROCEEDING.

Getting started with <canvas>: shapes, images, and text

The <canvas> element is an image you can create with JavaScript. The markup for it is similar to an <image> element in that you can specify a width and a height; but it has starting and closing tags that can enclose fallback content, and it doesn't reference an external source:

```
<canvas id="mycanvas" width="320" height="240"
        style="outline: 1px solid #999;">
    Your browser does not support the canvas element.
</canvas>
```

In a browser that doesn't support <canvas> the fallback content is displayed, as in this screenshot.

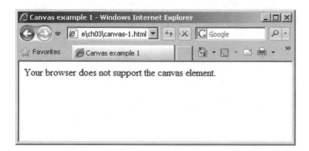

		Canvas 2D context	Canvas text
		4.0	4.0
		2.0	3.5
		9.0	9.0
		9.0	10.5
		3.1	4.0

Browser support quick check: <canvas>

YOU MIGHT HAVE A STATIC IMAGE AS THE FALLBACK IF IT COULD ADEQUATELY PRESENT SOME OF THE INFORMATION THAT WOULD BE DISPLAYED IN <canvas> IN SUPPORTING BROWSERS. OR, IF YOU WERE PARTICULARLY AMBITIOUS, YOU COULD USE AN ALTERNATIVE RENDERING METHOD SUCH AS FLASH.

You may be more interested to see what the page looks like in a browser that *does* support <canvas>.

If you're wondering where all the whizzy graphics promised in the introduction are, well, they don't appear by magic. To create pictures with <canvas>, there needs to be a JavaScript program that tells the browser what to draw.

Before you get to drawing something, you need to understand a couple of things. You need to know how to get a reference to your canvas object so you can send it drawing commands; and, because you'll be telling the <canvas> element to draw shapes on a grid, you need to know how the grid is defined. First, here's how to get a reference in JavaScript:

```
function draw() {
    var canvas = document.getElementById('mycanvas');
    if (canvas.getContext) {
        var ctx = canvas.getContext('2d');
        //do stuff
    }
}
window.addEventListener("load", draw, false);
```

Add this code between <script> tags in the <head> of an HTML document containing a <canvas> element like that shown in the first listing in this section. In the following sections, you'll update the draw() function to create graphics. If you're confused about what this document should look like, please download the code samples from www.manning.com/crowther/ and look at the file ch03/canvas-1.html.

YOU HAVE TO PASS A PARAMETER, 2d, TO THE getContext METHOD. THIS GIVES YOU A TWO-DIMENSIONAL DRAWING CONTEXT. CURRENTLY THIS IS THE ONLY PARAMETER SUPPORTED. SEVERAL BROWSER VENDORS ARE EXPERIMENTING WITH A THREE-DIMENSIONAL DRAWING CONTEXT WITH DIRECT ACCESS TO GRAPHICS HARDWARE, WHICH WILL OPEN UP POSSIBILITIES SUCH AS 3D GAMES, VIRTUAL-REALITY EXPERIENCES, AND MODELING TOOLS.

Drawing shapes

To draw on the canvas, you need to get a drawing context. The context then gives you access to methods that allow the drawing of lines and shapes.

Basic shapes are easy. If you replace the previous draw() function, you can draw a rectangle by using the fillRect method. The only prerequisite is that you first set the fill color using the fillStyle method. You call the fillRect method with four arguments: the x and y values of the upper-left corner and the width and height to fill:

```
function draw() {
 if (canvas.getContext) {
  var ctx = canvas.getContext('2d');
  ctx.fillStyle = 'rgb(255,0,0)';
  ctx.fillRect(50,50,100,100);
 }
}
```

 IN ADDITION TO fillRect(), THERE ARE ALSO METHODS TO CLEAR AN AREA OF PIXELS AND TO DRAW AN EMPTY RECTANGLE: clearRect() AND strokeRect(), RESPECTIVELY. THEY TAKE THE SAME PARAMETERS AS fillRect().

Let's extend the code to draw a line. Lines are a little more complex. You have to first draw a path, but the path doesn't appear until you apply a stroke. If you've ever used graphics software like Photoshop, this process should be familiar to you.

The moveTo method moves the "pen" without recording a path, and the lineTo method moves the pen and records a path:

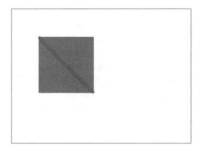

```
function draw() {
 var canvas = document
    .getElementById('mycanvas');

 if (canvas.getContext) {
  var ctx = canvas.getContext('2d');
  ctx.fillStyle = 'rgb(255,0,0)';
  ctx.fillRect(50,50,100,100);
  ctx.strokeStyle =
          'rgb(0,127,127)';
  ctx.moveTo(50,50);
  ctx.lineTo(150,150);
  ctx.lineWidth = 5;
  ctx.stroke();
 }
}
```

Now for a little experiment. What happens if the line is drawn first and then the box?

```
function draw() {
 var canvas = document
    .getElementById('mycanvas');

 if (canvas.getContext) {
  var ctx = canvas.getContext('2d');
  ctx.strokeStyle =
          'rgb(0,127,127)';
  ctx.moveTo(50,50);
  ctx.lineTo(150,150);
  ctx.lineWidth = 5;
  ctx.stroke();
  ctx.fillStyle = 'rgb(255,0,0)';
  ctx.fillRect(50,50,100,100);
 }
}
```

As you can see, the line is mostly obscured by the rectangle. You might think that if you could remove the rectangle the line would still be there underneath; but after you've drawn over it, the line is gone.

THE ONLY WAY TO GET THE LINE BACK IS TO ERASE BOTH THE RECTANGLE AND THE LINE AND THEN DRAW THE LINE AGAIN. THE <canvas> ELEMENT DOESN'T STORE THE ELEMENTS DRAWN, ONLY THE RESULTING PIXELS.

What about other shapes? The path-then-stroke approach is the way to do it. You can use the arc method to draw a circle and then fill it. The arc method accepts parameters for the location of the center; the radius; how far around, in radians, the arc should extend; and whether that should be clockwise or counterclockwise:

```
function draw(){
 var canvas = document
    .getElementById('mycanvas');
 if (canvas.getContext) {

  var ctx = canvas.getContext('2d');
  ctx.fillStyle = 'rgb(255,0,0)';
  ctx.fillRect(50,50,100,100);
  ctx.fillStyle = 'rgb(0,255,0)';
  ctx.arc(250, 100,
          50, 0,
          Math.PI*2,
          false);
  ctx.fill();
  ctx.strokeStyle =
          'rgb(0,127,127)';
  ctx.moveTo(50,50);
  ctx.lineTo(150,150);
  ctx.lineWidth = 5;
  ctx.stroke();
 }
}
```

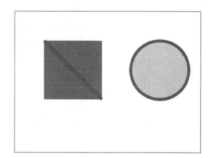

NOTE THAT THE STROKE YOU USE TO DRAW THE LINE AT THE
END ALSO GETS APPLIED TO THE CIRCLE. EVEN THOUGH THE
strokeStyle WAS SET AFTER THE ARC WAS CREATED.

To ensure that the stroke for the line doesn't apply to the circle, you need to explicitly put them on different paths with the beginPath() method:

```
function draw(){
 var canvas = document
    .getElementById('mycanvas');
 if (canvas.getContext) {

  ctx.fillStyle = 'rgb(255,0,0)';
  ctx.fillRect(50,50,100,100);
  ctx.beginPath();
  ctx.fillStyle = 'rgb(0,255,0)';
  ctx.arc(250, 100, 50, 0,
          Math.PI*2, false);
  ctx.fill();
  ctx.beginPath();
  ctx.strokeStyle =
          'rgb(0,127,127)';
  ctx.moveTo(50,50);
  ctx.lineTo(150,150);
  ctx.lineWidth = 5;
  ctx.stroke();
 }
}
```

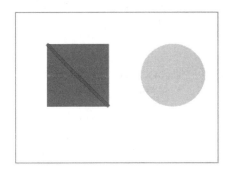

Other shapes are just a matter of creating a path and then stroking or filling, or both. If you move the first two shapes over a little, there's room to add a triangle. First draw the square and the circle again slightly further to the left:

```
ctx.fillStyle = 'rgb(255,0,0)';
ctx.fillRect(5,50,100,100);
ctx.beginPath();
ctx.fillStyle = 'rgb(0,255,0)';
ctx.arc(165, 100, 50, 0, Math.PI*2, false);
```

```
ctx.fill();
ctx.beginPath();
ctx.strokeStyle = 'rgb(0,127,127)';
ctx.moveTo(5,50);
ctx.lineTo(105,150);
ctx.lineWidth = 5;
ctx.stroke();
```

Put this code in your draw() function inside the if (canvas.getContext) {} block, replacing what you had previously, and then add the code for the triangle to it:

```
ctx.beginPath();
ctx.moveTo(265,50);
ctx.lineTo(315,150);
ctx.lineTo(215,150);
ctx.lineTo(265,50);
ctx.strokeStyle = 'rgb(51,51,51)';
ctx.fillStyle = 'rgb(204,204,204)';
ctx.stroke();
ctx.fill();
```

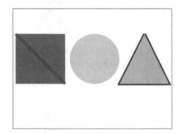

Notice that, even though the triangle starts and ends at the same point, there's a slight gap at the top.

To prevent this, you need to close the path using the closePath method; the additional line required is highlighted bold:

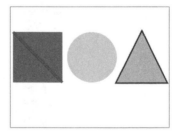

```
ctx.beginPath();
ctx.moveTo(265,50);
ctx.lineTo(315,150);
ctx.lineTo(215,150);
ctx.lineTo(265,50);
ctx.closePath();
ctx.strokeStyle = 'rgb(51,51,51)';
ctx.fillStyle = 'rgb(204,204,204)';
ctx.stroke();
ctx.fill();
```

You don't have to restrict yourself to straight lines in paths. Instead of lineTo, you can use either of two types of curve: quadratic or Bézier.

Let's replace the first straight line with a Bézier curve. Instead of

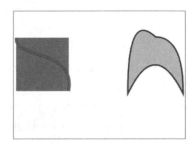

```
ctx.moveTo(5,50);
ctx.lineTo(105,150);
```

use the lines

```
ctx.moveTo(5,50);
ctx.bezierCurveTo(0,90, 120,70,
                      105,150)
```

The last pair of numbers is the end point. Preceding that are coordinates for the two control points.

To simplify things the circle has been removed for now, but the sides of the triangle have also been made curvy, this time with a quadratic curve. A quadratic curve is similar, but only needs one control point. This is the code that drew the triangle, using quadraticCurve instead of lineTo. Here's the original triangle drawing code:

```
ctx.moveTo(265,50);
ctx.lineTo(315,150);
ctx.lineTo(215,150);
ctx.lineTo(265,50);
```

Replace it with this:

```
ctx.moveTo(265,50);
ctx.quadraticCurveTo(315,50, 315,150);
ctx.quadraticCurveTo(265,50, 215,150);
ctx.quadraticCurveTo(215,0, 265,50);
```

In this version of the earlier diagram, the control points have been drawn along with lines connecting the control points to the start and end of the path; this should help you visualize what's going on. The drawn lines are distorted from their direct path so they approach an imaginary line drawn between the start or end point and the control point. Check out the full listings for these examples in ch03/canvas-6.html and ch03/canvas-6-controls.html of the code download at www.manning.com/crowther/.

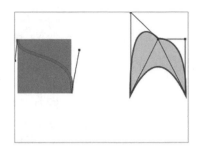

 AS YOU CAN SEE, IT'S EASY TO CREATE SOME INTERESTING SHAPES. BUT DRAWING CURVED LINES CAN BE HIT OR MISS, ESPECIALLY IF YOU'RE TRYING TO GET THE CURVE TO LINE UP WITH SOME OTHER DRAWN OBJECT. THE BEST APPROACH IS USUALLY TRIAL AND ERROR.

Placing images

One of the great features of <canvas> is that you can use it to manipulate images and achieve effects that are otherwise difficult to do with HTML and CSS. Here's an example of what can be achieved: a reflection effect.

The <canvas> element can't download images—you can't give it a URL and expect it to fetch the image. Any image you want to use must already be available in your page content. There are various ways to do this, but the easiest is to include the element in the normal way. In this case, it's hidden:

SOMETIMES I LIKE TO JUST SIT AND REFLECT

AM KNOWINK WHAT YOU MEANINK

```
<div style="display: none;">
    <img id="myimage" src="example.png" width="236" height="260">
</div>
```

The next few examples take the image at right and import it into the `<canvas>` element. The simplest example is to import the image and place it on the `<canvas>`.

You call `drawImage` with three parameters — the `img` element and the x and y coordinates:

```
function draw(){
 var canvas = document
    .getElementById('mycanvas');
 if (canvas.getContext) {
  var ctx = canvas.getContext('2d');
  var img =
document.getElementById('myimage');
  ctx.drawImage(img, 10, 10);
 }
}
```

The example image is too large to fit into the `<canvas>` frame. You can easily fix this by defining a width and height for the placed image:

```
if (canvas.getContext) {
  var ctx = canvas.getContext('2d');
  var img = document
    .getElementById('myimage');
  ctx.drawImage(
    img, 10, 10, 118, 130
  );
}
```

Now you're calling `drawImage` with five parameters. The additional two are the width and height of the placed image.

You may not even want all of the original image:

```
if (canvas.getContext) {
  var ctx = canvas.getContext('2d');
  var img =
document.getElementById('myimage');
  ctx.drawImage(img,
        80, 100, 80,  160,
        10, 10,  160, 200);
}
```

The previous example calls `drawImage` with nine parameters. Let's examine them in more detail:

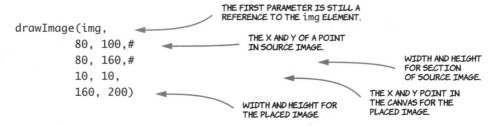

Drawing text

Let's now turn our attention to text. The <canvas> element has a limited ability to draw single lines of text on the context. The text-drawing methods are more suitable for drawing labels and titles than for rendering large blocks of text. But the full graphical-processing ability of the

<canvas> element can be applied to the text that's drawn, allowing for effects like this.

THIS EXAMPLE TAKES ADVANTAGE OF THE TRANSFORMATION AND GRADIENT FILL FEATURES OF THE <canvas> ELEMENT. MORE DETAILS ABOUT THEM ARE IN THE SECTION "ADVANCED <canvas>: GRADIENTS, SHADOWS, AND ANIMATION."

Drawing text on the <canvas> is easy with the fillText method:

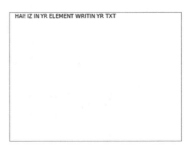

```
function draw(){
 var canvas = document
    .getElementById('mycanvas');
 if (canvas.getContext) {
  var ctx = canvas.getContext('2d');
  ctx.fillText(
    'HAI! IZ IN YR ELEMENT
    WRITIN YR TXT',
    10,10);
 }
}
```

The fillText method has three required parameters: a string that is the text to be drawn, and x and y coordinates to determine where it's to be drawn.

The text is drawn in the current font, which is determined by setting the font property of the drawing context. The <canvas> element's font property behaves like the CSS font property, allowing size and font to be specified simultaneously:

```
ctx.font = "10pt serif";
```

If you set the font size a little larger, you can see an alternative method for drawing text. As with rectangles, you can draw the fill and the stroke separately:

```
function draw(){
 var canvas = document
    .getElementById('mycanvas');
 if (canvas.getContext) {
  var ctx = canvas.getContext('2d');
  ctx.font = "12pt sans-serif";
  ctx.fillText(
    'HAI! IZ IN YR ELEMENT
    WRITIN YR TXT',
    10,20);
  ctx.strokeText(
    'HAI! IZ IN YR ELEMENT
```

```
    WRITIN YR TXT',
    10,40);
 }
}
```

You can of course draw both fill and stroke on a single line of text if you want.

Let's see what happens if you increase the font size a bit more. Remember, the example <canvas> element is 320 pixels wide:

```
ctx.font = "20pt sans-serif";
ctx.fillText(
  'HAI! IZ IN YR ELEMENT
  WRITIN YR TXT',
  10,80);
ctx.strokeText(
  'HAI! IZ IN YR ELEMENT
  WRITIN YR TXT',
  10,110);
```

As you can see, the text that doesn't fit flows off the edge of the element without wrapping.

To work around this issue, you can use the fourth, optional, parameter to the fillText and strokeText methods. This parameter sets a maximum width for the text; if the text will be wider than the value passed, the browser makes the text fit either by narrowing the spacing between the letters or scaling down the font:

```
ctx.fillText(
  'HAI! IZ IN YR ELEMENT
  WRITIN YR TXT',
  10,150,300);
ctx.strokeText(
  'HAI! IZ IN YR ELEMENT
  WRITIN YR TXT',
  10,180,300);
```

If you've added all three of these examples to the original listing, then you should have something similar to the ch03/canvas-text-4.html file in the code download.

To further control the text position you can set the baseline of the text, which will adjust where it's drawn in relation to the coordinates you provide. This is useful if you're trying to position labels next to things on your canvas because it saves you having to work out exactly how tall the letters will be drawn.

The default value is alphabetic, which means the bottom of an upper-case letter is placed at the y coordinate you provide in fillText. The following line sets the baseline to top, which means the top of an upper-case letter will be placed in line with the provided y coordinate:

```
ctx.textBaseline = "top";
```

The following figure shows the previous example alongside a similar example, except with textBaseline set differently.

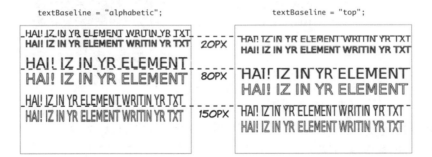

Other values for text-Baseline are hanging, middle, ideographic, and bottom.

YOU CAN NOW DRAW IMAGES AND TEXT ON YOUR <canvas> ELEMENT. THE SIMPLE EXAMPLES WE'VE COVERED HERE MAY NOT SEEM MUCH MORE EXCITING THAN WHAT CAN BE ACHIEVED WITH PLAIN HTML AND CSS, BUT WE'VE BARELY SCRATCHED THE SURFACE. IN THE NEXT SECTION, YOU'LL LEARN ABOUT SOME MORE ADVANCED TECHNIQUES: GRADIENTS, DROP SHADOWS, AND TRANSFORMATIONS.

Advanced <canvas>: gradients, shadows, and animation

With the ability to draw a single-pixel shape on any part of the canvas, it's possible for you to create any effect you want by implementing it yourself in JavaScript. But the <canvas> element has some built-in shortcuts for particular effects. This section covers them.

Creating gradients

The strokeStyle and fillStyle methods you used in "Drawing shapes" to set the color of lines and shapes can also accept a gradient object where the color changes smoothly across a defined space. The <canvas> element can create two types of gradient:

○ *Linear*—The gradient follows a straight line.

○ *Radial*—The gradient is circular.

In this section, you'll create one example of each. There are three steps to creating either gradient type in the <canvas> element:

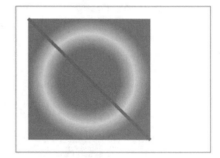

1 Create a gradient.
2 Specify the color stops.
3 Apply the gradient as a fill to a shape.

Here's a simple linear gradient in place of the solid fill from the earlier examples.

You define the extents of the gradient with the createLinearGradient() method. This method takes four parameters that define the upper-left and lower-right corners. The following diagram contains the code and indicates what the parameters refer to in the screenshot.

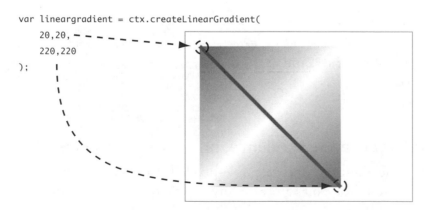

```
var lineargradient = ctx.createLinearGradient(
    20,20,
    220,220
);
```

Next you need to add color stops to the lineargradient you just created. A *color stop* is a point on the gradient at which you're setting a specific color. The browser interpolates between the color stops to create the gradient. The gradient object has an addColorStop() method for this. It accepts two parameters: a position and a color. The position is a number between 0 and 1, where 0 is the start of the gradient and 1 is the end. The code in the next diagram adds three color stops to your gradient.

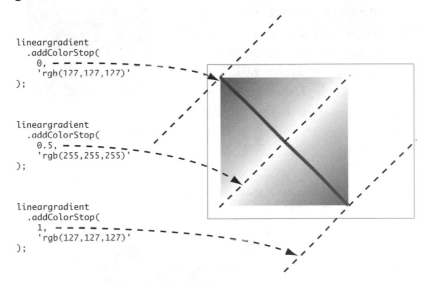

```
lineargradient
  .addColorStop(
     0,
     'rgb(127,127,127)'
);

lineargradient
  .addColorStop(
     0.5,
     'rgb(255,255,255)'
);

lineargradient
  .addColorStop(
     1,
     'rgb(127,127,127)'
);
```

All that remains is to add the gradient to the context as a fillStyle and draw a shape. Here's the complete draw() function from ch03/canvas-9.html:

```
function draw(){
    var canvas = document.getElementById('mycanvas');
    if (canvas.getContext) {
        var ctx = canvas.getContext('2d');
        var lineargradient = ctx.createLinearGradient(20,20,220,220);
        lineargradient.addColorStop(0,'rgb(127,127,127)');
        lineargradient.addColorStop(0.5,'rgb(255,255,255)');
        lineargradient.addColorStop(1,'rgb(127,127,127)');
        ctx.fillStyle = lineargradient;
        ctx.fillRect(20,20,200,200);
        ctx.strokeStyle = 'rgb(0,127,127)';
```

```
        ctx.moveTo(20,20);
        ctx.lineTo(220,220);
        ctx.lineWidth = 5;
        ctx.stroke();
    }
}
```

Now let's create a radial gradient.

For a radial gradient, you use the createRadialGradient() method. Six values are required: a center point and a radius for the inner bound, and a center point and a radius for the outer bound. This creates two circles between which the gradient is drawn. The two circles and their corresponding parameters are shown here.

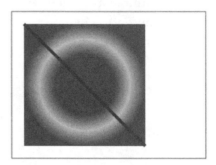

```
var radialgradient = ctx.createRadialGradient(
    120,120,50,
    120,120,100
);
```

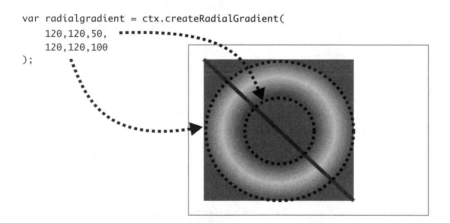

Adding color stops is exactly the same as with the linear gradient, except that now those stops define circles between the two described in the createRadialGradient method:

```
radialgradient.addColorStop(0, 'rgb(127,127,127)');
radialgradient.addColorStop(0.5, 'rgba(127,127,127,0.25)');
radialgradient.addColorStop(1, 'rgb(127,127,127)');
```

Finally, the gradient is applied as a `fillStyle` as before:

```
ctx.fillStyle = radialgradient;
ctx.fillRect(20,20,200,200);
```

Check out the full listing in the file ch03/canvas-10.html in the code download.

NOTE THAT YOU DEFINE BOTH LINEAR AND RADIAL GRADIENTS WITH COORDINATES RELATIVE TO THE ENTIRE CANVAS CONTEXT, NOT THE SHAPE YOU WANT TO APPLY THEM TO. IF YOU WANT THE GRADIENT TO EXACTLY FILL THE SHAPE, YOU HAVE TO MAKE SURE YOU CHOOSE THE COORDINATES SO THAT THE GRADIENT APPEARS IN THE SHAPE YOU WANT TO FILL IT WITH.

THE GRADIENT ISN'T CONFINED TO THE COORDINATES YOU SPECIFY—IT EXTENDS ACROSS THE CANVAS. THE FOLLOWING EXAMPLES SHOW A LINEAR GRADIENT CREATED WITH THREE DIFFERENT SETS OF COORDINATES.

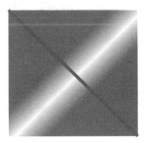

```
createLinearGradient(
   0,0,320,0
);
```

```
createLinearGradient(
   0,0,100,100
);
```

```
createLinearGradient(
   100,100,150,150
);
```

Drawing drop shadows

Drop shadows are an effect much loved by designers, and the <canvas> element has built-in support. To create a shadow, define the `shadowOffsetX`, `shadowOffsetY`, `shadowBlur`, and `shadowColor` properties on the context object; the shadow will then be applied to any shape you draw.

This example shows the earlier square with a line through it, now with a shadow in place:

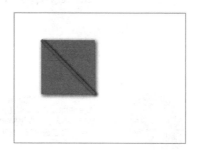

```
ctx.shadowOffsetX = 2;
ctx.shadowOffsetY = 2;
ctx.shadowBlur = 8;
ctx.shadowColor =
    "rgba(0, 0, 0, 0.75)";
```

Using shadows, you can create effects such as cutout text:

```
ctx.shadowOffsetX = 4;
ctx.shadowOffsetY = 2;
ctx.shadowBlur = 5;
ctx.shadowColor =
    "rgba(0, 0, 0, 0.9)";
ctx.fillStyle = 'rgb(0,0,0)';
ctx.fillText('HAI!',170,50);
ctx.fillStyle = 'rgb(255,255,255)';
ctx.fillText('IZ IN YR ELEMENT'
    ,170,70);
ctx.strokeStyle = 'rgb(0,0,0)';
ctx.strokeText('WRITIN YR TXT'
    ,170,90);
```

Transformations

THE <canvas> 2D CONTEXT SUPPORTS A NUMBER OF TRANSFORMATIONS. THESE WORK ON THE CONTEXT ITSELF, SO YOU APPLY THE TRANSFORMATION AND THEN DRAW WHATEVER YOU WANT TO APPEAR SUBJECT TO THAT TRANSFORM.

Let's start with a simple translate transformation. This moves the origin of the <canvas> element according to the x and y offsets you pass in as arguments:

```
var img = document
    .getElementById('myimage');
ctx.translate(120,20);
ctx.drawImage(
    img, 10, 10, 118, 130
);
```

If you compare this example with the similar one in "Placing images" without the transformation, you'll see you've basically moved the image down and to the right. Not particularly useful when you could have drawn the image there in the first place, but this technique would be useful if you wanted to move a collection of objects around while keeping their relative positions the same.

Next, let's try rotation:

```
var img =
document.getElementById('myimage');
ctx.rotate(Math.PI/4);
ctx.drawImage(img, 10, 10, 118, 130);
```

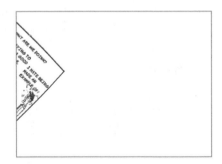

The rotate() method takes a value in radians and rotates the drawing context by that angle. As with translate, the values you provide to the drawImage() method are now relative to the transformation.

You don't want the image off the <canvas> like that, so let's translate it and then rotate it:

```
var img =
document.getElementById('myimage');
ctx.translate(120,20);
ctx.rotate(Math.PI/4);
ctx.drawImage(img, 10, 10, 118, 130);
```

The transformations affect the whole context, so the order in which you apply them is important.

Let's try the opposite order:

```
var img =
document.getElementById('myimage');
ctx.rotate(Math.PI/4);
ctx.translate(120,20);
ctx.drawImage(img, 10, 10, 118, 130);
```

You can see that the rotate now changes the direction the translate goes in.

Animation

ONE POTENTIAL USE OF THE <canvas> ELEMENT THAT HAS MANY DEVELOPERS EXCITED IS CREATING GAMES. ALREADY, MANY ARCADE CLASSICS OF THE 1980S AND '90S HAVE BEEN RE-CREATED USING <canvas>. IN ORDER TO CREATE GAMES, YOU NEED TO HAVE ANIMATION. LET'S LOOK AT HOW YOU CAN ANIMATE YOUR CANVAS DRAWINGS.

Mon 21 Jun 2010 15:00:03 BST

Mon 21 Jun 2010 15:00:24 BST

Mon 21 Jun 2010 15:00:47 BST

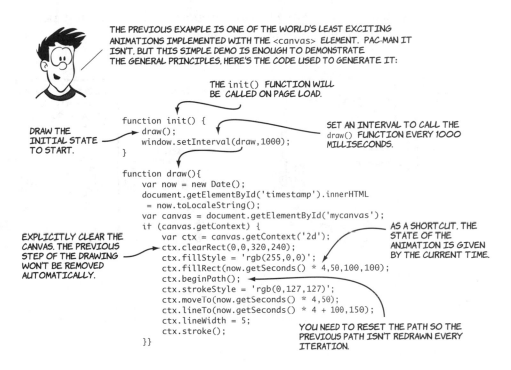

THE PREVIOUS EXAMPLE IS ONE OF THE WORLD'S LEAST EXCITING ANIMATIONS IMPLEMENTED WITH THE <canvas> ELEMENT. PAC-MAN IT ISN'T, BUT THIS SIMPLE DEMO IS ENOUGH TO DEMONSTRATE THE GENERAL PRINCIPLES. HERE'S THE CODE USED TO GENERATE IT:

THE init() FUNCTION WILL BE CALLED ON PAGE LOAD.

DRAW THE INITIAL STATE TO START.

SET AN INTERVAL TO CALL THE draw() FUNCTION EVERY 1000 MILLISECONDS.

```
function init() {
    draw();
    window.setInterval(draw,1000);
}

function draw(){
    var now = new Date();
    document.getElementById('timestamp').innerHTML
     = now.toLocaleString();
    var canvas = document.getElementById('mycanvas');
    if (canvas.getContext) {
        var ctx = canvas.getContext('2d');
        ctx.clearRect(0,0,320,240);
        ctx.fillStyle = 'rgb(255,0,0)';
        ctx.fillRect(now.getSeconds() * 4,50,100,100);
        ctx.beginPath();
        ctx.strokeStyle = 'rgb(0,127,127)';
        ctx.moveTo(now.getSeconds() * 4,50);
        ctx.lineTo(now.getSeconds() * 4 + 100,150);
        ctx.lineWidth = 5;
        ctx.stroke();
    }}
```

EXPLICITLY CLEAR THE CANVAS. THE PREVIOUS STEP OF THE DRAWING WON'T BE REMOVED AUTOMATICALLY.

AS A SHORTCUT, THE STATE OF THE ANIMATION IS GIVEN BY THE CURRENT TIME.

YOU NEED TO RESET THE PATH SO THE PREVIOUS PATH ISN'T REDRAWN EVERY ITERATION.

Here's what happens if you forget to explicitly start a new path.

Sat 11 Dec 2010 16:18:03 GMT   Sat 11 Dec 2010 16:18:23 GMT   Sat 11 Dec 2010 16:18:42 GMT

If you forget to close any paths you have open, they'll be redrawn as you iterate through your animation steps along with any additions to the path. Clearing the pixels on the context doesn't reset the path.

The <canvas> element allows precise, pixel-level control over what is displayed and is already considered a rival to Flash in the browser game marketplace because it works on iPhones and iPads. Experimental versions of <canvas> have full 3D support, and several first-person shoot-ers from the 1990s have already been ported to allow play in a browser.

 NOW THAT YOU'VE LEARNED ABOUT THE <canvas> ELEMENT, IT'S TIME TO LOOK AT THE SECOND TECHNOLOGY AVAILABLE IN HTML5 FOR DRAWING GRAPHICS: SVG.

Getting started with SVG

Scalable Vector Graphics (SVG) is an XML language for displaying vector graphics. It has long been possible to embed SVG within XML-based XHTML documents; but because HTML5 leads you back to HTML-based markup, it adds the useful feature that SVG can be embedded directly.

Browser support quick check: SVG in HTML		
	●	7.0
	●	4.0
	●	9.0
	●	11.6
	●	5.1

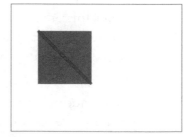

Let's create a simple SVG drawing.

You're probably thinking it looks familiar, and you're right. Many of the things that can be achieved with <canvas> can also be easily achieved with SVG. You'll learn more about the relative strengths and weaknesses of each in the section "SVG vs. <canvas>," but for now all you need to understand is that <canvas> and SVG are based on different conceptual models of how to create images. <canvas> is what programmers call *imperative*; you provide a detailed list of operations to be performed that will produce a particular result. SVG is *declarative*; you provide a description of the final result and let the browser get on with it. Where <canvas> requires JavaScript, SVG requires markup, much like HTML, and it can be included directly in HTML5:

```
<!DOCTYPE html>
<html>
<head>
    <title>SVG example 2</title>
</head>
<body>
    <svg id="mysvg" viewBox="0 0 320 240"
        style="outline: 1px solid #999; width: 320px; height:
  240px;">
        <rect x="50" y="50" width="100" height="100"
            style="fill: rgb(255,0,0)">
        </rect>
        <line x1="50" y1="50" x2="150" y2="150"
            style="stroke: rgb(0,127,127); stroke-width: 5;">
        </line>
    </svg>
</body>
</html>
```

There are several interesting things to be seen in this simple example. First, note that the size of the element on the page is determined by CSS in the style attribute, but you also define a viewBox with the same values. Because SVG is a vector format, pixels aren't as significant; you can use viewBox to define a mapping between the physical dimensions of the element, defined in CSS, and the logical coordinates of everything displayed within.

Look what happens if you use these values: `viewBox="0 0 640 480"`. It's the same SVG graphic as before, but rendered into a larger viewport.

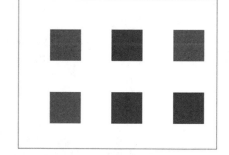

Applying styles to SVG

The previous examples used an inline style to apply colors and stroke thicknesses. Those properties can also be applied directly to the elements in question, like this:

```
<rect x="50" y="50" width="100" height="100"
      fill="rgb(255,0,0)"></rect>
<line x1="50" y1="50" x2="150" y2="150"
      stroke="rgb(0,127,127)" stroke-width="5"></line>
```

But you can alternatively leave off the style and inline attributes and use this in your CSS file, and achieve the same results:

```
rect { fill: rgb(255,0,0); }
line { stroke: rgb(0,127,127); stroke-width: 5; }
```

It looks much like any other CSS, albeit with some unusual properties. As with regular HTML, CSS can make life much easier if you have a lot of similar objects because you can use a class to apply a set of styles to several elements.

In this example there are three green squares (upper left, upper right, lower left) and three blue squares. Rather than specify inline styles on each one, you can declare their commonality with the `class` attribute:

```
<svg id="mysvg" viewBox="0 0 320 240">
    <rect x="50" y="50" width="50" height="50" class="earth"></rect>
    <rect x="150" y="50" width="50" height="50" class="water"></rect>
    <rect x="250" y="50" width="50" height="50" class="earth"></rect>
    <rect x="50" y="150" width="50" height="50" class="earth"></rect>
```

```
    <rect x="150" y="150" width="50" height="50" class="water"></rect>
    <rect x="250" y="150" width="50" height="50" class="water"></rect>
</svg>
```

Then you style the common elements with CSS in the <head> of your document in the usual way:

```
<style>
  rect.earth { fill: rgb(0,127,0); }
  rect.water { fill: rgb(0,0,255); }
</style>
```

Drawing common shapes

Let's carry on and re-create the rest of the <canvas> example shapes in SVG. In addition to the rectangle and line elements you've seen already, SVG has elements for circles and arbitrary polygons.

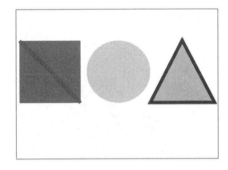

For a circle, you need to provide the x and y coordinates of the center and the radius as appropriate attributes. A polygon is slightly more complex; it has an attribute points that you use to supply a space-separated list of x,y coordinates. This code, when placed inside the <svg> element from the listing in the introduction, generates the previous image:

```
<rect x="5" y="50" width="100" height="100"
      style="fill: rgb(255,0,0);"></rect>
<line x1="5" y1="50" x2="105" y2="150"
      style="stroke: rgb(0,127,127); stroke-width: 5;"></line>
<circle cx="165" cy="100" r="50"
        style="fill: rgb(0,255,0);"></circle>
<polygon points="265,50  315,150  215,150"
         style="stroke: rgb(51,51,51); fill: rgb(204,204,204);
                stroke-width: 5;"></polygon>
```

With the polygon element you don't have to provide the starting point a second time; it assumes the shape is closed, and the path drawn returns to the first point. If you want to draw an open shape, you can use the

`<polyline>` element instead; it uses an identical `points` attribute but doesn't close the path around the shape.

```
<polygon
  points="265,50  315,150  215,150"
  style="stroke: rgb(51,51,51);
         fill: rgb(204,204,204);
         stroke-width: 5;">
</polygon>
```

```
<polyline
  points="265,50  315,150  215,150"
  style="stroke: rgb(51,51,51);
         fill: rgb(204,204,204);
         stroke-width: 5;">
</polyline>
```

YOU'VE SEEN SEVERAL ELEMENTS MAKE DIFFERENT SHAPES IN A SINGLE SVG DRAWING, BUT THERE'S ALSO A WAY TO DRAW SEVERAL DIFFERENT SHAPES IN A SINGLE SVG ELEMENT. FOR THIS YOU USE THE `<path>` ELEMENT. LET'S LOOK AT AN EXAMPLE.

ALTHOUGH YOU CAN SEE THREE SHAPES IN THE PREVIOUS IMAGE, THEY'RE A SINGLE SVG ELEMENT: A PATH. THE `<path>` ELEMENT IN SVG IS VERY POWERFUL. HERE'S THE CODE:

THE `<path>` ELEMENT WORKS AS IF IT WAS AN IMAGINARY PEN. YOU THEN USE THE ATTRIBUTE TO PASS A SERIES OF COMMANDS TO THE PEN TO TELL IT WHAT TO DRAW.

```
<path d="M5,50
```

MOVE TO COORDS 5,50.

```
l0,100 l100,0 l0,-100 l-100,0
```

DRAW A LINE TO -100,0 RELATIVE TO THE CURRENT POSITION.

UPPERCASE LETTERS MEAN ABSOLUTE COORDINATES

```
M215,100
```

```
a50,50 0 1 1 -100,0 50,50 0 1 1 100,0
```

LOWERCASE LETTERS MEAN COORDINATES RELATIVE TO THE CURRENT PEN POSITION.

```
M265,50
```

DRAW TWO ARCS TO MAKE A CIRCLE.

```
l50,100 l-100,0 l50,-100
```

CLOSE THE PATH.

```
z"
style="stroke: rgb(51,51,51);
       fill: rgb(204,204,204);
       stroke-width: 5;"/>
```

It seems like a path can do anything, so why bother to use anything else? The `<path>` element is difficult to understand and manipulate because of its reliance on a single attribute value. In addition, any style will apply to all shapes on the same path, so all your shapes will have the same border and color. Of course, nothing is stopping you from using more than one path with a different style applied to each.

Images, text, and embedded content

Images are easy to embed within your SVG drawing. The syntax is similar to that of HTML, and the only additional information you need to provide over and above the `<image>` element are the coordinates of the upper-left corner:

```
<image x="10" y="10"
       width="236" height="260"
       xlink:href="example.png">
</image>
```

You use an `xlink:href` to link to the image. The `xlink` is a namespace, a legacy of SVG's XML heritage that leaks through to HTML5; more on that shortly. Text is handled a little differently in SVG compared to HTML. In HTML, any text within the body is rendered to the screen—no special wrapping is required. In SVG, text has to be explicitly wrapped within a containing element:

```
<text x="10" y="20">
    HAI! IZ IN YR ELEMENT WRITIN
    YR TXT
</text>
<text x="10" y="60">
    HAI
    CAN HAS STDIO?
    VISIBLE "HAI WORLD!"
    KTHXBYE
</text>
```

The previous example highlights another problem: text that won't fit in the view isn't automatically wrapped. Line breaks also have to be explicitly coded using the <tspan> element:

```
<text x="10" y="20">
    HAI! IZ IN YR ELEMENT WRITIN
    YR TXT
</text>
<text x="10" y="60">
    <tspan x="10">HAI</tspan>
    <tspan x="10" dy="20">
        CAN HAS STDIO?
    </tspan>
    <tspan x="10" dy="20">
        VISIBLE "HAI WORLD!"
    </tspan>
    <tspan x="10" dy="20">
        KTHXBYE
    </tspan>
</text>
```

A nice effect you can achieve on short runs of text is to make the text follow a path. If you extract the circle part of the path from the earlier example, you can spread the text along it with the <textpath> element:

```
<defs>
  <path id="myTextPath"
        d="M215,100
            a50,50 0 1 1
            -100,0 50,50 0 1 1
            100,0">
  </path>
</defs>
<text>
  <textPath
      xlink:href="#myTextPath">
      HAI! IZ IN YR ELEMENT
      WRITIN YR TXT
  </textPath>
</text>
```

The path is created in the `<defs>` element, and then you link to it using an `xlink:href` like you used for the image earlier. The link works like other web content, so you could refer to the path in a separate file if you wanted to.

You can also apply gradient fills and any number of other SVG effects to the text. We'll cover this in detail in the next section, but this example shows a gradient from transparent light green to solid dark green applied as a fill to a slightly larger version of the circular text. See ch03/svg-10.html for the full code for this example.

AS WITH THE `<canvas>` ELEMENT, LARGE BLOCKS OF TEXT ARE SOMEWHAT CUMBERSOME IN SVG. THE TEXT ELEMENTS ARE ONLY REALLY USEFUL FOR LABELS AND SHORT DESCRIPTIONS. BUT SVG OFFERS AN ALTERNATIVE—YOU CAN EMBED HTML CONTENT INSIDE ANY ELEMENT WITH `<foreignObject>`.

```
<rect x="5" y="5" width="10" height="160"
      style="stroke-width: 5; stroke: rgb(102,102,102); fill: none;">
</rect>
<foreignObject x="10" y="10" width="100" height="150">
    <body>
      <p>
        <strong>HAI!</strong><br/>
        IZ IN YR ELEMENT
        <em>WRAPPIN</em> YR TXT
      </p>
    </body>
</foreignObject>
```

Everything inside the `<foreignObject>` element is HTML; and unlike the SVG `<text>` element, HTML can cope with wrapping text just fine by itself. It's important to remember that the browser isn't rendering the contents of `<foreignObject>` as if they were HTML; the content is HTML and can be interacted with in the normal way.

A second example will make this clearer.

On the right is a screenshot of the entire browser window; on the left it's zoomed in to just the content of the foreignObject element. The Duck Duck Go home page has been scaled down and rendered upside down inside the browser, but it's still possible to type search terms and see results returned (even if they're too small to read!). This was achieved by wrapping an HTML document inside a <foreignObject> element in SVG and then applying some transforms:

```
<svg id="mysvg" viewBox="0 0 800 600">
    <g transform="rotate(180) translate(-800,-600)">
        <foreignObject x="10" y="10" width="800" height="600">
            <body>
                <iframe src="http://duckduckgo.com/"
                    style="width:780px;height:580px">
                </iframe>
            </body>
        </foreignObject>
    </g>
</svg>
```

This example shows a few things you've seen before. The viewBox is set to 800 × 600 pixels, even though the element is 320 × 240 pixels; this takes care of the scaling. And an <iframe> element is used inside the <foreignObject> to fetch the Duck Duck Go page. New in this example are the <g> element for grouping SVG content and the transform attribute, both of which we'll look at in the next section.

USER FRIENDLY by Illiad

NOTE THAT IN REAL LIFE, IT'S POSSIBLE FOR WEBSITES TO BLOCK EMBEDDING LIKE THIS BY SENDING INFORMATION TO THE BROWSER TO TURN ON EXTRA SECURITY FEATURES. THIS IS DONE TO PROTECT USERS FROM MORE NEFARIOUS VERSIONS OF MIKE'S TRICK ON STEF.

Transforms, gradients, patterns, and declarative animation

SVG is a huge topic, worthy of a book by itself, and we've barely scratched the surface so far. In this section, we'll finish by taking a quick look at some of the more advanced features.

WHEN YOU WANT TO APPLY AN EFFECT TO A COLLECTION OF ELEMENTS, YOU USE THE GROUPING ELEMENT, <g>. GROUPING IS ALSO USEFUL FOR OTHER PURPOSES, FOR EXAMPLE, IF YOU WANT TO MOVE SEVERAL ELEMENTS AT THE SAME TIME.

You saw a transform in action in the last example of the previous section. Here it is again:

```
<g transform="rotate(180) translate(-800,-600)">
```

The transform attribute accepts a space-separated list of commands that are applied in order. The element is rotated 180 degrees and then, because the rotation point by default is the upper-left corner, it's moved back into view with the translate transform. You could instead pass a set of coordinates to the rotate transform and achieve the same result in a single step:

```
<g transform="rotate(180,400,300)">
```

In addition to rotate and translate, there are several other transformation commands:

- scale()—You've seen examples of scaling already. Earlier examples scaled the entire viewBox. This command allows you to control it for specific elements.

- matrix()—This is a powerful transformation that allows you to emulate all the others in combination, if you understand the mathematics of matrix transformations. If, like me, you missed that particular part of the curriculum, it's easiest to stick to the other transformations.

- skewX() and skewY()—See the following table.

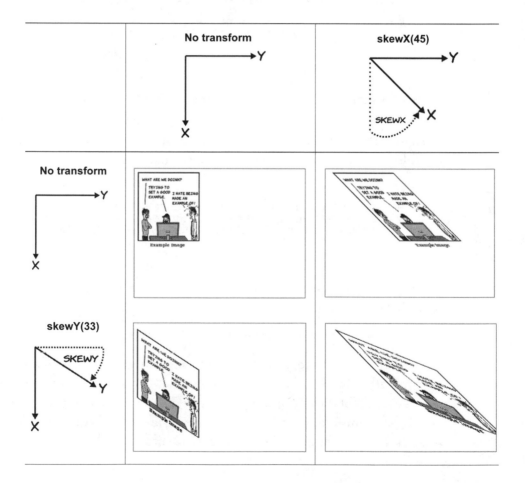

THE TRANSFORMATION FUNCTIONS FOR SVG AND <canvas> LOOK SIMILAR,
AND THEY ARE. THE MAIN DIFFERENCE FROM A DEVELOPER PERSPECTIVE IS
THAT SVG TRANSFORMATIONS EXPECT ANGLES IN DEGREES, WHEREAS
<canvas> TRANSFORMATIONS EXPECT ANGLES IN RADIANS.

GRADIENTS

As with <canvas>, an SVG gradient is defined in a separate object. You
can define this object at the top of your SVG file or element inside a
<defs> element, and then reference the gradient object through CSS:

```
<svg viewBox="0 0 320 240">
 <defs>
  <linearGradient id="grad1"
   x1="0%" y1="0%" x2="100%"
   y2="100%">
    <stop offset="0%" style="
     stop-color:rgb(127,127,127);
     stop-opacity:1"/>
    <stop offset="50%" style="
     stop-color:rgb(255,255,255);
     stop-opacity:1"/>
    <stop offset="100%" style="
     stop-color:rgb(127,127,127);
     stop-opacity:1"/>
  </linearGradient>
 </defs>
 <rect x="20" y="20"
    width="200" height="200"
    style="fill: url(#grad1)">
 </rect>
</svg>
```

The <rect> element references the grad1 gradient through its fill style.
See the full listing in the ch03/svg-15.html file in the code download.

PATTERNS AND MASKS

You might expect that you could create a repeating background by
specifying something like fill="url(example.png)", but that won't work.
You have to add the image to a <pattern>:

```
<defs>
  <pattern id="img1"
   patternUnits="userSpaceOnUse"
   width="315" height="212">
    <image xlink:href="uf009705.png"
     x="0" y="0"
     width="305" height="212">
  </pattern>
</defs>
```

Then use the pattern to fill:

```
<path d="M5,50
    l0,100 l100,0 l0,-100 l-100,0
    M215,100
    a50,50 0 1 1 -100,
    0 50,50 0 1 1 100,0
    M265,50
    l50,100 l-100,0 l50,-100
    z"
  fill="url(#img1)">
```

The full listing is in ch03/svg-16.html.

You can apply the same pattern to a
<text> element, although you should
pick your image carefully to ensure
that things are readable:

```
<text x="0" y="120"
 font-family="sans-serif"
 font-size="80"
 font-weight="bold"
 fill="url(#img1)" >
    <tspan>HTML5</tspan>
    <tspan x="0" y="180"
        font-size="70">
            ROCKS!
    </tspan>
</text>
```

This code is taken from the file ch03/
svg-17.html.

SVG is a large specification, and there's more than one way to achieve this same effect. Instead of applying the image as a background to the text, the text can be used to clip the image. To create a mask, the main change is that the text should be filled with white:

```
<mask id="img1" clipPathUnits="userSpaceOnUse" width="320"
height="200">
    <text x="0" y="120" font-family="sans-serif"
      font-size="80" font-weight="bold" fill="white">
        <tspan>HTML5</tspan>
        <tspan x="0" y="180" font-size="70">ROCKS!</tspan>
    </text>
</mask>
```

Then attach the mask to the <image> element with the mask attribute:

```
<image xlink:href="uf009705.png"
  mask="url(#img1)"
  x="-10" y="-5"
  width="340" height="220" />
```

The image is positioned to approximate the previous example; see the code in ch03/svg-17-clippath.html.

WE'LL FINISH OUR TOUR OF THE ADVANCED FEATURES OF SVG WITH A QUICK LOOK AT THE DECLARATIVE ANIMATION CAPABILITIES IT OFFERS. IN THE FOLLOWING SCREENSHOTS, THE TEXT-PATTERN EXAMPLE HAS BEEN ANIMATED TO MOVE DOWN AND THEN BACK UP AGAIN.

Wed 22 Dec 2010 14:45:46 GMT   Wed 22 Dec 2010 14:45:50 GMT   Wed 22 Dec 2010 14:45:55 GMT

Let's look in detail at how this is done in the listing from ch03/svg-18.html.

UNLIKE THE `<canvas>` ELEMENT YOU DON'T NEED TO RESORT TO JAVASCRIPT TO GET ANIMATION. ANIMATIONS CAN BE DESCRIBED USING THE SAME XML MARKUP USED TO DESCRIBE THE SHAPES THEMSELVES.

THIS IS THE SAME `<text>` ELEMENT USED IN THE PREVIOUS EXAMPLE.

```
<text x="0" y="120" font-family="sans-serif" font-size="80"
 font-weight="bold" fill="url(#img1)" >
    <tspan>HTML5</tspan>
    <tspan x="0" y="180" font-size="70">ROCKS!</tspan>
    <animateTransform fill="freeze"

    attributeName="transform" type="translate"

    values="0,0;0,220;0,0"

    begin="0s" dur="10s"

    repeatCount="indefinite">
  </text>
```

TO ANIMATE, ADD AN EXTRA CHILD NODE. THE ATTRIBUTES DETERMINE THE ANIMATION.

YOU'LL ANIMATE THE `translate` PROPERTY OF THE TRANSFORM.

A SEMICOLON-SEPARATED LIST OF VALUES FOR `translate`.

ONCE COMPLETE, REPEAT INDEFINITELY.

THE ANIMATION WILL BEGIN IMMEDIATELY AND RUN FOR A DURATION OF 10 SECONDS.

NOTE THAT, UNLIKE WITH ANIMATIONS ON `<canvas>`, YOU DON'T HAVE TO WRITE PROGRAMS TO REDRAW THE SCENE EVERY SECOND. YOU JUST DECLARE WHAT THE ANIMATION SHOULD BE AND LET THE BROWSER GET ON WITH IT. THIS IS WHY SVG ANIMATION WAS EARLIER REFERRED TO AS DECLARATIVE ANIMATION.

SVG animations aren't limited to simple attribute manipulations. Just as you were able to make text follow a path, it's also possible to make an animation follow a path. Here's an animation around a triangle.

Wed 22 Dec 2010 17:52:22 GMT   Wed 22 Dec 2010 17:52:25 GMT   Wed 22 Dec 2010 17:52:29 GMT

You can see the changes for yourself in ch03/svg-19.html. Here are the key points:

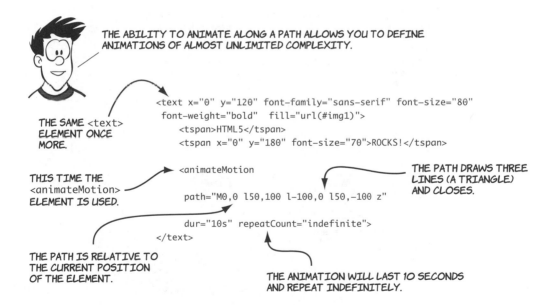

THE ABILITY TO ANIMATE ALONG A PATH ALLOWS YOU TO DEFINE ANIMATIONS OF ALMOST UNLIMITED COMPLEXITY.

THE SAME `<text>` ELEMENT ONCE MORE.

```
<text x="0" y="120" font-family="sans-serif" font-size="80"
  font-weight="bold"  fill="url(#img1)">
    <tspan>HTML5</tspan>
    <tspan x="0" y="180" font-size="70">ROCKS!</tspan>
```

THIS TIME THE `<animateMotion>` ELEMENT IS USED.

```
<animateMotion

  path="M0,0 l50,100 l-100,0 l50,-100 z"

    dur="10s" repeatCount="indefinite">
</text>
```

THE PATH DRAWS THREE LINES (A TRIANGLE) AND CLOSES.

THE PATH IS RELATIVE TO THE CURRENT POSITION OF THE ELEMENT.

THE ANIMATION WILL LAST 10 SECONDS AND REPEAT INDEFINITELY.

SVG vs. <canvas>

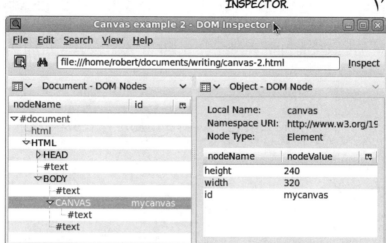

I AM LIKINK THE <canvas> ELEMENT. CLEAN AND SIMPLE API MAKINK HAPPY DEVELOPER.

SVG HAS AN API TOO, BUT IT'S THROUGH THE BROWSER DOM, WHICH DOUBLES AS A PERSISTENT OBJECT MODEL.

WITH <canvas>, YOU HAVE TO MANAGE YOUR OWN OBJECTS. AND IT HAS NO INTERNAL STRUCTURE, AS YOU CAN SEE BY COMPARING THE FOLLOWING TWO SCREENSHOTS OF DOM INSPECTOR.

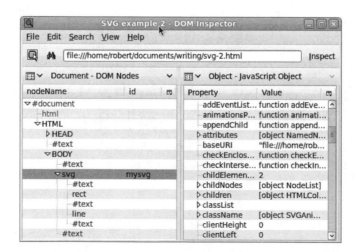

IS TRUE. BUT BROWSER DOM
IS BEINK TOO HEAVYWEIGHT. IS GOOD
THAT I AM CHOOSING OWN OBJECT
MODEL IN <canvas> WHEN MAPPINK
SEVERAL THOUSANDS OF MINIONS.

WELL, THERE ARE ISSUES
ONCE YOU HIT A CERTAIN THRESHOLD IN
THE NUMBER OF OBJECTS, BUT SVG HAS
OTHER ADVANTAGES.

THE NEXT TWO SCREENSHOTS
SHOW THE EFFECT OF ZOOMING IN
EIGHT TIMES ON A <canvas>
ELEMENT COMPARED TO AN SVG
ELEMENT.

YA. NATURAL VECTORS IS BEINK NICE
FEATURE. BUT BEINK PRACTICAL, CAN
JUST BE RESIZINK AND REDRAWINK
<canvas> ELEMENT TO BE MATCHINK
PAGE DIMENSIONS.

TRUE, BUT WHY
MAKE EXTRA WORK
FOR YOURSELF?

SVG HAS OTHER ADVANTAGES: FOR
INSTANCE, IT'S EASIER TO INTEGRATE IT
WITH OTHER WEB CONTENT. ALSO, THE
DECLARATIVE STYLE OF SVG MAY BE MORE
COMFORTABLE FOR WEB AUTHORS WHOSE
STRENGTHS LIE IN HTML AND CSS.

HAVE BEEN DISCUSSINK THIS BEFORE. AM
NOT BELIEVINK MARKUP MONKEYS IS BEINK
THE SAME THINK AS REAL DEVELOPERS.

NOT ALL WEB AUTHORS NEED TO BE HARD-CORE
DEVELOPERS. THERE ARE OTHER BENEFITS TO THE
OBJECT MODEL AND DECLARATIVE MARKUP—SVG
WILL BE MUCH EASIER TO MAKE ACCESSIBLE.

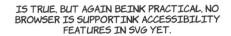

IS TRUE, BUT AGAIN BEINK PRACTICAL, NO
BROWSER IS SUPPORTINK ACCESSIBILITY
FEATURES IN SVG YET.

SOUNDS LIKE A GOOD TIME TO LOOK AT
BROWSER SUPPORT FOR <canvas> AND SVG.

Browser support

Both <canvas> and SVG have wide support in current browsers, with prospects for even better support in the respective next releases. <canvas> support tends to be all or nothing, but the situation with SVG is a lot more complex.

The SVG spec itself is about as complex as the HTML one, and no browser fully supports it, so the following table lists the percentage of the W3C SVG test suite that each browser passes. Figures aren't available for all browser versions, so the results for the most recent test in each browser are shown (thanks to www.codedread.com/svg-support.php for the figures).

	IE		Firefox		Chrome			Opera		Safari	
	12	14	4	6	8	9	10	11.5	12	5	5.1
<canvas>	•	•	•	•		•	•	•	•	•	•
<canvas> text	•	•	•	•		•	•	•	•	•	•
SVG score	89.23%		82.30%		-	59.64%		95.44%		82.48%	
SVG as image	•	•	•	•		•	•	•	•	•	•
SVG in CSS	•	•	•	•		•	•	•	•	•	•
SVG as object	•	•	•	•		•	•	•	•	•	•
SVG in XHTML	•	•	•	•		•	•	•	•	•	•
SVG in HTML	•	•	•	•		•	•		•		•

Key:
- Complete or nearly complete support
○ Incomplete or alternative support
  Little or no support

Supporting <canvas> in older versions of IE with explorercanvas

Internet Explorer was the only major browser that had no support for the <canvas> element, although support has been added in IE9. But older versions of IE have support for Vector Markup Language

(VML). VML is a predecessor of SVG, and you've already seen that SVG and <canvas> can do a lot of similar things. The explorercanvas library implements <canvas> in IE8 and earlier using VML. Activating explorercanvas is as simple as including a <script> element in the head of your HTML document:

```
<head>
<!--[if IE lte 8]><script src="excanvas.js"></script><![endif]-->
</head>
```

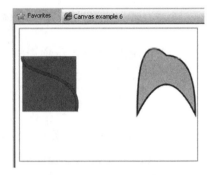

If you add that to any of the examples you've seen in this chapter, you should see them rendering in IE8 as the screenshot at right.

SVG in XML vs. SVG in HTML

I mentioned earlier that SVG support isn't as clear-cut as <canvas> support. This isn't just because the SVG specification is more complex but also because there are more ways to use SVG from within a web page. This is largely because SVG was originally envisioned as one of a family of XML-based languages that would be used for web content.

In nearly all the major browsers, it has long been possible to embed SVG content in the XML version of HTML/XHTML. Unfortunately, there has been one major obstacle to this happening.

FULLY COMPLIANT XHTML SHOULD BE DELIVERED FROM THE SERVER AS XML CONTENT. THE SERVER TELLS THE BROWSER THE CONTENT TYPE OF THE FILE IN THE HEADER OF THE HTTP RESPONSE. UNFORTUNATELY, IF YOU TRY TO SEND AN XML WEB PAGE TO A VERSION OF INTERNET EXPLORER EARLIER THAN 9, IT REFUSES TO PARSE THE PAGE. BECAUSE DEPLOYING SVG IN XHTML REQUIRES BREAKING IE, FEW PEOPLE HAVE CONSIDERED IT PRACTICAL.

Embedding SVG as an image

SVG can be used in the <img> element in the same way as any other image format:

```
<img src="svg-2.svg">
```

When used this way, SVG still has the advantage of being scalable; you can set it to take up half the browser window, and it will remain sharp no matter how high or low your user's screen resolution. But you lose the advantage of being able to manipulate the image from the Java-Script—the elements of the image aren't present in the DOM.

Referencing an SVG image from CSS

In the same way that it can be used as an image in HTML, SVG can be referenced as an image in CSS:

```
div { background: url(svg-2.svg) top right no-repeat; }
```

THIS IS PARTICULARLY USEFUL IN CONCERT WITH CSS3'S background-size PROPERTY, WHICH YOU'LL LEARN MORE ABOUT IN CHAPTER 10. YOU CAN CREATE BACKGROUND IMAGES THAT SCALE WITH THE SCREEN RESOLUTION BUT STAY SHARP.

Embedding SVG as an object

The <object> element is a general-purpose method to embed any exter-nal content in your web page. To embed SVG with <object>, you need to supply two parameters specifying the filename and the file type:

```
<object type="image/svg+xml" data="svg-2.svg"></object>
```

In browsers with native support for SVG, the object-embedding approach has results similar to including the SVG inline: the SVG ele-ments are available in the DOM and can be manipulated. This tech-nique works in every browser that has SVG support; and if you're using the same SVG image on different pages of your site, it's cached the same way a normal image would be, making your site load slightly faster. The corollary of this, of course, is that if you use the image only once it will require a second request to the server, making your site slightly slower to load.

SVG support in older browsers with SVG Web and Raphaël

YOU DON'T HAVE TO RELY ON DIRECT BROWSER SUPPORT FOR SVG. OLDER BROWSERS AND IE OFFER A COUPLE OF JAVASCRIPT LIBRARIES THAT ENABLE SVG SUPPORT THROUGH ALTERNATIVE MEANS.

SVG Web is a JavaScript library that, if it detects the browser has no native support for SVG, will replace any SVG graphics it finds with a Flash movie. The Flash movie will then take care of rendering the SVG in the browser. You have to make some slight modifications to your web page in order to enable SVG Web. The first is in the head of the document, where you reference the SVG Web JavaScript library:

```
<script src="svg.js"></script>
```

Then you have to surround each of your SVG graphics with `<script>` tags:

```
<script type="image/svg+xml">
    <svg viewBox="0 0 320 240">
        <rect x="50" y="50" width="100" height="100"
                style="fill: rgb(255,0,0)"></rect>
        <line x1="50" y1="50" x2="150" y2="150"
                style="stroke: rgb(0,127,127); stroke-width: 5;"></line>
    </svg>
</script>
```

Your SVG graphics will then render as SVG in browsers that support it and as Flash movies in browsers that don't support SVG. In the following examples, at left you can see that SVG Web allows Internet Explorer to render inline SVG, although it doesn't match the native support offered by browsers such as Firefox (shown on the right).

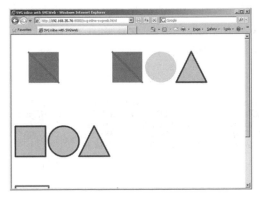 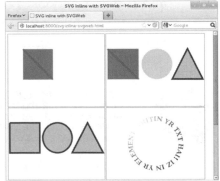

The Raphaël JavaScript library takes a different approach. Instead of making existing SVG work in IE, it presents an API for creating graphics. In Firefox, Chrome, Safari, and Opera it creates SVG; in IE, it creates VML. The interface Raphaël provides looks similar to the <canvas> API:

```
var paper = Raphael(10, 50, 320, 200);
var circle = paper.circle(50, 40, 10);
circle.attr("fill", "#f00");
circle.attr("stroke", "#fff");
```

RAPHAËL LOOKS SIMILAR TO <canvas>, BUT IT'S STILL SVG UNDERNEATH. THIS MEANS THAT WHEN YOU CALL THE CIRCLE FUNCTION, IT RETURNS AN OBJECT. THIS OBJECT CAN LATER BE MODIFIED, AND THE DRAWING WILL UPDATE TO REFLECT THE CHANGES; YOU DON'T HAVE TO CLEAR EVERYTHING AND REDRAW IT AS YOU DO WITH <canvas>.

Summary

In this chapter you've learned how you can generate graphics in your web page on the fly using two different HTML5 technologies — <canvas> and SVG. Because both can be created and updated dynamically, they don't need the user to reload the page in order to present new information to the user.

You've learned the basic techniques for drawing shapes and lines with both technologies, as well as how to import images and apply effects and transformations. With <canvas> you've looked at how to do simple animation while with SVG you saw how you can import whole web pages and apply transformations to them.

NOW THAT YOU CAN CREATE YOUR OWN GRAPHICS ON THE FLY, IT'S TIME TO COMPLETE YOUR EDUCATION ON THE MULTIMEDIA POSSIBILITIES OF HTML5 WITH A LOOK AT THE NEW AUDIO AND VIDEO ELEMENTS. IN THE NEXT CHAPTER, YOU'LL SEE THAT HTML5 MAKES ADDING AUDIO AND VIDEO TO WEB PAGES AS EASY AS ADDING IMAGES TO WEB PAGES IS IN HTML4.

4

Audio and video

This chapter covers

- *Why audio and video are important on the web*

- *Adding audio and video to your web pages*

- *Encoding audio and video files for the web*

- *Integrating video with other web platform features and content*

Native media support is one of the best known as well as one of the most controversial HTML5 features. In this chapter, you'll learn why HTML5 media support is great, why it's frustrating, and the practical factors you need to consider when using it.

Audio and video on the modern web

Audio and video are key parts of the modern web. For many sites, video and audio are parts of the content as integral as the text and pictures—and in some cases, they're more important.

For sites like BBC Radio 6 and last.fm, audio is the whole point of the page. And for podcasts like Buzz Out Loud, visitors expect to hear or see the content.

News sites like BBC News often offer video and audio as alternative content, and sites such as YouTube are all about the video content and are often used to add video to other sites such as I Can Has Cheezburger.

Despite their rising importance, HTML4 offers no built-in method for adding audio or video to a web page. This makes embedding audio and video relatively complex. Compare the markup required to add an image to a web page with that typically required to add a video.

Image	Video

``
<img
 width="320"
 height="240"
 id="myimage"
 src="myimage.png">
``
	``
	<object
	 classid="clsid:d27cdb6e-ae6d-11cf-96b8-444553540000"
	 codebase="http://download.macromedia.com/
	    pub/shockwave/cabs/flash/
	    swflash.cab#version=6,0,40,0"
	 width="320" height="240"
	 id="myvideoname">
	    <param name="movie"
	      value="myvideo.swf">
	    <param name="quality" value="high">
	    <param name="bgcolor" value=#ffffff>
	    <embed href="myvideo.swf"
	           quality="high" bgcolor="#ffffff"
	           width="320" height="240"
	           name="myvideoname"
	           type="application/x-shockwave-flash"
	           pluginspage="http://www.macromedia.com/
	             go/getflashplayer">
	    </embed>
	</object>
	``

Because there's no native support for audio and video, web authors have had to resort to browser plug-ins. The web has largely settled on Adobe Flash as a de facto standard, but as the previous code shows, this is still a good deal more complex than putting an image on a page. And that's not all the code that's required: to add controls such as Play and Pause, there must be code written inside Flash, and even more code if the player needs to be integrated into other page content.

ONE OF THE REASONS FOR YOUTUBE'S POPULARITY IS THAT IT REDUCES THE COMPLEXITY OF DISPLAYING VIDEO ON THE WEB—INSTEAD OF DOING ALL THE WORK YOURSELF, YOU UPLOAD THE VIDEO TO YOUTUBE AND THEN COPY AND PASTE SOME CODE. BUT HTML SHOULD MAKE IT THAT SIMPLE WITHOUT THE NEED FOR A THIRD-PARTY SITE. THIS IS A PROBLEM REMEDIED IN HTML5 WITH THE INTRODUCTION OF THE <audio> AND <video> ELEMENTS.

What is a plug-in?

A plug-in is a generic extension method for HTML that allows the page author to indicate embedded content that is to be rendered by an external program. The web browser hands over control of that region of the web page to the external program. This external program is referred to as a *plug-in*.

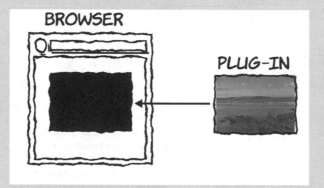

The content rendered by the plug-in is like a black box to the browser. Browser features like keyboard shortcuts, cookie preferences, and pop-up blockers don't apply.

Following is the HTML5 code for embedding audio and video, which compares favorably with the <img> element. The screenshots show the default presentation of the <video> and <audio> elements in Firefox with the controls visible.

Audio	Video
`<audio src="myaudio.ogg" controls>` `</audio>`	`<video src="myvideo.ogv" controls>` `</video>`

FIREFOX SHOWS THE CONTROLS ON THE <video>
ELEMENT ONLY WHEN THE USER MOUSES OVER AND AT
INITIAL PAGE LOAD, BUT OTHER BROWSERS HAVE THEM
VISIBLE UNTIL THE VIDEO STARTS PLAYING.

Both elements in the previous example have been set to 320 × 240 pixels with CSS, although in the case of the <audio> element you can see this doesn't achieve much. The <video> element is showing the first frame of the video. Note that the video is 320 × 180 pixels, but instead of stretching the video and changing the aspect ratio, the video is made as wide as possible and centered vertically.

NOW YOU KNOW WHY HTML5 HAS <audio> AND <video> ELEMENTS
AND WHAT THE BASIC CODE LOOKS LIKE. IN THE FOLLOWING
SECTIONS, YOU'LL LEARN ABOUT THE <audio> AND <video>
ELEMENTS IN MORE DETAIL, STARTING WITH THE <audio> ELEMENT.

The <audio> element

	Standard
	4.0
	3.5
	9.0
	10.5
	4.0

Browser support quick check: audio

Audio on the web gained something of a bad rap in the 1990s as thousands of people happily attached background music to their GeoCities pages, but there are plenty of legitimate uses for audio in a web page. Sometimes, websites are entirely about sound—band home pages should have samples of the band's work; dictionaries should allow you to listen to pronunciation; games need sound effects. As you've learned, until the <audio> element, the only available option was a browser plug-in. In this section, you'll learn about the <audio> element, its supported attributes, file formats, and how to convert between them.

Common attributes: controls, autoplay, loop, and preload

The <audio> element has several attributes that control its behavior, including src and controls, which you saw in the simple example. It's possible to add the element with no attributes at all:

```
<audio src="myaudio.ogg">
</audio>
```

HEY! WHERE IS IT?!!

The screenshot isn't interesting because there's nothing to see—without the controls attribute, the element isn't visible on the page. Having no visible controls means you have to start the audio playing by other means—either by using the autoplay attribute (discussed in a moment) or by providing your own controls (which you'll learn about in the section "The <video> element").

Adding the controls attribute means the <audio> element has visible properties:

```
<audio src="myaudio.ogg"
 controls>
</audio>
```

The preload attribute lets you hint to the browser whether a file is likely to be needed, so you can avoid excessive server load:

```
<audio src="myaudio.ogg" controls preload="metadata">
</audio>
```

It can take the following values:

- none—You don't believe the audio resource is likely to be used.
- metadata—You don't believe the audio is likely to be used, but the browser should fetch information such as the dimensions, first frame, and duration.

- auto — The server will have no problem with the browser download-ing the entire video even if the user doesn't explicitly create it.

The browser is free to ignore the preload attribute — for example, a mobile browser may choose not to download any media over a limited cell connection unless the user explicitly requests it.

The autoplay and loop attributes specify that the file is to start playing as soon as the user loads the page and to continue to play repeatedly after it's started:

```
<audio src="myaudio.ogg" controls
autoplay loop>
</audio>
```

Until recently the loop attribute didn't have any effect in browsers, but you can simulate the effect in older browsers with a little JavaScript:

```
<audio src="myaudio.ogg" controls autoplay onended="this.play();">
</audio>
```

The ended event is fired when the video has finished playing. The code waits for that event and starts the audio playing again when it happens.

Be careful with autoplay. Remember, your users may be working in a quiet environment, or listening to music while they're browsing, or depending on the audio provided by their screen-reader software, and they may not appreciate an audible interruption from a website they were only visiting to find a phone number.

IF YOU'RE WONDERING WHY THE <audio> ELEMENT HAS OPENING AND CLOSING TAGS, IT'S BECAUSE <audio> IS ALSO A CONTAINER FOR OTHER CONTENT. THAT CONTENT IS DISPLAYED ONLY IF THE BROWSER DOESN'T SUPPORT THE <audio> ELEMENT. THIS ALLOWS YOU TO WORK AROUND A LACK OF BROWSER SUPPORT.

The next example shows an <audio> element in IE8. The <audio> element itself is ignored, and just the contained content is displayed:

```
<audio src="myaudio.ogg" controls>
    Audio not supported.
</audio>
```

AUDIO NOT SUPPORTED.

Normally you would want to display something more useful than just the fact that the <audio> element isn't supported. At least if you show a link, the user has the chance to download the audio file and listen to it in an external player:

```
<audio src="myaudio.ogg" controls>
    <a href="myaudio.ogg">
        Download myaudio.ogg
    </a>
</audio>
```

DOWNLOAD MYAUDIO.OGG

Compare that with a browser like Firefox that does support the <audio> element, but not the media type specified in the src:

```
<audio src="myaudio.ogg" controls>
    Audio not supported.
</audio>
<audio src="myaudio.mp3" controls>
    Audio not supported.
</audio>
```

Firefox doesn't support MP3, so the user still sees an audio control, but it's inactive. In other browsers, you may see a broken image icon or some other indication that the media is invalid.

The <audio> element controls allow for a limited amount of styling with CSS. Here it's been set to 200 pixels square in Firefox:

```
audio {
    width: 200px;
    height: 200px;
    outline: 1px solid #ccc;
}
```

The outline shows the extent of the element. As you can see, the width is applied to the controls but the height is ignored. The next example makes that clearer:

```
audio {
    width: 100px;
    height: 50px;
    outline: 1px solid #ccc;
}
```

The controls have a minimum intrinsic width. If you try to make them smaller than that, the width will be ignored, as you can see from the still-visible outline in this example:

```
audio {
    width: 50px;
    height: 25px;
    outline: 1px solid #ccc;
}
```

Other browsers display slightly differently, as you can see in the next examples. Chrome (left) behaves similarly to Firefox: the controls extend out of the defined width and height. But Opera (right) is a little cleaner-looking at narrow width.

It's currently impossible to change the colors of the controls in any browser. CSS like the following sets the background color, but it doesn't make any difference to the controls themselves:

```
audio {
    width: 200px;
    height: 50px;
    outline: 1px solid #ccc;
    background-color: #000;
    color: #fff;
}
```

But it's possible to use the background in concert with the otherwise-ignored height property:

```
audio {
    width: 200px;
    height: 200px;
    outline: 1px solid #ccc;
    background:
      url('dust-puppy.svg')
      no-repeat top center;
    background-size: contain;
}
```

You could use this CSS to provide an image of the artist or some sort of cover art.

DESIGNERS MAY BE SEVERELY DISAPPOINTED WITH THE LACK OF STYLING OPTIONS AVAILABLE FOR THE AUDIO CONTROLS, BUT ALL ISN'T LOST. IN THE LATER SECTION "CONTROLLING AUDIO AND VIDEO WITH JAVASCRIPT," YOU'LL SEE HOW YOU CAN WRITE "YOUR OWN CONTROLS, WHICH YOU CAN THEN STYLE HOWEVER YOU WISH.

YOU'VE SEEN HOW SIMPLE IT IS TO EMBED AUDIO FILES, BUT UNFORTUNATELY THAT'S NOT THE END OF THE STORY. IN THE SAME WAY THE HTML5 STANDARD DOESN'T SPECIFY WHICH TYPES OF IMAGES A BROWSER SHOULD SUPPORT ON <img>, IT ALSO DOESN'T SPECIFY WHAT TYPES OF FILE SHOULD BE SUPPORTED BY <audio>; BUT UNLIKE IMAGES, THERE ARE NO AUDIO FORMATS THAT ALL THE BROWSER MAKERS HAVE DECIDED TO SUPPORT. THE NEXT SECTION DISCUSSES THESE ISSUES.

Codecs and license issues

Audio files are usually stored in a compressed format. To be stored on a computer, they must be encoded into that format; to be played back, they have to be decoded once again. The software that performs this encoding and decoding is called a *codec*. Music files on your computer usually have a file extension that identifies which codec is needed to decode them.

What is a codec?

In principal, it's possible to describe the raw data of audio and video streams to an arbitrary accuracy. For audio, you'd store the amplitude of the sound wave for each moment in time you wanted to play the sound back; for video, you'd store the color of each pixel for each frame (usually 25–30 per second) as well as the sound. But this would lead to impossibly large files for anything of a useful length.

In practice, you want to compress the audio and video data in the same way you might compress a large file into a zip archive. A codec is what's used to compress audio and video data for storage and later to decompress the same audio and video to be played through speakers and displayed on screens in real time.

Codecs can be split into two broad categories: *lossless* and *lossy*. Think about a zip archive: when you extract the content from it, you expect to get back the exact same files you put in—it's a lossless compression. In the same way, some codecs are capable of compressing audio and video with no loss of information. But these files are necessarily still large. The more interesting set of codecs for the web are lossy—each time they're used to encode a video stream, some information is thrown away, never to be seen again. These codecs can achieve far greater compression at the expense of some loss of audible or visual quality; the trick is to throw away data that makes as little difference to human perception as possible.

YOU'VE ALMOST CERTAINLY HEARD OF AT LEAST ONE CODEC: MPEG-1 (OR 2) AUDIO LEVEL III, COMMONLY KNOWN AS MP3. MP3 IS A PERFECTLY GOOD CODEC TECHNICALLY—IT WAS THE FIRST POPULAR CODEC ABLE TO MAKE A TYPICAL POP SONG SMALL ENOUGH TO BE DOWNLOADABLE WHILE RETAINING CD QUALITY—BUT THERE ARE ISSUES OTHER THAN THE TECHNICAL ONES.

The problem with the MP3 codec is that there are several patents on it; and if you want to distribute software that encodes and decodes MP3, you need to pay to license those patents. Mozilla, the makers of Firefox, takes the position that the web should be built out of free and open standards and so doesn't support MP3; instead, Firefox supports the open Ogg Vorbis (OGG) format. Opera agrees. Google also agrees in principal but for practical reasons distributes Chrome with MP3 support; Google has also released its own video format, WebM (which will be discussed further in the video section), which can also be used in audio-only mode. Apple and Microsoft both already have licenses to distribute MP3 codecs, so Safari and IE do support it; but, crucially, they don't support the free and open OGG format out of the box.

The different format support is summarized in the next table. The short version is this: no one file format works on all browsers. You'll need multiple files to support them all.

		WAV	OGG	MP3	AAC	WebM
Browser support quick check: audio codecs		8	5	5	5	8
		3.5	3.5	~	~	4
		~	~	9	9	*
		10.5	10.5	~	~	11.1
		4	**	4	4	**

* IE9 will support WebM if the user downloads an additional codec.

** Safari will support anything that can be played by Quick-Time. Users have to download additional codecs.

To encode a file to OGG, you can use the oggenc command-line utility available from www.rarewares.org. Use it to convert an uncompressed WAV file like this:

```
oggenc myaudio.wav
```

The output is a file called myaudio.ogg. To improve the quality of the encoding, use the –b flag to set the bitrate. The –o flag allows you to specify the output filename:

```
oggenc myaudio.wav –b 256 –o myhighqualityaudio.ogg
```

For MP3 audio, you can use the `lame` command-line utility, also available from www.rarewares.org:

```
lame myaudio.wav myaudio.mp3
```

Again, you can set the minimum bitrate with a command-line flag:

```
lame –b 256 myaudio.wav myhighqualityaudio.mp3
```

Bitrate

Bitrate is the number of bits (individual units of information) that are conveyed or processed per unit of time. Higher bitrates mean greater sound fidelity but also larger file sizes. Typical bitrates for CD-quality audio are in the 100–160 kbit/s range.

OGG AND MP3 BOTH WORK BY THROWING AWAY DATA THAT MAKES LITTLE AUDIBLE DIFFERENCE TO THE HUMAN EAR, BUT THEY TEND TO THROW AWAY DIFFERENT PARTS OF THE AUDIO DATA. FOR THIS REASON, YOU SHOULDN'T CONVERT BETWEEN OGG AND MP3 EXCEPT AS A LAST RESORT—IT'S FAR BETTER TO CONVERT FROM A LOSSLESS FORMAT (FREE LOSSLESS AUDIO CODEC [FLAC], WAV, OR AN ORIGINAL CD) TO BOTH OGG AND MP3.

Command-line utilities are handy, especially if you have a large collection of audio files, because you can write a script to convert them all in a single batch. If you just have one or two files to convert, you may prefer a GUI-driven approach. For this, there's a handy website: http://media.io. Visit the site, and select the file you want to encode from your hard drive.

media.io

Online Audio Converter

Select your file and upload it. media.io will convert it immediately. Supported file formats and file sizes.

Upload   [   ] [Browse...]
                                    [Upload]

After the file is uploaded, you're given a choice of four options for the codec and, if appropriate, a choice for audio quality.

Select the options you need, and click Convert; a few seconds later, your encoded file will be available to download. Note that the 192 kbps OGG encoded file is approximately 20% of the file size of the lossless original.

You'll have noticed that the file used in this example, despite being originally encoded with the free FLAC codec, isn't free content. Although it's in the OGG format supported by Firefox, Chrome, or Opera, I'm not allowed to upload it to my website because I have no rights to redistribute it. But it will now take up less space on my phone!

Even if I could upload it, the audio wouldn't play in IE or Safari. Unless users have installed additional codecs in their operating systems, Safari and IE won't play the OGG file—they need MP3.

If different browsers require different file types, how can you support multiple browsers with a single src attribute? HTML5 anticipates this issue and provides an easy mechanism for providing the correct source to each browser. Let's look at that in the next section.

Using multiple sources

As you've just seen, you need to be able to provide different audio files to different browsers. But each <audio> element only allows you a single src attribute, so how can you manage that? The design of the <audio> element has anticipated this requirement. Multiple sources can be provided for the <audio> element by using the <source> element:

```
<audio id="myaudio" controls>
    <source src="myaudio.mp3" type="audio/mp3">
    <source src="myaudio.ogg" type="audio/ogg">
    No audio support!
</audio>
```

The following tables list the common file extensions and MIME types for audio.

Audio type	File extensions	MIME types
MP3	.mp3	audio/mpeg
MP4	.m4a, .m4b, .m4p, .m4v, .m4r, .3gp, .mp4, .aac	audio/mp4 audio/aac
OGG	.ogg, .oga	audio/ogg
WebM	.webm	audio/webm
WAVE	.wav	audio/wave (preferred) audio/wav audio/x-wav audio/x-pn-wav

Browsers are expected to scan the list of <source> elements from top to bottom and load the first one they believe they can play. By using some

JavaScript, you can interrogate the `<audio>` element and find out which file is loaded.

PLAYING FILE MYAUDIO.OGG

PLAYING FILE MYAUDIO.MP3

Firefox plays the .ogg file.   Internet Explorer plays the .mp3 file.

Here's the snippet of JavaScript used in the previous screenshots. Add it to the `<audio>` element as an attribute, and add a `<div id="source"></div>` after the `<audio>` element to display the output:

```
onloadeddata="document.getElementById('source')
    .innerHTML = 'Playing file ' +
        this.currentSrc.slice(this.currentSrc.lastIndexOf('/')+1);"
```

This code is executed in the `loadeddata` event, which means after the browser has loaded identifying information about the file. You'll learn more about manipulating HTML5 media elements with JavaScript in the section "The <video> element."

AUDIO IS FINE, BUT IT LACKS VISUAL IMPACT. LET'S MOVE ON TO EMBEDDING VIDEO. IN THE NEXT SECTION, YOU'LL SEE THAT ADDING VIDEO TO A PAGE IN HTML5 IS JUST AS SIMPLE AS ADDING AUDIO.

The <video> element

For the many people who don't obsessively read standards groups' mailing lists, the first time they became aware of HTML5 was when they found out that Flash video doesn't work on the iPhone but HTML5 video does. As you saw in the introduction, the goal of the HTML5 `<video>` element is to make embedding video in your pages as easy as embedding images. This section looks at the details of making it work. We'll follow a pattern similar to the previous section: first the

allowed attributes, then the various encoding issues, and finally how to convert between file formats

Browser support quick check: video		Standard
		4.0
		3.5
		9.0
		10.5
		4.0

The sample video

The sample video used in this section's examples is of the author playing American football. Because this video was taken by the author's mother, we can neatly sidestep any issues involving media distribution rights.

<video> element attributes

The <video> element supports the same attributes as the <audio> element, with similar results. This section quickly runs through them in the same way as the section on audio.

The basic <video> element looks like this:

```
<video src="00092.webm"></video>
```

A <video> element without controls is a little more interesting than the equivalent <audio> element because you at least have the first frame of the video to look at. This screenshot was taken in Firefox; Opera and Chrome should work just as well for the WebM format.

As with audio, you can enable the standard controls with an attribute:

```
<video src="00092.webm"
  controls preload="metadata">
</video>
```

As with the `<audio>` element, the `preload` attribute provides a hint to the browser about how likely this video is to be played by the user.

If you add the `autoplay` attribute, on desktop browsers, the video will download and start playing as soon as possible:

```
<video src="00092.webm"
  controls autoplay loop>
</video>
```

The controls are available, but they auto-hide as the video starts playing.

As with the `<audio>` element, `loop` only works on the most recent browser versions, but it can be simulated with the same bit of JavaScript:

```
onended="this.play();"
```

Also as with the `<audio>` element, the `<video>` element can contain fall-back content. At the end of this chapter, we'll look at using that content to embed an alternative player for your videos using a plug-in, falling back to HTML4 technologies for browsers that don't support HTML5.

The `<video>` element also has its own specific attributes: `poster`, `width`, `height`, and `audio`. Let's look at each of those in turn.

The `poster` attribute lets you control what's shown in the `<video>` element when a video isn't playing. By default, browsers show the first frame of the video, but you can supply your own image:

```
<video src="videofile.ogv"
  poster="posterimage.jpg">
</video>
```

The width and height attributes set the width and height of the <video> element:

```
<video src="videofile.ogv"
  width="400px" height="300px">
</video>
```

Note that this doesn't directly set the width and height of the video itself; the aspect ratio of the video is always preserved. You can also set the width and height with CSS:

```
video {
    width: 400px;
    height: 300px;
}
```

If you set width and height attributes and also set the width and height with CSS, the CSS wins:

```
<video src="videofile.ogv"
  width="400px" height="300px"
  style="width: 320px;
         height: 180px;">
</video>
```

The muted attribute sets the default volume of the video to 0:

```
<video src="videofile.ogv" muted>
</video>
```

Unfortunately it doesn't yet work in any browsers, but you can fake it with this bit of JavaScript:

```
onloadeddata="this.volume = 0;"
```

YOU NOW KNOW ABOUT ALL THE ATTRIBUTES AVAILABLE ON THE `<video>` ELEMENT. IT'S TIME TO ADDRESS THE THORNY ISSUE OF VIDEO CODECS, WHICH IS EVEN MORE OF A MESS THAN THE SITUATION WITH AUDIO CODECS. THIS HAS BEEN ONE OF THE MORE CONTENTIOUS ISSUES IN THE WRITING OF THE HTML5 SPEC, NOT LEAST BECAUSE VIDEO SUPPORT IS SEEN AS BEING SO IMPORTANT.

Containers, codecs, and license issues

The situation with video is even more complex than with audio because video files need both a visual and an auditory stream, so they need both video and audio codecs. A format to contain both audio and video also needs to be defined.

UNLIKE AUDIO FILES, WHERE THE FILE EXTENSION IS LINKED DIRECTLY TO THE CODEC BEING USED, WITH VIDEO THE FILE EXTENSION IS LINKED TO THE CONTAINER FORMAT. TO BE ABLE TO PLAY THE VIDEO, THE BROWSER NEEDS TO SUPPORT THE CONTAINER FORMAT, THE VIDEO CODEC, AND THE AUDIO CODEC. IN PRACTICE, THIS ISN'T TOO MUCH OF A FACTOR BECAUSE AUDIO CODECS WITHOUT LICENSE FEES ARE ALWAYS PAIRED WITH VIDEO CODECS THAT DON'T REQUIRE A LICENSE, AND VICE VERSA.

Browser support quick check: video formats		MPEG-4	Ogg/Theora	WebM
	(Chrome)	5*	5	8
	(Firefox)	~	3.5	4
	(IE)	9	~	**
	(Opera)	~	10.5	11.1
	(Safari)	4	***	***

* Google has announced that Chrome will stop supporting MP4 in a future release.

** IE9 will support WebM if the user downloads an additional codec.

*** Safari will support anything that can be played by Quick-Time. Users have to download additional codecs

Following are the common file extensions and MIME types for video.

Video type	File extensions	MIME types
MPEG-4	.mp4	video/mp4
OGG	.ogg, .ogv	video/ogg
WebM	.webm	video/webm

MPEG-4 profiles

The MPEG-4 standard contains several different profiles in order to support a variety of different expected use cases, ranging from Blu-ray and HDTV to mobile phones with low screen resolutions. Mobile devices aren't expected to support the same profiles as desktop PCs or dedicated home multimedia equipment, so when you're encoding videos for use on iPhones make sure you're targeting the Simple Profile.

Easy encoding with Miro Video Converter

Rather than mess around with the different codecs and encoding options yourself, there are tools that make things easy for you. One of the simplest is the Miro Video Converter, available from www. mirovideoconverter.com.

Miro Video Converter doesn't present you with a lot of options—just a place to drop the file you want to convert; a drop-down list to say what

you want to convert it to; and a button to start the conversion. After you drop a video file on the central area, only the output format needs to be selected before you're ready to go.

The first three options are the main ones that interest us:

⊙ Theora is the OGG video format supported by Opera and Firefox.

- WebM (VP8) is Google's new video codec, supported by Chrome and newer versions of Opera and Firefox.
- MP4 video is the format supported by Safari and IE.

The additional options are variations of these main three, except that the output video is scaled for the particular device.

After you set the option, click Convert and, depending on how large your video is, wait a few minutes or a few hours. Repeat the process for as many encodings as you require.

The main advantage of this approach is that it's easy and requires little expertise. The disadvantage is that if you don't like the results, you have to take a different approach—there are no configuration options for you to tweak.

MIRO VIDEO CONVERTER CAN GIVE YOU A HEAD START IF YOU WANT A MORE FINE-TUNED APPROACH. NOTE THE FFMPEG OUTPUT BUTTON AT LOWER RIGHT IN THE FIGURE. FFMPEG IS THE COMMAND-LINE UTILITY THAT MIRO VIDEO CONVERTER USES TO DO THE ENCODING. IN THE NEXT SECTION, YOU'LL SEE HOW YOU CAN USE FFMPEG DIRECTLY FOR FINER-GRAINED CONTROL OVER THE ENCODING PROCESS.

Advanced encoding with FFmpeg

FFmpeg is a command-line tool originally written for the Linux operating system. It's powerful and has thousands of options that you can set by passing options on the command line. Rather than get into the details of how FFmpeg works, which could easily take up a few chapters, let's use the Miro Video Converter output as a starting point and look at some easy ways to tweak things.

If you click the FFMPEG Output button while encoding a WebM video, you'll see that the command being used, on Windows, is something similar to this:

```
ffmpeg-bin\ffmpeg.exe -y -i "C:\00092.MTS" -f webm
    -vcodec libvpx -acodec libvorbis -ab 160000
    -crf 22 "C:\00092.webmvp8.webm"
```

You can run this yourself at the command prompt. Here's a quick rundown of what the parameters mean (don't worry too much about the details—for the most part you won't need to change these):

- -y—Overwrite any existing output without prompting.
- -f—Container format.
- -acodec—Audio codec to use.
- -crf—Set the constant rate factor (crf). This automatically varies the bitrate to maintain a consistent quality.
- -i—Input file.
- -vcodec—Video codec to use.
- -ab—Audio bitrate to use. Bigger numbers lead to larger files.

One easy change you might want to make is to change the size of the output video, using the -s parameter. This example sets the output to 320 pixels wide by 180 pixels high:

```
ffmpeg-bin\ffmpeg.exe -y -i "C:\00092.MTS" -f webm
    -vcodec libvpx -acodec libvorbis -ab 160000
    -s 320x180 -crf 22 "C:\00092.webmvp8.320.high.webm"
```

It's also easy to adjust the quality of the output file by specifying a bitrate. To do so, use the -b parameter:

```
ffmpeg-bin\ffmpeg.exe -y -i "C:\00092.MTS" -f webm
    -vcodec libvpx -b 3600k -acodec libvorbis -ab 160000
    -s 320x180 "C:\00092.webmvp8.high.webm"
```

The same options can be applied to the command for iPhone MP4 encoding, although that has a few extra options specified by default:

```
ffmpeg-bin\ffmpeg.exe -i "C:\00092.MTS" -f mp4
    -acodec aac -ac 2 -strict experimental -ab 160k
    -s 320x180 -vcodec libx264
    -vpre slow -vpre ipod640 -b 1200k
    -threads 0 "C:\00092.iphone.320.mp4"
```

One thing to watch for when running the Miro version of FFmpeg is the location of the preset files. The slow and ipod640 presets used in the previous command correspond to the libx264-slow.ffpreset and libx264-ipod640.ffpreset files. Put these files in C:\usr\local\share\ffmpeg so that ffmpeg.exe can find them.

Using multiple sources

Now that you have a collection of video files to support all the different browsers and devices your users may be using, you can add them to the <video> element using the <source> element, just as with the <audio> element earlier:

```
<video id="myvideo" controls>
    <source src="00092.webm" type="video/webm">
    <source src="00092.mp4" type="video/mp4">
    <source src="00092.low.mp4" type="video/mp4">
    <source src="00092.ogv" type="video/ogg">
    No video support!
</video>
```

IF YOU EXPECT TO HAVE USERS WITH OLDER VERSIONS OF IOS, THEN YOU SHOULD BE AWARE THAT ALTHOUGH THE <source> ELEMENT IS RECOGNIZED, ONLY THE FIRST ONE WILL EVER BE USED. IN THE PREVIOUS EXAMPLES, YOU SHOULD PUT THE 00092.LOW.MP4 SOURCE FIRST SO OLDER IOSS WILL PLAY IT. OF COURSE, THIS MEANS USERS OF MODERN DESKTOP BROWSERS THAT SUPPORT MPEG-4 WILL PLAY THIS LOW-QUALITY VIDEO INSTEAD OF THE HIGHER-QUALITY ONES FURTHER DOWN.

As with the <audio> element, it's possible to find out which file the browser has chosen by looking at the currentSrc property of the <video> element in JavaScript. Adding this snippet of code to the <video>

element reports the filename to an element with ID `'source'` when the video has loaded:

```
onloadeddata=
 "document.getElementById('source')
   .innerHTML = 'Playing file ' +
        this.currentSrc.slice(this.currentSrc.lastIndexOf('/')+1);"
```

Loading the page in a variety of different browsers shows how the multiple source elements are picked up.

Playing file 00092.low.mp4

Android browser uses the low-quality MP4.

PLAYING FILE 00092.WEBM

Firefox 4 uses the WebM video.

PLAYING FILE 00092.OGV

Firefox 3.6 uses the Ogg video.

PLAYING FILE 00092.OGV

Desktop Safari uses the high-quality MP4.

YOU'VE NOW LEARNED HOW TO ADD AUDIO AND VIDEO TO YOUR PAGES, AND HAD A BRIEF INTRODUCTION TO THE MINEFIELD THAT IS VIDEO ENCODING FOR DESKTOP BROWSERS AND MOBILE DEVICES. BUT SO FAR, YOU HAVEN'T SEEN MUCH OF THE MAIN ADVANTAGE OF USING HTML5 VIDEO AND AUDIO: INTEGRATION WITH THE REST OF YOUR PAGE CONTENT. IN THE NEXT TWO SECTIONS, YOU'LL LEARN ABOUT THE POSSIBILITIES THIS ALLOWS, STARTING WITH AN EXPLORATION OF THE JAVASCRIPT API.

Controlling audio and video with JavaScript

Earlier in this chapter, you saw that, by default, <audio> and <video> elements don't provide controls for the user to interact with them; it's up to the web author to explicitly ask for controls to be provided. At the time, you'd be forgiven for thinking that this is a bit pointless—what good is a video if you can't play it? In this section, you'll discover exactly how useful it can be to have complete control over the video from JavaScript.

To begin with, let's look at playing and pausing a video. This is straightforward—the <video> element provides play() and pause() methods:

```
<button
onclick="document.getElementById('myvideo')
.play();">
  Play
</button>
<button
onclick="document.getElementById('myvideo')
.pause();">
  Stop
</button>
```

PLAYING FILE 00092.WEBM

Instead of providing controls on the video, buttons are provided on the page. If your first thought when you saw the default controls was, "Ugh! I don't like the look of those. How can I style them myself?" then here is the answer: create your own elements to control the video, and style them however you wish.

You don't have to limit yourself to the standard operations of Play and Pause. This function starts the video play from a point in the middle of the stream; you pass in the point as a parameter:

```
function playFrom(secs) {
  var v = document
    .getElementById('myvideo');
  v.currentTime = secs;
  v.play();
}
```

PLAYING FILE 00092.WEBM

You can then provide buttons to start playback from significant points:

```
<button onclick="playFrom(4);">Play from 4
secs</button>
<button onclick="playFrom(8);">Play from 8
secs</button>
```

Obviously there aren't many significant points in a 15-second video clip, but this would be useful if you had a podcast or longer movie and wanted to provide bookmarks for when particular topics were being discussed or for the start of each scene.

In the example, although the buttons claim to start the video play at the fourth and eighth seconds, the user has no way of seeing if they really work. When the controls are hidden, you lose not just Play and Pause but also the timeline. Fortunately, HTML5 provides a new <meter> element that's excellent for measuring how much of a video or audio clip has been played:

PLAYING FILE OOO92.WEBM

```
<meter id="mymeter" min="0"></meter>
```

The value of the meter needs to be continually updated as the video is playing. For this you use the timeupdate event, adding that to the <video> element alongside the loadeddata event already being used to capture the filename of the video being played:

```
<video id="myvideo" ontimeupdate="updateTime(this);"
       onloadeddata="dataLoaded(this);">
```

Here's the dataLoaded function. It's been updated to set the max value of the <meter> element so that it exactly matches the duration of the loaded video:

```
function dataLoaded(v) {
    document.getElementById('source')
```

```
        .innerHTML = 'Playing file ' +
            v.currentSrc.slice(v.currentSrc.lastIndexOf('/')+1);
    m = document.getElementById('mymeter');
    m.max = v.duration;
    m.value = 0;
}
```

The code to update the meter element is even simpler; it just sets the value of the `<meter>` element to the currentTime of the `<video>` element:

```
function updateTime(v) {
    m = document.getElementById('mymeter');
    m.value = v.currentTime;
}
```

DIRECT ACCESS TO THE `<audio>` AND `<video>` ELEMENTS WITH JAVASCRIPT ISN'T THE ONLY BENEFIT OF HAVING MEDIA BE AN INTEGRAL PART OF YOUR PAGE CONTENT; OTHER BROWSER TECHNOLOGIES SUCH AS CSS AND SVG CAN ALSO BE APPLIED. THE NEXT SECTION SHOWS YOU HOW.

Integrating media with other content

The `<video>` and `<audio>` elements are just like any other element on the web page. They can be styled with CSS and used in JavaScript. To begin, let's look at applying CSS transforms and transitions. The following three screenshots show the same web page over the course of 10 seconds.

The code for this example, slightly elided, is shown next; see the full listing in ch04/video-css-transitions.html. Don't worry too much about the details for now; read the sections "2D transforms" and "CSS transitions"

in chapter 9 for a more in-depth discussion. In the meantime, remember that anything you can do to HTML elements with CSS can be done to the <video> element:

```css
div video {
    transition-duration: 10s;
}
div:hover video:nth-child(1) {
    transform-origin: bottom
right;
    transform: rotate(16.5deg);
}
div:hover video:nth-child(2) {
    transform-origin: top right;
    transform: rotate(33deg);
}
div:hover video:nth-child(3) {
    transform-origin: top left;
    transform: rotate(66deg);
}
```

```html
<div>
  <video id="myvideo1"
width="160"
        autoplay loop>
    <source src="00092.webm"
            type="video/webm">
    <source src="00092.mp4"
            type="video/mp4">
    <source src="00092.low.mp4"
            type="video/mp4">
    <source src="00092.ogv"
            type="video/ogg">
    No video!
  </video>
  <video id="myvideo2" ...
    <video id="myvideo3" ...
</div>
```

CSS TRANSITIONS ARE COVERED IN DETAIL IN CHAPTER 9; ANY OF THE EFFECTS DESCRIBED IN THAT CHAPTER CAN BE APPLIED TO THE <video> ELEMENT. THE PREVIOUS EXAMPLE APPLIES THREE TRANSFORMS TO THREE IDENTICAL <video> ELEMENTS WITH A 10-SECOND TRANSITION ON :hover.

In the previous chapter, you learned that the <canvas> element can grab an image from anywhere on the page and subject it to various transformations. One of the more exciting features of HTML5 is that those same canvas manipulation tricks also work with the <video> element. The next example looks at the basic process of getting a frame from the video into a <canvas> element by making a frame grabber.

First, let's get the HTML sorted out. Start with the usual <video> element, and add as many sources as required; you can use the code from "Using multiple resources" as a starting point.

```
<video id="myvideo" controls>
  <source src="00092.webm"
    media="video/webm">
  No video!
</video>
```

PLAYING FILE 00092.WEBM

You need something for the user to click to signal that they want to grab a frame. A <button> element is easiest:

```
<button onclick="snap();">
  Snap
</button>
```

Place that before the <video> element. You also need a <canvas> element to put the frame in later:

```
<canvas id="mycanvas"></canvas>
```

Put the <canvas> element after the div with id 'source'. All the action happens in the snap() function:

```
function snap() {
  var video  = document
    .getElementById('myvideo');
  var canvas = document
    .getElementById('mycanvas');
  canvas.width  = video.videoWidth;
  canvas.height = video.videoHeight;
  var ctx = canvas.getContext('2d');
  ctx.drawImage(video, 0, 0);
}
```

PLAYING FILE 00092.WEBM

Most of this function is plumbing — grabbing references to the relevant elements and setting the width and height of the canvas to match the video. The code that draws the current frame on the canvas is this:

```
ctx.drawImage(video, 0, 0);
```

It's that simple! If you want to have some fun, refer back to the canvas transformations in chapter 3 and try them on frames of a video.

The other thing you learned about in the previous chapter was SVG — in particular applying SVG effects such as transforms, clips, and masks to HTML content with `<foreignObject>`. Because the `<video>` element is HTML content just like any other, those same effects can be applied. The following screenshots show a `<video>` element clipped to appear inside some text and then animated.

Sat 30 Apr 2011 23:30:04 BST

Sat 30 Apr 2011 23:30:09 BST

Sat 30 Apr 2011 23:30:13 BST

Here's the content of the SVG embedded into the HTML. Note that the SVG has HTML embedded into it in turn:

```
<defs>
  <clipPath id="img1" clipPathUnits="userSpaceOnUse"          CLIP PATH TO
           width="320" height="200">                          USE ON VIDEO
    <text x="0" y="70" font-family="sans-serif"               TEXT USED TO
          font-size="80" font-weight="bold">                  CLIP VIDEO
      <tspan>HTML5</tspan>
      <tspan x="5" y="134" font-size="85">VIDEO</tspan>
      <tspan x="5" y="186" font-size="70">ROCKS!</tspan>
    </text>
  </clipPath>
</defs>
<g clip-path="url(#img1)">                                     HTML
  <foreignObject x="0" y="0" width="320" height="200">        INCLUDED
    <body>                                                     IN SVG
      <video id="myvideo" width="320" height="200"
```

```
        autoplay loop>
      <source src="00092.webm" type="video/webm">
      <source src="00092.mp4" type="video/mp4">
      <source src="00092.low.mp4" type="video/mp4">
      <source src="00092.ogv" type="video/ogg">
         No video!
    </video>
  </body>
</foreignObject>
<animateTransform attributeName="transform"
                  type="translate" values="0,0;0,220;0,0"
                  begin="0s" dur="10s" fill="freeze"
                  repeatCount="indefinite">
</g>
```

SVG ANIMATION

Does HTML5 video replace Flash?

The short answer is, no. There are several things for which Flash is the only option now, and some things for which HTML5 video is never likely to be an option. Flash has support for Real Time Streaming Protocol (RTSP) and the Real Time Messaging Protocol (RTMP), which provide facilities such as adaptive streaming, switching the bitrate of the video stream as the available bandwidth varies, and digital rights management (DRM).

It's possible that HTML5 video will one day support adaptive streaming, but it's extremely unlikely that it will ever support any features for DRM in a cross-browser fashion. If you want to use DRM on your video and audio content, then you'll need to continue using Flash.

AS YOU MAY HAVE GUESSED, BROWSER SUPPORT FOR AUDIO AND VIDEO IS SOMETHING OF A THORNY SUBJECT. LET'S LOOK AT THE DETAILS.

Browser support

Support for both <video> and <audio> elements is universal across all current browsers. The problem at this point is finding the minimum number of different encodings for maximum browser compatibility.

	12	14	4	6	8	9	10	11.5	12	5	5.1
`<audio>` element	●	●	●	●		●	●	●	●	●	●
WAV audio	●	●	●	●		●	●			●	●
MP3 audio	●	●				●	●			●	●
OGG audio	●	●	●	●		○	○	●	●	○	○
`<video>` element	●	●	●	●		●	●	●	●	●	●
OGG video	●	●	●	●		○	○	●	●	○	○
MP4 video	●	●				●	●			●	●
WebM video	●	●	●	●		○	○	●	●	○	○

Key:
- ● Complete or nearly complete support
- ○ Incomplete or alternative support
  Little or no support

Web server configuration for audio and video

The first thing you need to consider when serving video and audio is that you have to make sure the correct MIME types are sent in the headers. The MIME type sent by the server should match the value set in the type attribute. On the common Apache server, this means using the AddType directive. This can go in the server configuration files or in an .htaccess file in your website directory. The relevant values for HTML5 audio and video are as follows:

```
AddType audio/ogg     oga ogg
AddType audio/mp4     m4a

AddType video/ogg     ogv
AddType video/mp4     mp4 m4v
AddType video/webm    webm
```

Supporting legacy browsers with Flash video

It's possible to get the best of both worlds: HTML5 video for browsers that support it and Flash for browsers that don't. At its simplest, this is a matter of wrapping the code for Flash inside the <video> element:

```
<video id="myvideo" controls>
  <source src="myvideo.webm" type="video/webm">          SOURCES FOR
  <source src="myvideo.mp4" type="video/mp4">            HTML5 VIDEO
  <source src="myvideo.low.mp4" type="video/mp4">        AS NORMAL
  <source src="myvideo.ogv" type="video/ogg">
  <object
   classid="clsid:d27cdb6e-ae6d-11cf-96b8-444553540000"
   codebase="http://download.macromedia.com/           ADD FLASH
      pub/shockwave/cabs/flash/                          CODE IN
      swflash.cab#version=6,0,40,0"                       <video>
   width="320" height="240"                              ELEMENT
   id="myvideoname">
     <param name="movie" value="player.swf">             FLASH MOVIE
                                                          IS A PLAYER
     <param name="quality" value="high">
     <param name="bgcolor" value=#ffffff>                VIDEO
     <param name="flashvars" value="file=myvideo.mp4">   FILE
  </object>                                               TO PLAY
  No video support, <a href="myvideo.webm">try downloading</a>!
</video>
```

Browsers that support the <video> element will ignore the fallback content, whereas browsers that don't support the <video> element will ignore that and only see the <object> element that embeds the Flash plug-in. Browsers that support neither the <video> element nor the Flash player will see the link to download the video.

Summary

In this chapter, you've learned about multimedia on the web, playing audio and video with simple markup. You've seen the benefits of having multimedia content integrated with the rest of your web page content and looked at manipulating that multimedia with JavaScript.

HTML5 OFFERS MANY OTHER OPPORTUNITIES FOR MANIPULATING YOUR CONTENT IN NEW AND EXCITING WAYS WITH JAVASCRIPT, SUCH AS WYSIWYG EDITING AND DRAG-AND-DROP INTERACTION. THE NEXT CHAPTER LOOKS AT THEM IN MORE DETAIL.

5

Browser-based APIs

This chapter covers

- *Directly editing page content with* `contentEditable`
- *Simulating desktop-like interactions with the drag-and-drop API*
- *Convenient access to semantic metadata with the microdata API*
- *How to not break the Back button with the history API*
- *Keeping web apps responsive with web workers*

This chapter looks at HTML5 application programming interfaces (APIs) that work "in browser"—that is, APIs that work directly with loaded web pages rather than accessing the network or web and relying on server functionality.

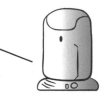

TO FOLLOW THE EXAMPLES IN THIS CHAPTER, YOU'LL NEED TO HAVE A BASIC UNDERSTANDING OF JAVASCRIPT. READ APPENDIX D FIRST IF YOU NEED MORE HELP. OR, IF YOU'RE MORE OF A DESIGNER THAN A DEVELOPER, SKIP AHEAD TO CHAPTER 7, WHERE WE START TO LOOK IN DETAIL AT CSS3.

What is an HTML5 API?

The HTML5 spec is ground-breaking in many ways, but one of the key ways is that it specifies both the syntax of the HTML markup and the APIs you should use to manipulate the document with JavaScript. Earlier specs kept those separate: the Web Hypertext Application Technology Working Group (WHATWG) felt this was both a source of needless duplication and a recipe for inconsistency. You've already seen several of HTML5's APIs in action—the form-validation API in chapter 2, the canvas in chapter 3, and the video and audio APIs in the last chapter—but there are many more.

The WHATWG produced a very long HTML spec that splits into 11 standards at the W3C, one of which is the HTML5 spec. In addition, several other specs, such as the Geolocation API, have never been part of the WHATWG spec but are considered part of the HTML5 buzzword nevertheless. In this book, we'll follow the more liberal definition because that lets you play with more fun stuff!

FIRST, LET'S LOOK AT ONE OF THE APIS THAT'S PART OF THE CORE HTML5 SPECIFICATION: contentEditable. IT ALLOWS RICH-TEXT EDITING IN THE BROWSER—A WHAT-YOU-SEE-IS-WHAT-YOU-GET (WYSIWYG) ENVIRONMENT SIMILAR TO THE EXPERIENCE PEOPLE ARE USED TO WITH MODERN WORD PROCESSORS.

Rich-text editing with the contenteditable attribute

The web was originally intended to be a place where people would create and share documents. But web browsers are complex to implement on their own, and existing text editors were good enough for creating web documents, so the creation and viewing of web content has historically been kept separate. Various solutions have arisen that enable the

Browser support quick check: contenteditable		Standard
		4.0
		3.0
		5.5
		9.00
		3.0

creation of content from a web page, but these have depended mostly on server capabilities rather than on any built-in support in HTML. This changes in HTML5 with the advent of the `contenteditable` and `spellcheck` attributes.

Basic text editing

Making an element editable is as easy as adding an attribute:

```
<p contenteditable="true">Stef works
as the Corporate Sales Manager. He
...
much more money than he does.</p>
```

If the user clicks the element, a cursor will appear, and they can start typing.

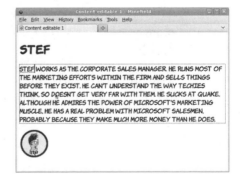

Any text the user types is added to the document. This requires no scripting on your part—the browser does all the work.

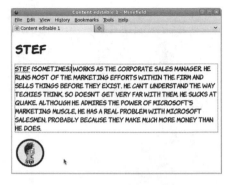

To make multiple elements editable, you can apply the `contenteditable` attribute to the parent, and the child elements will inherit the setting:

```
<section contenteditable="true">
  <h1>Stef</h1>
  <p>Stef works...
  ...than he does.</p>
  <img
   src="headshots/stef.gif"
   alt="Stef">
</section>
```

In the previous example, both the `<h1>` and the `<p>` elements are editable. So is the `<img>` element, but your only option is deletion—you can't edit the image from within the browser with the `contenteditable` API. It may be possible to build your own image editor using the `<canvas>` element (see chapter 3), but we don't have room to get into that here.

You can override the `contenteditable` value on a parent element by explicitly setting `contenteditable` on a child element:

```
<section contenteditable="true">
<h1 contenteditable="false">
  The Chief
</h1>
<p>The Chief is...
...meaningless.</p>
<img
  src="headshots/thechief.gif"
  alt="The Chief">
</section>
```

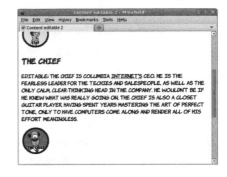

In this example, the <h1> element isn't editable, but every other child element of the <section> element is.

NOTE THAT IE8 DOESN'T TREAT contenteditable AS INHERITABLE. YOU'LL NEED TO SPECIFY contenteditable="true" ON EVERY ELEMENT YOU WANT TO BE EDITABLE IN IE.

The spellcheck attribute

A common feature of word processors is inline spell-checking—spelling mistakes are highlighted by a red squiggle. This feature is also available in `contenteditable` sections. To indicate to the browser that text should be spell-checked, set the `spellcheck` attribute to `true`:

```
<section
 contenteditable="true"
 spellcheck="true">
  <h1>The Chief</h1>
  <p>The Chief is Columbia...
  ...effort meaningless.</p>
```

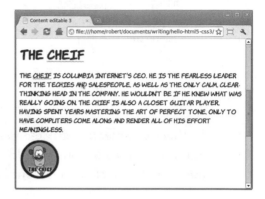

You can also recommend that browsers not spell-check text by setting the attribute to `false`. This might be useful if the user was expected to enter things like codes or part numbers:

```
<section
 contenteditable="true"
 spellcheck="false">
  <h1>Stef</h1>
  <p>Stef works as the...
  ...than he does.</p>
```

Note that, in both cases, the value of the `spellcheck` attribute is inherited by the child elements. You can override it by specifying it on particular elements.

The spellcheck attribute is just a suggestion; user preferences are allowed to override everything. If you look at the previous example in Firefox, you'll see that the spellcheck is active even though the attribute is set to false.

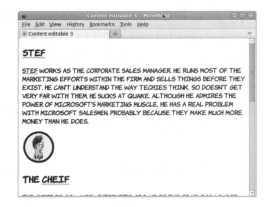

Saving the edited content

The contenteditable attribute only lets you edit the content in the page; it doesn't change the file stored on a web server. Although you could save the file locally to preserve the changes, to make this work as part of a content-management system (CMS) you would need to use JavaScript to get the results back to the server.

So far, we've only looked at what's achievable without JavaScript. For more advanced formatting, like setting text to bold or italic, or adding links, you have to start taking advantage of the API, as we'll discuss in the next section.

Applying formatting to the editable text

The HTML5 API provides the `execCommand()` function for manipulating text in the `contenteditable` region. The function has three parameters — one required, one ignored, and one optional.

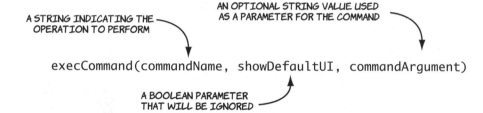

LET'S EXTEND THE PREVIOUS EXAMPLE BY ALLOWING THE USER TO APPLY FORMATTING TO THE TEXT THEY'RE EDITING. YOU'LL ADD BUTTONS TO THE PAGE THAT EXECUTE COMMANDS ON THE API WHEN CLICKED.

The commands for applying bold, italic, and underlined text are all fairly straightforward. Each requires the command name; all the other parameters can be left in their default state.

Here's the command for bold:

```
execCommand(
  'bold',false,''
);
```

If you add this code to the `onclick` attribute of a button, the formatting will be applied to the currently selected text when the button is clicked. Here are the equivalent commands for italic and underlined text:

```
execCommand(
  'italic',false,''
);
execCommand(
  'underline',false,''
);
```

The following screenshots show the process of applying these three different commands to selected text on the example page.

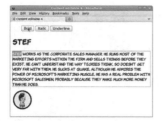  

ALTHOUGH SUPPORT FOR THE `execCommand()` METHOD IS CONSISTENT CROSS-BROWSER, THE IMPLEMENTATION OF THE INDIVIDUAL COMMANDS STILL VARIES CONSIDERABLY. FOLLOWING IS THE MARKUP GENERATED BY FOLLOWING THE PREVIOUS THREE STEPS IN CHROME AND OPERA ON THE LEFT, IE ON THE RIGHT, AND FIREFOX IN THE MIDDLE.

Chrome and Opera use `b` and `i`, so your styles apply.

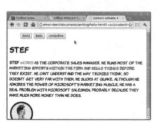

```
<b>
  Stef
</b>
<i>
  works
</i> as the
<u>
  Corporate Sales
  Manager
</u>.
```

Firefox inserts `span` elements with styles.

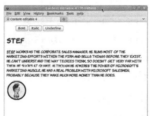

```
<span style="
  font-weight: bold;">
  Stef
</span>
<span style="
  font-style: italic;">
  works
</span> as the
<span style="
  text-decoration:
    underline;">
  Corporate Sales
    Manager
</span>.
```

IE inserts `strong` and `em` elements.

```
<strong>
  Stef
</strong>
<em>
  works
</em> as the
<u>
  Corporate Sales
  Manager
</u>.
```

YOU CAN MAKE FIREFOX USE THE SAME MARKUP AS CHROME AND OPERA WITH THE `styleWithCSS` COMMAND:

```
execCommand('styleWithCSS', false, false);
```

Support for more advanced formatting commands tends to be somewhat flaky cross browsers. Nevertheless, these commands can be useful, so we'll look at some of them.

The `formatblock` command allows you to wrap the current block in a new element:

```
execCommand(
  'formatblock',false,'<h1>'
);
```

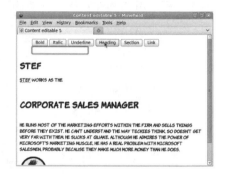

The *current block* refers to the block-level parent of the current insertion point. If you're focused on a `<paragraph>` element, that element will be converted to the type of element you specify in the argument.

AS EVER, WATCH OUT FOR BROWSER INCONSISTENCIES. FIREFOX REPLACES THE CURRENT BLOCK ELEMENT, SO A `<p>` BECOMES AN `<h1>` IN THE PREVIOUS EXAMPLE. IE, CHROME, AND OPERA WRAP THE OLD ELEMENT AROUND THE NEW ONE, SO THE `<p>` ENDS UP CONTAINING AN `<h1>`.

Only a limited number of elements can be passed in the argument for `formatblock`: IE allows `<h1>`–6, `address`, and `pre`. If you want to have more control over the exact markup inserted, you can use the `inserthtml` command. This means you have to deal with the currently selected text yourself. Use the HTML5 text-selection API to get the content of the user's current selection:

```
var selection =
        window.getSelection();
var range =
selection.getRangeAt(0); var
contents =
        range.extractContents();
```

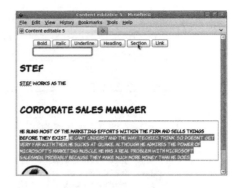

We're not going to cover the text-selection API in detail here. If you want to find out more, check out the specs.

Now you can insert the selection back into the document inside a `<section>` element. The current selection is replaced with the new content:

```
execCommand(
  'inserthtml',false,
  '<section>' +
   contents.textContent +
  '</section>');
```

Finally, a common requirement when editing web pages is inserting links. The command for this is `CreateLink`, but you also need to provide the user with a way of entering the link as well as the button to apply it:

```
if (
 document
  .getElementById('theURL')
  .checkValidity()
) {
  execCommand(
    'CreateLink',
    false,document
     .getElementById('theURL')
     .value
  );
}
```

Notice that for this example, rather than writing your own code to validate the email address, you take advantage of the HTML5 form-validation API (see chapter 2 for more details).

A BIG FEATURE OF DESKTOP APPLICATIONS IS THE ABILITY TO DRAG AND DROP-BLOCKS OF TEXT, IMAGES, AND FILES. WE'VE BECOME USED TO BEING ABLE TO SELECT WHAT WE WANT WITH THE MOUSE, DRAG IT WHERE WE WANT IT TO BE, AND DROP IT. IN THE NEXT SECTION, WE'LL LOOK AT THE HTML5 API THAT BRINGS DRAG-AND-DROP TO WEB APPLICATIONS.

Natural user interaction with drag-and-drop

Browser support quick check: drag-and-drop		Standard	Custom
	(Chrome)	2.0	-
	(Firefox)	3.5	-
	(Internet Explorer)	9.0	6.0
	(Opera)	-	-
	(Safari)	4.0	-

Drag-and-drop is a metaphor familiar on your desktop computers—you've probably used it for sorting files into folders, adding attachments to emails, and opening a file in a particular program. It's therefore useful when writing web applications to support this drag-and-drop metaphor both within your application and as an interaction method with other content on the user's computer. This functionality is provided in HTML5 in the drag-and-drop API.

THE DRAG-AND-DROP API WAS ORIGINALLY DEVELOPED BY MICROSOFT IN IE5.5. RATHER THAN INVENT AN INCOMPATIBLE API, THE WHATWG DECIDED TO EXHAUSTIVELY DOCUMENT WHAT IE HAD IMPLEMENTED. THIS HAS THE ADVANTAGE THAT THE STANDARD MOSTLY WORKS IN IE, BUT THE DISADVANTAGE THAT THE API IS SOMEWHAT MORE COUNTERINTUITIVE THAN MOST OTHER APIS IN THE HTML5 SPEC.

The drag-and-drop API makes use of a few properties and a lot of events. The following sequence of diagrams gives you an overview of which events fire when before we dive into code in the following section.

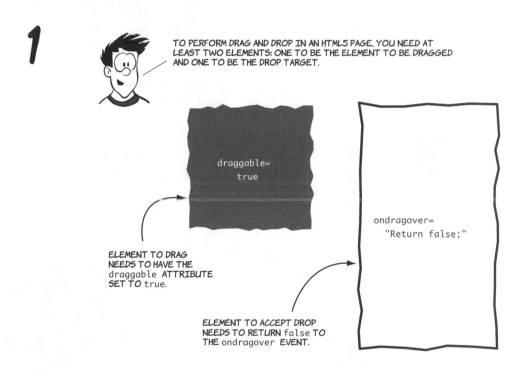

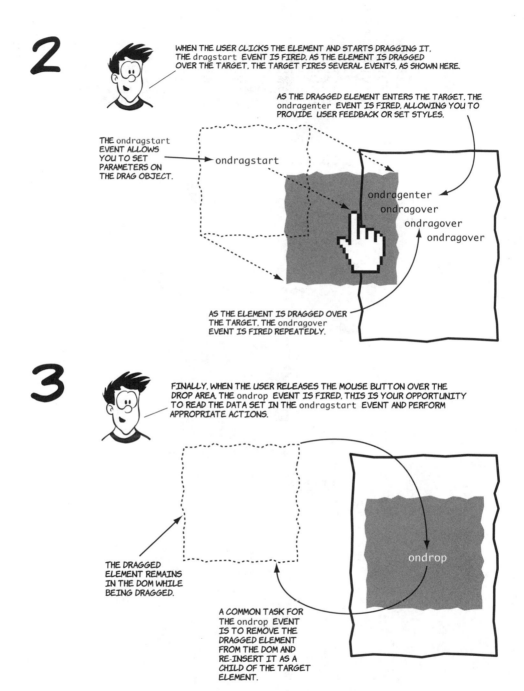

2 WHEN THE USER CLICKS THE ELEMENT AND STARTS DRAGGING IT, THE dragstart EVENT IS FIRED. AS THE ELEMENT IS DRAGGED OVER THE TARGET, THE TARGET FIRES SEVERAL EVENTS, AS SHOWN HERE.

AS THE DRAGGED ELEMENT ENTERS THE TARGET, THE ondragenter EVENT IS FIRED, ALLOWING YOU TO PROVIDE USER FEEDBACK OR SET STYLES.

THE ondragstart EVENT ALLOWS YOU TO SET PARAMETERS ON THE DRAG OBJECT.

ondragstart

ondragenter
ondragover
ondragover
ondragover

AS THE ELEMENT IS DRAGGED OVER THE TARGET, THE ondragover EVENT IS FIRED REPEATEDLY.

3 FINALLY, WHEN THE USER RELEASES THE MOUSE BUTTON OVER THE DROP AREA, THE ondrop EVENT IS FIRED. THIS IS YOUR OPPORTUNITY TO READ THE DATA SET IN THE ondragstart EVENT AND PERFORM APPROPRIATE ACTIONS.

THE DRAGGED ELEMENT REMAINS IN THE DOM WHILE BEING DRAGGED.

ondrop

A COMMON TASK FOR THE ondrop EVENT IS TO REMOVE THE DRAGGED ELEMENT FROM THE DOM AND RE-INSERT IT AS A CHILD OF THE TARGET ELEMENT.

Now that you have an overview, let's examine the details.

Basic drag-and-drop

To make an element draggable is simple, with a couple of browser compatibility caveats that we'll get to later: add a `draggable` attribute with value `true`. This first example, ch05/drag-and-drop-1.html, has a list of locations in the Columbia Internet offices that you'll make draggable:

```
<ul id="locations">
  <li draggable="true"
      id="recpt"
      ondragstart="drag(event)">
    Reception
  </li>
  ...
</ul>
```

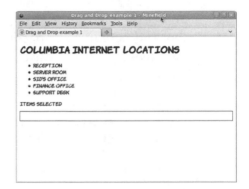

On each of the elements, the `ondragstart` attribute has been set. This function is used to set the data that will be passed by the drag-and-drop action. For now, you'll set the text data as the ID of the element:

```
function drag(event) {
  event.dataTransfer
    .setData('Text',
        event.target.id);
    log('drag ' + event.target.id);
}
```

Within the function there's also a `log` command so the sequence of events firing is recorded on the page. As the element with ID `'support'` is dragged, the messages are added at the bottom of the page.

The crucial event in the drag-and-drop process is dragOver. Any element that is to be a target for dropped elements must capture the dragOver event and cancel the default action on it:

```
function dragOver(event) {
  event.preventDefault();
  log('dragOver ' + event.target.id);
}
```

When the element is dropped, the drop event is fired. It's in this event that the actual work needs to be done. This example removes the list item from the source list and adds it to the selected list using the standard appendChild method:

```
function drop(event) {
  var id = event.dataTransfer.getData('Text');
  event.target.appendChild(document.getElementById(id));
  log('drop ' + event.target.id);
  event.preventDefault();
}
```

These two events can be bound declaratively to the drop target element:

```
    ondragover="dragOver(event)"
</ul>
<ul id="drophere"
    ondrop="drop(event)">
```

ITEMS SELECTED

    • SUPPORT DESK

DRAG SUPPORT
DRAGOVER DROPHERE
DRAGOVER DROPHERE
DRAGOVER DROPHERE
DRAGOVER DROPHERE
DRAGOVER DROPHERE
DRAGOVER DROPHERE
DRAGOVER DROPHERE
DRAGOVER DROPHERE
DRAGOVER DROPHERE
DRAGOVER DROPHERE
DROP DROPHERE

As you can see, the dragOver event is fired repeatedly while the dragged element is over the drop target.

If you only want drag-and-drop to work in Firefox, Chrome, and Safari, that's all the code you need—you're done! If you want it to work in IE too, read ahead to the next section.

Drag-and-drop in all browsers

Although the HTML5 drag-and-drop API is based on what IE5.5 implemented, it's not identical. What that means is that although it's possible to write cross-browser code for drag-and-drop that works across Firefox, Chrome/Safari, and IE, doing so isn't as straightforward as the code given in the previous section.

PROBLEM 1

The draggable attribute is an innovation of the HTML5 spec, and IE8 doesn't recognize it. By default, nothing in the previous example is draggable in IE.

SOLUTION 1

Links are draggable by default, so by making everything that should be draggable a link, IE can be supported.

B E F O R E

The initial code was simple—a draggable attribute and an event handler:

```
<li draggable="true"
    id="recpt"
    ondragstart=
      "dragstart(event)">
  Reception
</li>
```

A F T E R

Instead of making the list items draggable, add links around the text content:

```
<li id="recpt">
  <a ondragstart=
      "dragstart(event);"
    href="#"
    onclick="return false;">
   Reception
  </a>
</li>
```

The draggable attribute is no longer required because links are draggable by default.

The original `dragstart` event handler assumed that it was the `<li>`, with the `id`, that was draggable:

```
function dragstart(ev) {
  event.dataTransfer
    .setData('Text',
        event.target.id);
  log('drag ' +
event.target.id);
}
```

Now the `link` element is used as a proxy. The element you want to move is the parent of the one being dragged:

```
function dragstart(ev) {
  event.dataTransfer
    .setData('Text',
        event.srcElement
          .parentNode.id);
  log('drag ' +
        event.srcElement
          .parentNode.id);
}
```

PROBLEM 2

Older versions of IE use `srcElement` instead of `target`.

SOLUTION 2

Do the standard IE support bait-and-switch.

B E F O R E

The original code uses standard DOM events, methods, and properties:

```
function dragstart(ev) {
  event.dataTransfer
    .setData('Text',
        event.srcElement
          .parentNode.id);
  log('drag ' +
        event.srcElement
          .parentNode.id);
}
```

A F T E R

This is a fairly common problem in writing cross browser Java-Script. Test for the existence of `event.target`:

```
function dragstart(ev) {
  var target =
      event.target ?
        event.target :
        event.srcElement;
  event.dataTransfer
    .setData('Text',
        target.parentNode.id);
  log('drag ' +
        target.parentNode.id);
}
```

PROBLEM 3

The ondragover attribute doesn't work in IE8 and before.

SOLUTION 3

There are two possible approaches to solving this problem. The first approach is to handle the dragenter event, which older versions of IE recognize, instead of the dragover event, which they do not.

B E F O R E

If you don't need to support old versions of IE, you don't need to worry about the first approach, although it's simple to fix:

```
<ul id="drophere"
    ondrop="drop(event)"

ondragover="dragOver(event)">
```

A F T E R

In older versions of IE the dragenter event has to be cancelled instead of the dragover:

```
<ul id="drophere"
    ondrop="drop(event)"
    ondragover="dragOver(event)"
    ondragenter=
      "dragOver(event)">
```

Also note that IE8 and earlier need the dragOver event to return false;.

The second (and better) approach is to attach the event handler in script rather than declaratively in the HTML markup. The advantage of this approach is that, while attaching the handler declaratively will cause the event to fire, canceling that event won't make the element a drop target in IE8 and earlier. But if you use the proprietary attachEvent() method to attach to the dragOver event in script, canceling that will make the element a drop target. Attaching the event this way is straightforward; the code is shown here:

```
<!--[if lte IE 8]>
<script>
document.getElementById(
  'drophere'
).attachEvent(
  'ondragover', dragover
);
</script>
<![endif]-->
```

Note that for advanced developers the best practice is to always attach event handlers in script. For now, this snippet can be copied and pasted into your own code.

PROBLEM 4
Chrome is now broken!

SOLUTION 4
Find the closest parent ID.

B E F O R E

This is a strange one. Now that the draggable item is an anchor rather than a list item, Chrome inserts an extra element—the parentNode no longer has an ID, so this code doesn't work:

```
target.parentNode.id
```

Now take every place in the code where the ID is needed, like this

```
event.dataTransfer
  .setData('Text',
    target.parentNode.id);
```

A F T E R

The solution is to write a utility function to recurse up the document tree until an element with an ID is found:

```
function grabOuterId(el) {
    if (el.id) {
    return el.id;
    } else {
    return
grabOuterId(el.parentNode)
    }
}
```

And replace it with a call to the new function:

```
event.dataTransfer
  .setData('Text',
    grabOuterId(target)
  );
```

You can avoid this issue altogether if the elements you want to drag are links or images—add the ID directly to those draggable elements. An alternative approach for IE support on elements that aren't draggable by default is to add the links dynamically with script only in IE.

DRAG-AND-DROP IS A GREAT WAY FOR USERS TO INTERACT WITH YOUR WEB
APPLICATIONS. BUT THE USABILITY GAINS WILL BE LOST IF, AFTER SPENDING TIME
MOVING THROUGH YOUR APPLICATION, USERS CLICK THE BACK BUTTON EXPECTING
TO GO BACK A PAGE AND INSTEAD GO BACK TO THEIR START SCREEN. IN THE NEXT
SECTION, YOU'LL LEARN HOW TO USE THE HTML5 HISTORY API TO AVOID THAT FATE.

Managing the Back button with the history API

Browser support quick check: history API		popState	hashchange
		5.0	5.0
		4.0	3.6
		-	8.0
		11.5	10.6
		5.0	5.0

One major issue with JavaScript-based applications is that they break the Back button. If you update content on the page with JavaScript rather than loading a new page from the server, no entry made is in the browser history; so when the user clicks Back, expecting to go back to the previous state, they end up at the previous site instead.

The problem can be demonstrated simply. All you need is a function that updates the page in response to user activity

```
var times = 0;
function doclick() {
    times++;
    document.getElementById('message').innerHTML =
        'Recorded <b>' + times + '</b> clicks';
}
```

and a little markup:

```
<div onclick="doclick();">Click Me</div>
<div id="message">Recorded <b>0</b> clicks</div>
```

In real life, your web page would be doing something more complicated, like fetching new content from the server via AJAX, but a simple update is enough to demonstrate the concept. Let's see what happens when the user visits the page.

1 The user starts on their home page and decides to visit the amazing Click Me application they've heard about.

2 They type in the URL or follow a link from an email to get to the Click Me page.

3 After a few seconds of enjoyable interaction, the page state has changed several times.

4 But when the user clicks the Back button in the browser, they find that instead of going back to a previous page state, they leap to their home page.

The `doclick()` function can be updated to take advantage of the history API. Each time the page is updated it will also set the `location.hash`:

```
function doclick() {
    times++;
    location.hash = times;
    document.getElementById('message').innerHTML =
        'Recorded <b>' + times + '</b> clicks';
}
```

1   The user arrives at the Click Me page as before.

2   Notice that now the URL is updated after every click — "#3" has appeared at the end of it.

3   Clicking the Back button now takes the location back to #2, demonstrating that page states have successfully been added to the history. But note that clicking the Back button doesn't automatically return the page to its previous state.

Updating page state

Updating the history is only part of the problem; you also need to be able to update the state of the page to match the state in the history. Because you're the one managing the history, it's up to you to manage the page state. In order to update your page in response to `location.hash` being changed, you can listen to the `hashchange` event:

```
function doclick() {
    times++;
    location.hash = times;
}
window.onhashchange = function() {
    if (location.hash.length > 0) {
        times =
  parseInt(location.hash.replace('#',''),10);
    } else {
        times = 0;
```

1 UPDATE TIMES; CHANGE HASH

2 HASHCHANGE EVENT

3 CHECK THAT HASH EXISTS

4 SET TIMES VALUE

```
    }
    document.getElementById('message').innerHTML =
        'Recorded <b>' + times + '</b> clicks';
}
```

⑤ UPDATE PAGE STATE

The `doclick()` function **①** is now only responsible for updating the `times` variable and changing the hash. The `hashchange` event **②** is on the `window` object; when it takes place, you check that the hash exists **③**. In a real application, you'd also want to check that it had a valid value. Next, you set the value of `times` to be the number in the hash **④**. Finally, you update the document to reflect the correct page state **⑤**.

Let's look at this new code:

1 As before, the hash in the URL is updated as the user clicks.

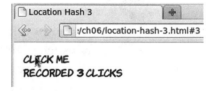

2 But now, when the Back button is clicked, the onhashchange function is triggered and the page state is reset to match the URL.

Using location.hash

The `location.hash` property and the associated `hashchange` event are useful if you want to tag particular views of your application and allow the user to navigate between them. Google Mail uses this approach by allowing you to navigate between your inbox (`#inbox`), contacts (`#contacts`), and other views—if you have a Gmail account, look at what happens to the URL as you navigate to various different pages and then click back.

But as far as state information goes, the hash only lets you store a string. You could encode a more complex object, but the URL would quickly become long and unwieldy and wouldn't be memorable for your users. If you need more complex information stored as part of the history, a better approach would be to use the hash as a key to pull further state information out of some store. Although you could roll your own approach to this, HTML5 has provided an API to do it for you through the `history.pushState()` method and the `popstate` event. These methods allow you to save and reload a complex object.

Example: Implementing an undo feature

The next example extends the content-editable example ch05/content-editable-5.html from the earlier section to include an undo feature. You can see the full listing in ch05/history-1.html. Here's how it works.

1 When the page is first loaded, an initial state is created and tagged in the URL with the hash undo0.

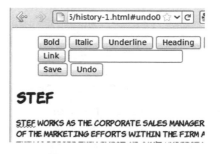

2 If the user makes a change in the text and then clicks the Save button, a new undo state is created and assigned to the hash undo1.

3 Clicking the Undo button or clicking the Back button in the browser returns the page to the previous state.

Now let's look at the implementation.

A. DECLARE A VARIABLE TO HOLD THE STATE

You start by declaring a global variable to hold your state:

```
var state;
```

B. CREATE THE INITIAL STATE

Now you need to set initial values of your state object. For this example, you need a property to hold a reference you can use in the hash, and the content of your editable region:

```
function init() {
    state = {
        undonum: 0,
        content: document.getElementById('content').innerHTML
    };
}
```

C. SAVE THE STATE WITH PUSHSTATE

When the user saves, that state needs to be updated and then pushed into the `history` object:

```
function save() {
    state.undonum++;
    state.content = document.getElementById('content').innerHTML;
    history.pushState(state, '', '#undo' + state.undonum);
}
```

The `pushState` function takes three parameters: the object to be stored as the state, a title for the state, and a hash to reference the state. Note that the title is advisory only; currently most browsers ignore it. The hash will be updated automatically by calling `pushState`.

D. WRITE A FUNCTION FOR THE POPSTATE EVENT

You also need a function to restore the state: it will be an event handler for the `popState` event. The `state` object is available on the event passed in, so you grab that and update the page from the `content` property:

```
function popState(event) {
    if (event.state) {
```

```
        state = event.state;
        document.getElementById('content').innerHTML = state.content;
    } else {
        history.replaceState(state, '', '#undo' + state.undonum);
    }
}
```

E. HANDLE THE INITIAL STATE, AND ATTACH THE EVENT HANDLER

If there isn't a state object on the event, then this is the first load; replace the current state with your initial state object. Now all that's needed is to wire up the events:

```
window.onload = init;
window.onpopstate = popState;
window.onpageshow = popState;
```

Both onpopstate and onpageshow are required because Firefox, unlike other browsers, doesn't fire popstate on the initial page load when no state is set.

F. SET UP THE MENU BUTTONS

Finally, link the buttons on the menu to appropriate functions:

```
<button onclick="save();">Save</button>
<button onclick="history.go(-1);">Undo</button>
```

THE HTML5 HISTORY API PRESENTS A POWERFUL TOOL FOR JAVASCRIPT-BASED APPLICATIONS AND HAS GOOD CROSS-BROWSER SUPPORT. IT'S ALREADY USED ON MAJOR WEBSITES SUCH AS GOOGLE MAIL AND TWITTER. IN THE NEXT SECTION, WE'LL LOOK AT HOW YOU CAN USE CONTENT THAT'S BEEN SEMANTICALLY ENHANCED WITH MICRODATA.

Getting semantic with the microdata API

The microdata API makes it convenient to examine and update content that's been marked up with microdata. Microdata was discussed in chapter 1; it's a method of flexibly extending the semantics of HTML to describe more than just text content—for example, contact information,

Browser support quick check: microdata API		Standard
	Chrome	-
	Firefox	16
	Internet Explorer	-
	Opera	12
	Safari	-

appointments, and licenses. In this section, we'll look at how to use the microdata API and then consider some useful applications.

So far, only Opera has implemented this API, although a Firefox implementation is in progress.

Using a single microdata format

Here's a simple example of contact information marked up with microdata using the hCard vocabulary. This code, along with the script that follows, is available in ch05/microdata-api-1.html:

```
<div id="aj" itemscope
            itemtype="http://microformats.org/profile/hcard">
    <h1 itemprop="fn">
        <meta itemprop="n" content="AJ">
        A.J.
    </h1>
    <img itemprop="photo" alt="AJ"
        src="http://www.userfriendly.org/cartoons/
            cartoons/aj/headshot_aj.gif" >
    <a itemprop="email" href="mailto:aj@userfriendly.org">
        aj@userfriendly.org
    </a>
</div>
```

With a little added CSS, you can make the item take on a business card–like appearance, as shown at right.

Now let's look at how the item data can be extracted with the microdata API. The first step is to get a list of all the items in the document:

```
var md = document.getItems();
```

The getItems() method returns a NodeList that represents all the top-level items in the document. This NodeList has three useful properties:

- itemType—Tells you what sort of item has been found. In this case, you're expecting it to be http://microformats.org/profile/hcard as per the itemtype attribute in the source.

- properties—An array that gives you access to values through an itemValue property on each member.
- names—An array of property names.

You can examine all three with a simple loop:

```
for (var i = 0; i < md.length; i++) {
    log('Found: ' + md[i].itemType);
    for (var j = 0; j < md[i].properties.length; j++) {
        log(md[i].properties.names[j] + ': '
            + md[i].properties[j].itemValue);
    }
}
```

The log function writes the string parameter out on the page so you can examine the output. Here are the results of running that code on the previous example markup:

```
Found: http://microformats.org/profile/hcard
fn: A.J.
n: AJ
photo: http://www.userfriendly.org/cartoons/cartoons/aj/
  headshot_aj.gif
email: mailto:aj@userfriendly.org
```

Note that the itemValue property performed a useful service for you because it understands how to get the value from different types of elements. For the fn property on the <h1> element, it returned the text content of the element; for the n property on the <meta> element, it returned the value of the content attribute; for photo on <img>, it returned the src value; and for email on an <a> element, it returned the href.

The email value is incorrect: emails shouldn't have mailto: appended to the front of them. You might also want to use the subproperties of n, such as given-name and family-name. Let's adjust the markup:

```
<h1 itemprop="fn">
    <span itemprop="n" itemscope>
        <span itemprop="given-name">A</span>.
        <span itemprop="family-name">J</span>.
    </span>
```

```
</h1>
<img itemprop="photo" alt="AJ"
    src="http://www.userfriendly.org/cartoons/
        cartoons/aj/headshot_aj.gif" >
<span itemprop="email">
    <a href="mailto:aj@userfriendly.org">
        aj@userfriendly.org
    </a>
</span>
```

You can see the full code in ch05/microdata-api-1a.html. Here are the results of running the same extraction loop used earlier:

```
Found: http://microformats.org/profile/hcard
fn: A. J.
n: [object HTMLElement]
photo: http://www.userfriendly.org/cartoons/cartoons/aj/
  headshot_aj.gif
email: aj@userfriendly.org
```

The email is fixed, but now there's something wrong with the n value. It's no longer a simple string, it's an HTMLElement. This is because if an item has child properties, itemValue doesn't contain a string; instead it contains another NodeList object. You can loop through that one the same way as before, but it's easier to define a recursive function:

```
function getMDProperties(name, props) {
    if (name.length > 0) name += '/';
    for (var i = 0; i < props.length; i++) {
        if (typeof(props[i].itemValue) == 'object') {
            getMDProperties(props.names[i],
                            props[i].itemValue.properties);
        } else {
            log(name + props.names[i] + ': '
                + props[i].itemValue);
        }
    }
}
```

This function is modeled on the loop used before, but it checks to see whether itemValue is an object. If it is, then the properties of the child object are passed recursively to the function. The name of the parent property is passed in as a parameter so the function can list that alongside its child properties. Now the loop is greatly simplified:

```
var md = document.getItems();
for (var i = 0; i < md.length; i++) {
    log('Found: ' + md[i].itemType);
    getMDProperties('',md[i].properties);
}
```

And the output, as you can see for yourself in ch05/microdata-api-2.html, is more like you want:

```
Found: http://microformats.org/profile/hcard
fn: A. J.
n/given-name: A
n/family-name: J
photo: http://www.userfriendly.org/cartoons/miranda/headshot_aj.gif
email: aj@userfriendly.org
```

Using multiple microdata formats

To finish this short exploration of the microdata API, let's consider what you might do with a more complex page that has multiple types of microdata items available. In ch05/microdata-api-3.html, an additional hCard has been added as well as an event using the http://microformats.org/profile/hcalendar#vevent vocabulary.

ADDRESSES

APPOINTMENTS

THE BIG DATE

31ST AUGUST @ 8PM UNTIL 10PM (OR ALL NIGHT, IF THINGS GO WELL)

LOCATION: MACMILLAN OBSERVATORY

This is what the event markup looks like:

```
<div itemscope
    itemtype="http://microformats.org/profile/hcalendar#vevent">
    <h2 itemprop="summary">The Big Date</h2>
    <p>
      <time itemprop="dtstart" datetime="2011-08-31T20:00:00Z">
        31st August @ 8pm
      </time>
      until
      <time itemprop="dtend" datetime="2011-08-31T22:00:00Z">
        10pm
      </time>
      (or all night, if things go well)
    </p>
    <p>Location:
      <span itemprop="location">Macmillan Observatory</span>
    </p>
</div>
```

Keeping the same function as before, all three microdata items are found and their properties enumerated. But maybe you're writing a calendar-event application and are only interested in the events; or, slightly more creepily, you might be writing context-sensitive advertising into the page with JavaScript and keen to pull out locations and dates. Rather than grab all the items and discard the ones you're not interested in, you can tell the getItems() method which sort of items you want:

```
document.getItems('http://microformats.org/profile/hcalendar#vevent');
```

The parameter is a space-separated list, so you can specify more than one type if necessary—for example, if you want to look for items of

THE MICRODATA API LETS YOU ACCESS STRUCTURED DATA WITHIN YOUR PAGE CONTENT. THIS IS USEFUL WHEN YOU'RE NOT IN CONTROL OF THE GENERATION OF THE CONTENT AND NEED TO GENERATE AN ALTERNATIVE VIEW OR INDEX OF THE DATA, OR GIVE THE USER THE OPTION OF CLICKING A LINK TO A CONTACT IN THEIR ADDRESS BOOK OR AN EVENT IN THEIR CALENDAR.

type http://schema.org/Event as well as the standard events. You can look at the type-specific example in ch05/ microdata-api-3a.html.

Lag-free interfaces with web workers

All JavaScript in a browser has traditionally been run in a single execution context (a *thread* in operating system terms). That changed with the release of IE8, which separated the execution of interface code and web-page code, and then the launch of Google Chrome, which was built from the ground up to be multithreaded. Other browsers have since followed suit. This made browsers quicker, more responsive, and more resilient to bad or malicious code, but all the JavaScript in a single page still used the one thread assigned to it. There was no way for a web author to take advantage of multiple threads to offload expensive processing to another thread while still responding to user input, as they could in a desktop application. For this purpose, web workers were created.

Single-threaded and multithreaded

Single-threaded means the web browser does only one thing at a time. After it starts executing a single JavaScript function, it carries on until that function is finished. While it's executing the function, the browser can't do anything else: respond to clicks, animate GIFs, scroll the page, and so on. This isn't unusual; if you have an old computer with only a single processor with one core, it can only do one thing at a time too. One of the primary jobs of an operating system is to switch between applications so quickly that the computer appears to be doing more than one thing at a time.

Normally, each JavaScript function also executes so quickly that you don't notice; but some heavy processing, a simple coding mistake, or even a malicious script could bring the browser to a halt.

If the browser is *multithreaded*, it can take advantage of the operating system's abilities to switch between tasks. If one thread starts eating up resources, the browser can recognize this on another thread and take corrective action. The advent of multicore processors, which can do more than one thing at a time, also opens up an opportunity to increase the performance of the entire browser by splitting execution across multiple cores.

		Standard
	Chrome	4.0
Browser support quick check: web workers	Firefox	3.5
	IE	10.0
	Opera	10.60
	Safari	4.0

To test the utility of web workers, all you need to do is write some bad code. This function runs a loop several million times and attempts to report progress to the page every so often:

```
function kill_browser() {
    log('Starting');
    var j = 0;
    var n = 1e9;
    var p = n/10;

    for (var i=0;i<n;i++) {
        if (j++ > p) { j=0; log(i); }
    }
    log('Done');
}
```

The page has two buttons: one that calls this function directly and one that calls it via a web worker. Depending on how fast (or slow) your machine is, you may need to adjust the n value to get the best effect. Change the exponent (the number after the *e*) either up or down if you don't see the following behavior.

Start by calling `kill_browser()` directly by clicking the button. Unfortunately, nothing happens—not even the initial "Starting" message. At this point you may find that your browser won't respond to clicks.

The timestamp claims that only 3 seconds have passed, but it stopped updating the moment the button was clicked. Eventually, the browser recognizes the issue and asks if you want to stop the script.

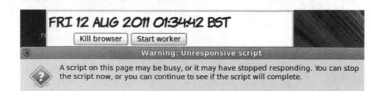

After you stop the script, the other functions—such as log() and the timestamp updater—get a chance to function. Suddenly all the information you were expecting appears.

All in all, this is a pretty bad user experience, and it doesn't even give you the results you were expecting. Let's look at what happens when you use a web worker instead.

With a worker, the difference is immediately obvious—the "Starting" message appears straight away.

The other noticeable differences are that the timestamp continues updating and the browser remains responsive.

Meanwhile, the computation updates are posted regularly.

To turn the kill_browser() function into a web worker, the first and most obvious change is that you need to put it in a separate file. You can then create the worker object from the main page like this:

```
var worker = new Worker("web-worker-1.js");
```

Workers don't have access to the DOM; they can't update elements on the page or access any global variables in your script. Data has to be passed to and from the worker by messages. Set up a listener for messages from the worker that logs the data using the usual function:

```
worker.onmessage = function(event) {
    log(event.data);
}
```

Similarly, you signal that the worker is to start computing by passing it a message using postMessage:

```
<button onclick="worker.postMessage('Starting'); return false;">
    Start worker
</button>
```

In the function, all attempts to access the DOM must be removed. This means replacing the log function with calls to postMessage():

```
function kill_browser() {
    var j = 0;
    var n = 1e9;
    var p = n/10;

    for (var i=0;i<n;i++) {
        if (j++ > p) { j=0; postMessage(i); }
    }
    postMessage('Done');
}
```

Finally, the worker needs to listen to messages so it knows when to start:

```
onmessage = function(event) {
    postMessage(event.data);
    kill_browser();
}
```

You can try this example for yourself with the files ch05/web-workers-1.html and ch05/web-worker-1.js.

WORKERS ARE A POWERFUL ADDITION TO THE WEB AUTHOR'S TOOLKIT, ALLOWING YOU TO WRITE MORE DESKTOP-LIKE APPLICATIONS WITHOUT RESORTING TO ADVANCED JAVASCRIPT TRICKERY. IN THE NEXT SECTION, WE'LL SUMMARIZE BROWSER SUPPORT FOR EVERYTHING COVERED IN THIS CHAPTER.

Browser support

With the exception of the microdata API, support for everything in this chapter is surprisingly complete across all major browsers. As mentioned in the relevant sections, there are some inconsistencies in the implementations of contentEditable and drag-and-drop, particularly in older versions of IE compared to the other browsers, but these aren't insurmountable. The richer web applications enabled by these APIs are already within your reach.

	12	14	4	6	8	9	10	11.5	12	5	5.1
contentEditable	•	•	•	•	•	•	•	•	•	•	•
Drag-and-drop	•	•	•	•	○	○	•		•	•	•
hashchange	•	•	•	•	•	•	•	•	•	•	•
popState	•	•	•	•		•	•	•	•	○	○
Microdata API									•		
Web workers	•	•	•	•		•	•	•	•	•	•

Key:
- Complete or nearly complete support
- ○ Incomplete or alternative support
- Little or no support

Summary

This chapter has presented the most interesting HTML5 APIs, focused on enriching the in-browser experience. We've covered creating word processor–style WYSIWYG editing interfaces and allowing natural drag-and-drop interactions. You've learned that managing the browser's history allows you make the Back button behave in a more sensible way in the context of your application, while the microdata API gives you access to structured semantic information in page contents. Finally, web workers make your app more responsive by running any heavy processing in a background thread that doesn't interfere with the UI.

The best way to learn more is to try coding for yourself. Download the book's sample code to get started.

NOW THAT YOU'VE LEARNED ABOUT APIS FOR CREATING RICH BROWSER APPS, IN THE NEXT CHAPTER YOU'LL LOOK AT HTML5 APIS RELATED TO NETWORKING AND COMMUNICATION.

6

Network and location APIs

This chapter covers

- *Finding the user's location and proximity to places and people of interest*
- *Communicating directly with content from other servers*
- *Having the server push information to the user rather than rely on pull*
- *Building websites that work when there's no network connectivity*

The previous chapter discussed HTML5 APIs that worked directly with the content in the browser, but one of the key features of the web is that it's not about standalone computers: it's about a connected network. HTML5 has a number of APIs related to connectivity and communication, and you'll learn about them in this chapter.

AGAIN, THE EXAMPLES IN THIS CHAPTER RELY ON A BASIC UNDERSTANDING OF JAVASCRIPT. READ APPENDIX D FIRST IF YOU NEED MORE HELP. OR, IF YOU'RE MORE OF A DESIGNER THAN A DEVELOPER, SKIP AHEAD TO CHAPTER 7, WHERE WE START TO LOOK IN DETAIL AT CSS3.

Finding yourself with the Geolocation API

Location-aware services and applications are a hot topic at the moment. Most of us are now familiar with navigation devices in our cars that constantly update position information using the Global Positioning System (GPS) network. These days, many mobile phones and other portable devices come with built-in GPS technology, as well as other positioning services, and the HTML5 Geolocation API exposes these to your web pages.

Google already uses the Geolocation API if you access its site from your mobile phone. The screenshot at left shows that Google is aware of my current location. One of my options upon searching is to choose Local, which provides search results that are tailored to my current location.

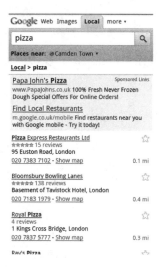

Browser support quick check: geolocation	Standard
Chrome	5.0
Firefox	3.5
Internet Explorer	9.0
Opera	10.6
Safari	5.0

Finding your location

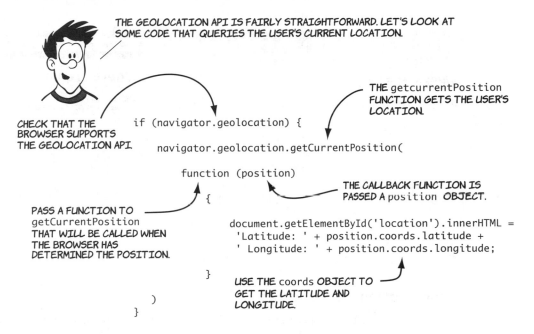

THE GEOLOCATION API IS FAIRLY STRAIGHTFORWARD. LET'S LOOK AT SOME CODE THAT QUERIES THE USER'S CURRENT LOCATION.

CHECK THAT THE BROWSER SUPPORTS THE GEOLOCATION API.

THE getcurrentPosition FUNCTION GETS THE USER'S LOCATION.

```
if (navigator.geolocation) {

    navigator.geolocation.getCurrentPosition(

        function (position)
        {

            document.getElementById('location').innerHTML =
            'Latitude: ' + position.coords.latitude +
            ' Longitude: ' + position.coords.longitude;

        }
    )
}
```

THE CALLBACK FUNCTION IS PASSED A position OBJECT.

PASS A FUNCTION TO getCurrentPosition THAT WILL BE CALLED WHEN THE BROWSER HAS DETERMINED THE POSITION.

USE THE coords OBJECT TO GET THE LATITUDE AND LONGITUDE.

The first thing the user will see when they run this code is the browser asking permission to share their location. Here are examples in Firefox, Chrome, and the Android browser.

After the user accepts, the browser looks up the location. When it finds the location, the function is called and the coordinates are displayed.

Where are you?

Latitude: 51.529110724999995
Longitude: -0.12772145000000001

Finding your location more accurately

Notice that the two screenshots at the end of the previous section are reporting different coordinates—they're about two miles apart. At the time when these were taken, my phone and my laptop were lying side by side on the same table—considerably closer than two miles! This discrepancy is because the browser on my laptop and the browser on my phone use different location service providers. There are four common ways of identifying location.

GEOLOCATION OPTIONS

SATELLITE
- VERY ACCURATE (1–20M) IN OPEN SPACE
- CAN BE SLOW TO ACQUIRE SATELLITE LOCK

CELL TOWER
- ACCURACY (20–200M) DEPENDS ON CELL TOWER SPACING
- NEEDS MOBILE SIGNAL

WI-FI
- VERY ACCURATE (10–15M) IN URBAN AREAS
- NEEDS NETWORK CONNECTION FOR LOOKUP

ADDRESS DATABASE
- NOT ACCURATE (1000–40000M)
- WORKS ON DESKTOPS
- NEEDS NETWORK CONNECTION

IT'S NOT POSSIBLE TO FIND OUT EXACTLY WHICH TECHNOLOGY WAS USED TO PROVIDE THE POSITIONING INFORMATION. BUT YOU CAN GET AN IDEA HOW ACCURATE THE FIGURE IS LIKELY TO BE, BECAUSE THE coords OBJECT ALSO INCLUDES AN accuracy PROPERTY.

Here's a new version of the previous example, this time displaying the accuracy.

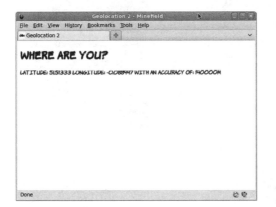

USING THE ACCURACY IS STRAIGHTFORWARD. THE ONLY CHANGE THAT NEEDS TO BE MADE TO THE PREVIOUS LISTING IS AN EXTRA LINE IN THE CODE WHERE YOU WRITE THE RESULTS TO THE PAGE.

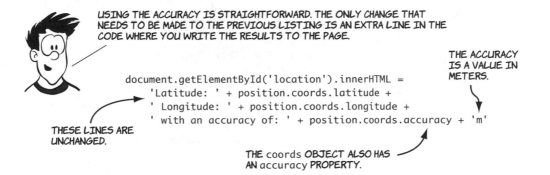

```
document.getElementById('location').innerHTML =
    'Latitude: ' + position.coords.latitude +
    ' Longitude: ' + position.coords.longitude +
    ' with an accuracy of: ' + position.coords.accuracy + 'm'
```

THESE LINES ARE UNCHANGED.

THE coords OBJECT ALSO HAS AN accuracy PROPERTY.

THE ACCURACY IS A VALUE IN METERS.

Finding your location continuously

What if you want to continuously track the user's position? You could just call getCurrentPosition() repeatedly, but that's a waste if the user is stationary, and it could drain battery life on hand-held devices. A better option is to have the browser tell you when there's an updated location. For this, the Geolocation API provides the `watchPosition()` method.

This screenshot shows my progress through North London over a couple of hours one afternoon. All I had to do to get this information was open the page in the phone's browser and then keep the phone in my pocket. When new geolocation information was available, the browser activated the callback function.

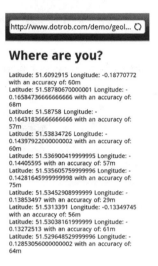

THE CODE IS ALMOST IDENTICAL TO THE PREVIOUS EXAMPLE. THE ONLY CHANGE IS IN THE METHOD CALLED.

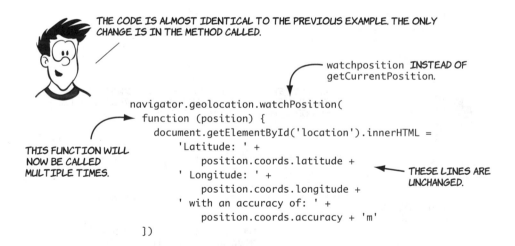

watchposition INSTEAD OF getCurrentPosition.

THIS FUNCTION WILL NOW BE CALLED MULTIPLE TIMES.

THESE LINES ARE UNCHANGED.

```
navigator.geolocation.watchPosition(
    function (position) {
        document.getElementById('location').innerHTML =
            'Latitude: ' +
                position.coords.latitude +
            ' Longitude: ' +
                position.coords.longitude +
            ' with an accuracy of: ' +
                position.coords.accuracy + 'm'
    })
```

Practical uses for geolocation

Now that you've seen the basics of acquiring position information, let's consider how you might use the Geolocation API in practice. We'll look at two simple examples: calculating how far the user is from a given point, and showing the user on a map.

The first example calculates how far the user is from the birthplace of Tim Berners-Lee. Although this example uses a single fixed point for simplicity, the techniques involved will work just as well for more advanced scenarios—working out how far apart two users of your website are, for example.

YOU MAY REMEMBER, FROM SCHOOL, WORKING OUT THE DISTANCE BETWEEN TWO POINTS ON A PLANE USING THE PYTHAGOREAN THEOREM. CALCULATING THE DISTANCE BETWEEN TWO LATITUDE/LONGITUDE POINTS ISN'T QUITE AS STRAIGHTFORWARD BECAUSE THESE AREN'T POINTS ON A FLAT SURFACE, BUT POINTS ON A SPHERE.

Rather than learn all that math for yourself, you can use an excellent set of JavaScript utilities from Chris Veness, available at www.movabletype .co.uk/scripts/latlong.html. This library allows you to create

LatLon objects that have several useful methods available. Starting with a blank HTML5 document, you can create the following page with five simple steps.

1 Start with an empty HTML5 page with a link to the LatLon.js library. All the JavaScript code goes in the empty init function:

```
<!DOCTYPE html>
<html>
<head>
    <meta charset="utf-8">
    <title>Geolocation 4</title>
    <script src="LatLon.js"></script>
    <script> function init() { } </script>
</head>
<body onload="init();">
</body>
</html>
```

2 For convenience, create a LatLon object for Tim Berners-Lee's birthplace, East Sheen in London:

```
var eastSheen = new LatLon(Geo.parseDMS('51?27\'49"N'),
                Geo.parseDMS('0?15\'49"W'));
```

3 As usual, add a template in your HTML to fit the data into:

```
<h1>
    You are <span id="accuracy"></span>
    <span id="distance"></span>
    kilometres from the birthplace of Tim Berners-Lee
</h1>
```

4 Add a function to update the template:

```
function writeLoc(message, accuracy) {
    document.getElementById('distance').innerHTML = message;
    if (accuracy > 100) {
        document.getElementById('accuracy').innerHTML =
'approximately';
    }
}
```

5 Take the usual geolocation boilerplate code, and adapt it so that it creates a LatLon object for the user's current location. You can then use the distanceTo method of LatLon to get the distance between the two points:

```
if (navigator.geolocation) {
    navigator.geolocation.getCurrentPosition(function
(position)
    {
        var you = new LatLon(position.coords.latitude,
                    position.coords.longitude);
        writeLoc(you.distanceTo(eastSheen),
                    position.coords.accuracy);
    });
}
```

Although it's neat that you can perform calculations on the coordinates you get from the Geolocation API, most users probably aren't bothered by exactly how far they are, as the crow flies, from Tim Berners-Lee's birthplace, or any other famous landmark. It's also likely that, outside of geocachers, most people aren't too interested in their exact latitude and longitude. They're far more likely to want to know where they are in some sort of sensible context—in other words, on a map.

GOOGLE OFFERS A FREE SERVICE FOR THE BASIC DISPLAY OF A MAP ON A WEB PAGE. THE NEXT EXAMPLE TAKES THE INFORMATION FROM THE GEOLOCATION API AND USES IT TO CALL UP A MAP OF THE USER'S CURRENT LOCATION.

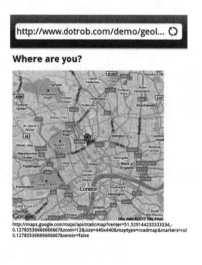

The Google Maps API requires some parameters as part of a URL. The URL can be built in the `writeLoc()` function and then set to be the source of an image element. For convenience, create an empty image element in your page where the map is to appear:

```
<img id="location">
```

In the callback function, set the URL of the image to the appropriate
Google Maps API call:

```
function init() {      if (navigator.geolocation) {
  navigator.geolocation.getCurrentPosition(function (position){
  writeLoc(position.coords);     });}
function writeLoc(coords) {
    var l = 'http://maps.google.com/maps/api/staticmap?center=' +
    coords.latitude + ',' + coords.longitude +
    '&zoom=12&size=440x440&maptype=roadmap' +
    '&markers=color:red|color:red|label:a|' +
    coords.latitude + ',' + coords.longitude +
    '&sensor=false';
    document.getElementById('location').src = l;
    document.getElementById('debug').innerHTML = l;
}
```

When the image URL is set, the browser will load the appropriate map
from the Google Maps API.

NOW YOU KNOW WHERE YOU ARE. WHAT ABOUT TELLING SOMEONE ABOUT IT?
COMMUNICATION IS CENTRAL TO THE WEB, BUT WEB PAGES HAVE BEEN
CONSTRAINED IN WHAT THEY'RE ALLOWED TO COMMUNICATE WITH AND HOW
THEY'RE ALLOWED TO DO IT. HTML5 OFFERS NEW COMMUNICATION APIS: FOR
COMMUNICATING IN A SAFE WAY IN BROWSER-BASED APPS, CROSS-DOCUMENT
MESSAGING; AND FOR COMMUNICATING EFFICIENTLY WITH A SERVER IN REAL TIME,
THE WEBSOCKET API. THE NEXT SECTION LOOKS AT THESE APIS IN MORE DETAIL.

Communication in HTML5

The communication model in HTML4 is pretty much the same as it was
in the first version of HTML. The user requests information from a
server, and then the server delivers it. Although innovations like the
XMLHTTPRequest object allow us to do some cunning things, the underly-
ing model is the same. In addition, content loaded from different servers is usually shielded from other servers—a policy known as *same
origin restriction.*

THIS SECTION NECESSARILY INVOLVES SOME INTERACTION WITH A
SERVER; DISCUSSING HOW TO GET EVERYTHING WORKING ON ALL
POSSIBLE ARCHITECTURES WILL TAKE TOO MANY PAGES. IF YOU'RE
NOT COMFORTABLE WITH THE SERVER SIDE OF THINGS, SKIP AHEAD.

Enabling more secure integration with cross-document messaging

In many situations, people like to use widgets from other websites inside their own pages. Common scenarios where this happens are Facebook's Like buttons, external commenting systems such as Disqus, and Google Ads. There are two basic approaches for this:

⚙ *The* <iframe>—An embedded window inside your page into which another web page is loaded. The page inside the <iframe> is completely separate from the page containing the <iframe>, and standard browser security prevents them from communicating with each other.

⚙ *JavaScript include*—An inline <script> element in the host page, which is allowed to create elements and fetch content from the server from which it came. The script is completely integrated in the host page and has access to all the information the host page does.

	Standard
Browser support quick check: cross-document messaging	
	3.0
	8.0
	9.5
	4.0

The problem is that there are two extremes. With the <iframe>, you can guarantee that the widget doesn't have access to any private data about your users that you happen to be manipulating with JavaScript, because it doesn't have access to anything in the host page, including any information that might be useful for the script. With the JavaScript include, the opposite is true: the script has access to everything in the page, including any cookies that may be set and any forms the user is filling in. What's needed is a solution that maintains the privacy and security allowed by <iframe>s but allows a controlled flow of infor-mation between the two domains. This is what cross-document messaging provides.

Faking multiple domains

Experimenting with multiple domains requires that you have multiple domains available. If you don't happen to be one of those people who collect domain names, you can fake it on your local machine by editing your hosts file. On Windows, this file is usually located at C:\Windows\System32\Drivers \etc\hosts (note that the filename doesn't have an extension) and on Linux and Unix systems at /etc/hosts. The file format is an IP address followed by a number of aliases:

```
127.0.0.1    myfirstfakedomain.com
127.0.0.1    myotherfakedomain.com
```

> **(continued)**
>
> If these two lines are added to your hosts file, then browsing to either http://myfirstfakedomain.com or http://myotherfakedomain.com will direct a request to a web server running on your local machine.

To experiment with cross-domain messaging, you'll need two files. The first, the parent page, contains an `<iframe>` element that will load the second child page:

```
<iframe width="600px"
 height="200px" src="child-1.html">
</iframe>
<textarea id="message">
  This is a message in
  the parent frame
</textarea>
```

This page also contains a `<button>` that will initiate communication with the child:

```
<button onclick="update_child()">
  Update child
</button>
```

The `update_child()` function attempts to directly edit the contents of the child page:

```
function update_child() {
  var el = document
    .getElementsByTagName(
      'iframe'
    )[0];
  var tb = el.contentDocument
    .getElementById('message');
  tb.value = 'Updated from parent';
}
```

The child page is similar:

```
<textarea id="message">
  This is a message in the child frame
</textarea>
```

But this time, the `<button>` attempts to communicate with the parent:

```
<button onclick="update_parent()">Update parent</button>
```

When both pages are on the same domain, it's possible to access the elements of the child page directly and do the same in reverse (access the parent from the child):

```
function update_parent() {
  var tb = parent.document
    .getElementById('message');
  tb.value = 'Updated from child';
}
```

But look what happens if the pages are served from different domains:

```
<iframe width="600px"
height="200px"
  src="http://www.boogdesign.com/
    examples/messaging/child-
2.html">
</iframe>
```

The pages are otherwise identical, but now when you click Update Child, the browser reports an error:

```
Exception: Permission denied for <http://localhost:8000> to get
property HTMLDocument.getElementById from <http://www.boogdesign.com>.
```

The cross-document messaging API allows you to work around this security restriction, but it's slightly more complex than accessing the documents directly. The first step is to add a listener to the page for the message event that will call a function when a message is received:

```
window.addEventListener('message', receiver, false);
function receiver(e) {
  document.getElementById('message').value = e.data;
}
```

This event listener can be added in both the parent and child pages. The update_child() function then needs to be changed to call the post-Message() method:

```
function update_child() {
  var el =
    document.getElementsByTagName(
      'iframe')[0];
  el.contentWindow
    .postMessage(
      'Updated from parent', '*'
    );
}
```

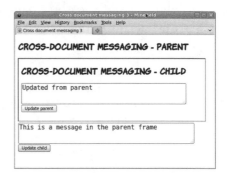

The same postMessage() method can be called from the child to the parent:

```
function update_parent() {
  parent
    .postMessage(
      'Updated from child',
      '*'
    );
}
```

ALTHOUGH THIS FUNCTIONALITY ALLOWS YOU, THE WEB DEVELOPER, GREAT POWER, IT ALSO INCREASES YOUR RESPONSIBILITY. NOW THAT THE BROWSER HAS PROVIDED A WAY AROUND A SECURITY RESTRICTION, YOU NEED TO PROVIDE YOUR OWN SECURITY CHECKS.

In the following code, the `receiver()` function has been modified to check the origin of the `onmessage` event:

```
function receiver(e) {
    if (e.origin == 'http://www.boogdesign.com') {
        document.getElementById('message').value = e.data;
    } else {
      alert('Unauthorized');
    }
}
```

Similarly, the `update` functions should be modified to send the origin:

```
function update_parent() {
    parent.postMessage('Updated from child', 'http://
  www.boogdesign.com');
}
```

Note that the origin argument here should be the parent's origin, not the child's.

Communicating between documents across domains is just one of the new communication features in HTML5. It also offers new options for communicating with the server. The next section will look at the most exciting of these technologies: WebSockets.

Real-time communication with the WebSocket API

WebSockets are a lightweight protocol, new to HTML5, allowing a server to communicate directly with a web browser without waiting for a request. You may be thinking that the web has always had a way for the browser and server to communicate, and that it's a fairly fundamental property, but it's always had a request-response model. This means that to receive a response from the server, the browser must first make a request. Although this is fine for web pages, it has limitations as far as web-based applications are concerned. If an application relies on frequent updates from the server—for instance, if it's a multiplayer game or a chat application—the browser could end up not requesting an update as it becomes available, or wasting bandwidth requesting updates when none are available.

The WebSocket API solves this problem by allowing the server to initiate a response to the browser without the browser asking for it. Updates can now be delivered as they're ready and only when they're ready, as the following diagram shows.

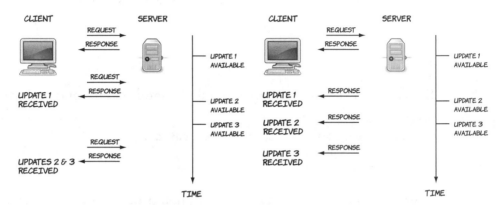

In a traditional AJAX model, updates from the server are sent when the client asks for them. If the client doesn't request an update, it sits on the server.

With WebSockets, the server is in control of sending updates. They can be sent to the client as soon as they're available.

		Standard
Browser support quick check: WebSockets	(Chrome)	4.0
	(Firefox)	4.0*
	(Internet Explorer)	10.0
	(Opera)	11.0
	(Safari)	5.0

*   The WebSocket API is disabled by default in Firefox 4 and 5 and Opera due to a security concern. It must be enabled manually.

> **A server for WebSockets: Node.js**
> Experimenting with WebSockets requires a server. The following example uses Node.js, a new server written using JavaScript. Download Node.js from http://nodejs.org, and follow the instructions for installing it on your operating system. The server-side files used for the example are ch06/messaging/server-1.js and ch06/messaging/server-2.js.

The first step on the client side is to create a new `WebSocket` instance:

```
var socket =
 new WebSocket(
        "ws://localhost:8080/"
    );
```

Then, assign event handlers to the socket object. In this first example, the server will wait 10 seconds and then close the connection, so you just need to watch the onopen and onclose events:

```
socket.onopen = function () {
  log("Socket has been opened!");
}
socket.onclose = function () {
  log("Socket has been closed");
}
```

Now let's look at what happens when the server sends a message. In the browser, you have to handle the onmessage event:

```
socket.onmessage = function(msg) {
  log(msg.data);
}
```

The data attribute of the event handler argument contains the message from the server; in this case, the current data and time every 10 seconds.

You can also control the connection from the browser with the close method on the socket object:

```
socket.close();
```

Finally, you may want to send a message to the server. This is done with the send() method on the socket object, passing the message as the parameter:

```
function send() {
  var msg = document
    .getElementById('message').value;
  socket.send(msg);
}
```

The server is set up to echo back any message it receives.

THE WEBSOCKETS COMMUNICATION PROTOCOL HAS CHANGED FREQUENTLY DURING DEVELOPMENT, SO IF YOU ENCOUNTER DIFFICULTIES, CHECK THAT BOTH CLIENT AND SERVER ARE USING THE SAME VERSION OF THE PROTOCOL.

Offline web applications

Although in the modern world we sometimes take connectivity for granted, there are plenty of situations where you might want access to web applications when you're offline—particularly when, as the authors of the HTML5 specification hope, more and more of the applications you use every day are web applications. For a web application to be available offline, there are two basic requirements:

- A mechanism for storing the pages and other files (images, scripts, and stylesheets) required by the application
- A place to store the user's data as it's accessed and updated while the user is offline

In this section, you'll learn about HTML5 technologies for the first of these requirements: the *application cache*—a way of placing a copy of your web app on your user's machine. In the following section, you'll learn about the offline storage of data.

Before going into the application cache, you'll set up a development environment and then get a reminder of how web applications work when they're online.

Setting up a development environment

THE EXAMPLES IN THIS SECTION USE A LOCAL WEB SERVER, THE PYTHON MODULE SimpleHTTPServer, SO YOU CAN SEE BOTH ENDS OF THE COMMUNICATION IN REAL TIME. IF YOU'RE RUNNING LINUX, THIS MODULE IS PROBABLY ALREADY INSTALLED; OTHERWISE YOU'LL HAVE TO INSTALL A STANDARD DISTRIBUTION OF PYTHON.

SimpleHTTPServer records a line like this every time a request is made (it's been split into three sections so it fits better on a single page):

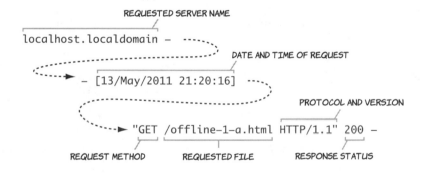

		App cache	Local storage
Browser support quick check: offline apps	Chrome	4.0	4.0
	Firefox	3,5	3,5
	Internet Explorer	-	8.0
	Opera	10.6	10.5
	Safari	5.0	5.0

The only parts we're interested in are the request and the status code, so I'll elide the extra details in the examples that follow.

In order to understand what's going on with offline web applications, you first need a good understanding of what normally happens as the browser and the web server communicate in order to display a web page. Let's first examine the interaction between the web browser and the server for a simple two-page website, without enabling any of HTML5's offline features. Here are the two pages you'll use.

ch06/offline-example/offline-1-a.html	ch06/offline-example/offline-1-b.html

<pre><!DOCTYPE HTML>
<html>
<head>
  <meta charset="utf-8">
  <title>
    Offline Web Applications 1
    - Page A
  </title>
  <link rel="stylesheet"
    href="offline-1.css">
</head>
<body>
  <h1>Page A</h1>
  <p>
    <a href="offline-1-b.html">
      Go to page B
    </a>
  </p>
</body>
</html></pre>
	<pre><!DOCTYPE HTML>
	<html>
	<head>
	  <meta charset="utf-8">
	  <title>
	    Offline Web Applications 1
	    Page B
	    </title>
	  <link rel="stylesheet"
	    href="offline-1.css">
	</head>
	<body>
	  <h1>Page B</h1>
	  <p>
	    <a href="offline-1-a.html">
	      Go to page A
	    </a>
	  </p>
	  <img src="example.png"
	    alt="An example image">
	</body>
	</html></pre>

First, start the local web server:

```
# python -m SimpleHTTPServer
Serving HTTP on 0.0.0.0 port 8000 ...
```

If you load the page in the browser, the server records the following requests:

```
"GET /offline-1-a.html HTTP/1.1" 200 -
"GET /offline-1.css HTTP/1.1" 200 -
```

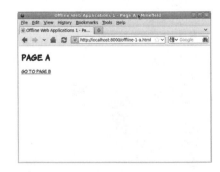

The page itself is requested, as is anything required to display that particular page (in this case the stylesheet), but none of the links within the page are loaded.

When you click the link, the server records the following two requests:

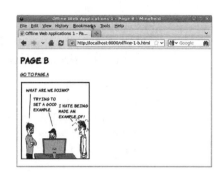

```
"GET /offline-1-b.html HTTP/1.1" 200 -
"GET /example.png HTTP/1.1" 200 -
```

Again, the page itself is requested as well as the image embedded in the second page.

Most browsers, in their default configurations, cache recently accessed pages. If you use the Back and Forward buttons in your browser at this point, no new requests will be made to the server.

Stop the server (press Ctrl-C/Cmd-C in the terminal):

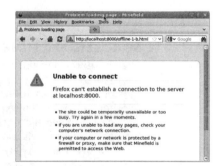

```
^CTraceback (most recent call last):
  ...
KeyboardInterrupt
```

In the browser, try going back and forward again. You'll see that the pages are still there in the browser's temporary cache. But if you try to reload the page, the browser tries to contact the server, finds it's unavailable, and shows an error.

The application cache

The application cache is a service provided by HTML5 web browsers in which you can store your web apps for offline use. To change the previous example into an offline application, it requires one small change and an additional file. At the top of the home page, you need to add a reference to a manifest file, like this from ch06/offline-example/example-2-a.html:

```
<!DOCTYPE HTML>
<html manifest="offline-2.appcache">
```

Then the manifest file itself needs to be created. This is a text file that begins with the words CACHE MANIFEST and then lists all the files in your web application, one per line:

```
CACHE MANIFEST
offline-2-a.html
offline-2-b.html
offline-2.css
example-2.png
```

Note that it's not necessary to list the file where the reference to the manifest appears, because the file that references the manifest is automatically added to the cache; but doing so may save you headaches later if you end up with a large application and you change the file from which the manifest is referenced. Also, note that paths are relative to the manifest file, not the file from which the manifest is referenced.

> **Manifests and MIME types**
>
> The file extension used here for the manifest file is .appcache. This is recommended by the HTML5 spec. Initially, manifest files were given a .manifest extension, but it was found that Microsoft was already using this extension for another purpose. To avoid collisions, the recommended file extension was changed. But the file extension isn't as important to the browser as the MIME type the server sends along with the file in the headers. The correct MIME type for manifest files is text/cache-manifest. MIME types were discussed in chapter 4, when we looked at video.

Start SimpleHTTPServer again, and access the new page. As before, the browser requests two files from the server:

PAGE A

```
"GET /offline-2-a.html HTTP/1.1" 200
"GET /offline-2.css HTTP/1.1" 200
```

But this time there's a difference in the browser—it's asking for permission to store files for offline use.

If you click Allow, the browser immediately makes several more requests:

```
"GET /offline-2.appcache HTTP/1.1" 200
"GET /offline-2-b.html HTTP/1.1" 200
"GET /example-2.png HTTP/1.1" 200
"GET /offline-2.appcache HTTP/1.1" 200
```

The entire website is now available offline. You can test this by again stopping `SimpleHTTPServer` and then, when no server is running, visiting the second page.

Even though you've never visited that page and the server is unavailable, the browser can display the page to you.

Let's try a little experiment. Start your local web server again, but edit the offline-2-a.html file:

```
<h1>Edited Page A</h1>
```

Now visit the page in the browser again. Notice that your edit isn't visible. This is because you've told the browser to store the page locally. Changes you make to the file on the server aren't seen because the browser doesn't go back to the server for the file, even if you reload.

If you look in the console, you'll see that the only request the browser made is for the manifest file:

```
"GET /offline-2.appcache HTTP/1.1" 200 -
```

In order to make the browser fetch a new version of any cached file, the manifest needs to be updated. Any change will do. The best approach is to add a comment with a version number:

```
CACHE MANIFEST
#v1
offline-2-a.html
offline-2-b.html
offline-2.css
example-2.png
```

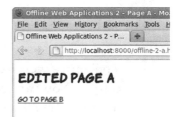

When you reload, the edited page appears. If you check the console, you'll see that all the files in the manifest have been downloaded again.

Beware the browser cache

There is a certain amount of caching built into HTTP, and browsers are often configured to minimize network traffic by serving pages out of local cache instead of downloading them again. This isn't the same as having them in the application cache; there are no guarantees or control for the web author. But the browser cache can interfere with the application cache, because the browser may not look on the network for new versions of files even if it detects that the manifest file has been updated. In this case, the application cache is updated with files from the browser cache. The situation is even worse if the manifest file is loaded into the browser cache—then the user might never see your application updates. You can avoid issues by explicitly setting caching values in the headers of your files in the server configuration. Here's the required line for Apache:

```
ExpiresByType text/cache-manifest        "access plus 0 seconds"
```

In case you missed that last part, if you want to update a single file in your application, all the files in your application will be downloaded again.

THE KEY POINT TO GRASP FROM THIS IS THAT THE APPLICATION CACHE ISN'T A GOOD PLACE TO STORE DATA THAT WILL CHANGE OFTEN; IF YOU'RE EXPECTING YOUR USER TO EDIT DATA AS PART OF THE APPLICATION, THEN YOU NEED TO STORE THAT DATA ELSEWHERE.

HTML5 provides several options for storing an application's dynamic data, as you'll see in the section "Storing data for offline use." In the meantime, the next section will cover the other key features of the application cache that you need to know about.

Managing network connectivity in offline apps

In this section, you'll learn about detecting the status of your offline application: is it currently online or offline? To understand how to do this, you'll need to explore some additional features of the manifest file; but first you'll see why the built-in Offline API isn't appropriate.

HTML5 provides the Offline API to detect whether the browser is offline or online. It consists of the `ononline` and `onoffline` events and a Boolean property, `navigator.onLine`. These would be an excellent way of managing when to attempt to sync data with the server—if they worked.

That's a little harsh—the API does work, but not in a way that's useful to web authors. The offline state in HTML5 is tied to the state of the browser, not the state of your network connection or the availability of the server. Here are the basics of the API:

- `navigator.onLine`—This property is `true` if the browser thinks it's online and `false` if the browser thinks it's offline.
- `window.online`—This event is fired whenever the browser changes from an offline state to an online state.
- `window.offline`—This event is fired whenever the browser changes from an online state to an offline state.

A function can be attached to the events either by declaring an `ononline` or `onoffline` attribute on the `body` element, or by binding an event listener to the `window` object in the standard way, as in the following example.

```
window.setInterval(
    function () { log('onLine: ' + navigator.onLine); },
    10000
);
window.addEventListener('online',
    function () { log('online event fired'); } ,
    false
);
window.addEventListener('offline',
    function () { log('offline event fired'); } ,
    false
);
```

The log function writes a message on the screen so you can see what's going on. The full listing is in ch06/offline-example/offline-events.html.

In the screenshot, the local web server was started and the page loaded. After a short time, the local web server was stopped. As you can see, it made absolutely no difference to the output in the browser.

OFFLINE EVENTS

ONLINE: TRUE
ONLINE: TRUE
ONLINE: TRUE
ONLINE: TRUE
ONLINE: TRUE
ONLINE: TRUE
ONLINE: TRUE
ONLINE: TRUE
ONLINE: TRUE

The reason is that these events and properties aren't designed to track what's going on with the network connection or the availability of the remote server. Instead, they're plumbed directly into a menu item in the browser UI: the Work Offline entry, which is usually on the File menu.

File	Edit	View	History	Bookma
New Tab				Ctrl+T
New Window				Ctrl+N
Open Location...				Ctrl+L
Open File...				Ctrl+O
Close Tab				Ctrl+W
Close Window				Ctrl+Shift+W
Save Page As...				Ctrl+S
Send Link...				
Page Setup...				
Print Preview				
Print...				Ctrl+P
Import...				
☐ Work Offline				
Quit				Ctrl+Q

If the local server is started up again and the page reloaded, you can see the effect of selecting and then deselecting Work Offline in the menu.

This is perfectly reasonable behavior from the browser if you think about it—there are so many reasons the server may not be contactable, that it can't be tied to a single property in the browser or the operating system, or linked to a simple event.

OFFLINE EVENTS

ONLINE: TRUE
ONLINE: TRUE
OFFLINE EVENT FIRED
ONLINE: FALSE
ONLINE EVENT FIRED
ONLINE: TRUE

Before you get too disappointed, there's an alternative approach that relies on detecting the property that an offline application really cares about: whether it can connect to the server. To understand this approach, you need to learn about some further features of the manifest file: sections introduced with the keywords FALLBACK or NETWORK. A NETWORK section lists resources that will always be fetched from the network—they won't be available when offline. The FALLBACK section lists replacements for certain files or directories when the user's offline. Here's ch06/offline-example/offline-3.appcache, which has a FALLBACK section:

```
CACHE MANIFEST
#v1
offline-3-a.html
offline-3-b.html
offline-3.css

FALLBACK:
example-3.png dust-puppy-3.png
```

Let's see what difference that makes in what files are requested when the browser makes an initial request for offline-3-a.html:

```
"GET /offline-3-a.html HTTP/1.1" 200
"GET /offline-3.css HTTP/1.1" 200
"GET /offline-3.appcache HTTP/1.1" 200
"GET /offline-3-b.html HTTP/1.1" 200
"GET /dust-puppy-3.png HTTP/1.1" 200
"GET /offline-3.appcache HTTP/1.1" 200
```

PAGE A

GO TO PAGE B

The file dust-puppy-3.png is fetched from the server even though it isn't listed in the opening section of the manifest file.

When offline-3-b.html is visited, it looks the same as before. Because the server is still running, the example-3.png image is loaded as normal.

PAGE B

GO TO PAGE A

But if the web server is stopped and the page reloaded, then, depending on browser settings, the dust-puppy-3.png fallback image is shown instead.

The significant browser settings are the ones to do with caching outside of the application cache. The browser may still choose to show the image out of the browser cache even when the server's unavailable—see the sidebar "Beware the browser cache" for a discussion of this issue. If the fallback image isn't shown when the page is reloaded, try a hard reload: Ctrl+F5 on Windows or Linux.

PAGE B

GO TO PAGE A

Listing ch06/offline-example/offline-4.appcache has a few more new features:

```
CACHE MANIFEST
#v1
offline-4.html

FALLBACK:
example-4.png dust-puppy-4.png

CACHE:
offline-4.css
```

```
FALLBACK:
headshots/ dust-puppy-4.gif

NETWORK:
*
```

In addition to multiple FALLBACK sections and a NETWORK section, this listing has two CACHE sections. There are two because CACHE is the default assumption at the start of the manifest file. It's possible to switch between sections at any point by adding one of the three keywords on a line by itself. This means the manifest file can be arranged to suit the application rather than forcing everything to fit into three sections.

The other interesting feature of this manifest file is that it demonstrates the pattern-matching and wildcard ability of the FALLBACK and NETWORK sections. The NETWORK section has a star in it, which means "match anything"— anything that isn't listed is requested from the network. This is the default behavior, so it's not necessary to include it here, but if you were developing real offline applications you'd include URL patterns for your API in this section.

The second FALLBACK section includes a directory. It's saying, "For anything in the folder headshots, fall back to dust-puppy-4.gif when offline."

This screenshot shows ch06/offline-example/offline-4.html when online. Here's the markup for this example:

```
<img src="example-4.png"
  alt="An example image">
<p>Example starring:</p>
<img src="headshots/pitr.gif"
  alt="Pitr">
<img src="headshots/mike.gif"
  alt="Mike">
<img src="headshots/stef.gif"
  alt="Stef">
```

And here's what the same page looks like when offline. Each image from the headshots folder has been replaced by the fallback image without having to explicitly list each image.

It's worth noting that in this particular example, the alt text no longer corresponds to the images displayed, so it might be a good idea to override the alt text with JavaScript if you can detect that the page is offline. As discussed at the beginning of the section, it's possible to do this now that you know how FALLBACK works.

There are several possible approaches to using a fallback to detect the application's online status, but they all boil down to the same thing: having a pair of files in the FALLBACK section of the manifest that have an easily detectable difference between the online and fallback versions. The complete listings for the two files this example uses are shown in the following table.

ch06/offline-example/online.txt	ch06/offline-example/offline.txt
ONLINE	OFFLINE

It would certainly be possible to add more complexity; but the online.txt file will be fetched from the server frequently, so the shorter the better. In real life, it would be best to stop pandering to human readability and use values of 1 and 0. Now add these two files in the FALLBACK section of the manifest file:

```
CACHE MANIFEST
#v1
```

```
offline-5.html
offline-5.css
offline-checker.js

FALLBACK:
online.txt offline.txt
```

These files can then be used to determine the online status. In this example it's linked to a button: each time the button is clicked, the online status is checked and reported.

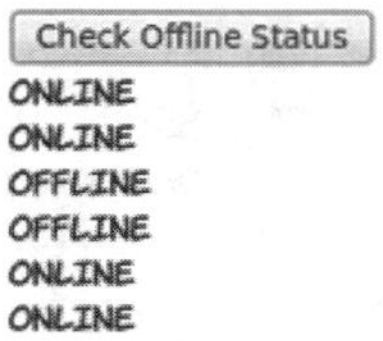

Check Offline Status

ONLINE
ONLINE
OFFLINE
OFFLINE
ONLINE
ONLINE

The full listing is in the files ch06/offline-example/offline-5.html and ch06/offline-example/offline-checker.js. The key parts of the code are shown next.

Here's the function that's called when the button is clicked. It calls another function in the external JavaScript file, passing two functions as parameters. The first function is executed if the server's available, the second if the server's offline:

```
function display_online_status() {
    check_online(
                function() { log('online'); },
                function() { log('offline'); }
            );
    return false;
}
```

In a real application, the functions passed in would do something useful, such as synchronize the application data with the server or queue it for later delivery. But in this example, all they do is log the state of the connection to the page.

Finally, here's the function that does all the real work. Most of this is standard AJAX boilerplate; using any one of the popular JavaScript libraries will reduce the function to about four lines of code. The key

line is about halfway down, where req.responseText is checked to see if
it contains the string 'OFFLINE':

```
function check_online(online_fn, offline_fn) {
    var currentTime = new Date()
    req = window.XMLHttpRequest ?
            new XMLHttpRequest() :
            new ActiveXObject("MSXML2.XMLHTTP.3.0");
    var freshUrl = 'online.txt?brk=' + currentTime.getTime();
    req.open("GET", freshUrl, true);
    req.onreadystatechange = function() {
        if (req.readyState == 4) {
            if (req.status == 200) {
                if (req.responseText.indexOf('OFFLINE') > -1) {
                    offline_fn();
                } else {
                    online_fn();
                }
            } else {
                offline_fn();
            }
        }
    }
    req.send(null);
}
```

HAVING YOUR APPLICATION AVAILABLE WHEN THERE'S NO CONNECTIVITY IS ONE
THING, BUT MOST APPLICATIONS NEED TO INTERACT WITH DATA TO BE USEFUL.
IF ALL THE DATA IS ON THE SERVER, THEN HAVING THE APPLICATION WORK
OFFLINE ISN'T OF MUCH USE IN ITSELF. IN THE NEXT SECTION, YOU'LL LEARN
ABOUT STORING DATA SO IT'S AVAILABLE FOR OFFLINE APPLICATIONS.

Storing data for offline use

In this section, you'll learn about the Web Storage API, a convenient
way to store data in the browser. Although web storage is crucial for
any sort of offline application, it's also useful for providing quick access
to data in the browser without having to repeatedly request it from the
server. Web storage comes in two flavors: local storage, which is persistent across browser sessions, and session storage, which is lost when
the user ends their browsing session. The storage APIs are also available to offline apps, making them extremely useful for caching your

user's data for access while they're offline. The API for each is identical, so this section concentrates on local storage and then provides a quick comparison with session storage before finishing with a look at using web storage in an offline application.

Local storage

For many years, the only option web authors have had for storing data on the client has been cookies. These are small strings stored in the client browser along with an expiry date and a key to reference them by. They're then passed back by the browser along with any HTTP request made to the server that set them.

COOKIES ARE WIDELY USED—ANY WEBSITE YOU VISIT THAT ALLOWS YOU TO LOG IN OR REMEMBERS YOUR PAST ACTIVITY OR PREFERENCES IS USING COOKIES TO CORRELATE EACH REQUEST YOU MAKE WITH STORED INFORMATION ON THE SERVER, BUT THEY AREN'T WITHOUT ISSUES.

The local storage APIs create a client-side key-value store so that data doesn't have to be repeatedly fetched from the server. Cookies are useful for tracking things like whether a user is logged on, but they've been forced into a role where they end up storing a significant amount of data. This is a problem because each request the browser makes contains the full set of cookies it has. Local storage replaces cookies by providing a simple in-browser service for associating keys with values. The data stays in the browser and doesn't need to be sent back to the server.

This section builds a simple to-do list application using local storage. First you need some markup for a text input and a button:

```
<input type="text" id="new_item">
<button onclick="add_item()">
  Add
</button>
<ul id="todo_list">
</ul>
```

MY TO-DO LIST

[_____] [Add]

To add an item to the to-do list, the user must type a description into the text input and click the Add button. When the user clicks Add, three steps are required: add the item to the list element on the page, add the item to local storage, and finally clear the text input ready for the next item:

```
function add_item() {
  var new_item =
   document.
     getElementById('new_item');
  add_listitem(new_item.value);
  add_storageitem(new_item.value);
  new_item.value = '';
}
```

MY TO-DO LIST

Write simple to do list app | Add

This calls functions to add the item to the list on the page and to add the same item to local storage. The function that adds an element to the page is straightforward, using the same DOM scripting techniques that everyone's been using for years with HTML4:

```
function add_item() {
    var new_item = document.getElementById('new_item');
    add_listitem(new_item.value);
    add_storageitem(new_item.value);
    new_item.value = '';
}
```

The interesting thing is the call to the add_storageitem function:

```
function add_storageitem(item) {
  var key = new Date();
  window.localStorage.setItem(
    key.getTime(),item
  );
}
```

MY TO-DO LIST

| Add

- WRITE SIMPLE TO DO LIST APP
- THINK OF THINGS TO DO

The localStorage object is available from the window object. In this case, you call the setItem method that adds the provided key-value pair to the storage. It doesn't matter what the key is—it just has to be unique. If you call setItem with a key that already exists, it will overwrite the previously stored item, so the current time in milliseconds is used. The value has to be a string, and in this case the value is whatever the user has typed into the text input. The full code for this first example is in ch06/offline-example/local-storage-1.html.

Now that your to-do items are in local storage, they'll be there the next time you load the page. Restart your browser and load the page again to check. You should see something like the screenshot here.

MY TO-DO LIST

You've not been lied to, your items are in local storage, but that doesn't mean they'll appear in your page automatically. You have to write application logic to grab the contents of localStorage and display it, just as you had to write code to add the to-do items to the page in the first place.

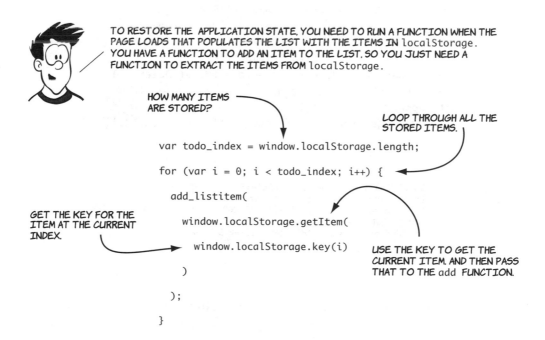

TO RESTORE THE APPLICATION STATE, YOU NEED TO RUN A FUNCTION WHEN THE PAGE LOADS THAT POPULATES THE LIST WITH THE ITEMS IN localStorage. YOU HAVE A FUNCTION TO ADD AN ITEM TO THE LIST, SO YOU JUST NEED A FUNCTION TO EXTRACT THE ITEMS FROM localStorage.

HOW MANY ITEMS ARE STORED?

LOOP THROUGH ALL THE STORED ITEMS.

GET THE KEY FOR THE ITEM AT THE CURRENT INDEX.

USE THE KEY TO GET THE CURRENT ITEM, AND THEN PASS THAT TO THE add FUNCTION.

```
var todo_index = window.localStorage.length;

for (var i = 0; i < todo_index; i++) {

  add_listitem(

    window.localStorage.getItem(

      window.localStorage.key(i)

    )

  );

}
```

You can find the complete listing in ch06/offline-example/local-storage-2.html. Look for the init() function for the previous code.

There are some other functions you'll need for a complete application. A to-do list isn't much use if it's impossible to remove a task after completion. To delete a single item from localStorage, pass its key to the removeItem() method:

MY TO-DO LIST

- WRITE A SIMPLE TO-DO LIST APP [Delete]
- THINK OF MORE THINGS TO DO [Delete]

[Clear All]

```
window.localStorage.removeItem(key);
```

This depends on knowing which element on the page is associated with which key in local storage. If a data-* attribute is used to store that information, then removal is straightforward. That attribute can be created in the add_listitem() function if it's modified to accept both the key and the item as parameters:

```
function add_listitem(key, item) {
    var li = document.createElement('li');
    li.appendChild(document.createTextNode(item));
    li.setAttribute("data-key", key);
    var but = document.createElement('button');
    but.appendChild(document.createTextNode('Delete'));
    but.onclick = remove_item;
    li.appendChild(but);
    document.getElementById('todo_list').appendChild(li);
}
```

IN A FULLY HTML5-COMPLIANT BROWSER, THE LINE li.setAttribute("data-key", key) WOULD BECOME li.dataset.key = key. BECAUSE NO BROWSER HAS SO FAR IMPLEMENTED THE CUSTOM DATA ATTRIBUTE API, THIS EXAMPLE STICKS WITH THE TRADITIONAL DOM API.

Another change is required to support this. Previously it didn't matter what the key was when adding a new item, but now it needs to be added to the list item as entries are created. The key is created in the add_item() method and passed in to both add_listitem() and add_storageitem():

```
function add_item() {
    var new_item = document.getElementById('new_item');
    var key = new Date();
    add_listitem(key.getTime(), new_item.value);
    add_storageitem(key.getTime(), new_item.value);
    new_item.value = '';
}
```

Finally, a user may want to delete everything in local storage rather than individual items one at a time. This is easy using the clear() method:

```
window.localStorage.clear();
```

You can look at the finished listing in ch06/offline-example/local-storage-3.html.

Session storage

So far, the example has used local storage, but the section introduction also mentioned session storage. Local storage and session storage have exactly the same API: if you go back through the example and replace every instance of localStorage with sessionStorage, it will still work. Here's the sessionStorage version of the add and remove functions:

```
function add_storageitem(key, item) {
    window.sessionStorage.setItem(key, item);
}
function remove_storageitem(key) {
    window.sessionStorage.removeItem(key);
}
```

There's a full sessionStorage example in the listing ch06/offline-example/session-storage-1.html.

The only difference between the two types of storage is the length of time the items are stored. Session storage is only guaranteed to last as long as the browser process; if the browser's closed, then any data stored is lost (unless the session-restore features of the browser are enabled). Local storage lasts until your application clears it, or until the user manually deletes the data, no matter how many times the browser's closed in the meantime.

One note before we proceed: while the capacity of local and session storage is much larger than that of cookies, it's still finite, and varies substantially between browsers. Web storage can be a useful way to store large amounts of data on the client side but, like all client-side technologies, you should never rely on it being available all the time.

Putting it all together

Now that the to-do list app is functional, it would be nice to enable it to work offline. Because the entire thing is self contained—no external files of any kind, just the single HTML file—you just need an empty manifest file

```
CACHE MANIFEST
#v1
```

and a reference to that manifest in the markup:

```
<!DOCTYPE HTML>
<html manifest="storage.appcache">
```

Remember that the file that references the manifest is always cached and doesn't need to be listed in the manifest file explicitly. If you have a set of single-page applications on the same site, then they can all reference this one manifest file and they'll be cached the first time the user visits them. You can try it for yourself on your local web server with the example file in ch06/offline-example/local-storage-4.html.

YOU'VE LEARNED ABOUT A LOT OF DIFFERENT HTML5 FEATURES IN THIS CHAPTER, BUT HOW MANY OF THEM CAN YOU USE RIGHT NOW? BROWSER COMPATIBILITY IS SUMMARIZED IN THE NEXT SECTION.

Browser support

Browser support for most of the APIs discussed in this chapter is very good. Only Internet Explorer lets things down by not supporting Web-Sockets or the application cache, but support is being considered for a future release.

	12	14	4	6	8	9	10	11.5	12	5	5.1
Geolocation	●	●	●	●		●	●	●	●	●	●
Cross-document messaging	●	●	●	●	●	●	●	●	●	●	●
WebSockets	●	●	●	●			●	●	●	●	●
App cache	●	●	●	●			●	●	●	●	●
Session storage	●	●	●	●	●	●	●	●	●	●	●
Local storage	●	●	●	●		●	●	●	●	●	●

Key:
- ● Complete or nearly complete support
- ○ Incomplete or alternative support
  Little or no support

Summary

This chapter has covered a selection of the most interesting HTML5 APIs associated with networking and connectivity. You should now be able to build apps that

- Take advantage of the user's location, thanks to the Geolocation API
- Communicate in a controlled way with pages on other domains
- Write real-time chat and game apps with WebSockets

- Build apps that work even when there's no internet connection
- Store data in the browser with the storage APIs

The best way to learn more is to try coding for yourself. Download the book's sample code to get started.

THIS CHAPTER IS THE LAST IN THIS BOOK SPECIFICALLY ABOUT HTML5. YOU'VE LEARNED HOW TO BUILD HTML5 WEB PAGES AND SEEN SOME OF THE MANY NEW POSSIBILITIES FOR WEB APPLICATIONS THAT HTML5 ENABLES. BUT YOU DON'T JUST WANT YOUR APPLICATIONS TO BE FUNCTIONAL; YOU ALSO WANT THEM TO LOOK BEAUTIFUL. IN THE NEXT CHAPTER, YOU'LL START TO EXPLORE CSS3 AND THE NEW OPTIONS IT OFFERS FOR THE VISUAL PRESENTATION OF WEB PAGES.

Learning CSS3

The second part of the book begins by exploring the basics of CSS3 and selectors in chapters 7 and 8. Then, chapter 9 discusses how to use motion and color, chapter 10 covers borders and backgrounds, and chapter 11 wraps things up with a look at fonts and text formatting.

7

New CSS language features

Let's remind ourselves what a CSS rule looks like.

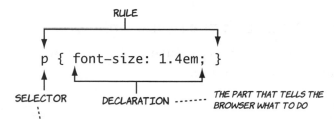

In this chapter we're concerned entirely with the parts of CSS that appear outside of the curly brackets—the selectors and associated syntax that makes up a CSS document. After this chapter, we'll concentrate almost completely on the stuff that appears inside the curly brackets—the properties and values that define the visual effect to be applied. The stuff that appears inside the curly brackets is naturally more interesting, because

THERE'S AN INTRODUCTION TO CSS IN APPENDIX C. IF YOU DIDN'T KNOW ANY CSS BEFORE PICKING UP THIS BOOK, YOU SHOULD READ THAT BEFORE PROCEEDING.

that's what lets you change the style of your pages. But being able to choose what elements your styles affect is crucially important for the whole thing to work.

What is CSS3?

CSS3 is the third major revision of the W3C CSS specification. Unlike the previous two revisions, CSS3 is divided into modules—instead of being one, long document like CSS1 and CSS2/2.1, there are currently more than 30 individual documents that are part of CSS3. These are all allowed to progress and mature at their own rates; depending on the level of interest, some modules will progress to level 4 before the level-3 work is completed.

Like the term *HTML5*, the term *CSS3* is often given a wider definition than just the specifications. Many of the features people consider to be CSS3 are actually in CSS2.1.

CSS3 HAS MANY MORE TOOLS FOR SELECTING ELEMENTS, SO YOU'RE BETTER EQUIPPED TO KEEP YOUR MARKUP FREE FROM ELEMENTS, CLASSES, AND IDS THAT HAVE NO MEANING AND ARE ONLY THERE TO SUPPORT STYLING. IN THE NEXT SECTION, YOU'LL SEE SOME COMMON DESIGN PROBLEMS AND LEARN HOW CSS3 SELECTORS MAKE SOLVING THESE PROBLEMS EASY.

Choosing elements through their relationships

Here are screenshots of three popular websites, showing three different but common design requirements.

Alternating table rows have a different style.

Links to the current page or section have a different style.

The first and last elements have a different style.

Using traditional approaches, you would have to apply classes to each element. For the previous three examples, the code would be something like the following, where the class names don't add any further meaning to the markup—they just make explicit relationships that are already present:

```
<table>                  <ul>                     <ul>
 <tr class="odd">         <li>                     <li class="first">
  <td></td>                <a href="/home"           top + right border
 </tr>                        class="current">      </li>
 <tr class="even">        Home                      <li>
  <td></td>               </a>                      right border
 </tr>                   <a href="/other">         </li>
</table>                  Other                     <li class="last">
                         </a>                       bottom + right
                         </li>                      border
                        </ul>                       </li>
                                                  </ul>
```

In CSS3, thanks to all the new selectors available, you can take advantage of those relationships directly with no need to add extra class attributes. In this section, you'll learn about the key ways of selecting elements with CSS combinators and pseudo-classes.

Selecting sets of elements with combinators

Combinators allow you to chain simple selectors together. They're the workhorses of CSS. The following diagrams show a simple HTML fragment as a tree structure and then highlight the elements that the different rules select using the common CSS2 combinators.

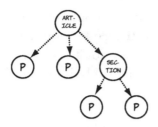

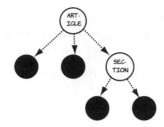

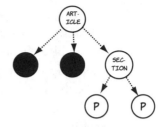

```
<article>
    <p></p>
    <p></p>
    <section>
        <p></p>
        <p></p>
    </section>
</article>
```

article p {}

A space is the descendant combinator, selecting any p that is a descendant of an article element.

article > p {}

The greater-than symbol is the child combinator, selecting only the p elements that are direct children of an article.

FIRST WE'LL LOOK AT THE ADJACENT-SIBLING COMBINATOR. IT WAS INTRODUCED IN CSS2.1, BUT IT ISN'T SUPPORTED BY IE6 OR 7 AND SO HASN'T BEEN WIDELY USED. IT SELECTS AN ELEMENT THAT IMMEDIATELY FOLLOWS ANOTHER ELEMENT.

THE ADJACENT-SIBLING COMBINATOR

Rather than use tree diagrams to illustrate the new selectors, we'll use this simple document:

```
<header>
    <h1>Header</h1>
</header>
<article>
    <h1>Article</h1>
    <p>Paragraph 1</p>
    <p>Paragraph 2</p>
    <footer>Article footer</footer>
</article>
<footer>
    Body footer
</footer>
```

The complete listing is available in ch07/sibling-combinator-1.html.

This rule selects any paragraph elements that immediately follow a level-one heading element:

```
h1 + p { background-color: #000; }
```

You can see in the screenshot that only the first paragraph is selected. The + is known as the *adjacent-sibling combinator*. This example is from ch07/sibling-combinator-1a.html.

The target element is always listed last. This rule has no effect because there are no paragraph elements immediately after footer elements:

```
footer + p {
  background-color: #000;
}
```

Switch the two simple selectors around, and you can see that there are footers that follow paragraphs:

```
p + footer {
 background-color: #000;
}
```

See the files sibling-combinator2a.html and sibling-combinator2b.html in the ch07 folder for these two examples.

THE ADJACENT-SIBLING COMBINATOR IS USEFUL FOR SITUATIONS WHERE YOU MIGHT WANT TO ALLOW A DIFFERENT AMOUNT OF SPACE DEPENDING ON WHAT THE PREVIOUS ELEMENT WAS. FOR EXAMPLE, IF YOU HAVE A HEADING DIRECTLY AFTER A PARAGRAPH, YOU WANT TWO LINES OF SPACE. A HEADING THAT FOLLOWS ANOTHER HEADING NEEDS ONLY ONE LINE OF SPACE, BUT THE ELEMENTS HAVE TO DIRECTLY FOLLOW ONE ANOTHER.

THE GENERAL-SIBLING COMBINATOR

Suppose another element is inserted between the paragraph and the footer, like this:

```
<p>Paragraph 2</p>
<img src="example.png">
<footer>Article footer</footer>
```

The footer is no longer selected by p + footer because it doesn't immediately follow the paragraph.

 FOR SITUATIONS WHERE THE ELEMENTS YOU WANT TO SELECT WILL SHARE THE SAME PARENT AS ANOTHER ELEMENT, BUT NOT NECESSARILY BE DIRECTLY ADJACENT, CSS3 OFFERS THE GENERAL-SIBLING COMBINATOR.

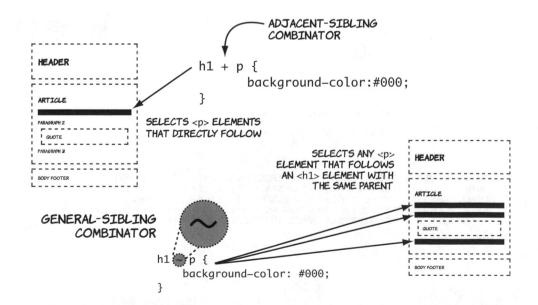

ADJACENT-SIBLING COMBINATOR

```
h1 + p {
        background-color:#000;
}
```

SELECTS <p> ELEMENTS THAT DIRECTLY FOLLOW

SELECTS ANY <p> ELEMENT THAT FOLLOWS AN <h1> ELEMENT WITH THE SAME PARENT

GENERAL-SIBLING COMBINATOR

```
h1 ~ p {
        background-color: #000;
}
```

For this set of examples, we'll make a slight modification to the HTML. Instead of an article footer, a `blockquote` element and a third paragraph have been added.

```
<header>
    <h1>Header</h1>
</header>
<article>
    <h1>Article</h1>
    <p>Paragraph 1</p>
    <p>Paragraph 2</p>
    <blockquote>Quote</
blockquote>
    <p>Paragraph 3</p>
</article>
<footer>
    Body footer
</footer>
```

Browser support quick check: combinators		+	~
	Chrome	1.0	1.0
	Firefox	1.0	1.0
	Internet Explorer	7.0	8.0
	Opera	6.0	9.5
	Safari	1.0	1.0

Elements targeted by the general-sibling combinator have to occur after the elements targeted by the preceding selector in the document. Compare the results of these two rules. There are three paragraphs after the h1, but only one of those is after the blockquote.

```
h1 ~ p {
    background-color: #000;
}
```

Listing: ch07/sibling-combinator-1b.html

```
blockquote ~ p {
    background-color: #000;
}
```

Listing ch07/sibling-combinator-1c.html

THE REASON ONLY THE ELEMENTS AFTER THE blockquote ARE AFFECTED IS THAT THE BROWSER RECEIVES THE WEB PAGE AS A STREAM, ONE CHARACTER AT A TIME, AND APPLIES STYLES AS IT GOES ALONG. IT TRIES TO AVOID GOING BACK AND RESTYLING ALREADY-RENDERED ELEMENTS, BECAUSE DOING SO IMPACTS PERFORMANCE.

YOU'VE JUST LEARNED ABOUT CSS3'S NEW COMBINATORS, BUT CSS3 ALSO PROVIDES SEVERAL PSEUDO-CLASSES FOR TARGETING ELEMENTS ACCORDING TO THEIR RELATIVE POSITION IN THE DOM. PSEUDO-CLASSES ACT AS MODIFIERS TO SIMPLE SELECTORS— SO INSTEAD OF SELECTING ALL THE PARAGRAPHS, YOU CAN SELECT JUST THE FIRST ONE, OR JUST THE LAST ONE, OR EVERY THIRD ONE. IN THE NEXT SECTION, YOU'LL LEARN HOW TO USE CSS3 PSEUDO-CLASSES TO SOLVE COMMON DESIGN PROBLEMS.

Selecting among a set of elements with pseudo-classes

Combinators allow you to select all elements that fit a particular relationship. But what if you don't want to select all of the `<p>` elements that are descendants of an `<article>` element for the same styling? Or all the rows of a table? CSS pseudo-classes allow you to select the first element, the last element, or a subset of the elements according to a pattern. They remove the need to add classes to your markup for purely stylistic purposes. Before you learn about pseudo-classes, let's consider what you would need to do if pseudo-classes didn't exist, and why that's not good practice, with a couple of examples.

The IE6 problem

IE6 is the most successful browser of all time in terms of market share, managing as much as 90% market share in its heyday. Unfortunately, it's missing several key features of CSS2.1.

The ubiquity of IE6 allowed many organizations to get away with shortcuts in web app development. The result is that they have since been stuck with expensive-to-replace applications that only work on IE6. It's impossible to upgrade the web browser without first replacing all those applications a slow process. The end result is that several CSS2.1 features couldn't be used on most websites until recently, one of which is pseudo-classes.

In the old days (you know, around 2005) when IE6 was predominant, the only way to do this consistently was to add classes all over your HTML that anticipated the styling you wanted. With CSS2.1 and CSS3 approaching 90% browser support, you should now be doing this with pseudo-classes.

SELECTING THE FIRST AND LAST ELEMENT

Styling the first element of any set differently is common on the web today. This blog renders the first paragraph in a larger font to make it stand out.

The old way to approach this was to explicitly add a class to the first paragraph:

```
<h1>Heading</h1>
<p class="first">
  First paragraph...
</p>
```

This blog goes even further—the first post is styled differently than the other posts previewed on the home page. The first post takes up the full width and is divided into columns; the rest of the posts are in a single column further down. Again, the usual approach to this is to add a class in the markup:

```
<div class="post first">
  <h1>Post 1</h1>
  <p>...
</div>
<div class="post">
  <h1>Post 2...
```

For details on CSS columns, check out chapter 11.

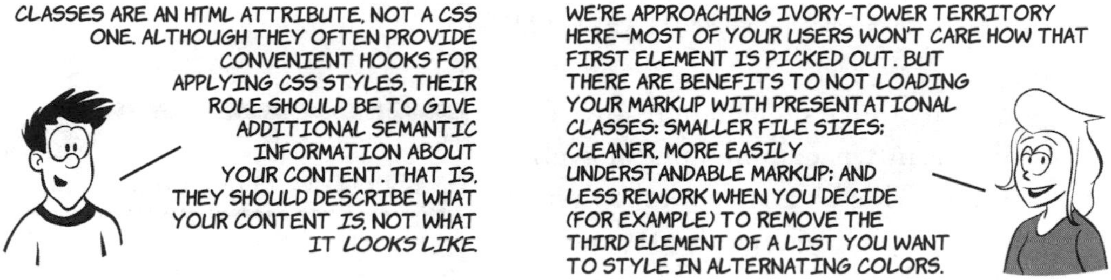

CLASSES ARE AN HTML ATTRIBUTE, NOT A CSS ONE. ALTHOUGH THEY OFTEN PROVIDE CONVENIENT HOOKS FOR APPLYING CSS STYLES, THEIR ROLE SHOULD BE TO GIVE ADDITIONAL SEMANTIC INFORMATION ABOUT YOUR CONTENT. THAT IS, THEY SHOULD DESCRIBE WHAT YOUR CONTENT *IS*, NOT WHAT IT *LOOKS LIKE*.

WE'RE APPROACHING IVORY-TOWER TERRITORY HERE—MOST OF YOUR USERS WON'T CARE HOW THAT FIRST ELEMENT IS PICKED OUT. BUT THERE ARE BENEFITS TO NOT LOADING YOUR MARKUP WITH PRESENTATIONAL CLASSES: SMALLER FILE SIZES; CLEANER, MORE EASILY UNDERSTANDABLE MARKUP; AND LESS REWORK WHEN YOU DECIDE (FOR EXAMPLE) TO REMOVE THE THIRD ELEMENT OF A LIST YOU WANT TO STYLE IN ALTERNATING COLORS.

For the next few examples, we'll use a markup fragment in a style that's commonly used for site navigation—an unordered list of links. The screenshot shows some default styling, putting a dotted outline around each major element so you can see where it is.

```
<nav>
  <ul>
    <li>
      <a href="#item1">Item 1</a>
    </li>
    <li>
      <a href="#item2">Item 2</a>
    </li>
    <li>
      <a href="#item3">Item 3</a>
    </li>
    <li>
      <a href="#item4">Item 4</a>
    </li>
    <li>
      <a href="#item5">Item 5</a>
    </li>
    <li>
      <a href="#item6">Item 6</a>
    </li>
  </ul>
</nav>
```

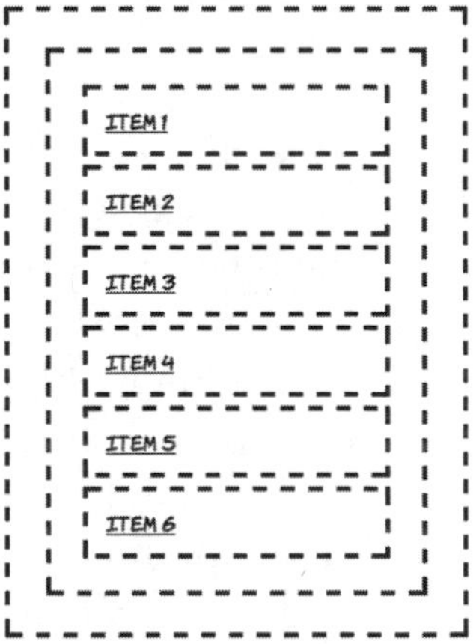

To select the first element in the list without adding additional markup, you can use the :first-child pseudo-class:

```
ul li:first-child {
  background-color: #000;
}
```

This selector is saying, "Select the <li> elements that are the first child of their respective <ul> elements."

Selecting the last element is also straightforward with the :last-child pseudo-class:

```
ul li:last-child {
  background-color: #000;
}
```

This selector is saying, "Select the <li> elements that are the last child of their <ul> parent elements."

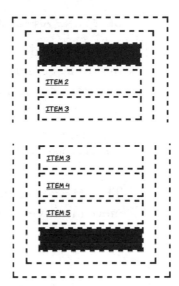

YOU DON'T HAVE TO APPLY THESE PSEUDO-CLASSES TO A PARTICULAR ELEMENT. THEY CAN BE USED STANDALONE. SEE IF YOU CAN WORK OUT WHICH ELEMENTS THIS CSS RULE WILL SELECT. THE ANSWER IS FURTHER DOWN:

```
ul :last-child { background-color: #000; }
```

Pseudo-classes can be used with descendent or child combinators like any other simple selector. Compare this with the previous example:

```
li:last-child {
  background-color: #000;
}
li:last-child a {
  background-color: #fff;
}
```

The extra rule selects all <a> elements that descend from an <li> element that is a last child. This rule has been used to make the link visible.

SELECTING AN ELEMENT BY ITS ORDERING

What if you don't want to select just the first or last child? With :nth-child you can easily select specific elements by specifying a numeric parameter:

```
li:nth-child(3), li:nth-child(5) {
  background-color: #000;
}
```

The :first-child pseudo-class is just a more intuitive way of saying :nth-child(1).

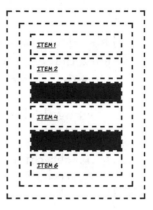

OFTEN YOU WANT TO SELECT, NOT INDIVIDUAL ELEMENTS OUT OF A SET, BUT A SUBSET OF THE ELEMENTS ACCORDING TO SOME REPEATING PATTERN. A COMMON EXAMPLE IS LARGE TABLES OF DATA IN WHICH IT'S HELPFUL TO GIVE THE ROWS ALTERNATING BACKGROUND COLORS TO AID THE EYE AS IT TRACKS ACROSS THE VALUES.

COUNTRY	🥇	🥈	🥉	Total
AUSTRALIA	74	55	48	177
INDIA	38	27	36	101
ENGLAND	37	59	46	142
CANADA	26	17	32	75
SOUTH AFRICA	12	11	10	33
KENYA	12	11	9	32
MALAYSIA	12	10	13	35
SINGAPORE	11	11	9	31
NIGERIA	11	10	14	35
SCOTLAND	9	10	7	26
NEW ZEALAND	6	22	8	36
CYPRUS	4	3	5	12
NORTHERN IRELAND	3	3	4	10
SAMOA	3	0	1	4
WALES	2	7	10	19
JAMAICA	2	4	1	7
PAKISTAN	2	1	2	5

Date	RSS/Atom	Robots	Browsers	Unknown	Total
18/11/10	341	13	91	27	472
17/11/10	484	38	59	84	665
16/11/10	455	39	61	25	580
15/11/10	456	29	54	14	553
14/11/10	479	37	55	41	612
13/11/10	474	22	47	41	584
12/11/10	469	39	46	29	583
11/11/10	451	24	50	45	570
10/11/10	429	32	331	45	837
09/11/10	426	35	73	39	573
08/11/10	421	31	52	46	550
07/11/10	436	33	75	35	579
06/11/10	416	31	43	18	508
05/11/10	477	18	52	33	580
04/11/10	482	42	67	60	651
03/11/10	471	15	59	33	578
Total	7167	478	1215	615	9475

These examples were taken from the 2010 Commonwealth Games website (left) and the admin pages of my own blog (right). The markup for the two is remarkably similar—each gives a specific class to each <tr> element in the table.

```
<table>
  <tr class="odd">...
  <tr class="even">...
  <tr class="odd">...
  <tr class="even">...
  <tr class="odd">...
  <tr class="even">...
```

You could use `:nth-child(1)`, `:nth-child(2)`, `:nth-child(3)`, and so on to apply a style to each row in the table in order, but that would be as much work as adding a class to each row. Instead of specifying a number as the parameter to `:nth-child`, you can specify a pattern. Let's look at that next.

To select every second element, use the pattern 2n:

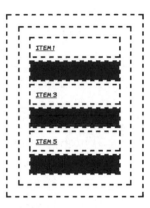

```
li:nth-child(2n) {
  background-color: #000;
}
```

If you imagine that all the elements are numbered in order, this selects all the `<li>` elements with a number that matches the pattern 2n for whole number values of n.

Selecting the odd-numbered children this way looks a little more complex but follows the same pattern:

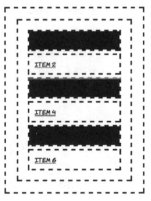

```
li:nth-child(2n-1) {
  background-color: #000;
}
```

The odd-and-even requirements are so common that there's a shortcut keyword for each. This creates a red-and-blue striped list:

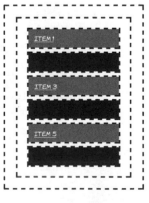

```
li:nth-child(odd) {
  background-color: #f00;
}
li:nth-child(even) {
  background-color: #006;
}
```

SELECTING FROM THE END BACKWARD

You don't have to select from the top
down. You can select from the bottom up
with :nth-last-child. It works in the same
way as :nth-child:

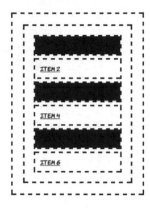

```
li:nth-last-child(2n) {
  background-color: #000;
}
```

The hypothetical values for n extend to
negative numbers, as can be seen if you
try this:

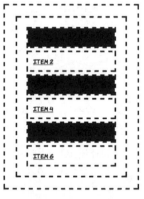

```
li:nth-last-child(2n+2) {
  background-color: #000;
}
```

You'll notice that 2n+2 has results identical
to 2n and to 2n-2.

But if n is negative, different rules apply.
Now n will count backwards from the
elements you see; if there are six elements
it will count six back. So adding a fixed
number to it will move the range of
selected elements so that it selects that
number of visible elements. This selector
will target just the first three elements:

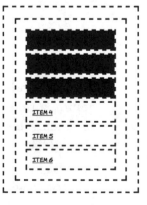

```
li:nth-child(-n+3) {
  background-color: #000;
}
```

The same trick works with `:nth-last-child` except, as with last child, the counting is from the end of the set of elements up. This selects just the last two odd-numbered items:

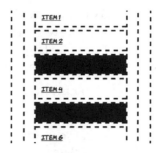

```
li:nth-last-child(-2n+4) {
    background-color: #000;
}
```

MORE COMPLEX SELECTION PATTERNS

If you increase the number in front of n, then the pattern extends over more elements. This rule selects the middle element out of each set of three:

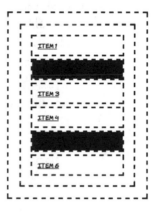

```
li:nth-last-child(3n-1) {
    background-color: #000;
}
```

Of course, this still targets only one element out of every three. You'd need an extra rule if you wanted a pattern *ABC* instead of *ABA*.

Now the answer to the mini-quiz AJ posed earlier. Here's the code again. The result is shown in the screenshot:

```
ul :last-child {
    background-color: #000;
}
```

Did you guess right? Without specifying that only `<li>` elements that were last children should be styled, the rule now selects any element that is a last child. The `<a>` elements are all the last child of their respective parent `<li>` elements.

You may be thinking to yourself that there are a few situations in which you would like to select elements that are both first and last child, like the links in this example. You can do this by combining the two pseudo-classes:

```
ul :first-child:last-child {
  background-color: #000;
}
```

This rule selects elements that are both a first and a last child and are descendants of the `<ul>` element. It's a bit of a mouthful, though, so fortunately there's an alternative pseudo-class that has the same effect:

```
ul :only-child {
  background-color: #000;
}
```

Browser support quick check: child selectors		:first-child	:last-child	:nth/:nth-last child/of type
		1.0	1.0	1.0
		1.0	1.0	3.5
		7.0	9.0	9.0
		7.0	9.5	10.10
		1.0	1.0	3.0

SELECTING BY TYPE OF ELEMENT

Sometimes, if the structure is likely to vary, the element you want to select isn't consistently the first or last (or second or third) child. Here each article has a picture, but it's located in a different place in each one:

```
<header>
  <h1>Header</h1>
</header>
<article>
  <h1>Article 1</h1>
  <img src="example.png">
  <p>Paragraph 1</p>
  <p>Paragraph 2</p>
</article>
<article>
  <h1>Article 2</h1>
  <p>Paragraph 1</p>
  <p>Paragraph 2</p>
  <img src="example.png">
</article>
<footer>
  Body footer
</footer>
```

How would you write a selector for the last paragraph of each article? Or could you select the first article? Let's try using `:first-child` and `:last-child`:

```
article:first-child {
  background-color: #000;
}
p:last-child {
  background-color: #000;
}
```

As the screenshot shows, these rules have no effect. The naive solution fails because neither <article> nor <p> is the first child of any container.

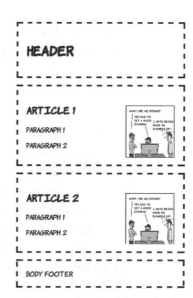

The first article is the second element on the page. You could select it with article:nth-child(2), but that would be a fairly fragile solution—it would break if someone decided to add an advertising banner between the header and the first article. Each article starts with an <h1>, but then one article leads with a picture, and the other leads with a paragraph. In this case, p:nth-child(2) would only select the last paragraph in the first article.

It's for situations exactly like these that we have the :first-of-type pseudo-class:

```
article:first-of-type {
  background-color: #000;
}
```

This selector will always apply to the first article element on the page, as well as any other first article elements further down the tree. Note that the image isn't transparent so you can't see the background behind it.

The last-of-type pseudo-class works in the same way, except in reverse:

```
p:last-of-type {
  background-color: #000;
}
```

If you don't want the last or the first, or you want to style according to a pattern, you can use :nth-first-of-type and :nth-last-of-type. This work in the same way as :nth-child except that the only elements that take part in the count are those specified by the simple selector to which you apply the pseudo-class.

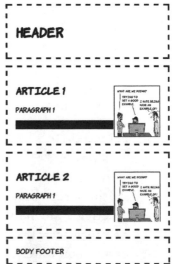

YOU NOW KNOW ALL THERE IS TO KNOW ABOUT CSS3 SELECTORS BASED ON THE STRUCTURE OF THE DOCUMENT, BUT THERE'S MORE TO CSS3 THAN THAT. IN THE NEXT SECTION YOU'LL LEARN ABOUT SELECTING ELEMENTS BASED ON THEIR ATTRIBUTES.

Choosing elements by their attributes

You should by now be aware that CSS provides convenient shorthand for selecting elements according to their class and ID. But class and ID are just two of many attributes that can be applied to HTML elements. Here are some common scenarios with another common attribute, the `href` on links.

• *Sketch of the Analytical Engine Invented by Charles Babbage, Esq. @ with notes by trans. Ada Lovelace, in Scientific Memoirs, Vol 3 (1842)*

29. ^ "PDF Referencem Sixth Edition, version 1.7, table 5.11" 📄.

Different styling for external links

Different styling for an element based on the URL

Different styling for file downloads

If you were using HTML4 and IE6-compatible CSS2, you'd probably implement these examples by adding an explicit class to the elements concerned:

```
<a
 class="external"
 href="http://site.com/
">
  Visit site
</a>
```

```
<a
 class="home"
 href="/home">
  Home
</a>
```

```
<a
 class="pdf"
 href="doc.pdf">
  Download document
</a>
```

In these examples, the `class` attribute is really just duplicating information available in the `href` attribute. Whenever there's duplicate information, there's an opportunity for the two sets of information to get out of sync. For example, what if the document in the third example changes

Browser support quick check: attribute selectors	[] =	^ $ * ~
	1.0	1.0
	1.0	2.0
	7.0	7.0
	7.0	9.0
	1.0	1.0

from a PDF to a Word document, so someone updates the link but forgets to update the class? The link would be styled as a PDF, but it would actually be a Word document. Wouldn't it be handy if there was some way you could select elements based on those other attributes rather than relying on classes and IDs?

CSS3 makes it possible to write selectors that target these elements based on the values in the href attribute; these are called *attribute selectors*. One excellent opportunity to use attribute selectors is microdata. Remember the sample hCard from chapter 2? Here's the listing again.

THE FOLLOWING EXAMPLE HAS BEEN CHOSEN BECAUSE IT PRESENTS LOTS OF SUITABLE ATTRIBUTES TO DEMONSTRATE STYLING. BUT, BECAUSE MICRODATA CAN ALSO BE REPRESENTED ENTIRELY ON INVISIBLE meta ELEMENTS, THIS ISN'T NECESSARILY A GOOD GENERAL-PURPOSE APPROACH FOR STYLING UNKNOWN MICRODATA MARKUP.

```
<section id="rob" itemscope
  itemtype="http://microformats.org/profile/hcard">
  <h1 itemprop="fn">Rob Crowther</h1>
  <p itemprop="n" itemscope>Full name:
    <span itemprop="given-name">Robert</span>
    <span itemprop="additional-name">John</span>
    <span itemprop="family-name">Crowther</span>
  </p>
  <p itemprop="org" itemscope>
    <span itemprop="organization-name">Manning Publications Co.</span>
    (<span itemprop="organization-unit">Hello! Series</span>)
  </p>
</section>
```

This is what it looks like with no styling applied. Although you could apply classes to various elements to attach styles, you can use the various item* attributes instead.

ROB CROWTHER

FULL NAME: ROBERT JOHN CROWTHER

MANNING PUBLICATIONS CO. (HELLO! SERIES)

The simplest attribute selector is called the *existence selector*:

```
[itemscope] {
  outline: 4px dashed black;
}
```

When you put the attribute name inside square brackets, the selector will match any element that has the attribute.

Attribute selectors can be appended to other simple selectors. To select only paragraphs that have an `itemscope` attribute, use this selector:

```
p[itemscope] {
  outline: 4px dashed black;
}
```

Although attribute existence can be useful occasionally, it's more likely you'll be interested in selecting between attributes with values. The syntax for this is intuitive:

```
[itemprop="org"] {
  outline: 4px dashed black;
}
```

Note that three elements have an `itemprop` attribute that begins with the letters *org*, but only the one that exactly matches has been selected. It's possible to select the elements whose attribute begins with *org*:

```
[itemprop^="org"] {
  outline: 4px dashed black;
  display: block;
}
```

Similarly, you can select all the elements whose `itemprop` attribute ends with a particular value:

```
[itemprop$="name"] {
  outline: 4px dashed black;
  display: block;
}
```

In the examples so far, the attribute value you're trying to match is a simple string, so quotes are optional. You could also write this selector as `[itemprop$=name]`. If the value you're matching contains characters other than letters and numbers, then the quotes are required.

ROB CROWTHER

FULL NAME:

> ROBERT

> JOHN

> CROWTHER

> MANNING PUBLICATIONS CO.

(HELLO! SERIES)

If the significant part of the attribute value is in the middle rather than at the start or the end, there's also an attribute selector for that:

```
[itemprop*="tion"] {
  outline: 4px dashed black;
  display: block;
}
```

This rule matches any element which has an `itemprop` property with a value which contains *tion* somewhere within it.

ROB CROWTHER

FULL NAME: ROBERT

> JOHN

CROWTHER

> MANNING PUBLICATIONS CO.

(

> HELLO! SERIES

)

YOU CAN NOW WRITE SELECTORS THAT MATCH ALL THREE EXAMPLES YOU SAW AT THE START OF THIS SECTION:

EXTERNAL LINKS: `a[href^="http://"]`

SPECIFIC URLS: `a[href="/home"]`

FILE DOWNLOADS: `a[href$=".pdf"]`

The traditional CSS ID selector can now be seen as syntactic sugar for the attribute selector. These two selectors are equivalent:

`#myid`   `[id="myid"]`

But the class selector is slightly more difficult. What attribute selector we've considered so far would be equivalent to `.myclass`? Let's consider some options.

Attribute selector	Matches	Doesn't match
`[class="myclass"]`	`class="myclass"`	`class="myclass otherclass"`
`[class^="myclass"]`	`class="myclass otherclass"`	`class="otherclass myclass"`
`[class*="myclass"]`	`class="otherclass myclass"` `class="notmyclass"`	

It's clear that there's a gap in our toolkit. Fortunately, CSS3 fills this hole: `[class~="myclass"]` selects an element with a whitespace-separated list of values, one of which is `myclass`.

Attribute selector	Matches	Doesn't match
`[class~="myclass"]`	`class="myclass"` `class="myclass otherclass"`	`class="notmyclass"`

Choosing what isn't

So far, we've concerned ourselves with positive identification. We've selected the elements that are the first child, and we've selected elements that have a particular attribute. But CSS3 also gives us the ability to select elements that aren't the first child or don't have particular attributes, with the `:not` pseudo-class. To understand how this might be useful, consider how you might lay out a form:

```
<label>Text:
  <input type="text">
</label>
<label>Range:
  <input type="range">
</label>
<label>Radio:
  <input type="radio">
</label>
<label>Checkbox:
  <input type="checkbox">
</label>
```

It looks a little disorganized, so let's add some styles to make things more consistent:

```
input {
  margin: 1em;
  display: block;
  width: 12em;
}
```

Clearly you want to apply different styles to input elements of type radio and checkbox. By selecting positively, you have two basic options: select everything and then override (following, left), or explicitly select only the items you want to style (following, right):

```
input {
  margin: 1em;
  display: block;
  width: 12em;
}
input[type=radio],
 input[type=checkbox] {
  display: inline;
  width: auto;
}
```

```
input { margin: 1em; }
input[type=text],
input[type=search],
input[type=tel],
input[type=url],
input[type=email],
input[type=password],
input[type=datetime],
input[type=date],
input[type=month],
input[type=week],
input[type=time],
input[type=datetime-local],
```

```
input[type=number],
input[type=range],
input[type=color],
input[type=file],
input[type=submit],
input[type=image],
input[type=reset],
input[type=button] {
  display: block;
  width: 12em;
}
```

The :not pseudo-class allows you to be more succinct than either of those two examples:

```
input { margin: 1em; }
input:not([type=checkbox]):not([
type=radio]) {
  display: block; width: 12em;
}
```

You can also combine :not with other selectors you've seen in this chapter. Going back to the :nth-child examples in the section "Selecting among a set of elements with pseudo-classes," this is how you select everything except the first two list items:

```
li:not(:nth-child(-n+2)) {
  background-color: #000;
}
```

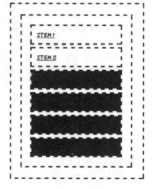

Pseudo-elements

Pseudo-elements are CSS selectors that allow you to style certain page elements as if an element existed in your markup. It sounds more complicated than it is, so let's dive into some examples. A common typographical feature, almost since the beginning of book publishing, is

Browser support quick check: pseudo-elements		:no	::first-letter/ ::first-line
		1.0	1.0
		3.0	3.0
		5.5.	5.5
		10.0	7.0
		1.0	1.0

to style the first line or first letter of a section differently than the following text. Following are some examples both from history and the present day.

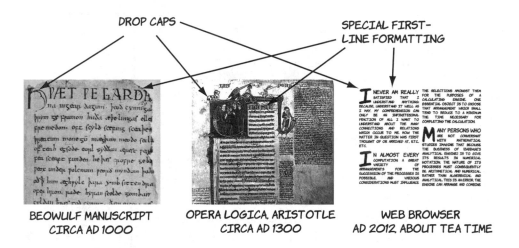

DROP CAPS

SPECIAL FIRST-LINE FORMATTING

BEOWULF MANUSCRIPT
CIRCA AD 1000

OPERA LOGICA, ARISTOTLE
CIRCA AD 1300

WEB BROWSER
AD 2012, ABOUT TEA TIME

In order to achieve similar effects, CSS3 has the ::first-line and ::first-letter pseudo-elements. To examine these, we need some suitably weighty prose to live up to our historical antecedents. I've chosen a selection of quotes from Ada Lovelace all marked up as paragraphs like this:

```
<p>I never am really satisfied that I
understand anything; because, understand
it well as I may, my comprehension can
only be an infinitesimal fraction of all
```

I NEVER AM REALLY SATISFIED THAT I UNDERSTAND ANYTHING; BECAUSE, UNDERSTAND IT WELL AS I MAY, MY COMPREHENSION CAN ONLY BE AN INFINITESIMAL FRACTION OF ALL I WANT TO UNDERSTAND ABOUT THE MANY CONNECTIONS AND RELATIONS WHICH OCCUR TO ME, HOW THE MATTER IN QUESTION WAS FIRST THOUGHT OF OR ARRIVED AT, ETC, ETC.

I want to understand about the many
connections and relations which occur to
me, how the matter in question was first
thought of or arrived at, etc., etc.</p>

If you want to style the first line differently, what do you do? One option is to insert elements to signify the first line:

```
<p><span class="first">I never am
really</span> satisfied that I
understand anything; because,
understand  it well as I may, my
comprehension can only be an
infinitesimal fraction of all I want
to understand about the many
connections and relations which
occur to me, how the matter in
question was first thought of or
arrived at, etc.</p>
```

I NEVER AM REALLY
SATISFIED THAT I UNDERSTAND ANYTHING; BECAUSE,
UNDERSTAND IT WELL AS I MAY, MY COMPREHENSION
CAN ONLY BE AN INFINITESIMAL FRACTION OF ALL I
WANT TO UNDERSTAND ABOUT THE MANY
CONNECTIONS AND RELATIONS WHICH OCCUR TO ME,
HOW THE MATTER IN QUESTION WAS FIRST
THOUGHT OF OR ARRIVED AT, ETC, ETC.

This looks OK in the example, but what if the user's screen is wider or narrower, or their font is larger, as in the following examples?

I NEVER AM REALLY SATISFIED THAT I
UNDERSTAND ANYTHING; BECAUSE, UNDERSTAND IT WELL AS I MAY, MY
COMPREHENSION CAN ONLY BE AN INFINITESIMAL FRACTION OF ALL I
WANT TO UNDERSTAND ABOUT THE MANY CONNECTIONS AND
RELATIONS WHICH OCCUR TO ME, HOW THE MATTER IN QUESTION
WAS FIRST THOUGHT OF OR ARRIVED AT, ETC, ETC.

**I NEVER AM
REALLY** SATISFIED THAT I
UNDERSTAND ANYTHING; BECAUSE,
UNDERSTAND IT WELL AS I MAY, MY
COMPREHENSION CAN ONLY BE AN
INFINITESIMAL FRACTION OF ALL I WANT
TO UNDERSTAND ABOUT THE MANY
CONNECTIONS AND RELATIONS WHICH
OCCUR TO ME, HOW THE MATTER IN
QUESTION WAS FIRST THOUGHT OF OR
ARRIVED AT, ETC, ETC.

Pseudo-elements vs. pseudo-classes

Pseudo-elements create virtual elements within your document, as opposed to pseudo-classes, which rely on properties of the document entered by the author. In CSS3, pseudo-elements are distinguished by a double colon (::) rather than the single colon of a pseudo-class. This differs from CSS2, where both used a single colon.

The `::first-line` pseudo-element puts the onus of calculating what constitutes the first line of text on the browser:

```
p::first-line {
  background-color: #000;
}
```

It applies styles as if there were an element wrapping all the text on the first line. But unlike a real element, you can't style children of the first line. The pseudo-element can only come as the last simple selector in a selector group.

The `::first-letter` pseudo-element is similar, except that it only selects the first letter:

```
p::first-letter {
  background-color: #000;
}
```

Although the background has been styled in this example because it stands out in the screenshots, it would be more common to use a decorative font for the first letter, or to increase its size.

████████████████████████
UNDERSTAND ANYTHING; BECAUSE, UNDERSTAND IT
WELL AS I MAY, MY COMPREHENSION CAN ONLY BE
AN INFINITESIMAL FRACTION OF ALL I WANT TO
UNDERSTAND ABOUT THE MANY CONNECTIONS AND
RELATIONS WHICH OCCUR TO ME. HOW THE
MATTER IN QUESTION WAS FIRST THOUGHT OF OR
ARRIVED AT, ETC, ETC.

████████████████████████
VARIETY OF ARRANGEMENTS FOR THE SUCCESSION
OF THE PROCESSES IS POSSIBLE, AND VARIOUS
CONSIDERATIONS MUST INFLUENCE THE
SELECTIONS AMONGST THEM FOR THE PURPOSES
OF A CALCULATING ENGINE. ONE ESSENTIAL
OBJECT IS TO CHOOSE THAT ARRANGEMENT
WHICH SHALL TEND TO REDUCE TO A MINIMUM THE
TIME NECESSARY FOR COMPLETING THE
CALCULATION.

█ NEVER AM REALLY SATISFIED THAT I
UNDERSTAND ANYTHING; BECAUSE, UNDERSTAND IT
WELL AS I MAY, MY COMPREHENSION CAN ONLY BE
AN INFINITESIMAL FRACTION OF ALL I WANT TO
UNDERSTAND ABOUT THE MANY CONNECTIONS AND
RELATIONS WHICH OCCUR TO ME. HOW THE
MATTER IN QUESTION WAS FIRST THOUGHT OF OR
ARRIVED AT, ETC, ETC.

█N ALMOST EVERY COMPUTATION A GREAT
VARIETY OF ARRANGEMENTS FOR THE SUCCESSION
OF THE PROCESSES IS POSSIBLE, AND VARIOUS
CONSIDERATIONS MUST INFLUENCE THE
SELECTIONS AMONGST THEM FOR THE PURPOSES
OF A CALCULATING ENGINE. ONE ESSENTIAL
OBJECT IS TO CHOOSE THAT ARRANGEMENT
WHICH SHALL TEND TO REDUCE TO A MINIMUM THE
TIME NECESSARY FOR COMPLETING THE
CALCULATION.

Using both `::first-line` and `::first-letter`, it's straightforward to create text that looks similar to the examples from the start of this section:

```
p {
  text-align:
justify;
  clear: left;
}
p::first-letter {
  font-size: 400%;
  float: left;
  line-height: 1em;
  padding-right:
0.1em;
}
p::first-line {
  font-size: 150%;
}
```

I NEVER AM REALLY SATISFIED THAT I UNDERSTAND ANYTHING; BECAUSE, UNDERSTAND IT WELL AS I MAY, MY COMPREHENSION CAN ONLY BE AN INFINITESIMAL FRACTION OF ALL I WANT TO UNDERSTAND ABOUT THE MANY CONNECTIONS AND RELATIONS WHICH OCCUR TO ME, HOW THE MATTER IN QUESTION WAS FIRST THOUGHT OF OR ARRIVED AT, ETC., ETC.

IN ALMOST EVERY COMPUTATION A GREAT VARIETY OF ARRANGEMENTS FOR THE SUCCESSION OF THE PROCESSES IS POSSIBLE, AND VARIOUS CONSIDERATIONS MUST INFLUENCE THE SELECTIONS AMONGST THEM FOR THE PURPOSES OF A CALCULATING ENGINE. ONE ESSENTIAL OBJECT IS TO CHOOSE THAT ARRANGEMENT WHICH SHALL TEND TO REDUCE TO A MINIMUM THE TIME NECESSARY FOR COMPLETING THE CALCULATION.

MANY PERSONS WHO ARE NOT CONVERSANT WITH MATHEMATICAL STUDIES IMAGINE THAT BECAUSE THE BUSINESS OF [BABBAGE'S ANALYTICAL ENGINE] IS TO GIVE ITS RESULTS IN NUMERICAL NOTATION, THE NATURE OF ITS PROCESSES MUST CONSEQUENTLY BE ARITHMETICAL AND NUMERICAL, RATHER THAN ALGEBRAICAL AND ANALYTICAL. THIS IS AN ERROR. THE ENGINE CAN ARRANGE AND COMBINE ITS NUMERICAL QUANTITIES EXACTLY AS IF THEY WERE LETTERS OR ANY OTHER GENERAL SYMBOLS; AND IN FACT IT MIGHT BRING OUT ITS RESULTS IN ALGEBRAICAL NOTATION, WERE PROVISIONS MADE ACCORDINGLY.

THE ANALYTICAL ENGINE HAS NO PRETENSIONS WHATEVER TO ORIGINATE ANYTHING. IT CAN DO WHATEVER WE KNOW HOW TO ORDER IT TO PERFORM. IT CAN FOLLOW ANALYSIS, BUT IT HAS NO POWER OF ANTICIPATING ANY ANALYTICAL REVELATIONS OR TRUTHS. ITS PROVINCE IS TO ASSIST US IN MAKING AVAILABLE WHAT WE ARE ALREADY ACQUAINTED WITH.

Choosing elements based on user interaction

Dynamic pseudo-classes allow you to assign different styles to elements based on user activity. One of the best known of these is the :hover pseudo-class, introduced in CSS2, which lets you apply a different style to an element when the mouse pointer is hovering over it (see appendix C for some examples). CSS3 adds several new dynamic pseudo-classes. In this section, you'll learn about styling form elements based on their properties. This will let you give cues to your users about the state of form elements—for example, whether they're required or whether they're currently valid. After that, you'll learn about the target selector that lets you style the page based on the current URL, which is useful for tabbed interfaces and slide shows.

Browser support quick check: dynamic pseudo-classes	Enabled/ disabled/ checked	Valid/ invalid/ required	Target
	1.0	10.0	1.0
	3.0	4.0	3.5
	9.0	10.0	9.0
	9.0	9.5	10.0
	3.0	5.0	3.0

Styling form elements based on state

YOU SAW SEVERAL OF CSS3'S NEW DYNAMIC PSEUDO-CLASSES FOR HTML5 FORMS IN CHAPTER 3 WHEN YOU LEARNED ABOUT HTML5 FORMS. IN THIS SECTION, YOU'LL SEE THE FULL SET IN ONE PLACE.

The first dynamic pseudo-classes we'll consider are :enabled and :disabled. Here are two text inputs, one of which is disabled:

```
<label>Enabled
  <input type="text">
</label>
<label>Disabled
  <input type="text" disabled>
</label>
```

Form elements are enabled by default, so this rule targets the first input:

```
input:enabled {
  outline: 4px solid #000;
}
```

Most browsers make it fairly obvious when a form control is disabled, but the pseudo-classes allow you to add additional styling:

```
input:disabled {
  outline: 4px solid #000;
}
```

If your form enables and disables controls dynamically based on user input, then :enabled and :disabled allow you to attach transitions to the changes between the two states; see chapter 9 for further details.

The :checked and :indeterminate pseudo-classes can only be applied to inputs of type checkbox:

```
<label>Not checked
  <input type="checkbox">
</label>
<label>Checked
  <input type="checkbox" checked>
</label>
```

As you might expect, :checked lets you style all checked check boxes:

```
input:checked {
  outline: 4px solid #000;
}
```

You might use this to replace the default check box with a graphic.

The indeterminate state has to be set by a script:

```
input:indeterminate {
  outline: 4px solid #000;
}
```

Note that :indeterminate is independent of :checked—both checked and unchecked check boxes can be in the indeterminate state.

You can also use CSS3 with the HTML5 form features, such as validity. Here are one valid and one invalid form field:

```
<label>Valid
  <input type="url"
    value="http://manning.com">
</label>
<label>Invalid
  <input type="url"
    value="Not a URL">
</label>
```

The pseudo-class for valid inputs is, unsurprisingly, :valid:

```
input:valid {
  outline: 4px solid #000;
}
```

And the corresponding pseudo-class is invalid:

```
input:invalid {
  outline: 4px solid #000;
}
```

It's also possible to style required inputs. Here are one required and one optional input (of course, inputs are optional by default):

```
<label>Required
  <input type="text" required>
</label>
<label>Optional
  <input type="text">
</label>
```

This is the CSS to select an input with the required attribute:

```
input:required {
  outline: 4px solid #000;
}
```

And this is the CSS to target just the optional input:

```
input:optional {
  outline: 4px solid #000;
}
```

Styling the page based on the target of the URL

Fragment identifiers — a string after a # symbol — are often used to identify sections within a long document, such as the table of contents at the top of a Wikipedia article. When the label in the fragment identifier matches an ID in the document, the browser scrolls the page down to where that element is displayed.

IN AJAX APPS, THE CURRENT STATE OF THE APPLICATION IS OFTEN
MAINTAINED THROUGH A FRAGMENT IDENTIFIER TO ALLOW EASY
BOOKMARKING, AS IN THE FOLLOWING GMAIL URL.

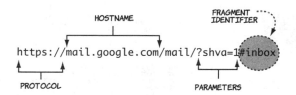

HOSTNAME

FRAGMENT
IDENTIFIER

`https://mail.google.com/mail/?shva=1#inbox`

PROTOCOL

PARAMETERS

If the URL has a fragment identifier, then the element with the ID matching it can be given special styling with the `:target` pseudo-class. This is useful for slideshows and tab-based interfaces.

This example uses four paragraphs, each of which has an `id` attribute:

```
<p id="one">I never am really satisfied
that...</p>
<p id="two">In almost every computation
a...</p>
<p id="three">Many persons who are not
conversant...</p>
<p id="four">The Analytical Engine has
no pretensions...</p>
```

This is what the page looks like if you load it into your browser with a bare URL:

```
http://host/target.html
```

I NEVER AM REALLY SATISFIED THAT I UNDERSTAND ANYTHING; BECAUSE, UNDERSTAND IT WELL AS I MAY, MY COMPREHENSION CAN ONLY BE AN INFINITESIMAL FRACTION OF ALL I WANT TO UNDERSTAND ABOUT THE MANY CONNECTIONS AND RELATIONS WHICH OCCUR TO ME, HOW THE MATTER IN QUESTION WAS FIRST THOUGHT OF OR ARRIVED AT, ETC., ETC.

IN ALMOST EVERY COMPUTATION A GREAT VARIETY OF ARRANGEMENTS FOR THE SUCCESSION OF THE PROCESSES IS POSSIBLE, AND VARIOUS CONSIDERATIONS MUST INFLUENCE THE SELECTIONS AMONGST THEM FOR THE PURPOSES OF A CALCULATING ENGINE. ONE ESSENTIAL OBJECT IS TO CHOOSE THAT ARRANGEMENT WHICH SHALL TEND TO REDUCE TO A MINIMUM THE TIME NECESSARY FOR COMPLETING THE CALCULATION.

MANY PERSONS WHO ARE NOT CONVERSANT WITH MATHEMATICAL STUDIES IMAGINE THAT BECAUSE THE BUSINESS OF [BABBAGE'S ANALYTICAL ENGINE] IS TO GIVE ITS RESULTS IN NUMERICAL NOTATION THE NATURE OF ITS PROCESSES MUST CONSEQUENTLY BE ARITHMETICAL AND NUMERICAL, RATHER THAN ALGEBRAICAL AND ANALYTICAL. THIS IS AN ERROR. THE ENGINE CAN ARRANGE AND COMBINE ITS NUMERICAL QUANTITIES EXACTLY AS IF THEY WERE LETTERS OR ANY OTHER GENERAL SYMBOLS; AND IN FACT IT MIGHT BRING OUT ITS RESULTS IN ALGEBRAICAL NOTATION, WERE PROVISIONS MADE ACCORDINGLY.

THE ANALYTICAL ENGINE HAS NO PRETENSIONS WHATEVER TO ORIGINATE ANYTHING. IT CAN DO WHATEVER WE KNOW HOW TO ORDER IT TO PERFORM. IT CAN FOLLOW ANALYSIS, BUT IT HAS NO POWER OF ANTICIPATING ANY ANALYTICAL REVELATIONS OR TRUTHS. ITS PROVINCE IS TO ASSIST US IN MAKING AVAILABLE WHAT WE ARE ALREADY ACQUAINTED WITH.

This CSS selector says, "Add a black background to the paragraph elements that are the target":

```
p:target { background: #000; }
```

Now, if the URL is adjusted to contain a fragment identifier, the `p:target` rule is triggered. The following screenshots show the same page with two different fragment identifiers appended to the URL. When the fragment is #one, the element with `id` value one matches the `p:target` rule and has a black background.

http://host/target.html#one

http://host/target.html#three

CHANGING THE FRAGMENT IDENTIFIER DOESN'T RELOAD THE PAGE, SO THE `:target` PSEUDO-CLASS MAKES IT EASY TO CREATE TABBED INTERFACES LIKE THAT IN THE NEXT EXAMPLE.

You can adjust the CSS from the previous example so the paragraphs are hidden by default but visible when they're the target:

```
p { display: none; }
p:target { display: block; }
```

Add a simple menu:

SHOW ONE SHOW TWO SHOW THREE SHOW FOUR

```
<menu>
    <a href="#one">Show one</a>
    <a href="#two">Show two</a>
    <a href="#three">Show three</a>
    <a href="#four">Show four</a>
</menu>
```

Initially all the tabs are hidden, so all you see is the menu and an empty space.

Clicking the Show Two link changes the URL to http://host/target.html#two. Now #two is the target. Thanks to the target selector, the element with `id` value two becomes `display: block` instead of `display: none`.

SHOW ONE SHOW TWO SHOW THREE SHOW FOUR

IN ALMOST EVERY COMPUTATION A GREAT VARIETY OF ARRANGEMENTS FOR THE SUCCESSION OF THE PROCESSES IS POSSIBLE, AND VARIOUS CONSIDERATIONS MUST INFLUENCE THE SELECTIONS AMONGST THEM FOR THE PURPOSES OF A CALCULATING ENGINE. ONE ESSENTIAL OBJECT IS TO CHOOSE THAT ARRANGEMENT WHICH SHALL TEND TO REDUCE TO A MINIMUM THE TIME NECESSARY FOR COMPLETING THE CALCULATION.

Clicking Show Four changes the target again: the element with an `id` value of four becomes visible.

SHOW ONE SHOW TWO SHOW THREE SHOW FOUR

THE ANALYTICAL ENGINE HAS NO PRETENSIONS WHATEVER TO ORIGINATE ANYTHING. IT CAN DO WHATEVER WE KNOW HOW TO ORDER IT TO PERFORM. IT CAN FOLLOW ANALYSIS, BUT IT HAS NO POWER OF ANTICIPATING ANY ANALYTICAL REVELATIONS OR TRUTHS. ITS PROVINCE IS TO ASSIST US IN MAKING AVAILABLE WHAT WE ARE ALREADY ACQUAINTED WITH.

NOW THAT YOU'VE SEEN ALL THE NEW FEATURES, LET'S CHECK OUT WHAT BROWSER SUPPORT THEY HAVE. YOU MAY BE PLEASANTLY SURPRISED.

Browser support

Browser support for CSS3 selectors is excellent across modern browsers. The main issue in browser support is the large numbers of people still using obsolete versions of Internet Explorer. As you'll see, it's easy to add support for these old browsers using jQuery.

	Chrome		Firefox		IE			Opera		Safari	
	12	14	4	6	8	9	10	11.1	11.5	5	5.1
Adjacent sibling	●	●	●	●	○	●	●	●	●	●	●
General sibling	●	●	●	●		●	●	●	●	●	●
First/last child	●	●	●	●		●	●	●	●	●	●
nth/last child	●	●	●	●		○	○	●	●	●	●
Only child	●	●	●	●			○	●	●	●	●
Of type	●	●	●	●		○	○	●	●	●	●
Attribute	●	●	●	●	●	●	●	●	●	●	●
=	●	●	●	●	●	●	●	●	●	●	●
^=	●	●	●	●	●	●	●	●	●	●	●
*=	●	●	●	●	●	●	●	●	●	●	●
$=	●	●	●	●	●	●	●	●	●	●	●
~=	●	●	●	●	●	●	●	●	●	●	●
Not	●	●	●	●		●	●	●	●	●	●
First letter	●	●	●	●	●	●	●	●	●	●	●
First line	●	●	●	●	●	●	●	●	●	●	●
Dis-/enabled	●	●	●	●			●	●	●	●	●
In-/valid	●	●	●	●			●	●	●	●	●
Checked	●	●	●	●	●	●	●	●	●	●	●
Indeterminate	●	●	●	●	●	●	●	●	●	●	●
Optional/required	●	●	●	●			●	●	●	●	●
Target	●	●	●	●		●	●	●	●	●	●

Key:
- ● Complete or nearly complete support
- ○ Incomplete or alternative support
  Little or no support

Using jQuery to support older browsers

The jQuery JavaScript library uses CSS selectors as a key part of its normal operation. In order for this to work cross-browser, the authors of jQuery had to implement CSS selectors in JavaScript. This is handy if you want to use the latest CSS features but still present more limited older browsers with your intended design.

Here's a CSS selector that doesn't work in IE8 and older:

```
tbody tr:nth-child(2n+1) {
    background: #999;
}
```

The screenshot shows that in IE8, the odd rows don't have the gray background that the rule specifies.

ONE	TWO	THREE	FOUR	FIVE
1	2	3	4	5
1	2	3	4	5
1	2	3	4	5
1	2	3	4	5
1	2	3	4	5
1	2	3	4	5

To add IE8 support without messing up your markup, you can add some jQuery. Start by adding the library itself:

```
<script src="jquery-1.5.2.min.js">
</script>
```

In an IE-only code block, use the jQuery selector engine to match the nodes using the same selector, and add a class to them:

```
<!--[if lte IE 8]>
<script>
$(document).ready(
  function() {
    $('tbody tr:nth-child(2n+1)')
      .addClass('odd');
  }
)
</script>
<style>
tr.odd { background: #999; }
</style>
<![endif]-->
```

ONE	TWO	THREE	FOUR	FIVE
1	2	3	4	5
1	2	3	4	5
1	2	3	4	5
1	2	3	4	5
1	2	3	4	5
1	2	3	4	5

All that's now required is to replicate the style elements with that class. In most cases, you can add the selector to your original rule. But the nth-child syntax will cause IE8 to treat the whole rule as invalid, so the style rule also has to be replicated.

USING JQUERY TO SUPPORT OLDER BROWSERS IS A HANDY WORKAROUND IF THERE ARE SOME CSS3 STYLES THAT ABSOLUTELY MUST BE APPLIED. IN LATER CHAPTERS, YOU'LL SEE OTHER JAVASCRIPT LIBRARIES THAT CAN ENABLE CSS3 FEATURES IN OLDER BROWSERS. THESE CAN BE MASSIVE TIME-SAVERS. BUT REMEMBER, THEY DO COME AT A COST—IF YOU RELY ON THEM HEAVILY, THEY CAN SIGNIFICANTLY INCREASE YOUR PAGE-LOADING TIMES.

Summary

In this chapter, you've learned about many new features available in CSS3 for selecting elements: combinators for selecting elements based on relationships with their parents; pseudo-classes for selecting elements based on their relationships with their siblings; attribute selectors that reduce your dependence on class and id attributes; and dynamic pseudo-classes for giving immediate feedback to users on the state of form elements. It's been a lot to get through, but these features make up the foundation on which all the rest of CSS is built.

AFTER YOU'VE PICKED OUT ELEMENTS WITH SELECTORS, PSEUDO-CLASSES, AND ATTRIBUTE SELECTORS, YOU'LL WANT TO APPLY STYLES TO THEM. CSS3 OFFERS MANY NEW OPTIONS IN THAT DEPARTMENT, AND IN THE REST OF THE BOOK YOU'LL LEARN ABOUT THEM. WE'LL START IN THE NEXT CHAPTER WITH THE NEW OPTIONS FOR LAYOUT.

8

Layout with CSS3

This chapter covers

- inline-block *and table display values from CSS2*
- calc *and* box-sizing *properties that make CSS2 layout more manageable*
- *Media queries to give different CSS to different devices*
- *New CSS3 layout modules: templates, grids, and regions*

Many people have complained over the years about the poor tools available for layout in CSS. This isn't an unwarranted criticism, because CSS1 had almost no layout tools. No one anticipated that people would start to do graphic design with web pages until it happened. Several options were added in CSS2, most of which didn't see broad browser support until the release of IE8 in 2009. Given that it's taken so long for CSS2 layout to be supported, support for CSS3 layout modules got off to a slow start; but recently there's been a lot of activity. This chapter covers both the old features of CSS2 that haven't seen much use and the new features in CSS3 that browsers are just starting to support.

> **An HTML5 contribution to tables for layout**
>
> The W3C HTML working group has acknowledged the incredible persistence of the layout table and, thanks to HTML5 and ARIA, has recommended a method for indicating that a particular table is semantically meaningless (that it's just for layout):
>
> ```
> <table role="presentation">
> ```
>
> This doesn't mean you should ignore all the best practice advice and convert your CSS layouts to tables, but it does mean you can easily make old pages more accessible without a major rewrite. See www.w3.org/html/wg/tracker/issues/130 for further details.

Underused CSS2 layout features

CSS2 had several new features for layout—`inline-block` and `table`, `table-row`, and `table-cell` values for the `display` property—but they've seen little use in real websites because of the lack of support for them in the most popular browser of all time (in terms of market share), IE6. In this section, we'll review these underused features of CSS2.

Placing elements on a line with inline-block

`inline-block` is a compromise between `<block>` elements and `<inline>` elements. A `<block>` element can have a defined width, height, padding, and margin and causes a break in the text. An `<inline>` element sits on the line of text but can't have a width, height, padding, or margin. An `inline-block` element combines features of both—it sits on the line of text, but it can be given a specific width, height, padding, and margin.

This simple markup will be used to demonstrate layout with `inline block`. If you check the code download for this chapter, you'll find an example layout done with floats, a method familiar to anyone who's done any CSS layouts in the last ten years. Achieving a similar layout with `inline-block` requires that you set the widths of the `<section>` and `<aside>` elements appropriately:

```
<header>
  <h1>Heading</h1>
</header>
<section>
  <p>I never am...</p>
</section>
<aside>Side bar</aside>
<footer>Footer</footer>
```

```
header, section, aside, footer {
    margin: 2%;
    padding: 2%;
    outline: 4px dashed black;
    vertical-align: top;
}
section, aside {
    display: inline-block;
    width: 54.5%;
}
aside {
    margin-right: 0;
    width: 28.5%;
}
```

Browser support quick check: inline-block		Full	Partial
	(Chrome)	1.0	-
	(Firefox)	3.0	2.0
	(Internet Explorer)	8.0	6.0
	(Opera)	9.0	-
	(Safari)	3.1	-

inline-block solves several issues that afflict floats. The first benefit of inline-block over floats is that the elements aren't removed from the normal document flow. This means that in a basic two-column layout, it doesn't matter which of the columns is the longest. Any full-width element will automatically be pushed below both columns—no clearing is required.

`inline-block` also makes the behavior of grids of items more consistent when there are elements of different sizes. Elements that are `inline-block` are aligned with the normal character grid, just like lines of text on a page. In this screenshot, you can see that the oversize element forces the entire next line down.

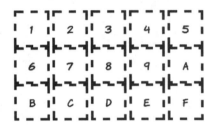

Being aligned with the normal character grid does present other issues. Spacing is no longer entirely controlled by margins. This code is from ch08/layout-inline-4.html:

```css
div {
    margin: 0;
    border: 4px dashed black;
    display: inline-block;
}
```

You can see that despite the margin being set to 0, there's still a gap between the elements on each row.

This gap is due to letter and word spacing. Elements that are `inline-block` behave as if they're letters or words. Setting negative spacing removes the gap, as in ch08/layout-inline-4a.html:

```css
body {
    letter-spacing: -0.4em;
    word-spacing: -0.4em;
}
```

Other text properties also affect `inline-block` elements — baseline alignment sometimes causes unexpected spaces to appear between rows of elements.

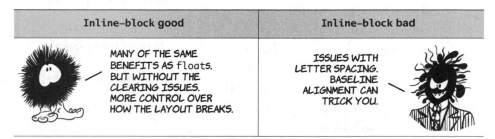

Inline–block good	Inline–block bad
MANY OF THE SAME BENEFITS AS floats, BUT WITHOUT THE CLEARING ISSUES. MORE CONTROL OVER HOW THE LAYOUT BREAKS.	ISSUES WITH LETTER SPACING. BASELINE ALIGNMENT CAN TRICK YOU.

Grouping element dimensions with display: table

One question you might well ask yourself: if browsers use CSS for their layout, what CSS do they use to lay out tables? The simple answer is that there's a special CSS display mode for `table`, as well as display modes for `table-row` and `table-cell`. All of these display modes can be applied to nontabular elements.

Here's a simple layout created with `display: table`. The following markup is taken from ch08/layout-table-1.html. It's based on the listing in ch08/layout-table-1-actualtable.html, which implements the same layout using an HTML table. If you've never done a layout with a table before, please check out that listing because there's no room to show it here:

```
<header>
  <h1>Heading</h1>
  <figure>
    <img src="dust-puppy.svg">
  </figure>
</header>
<div>
  <section>
    <p>I never am ...</p>
  </section>
  <aside>Side bar</aside>
</div>
<footer>
  <nav>
    <a href="/l1">Link 1</a>
    <a href="/l2">Link 2</a>
    </nav>
  <small>Footer credits</small>
</footer>
```

This listing was created by replacing each td, tr, and table element in the original table layout with more semantic container elements. The direct replacement means you have suitable elements to attach the table-row and table-cell styles to and, because this is a simple document, you can set body to be display: table rather than add an explicit wrapper in place of the table element.

```css
body {
  display: table;
  border-collapse: separate;
  border-spacing: 1em;
}
header, div, footer {
  display: table-row;
}
section, aside, figure, h1, nav,
 small {
  display: table-cell;
}
img { max-width: 100px; }
```

Browser support quick check: display: table		Full	Partial
		1.0	-
		2.0	-
		8.0	-
		9.0	-
		3.1	-

USER FRIENDLY by J.D. "Illiad" Frazer

SO WHAT BENEFITS DO WE GAIN WITH THIS DISPLAY: TABLE OVER JUST USING A LAYOUT TABLE?

NOW THE MARKUP MORE CORRECTLY DESCRIBES OUR CONTENT AND OUR LAYOUT IS WHERE IT BELONGS, IN THE STYLESHEET.

SO, JUST A WARM, SATISFIED FEELING INSIDE?

I CAN UNPLUG YOU, YOU KNOW.

The naive approach to using display: table might look something like this. You have classes for every element of the table hierarchy. The following images show this applied to two different markup fragments. (See the full listing in ch08/layout-table-4.html.)

```css
.grid {
    display: table;
    border-collapse: separate;
    border-spacing: 1em;
}
.row {
    display: table-row;
}
.cell {
    display: table-cell;
    width: 25%;
}
```

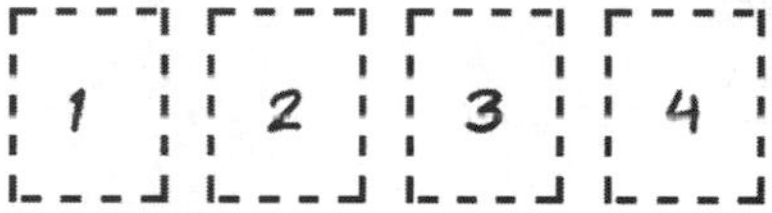

```html
<div class="grid">
  <div class="row">
    <div class="cell">1</div>
    <div class="cell">2</div>
    <div class="cell">3</div>
    <div class="cell">4</div>
  </div>
</div>
```

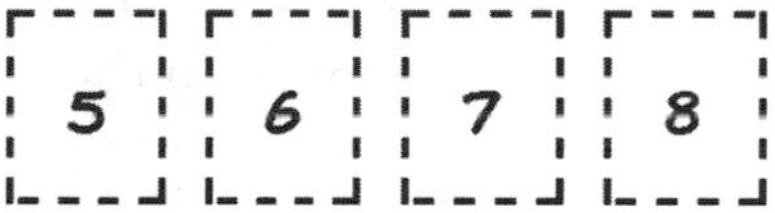

```html
<div class="grid">
  <div class="cell">5</div>
  <div class="cell">6</div>
  <div class="cell">7</div>
  <div class="cell">8</div>
</div>
```

There's no difference in rendering between the two versions of the code. This is because the browser inserts an *anonymous table object* in place of the missing table row. You can see more clearly how it works if you look at an example that doesn't work in your favor. The next listing is from ch08/layout-table-2.html; markup is on the left and CSS is on the right:

```html
<body>
    <header>
        <h1>Heading</h1>
    </header>
    <div>
        <article>...</article>
        <aside>...</aside>
    </div>
    <footer>Footer</footer>
</body>
```

```css
body {
    display: table;
}
header, footer, div {
    display: table-row;
}
article, aside {
    display: table-cell;
}
```

For this code, you might expect the header to extend across the entire width of the page because it's set to be `display: table-row`. But what actually happens is shown at right. Because there are no elements in the row with `display: table-cell`, `header` is promoted to that role, and an anonymous table object assumes the role of the table row. The result is that the header and footer both have the same width as the first `table-cell` element in the middle row.

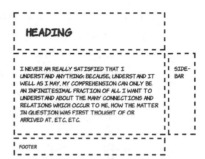

display: **table** good	display: **table** bad
 LIKE TABLES, ELEMENTS' VISUAL PROPERTIES ARE RELATED SO A SET OF ELEMENTS IN A ROW ALL SHARE THE SAME HEIGHT.	ABSOLUTE RESPONSIBILITY FOR LAYOUT. SOME OF THE SAME PERFORMANCE ISSUES AS TABLES. 

YOU NOW HAVE A GRASP OF WHAT CSS2 HAS TO OFFER IN TERMS OF LAYOUT. THE GOOD NEWS IS, SINCE THE LAUNCH OF IE8 IN MARCH 2009, EVERY MAJOR BROWSER SUPPORTS ALL THESE APPROACHES. IN THE NEXT SECTION, YOU'LL LEARN ABOUT TWO SMALL BUT USEFUL IMPROVEMENTS THAT CSS3 OFFERS FOR CSS2-COMPATIBLE LAYOUTS.

CSS3 improvements to CSS2 approaches

One of the major pain points that arise with the CSS layout approaches mentioned in the previous sections is the control of combined width, particularly when mixing percentage and pixel units as you saw with `inline-block`. CSS3 offers two new features that alleviate this pain:

- A `calc()` function
- The `box-sizing` property

The `calc` function allows the construction of widths from multiple units: for example, 25% — 4px. This is useful if several elements need to fit exactly in a percentage width, but each needs to have a border or margin of a certain number of pixels. `box-sizing` gives the web author control over the problematic CSS box model. Both are covered in more detail in this section.

Mixing different length units with calc

Many of the issues with using `floats` or `inline-block` for layout are due to the basic incompatibility of different length measurements — how many pixels to a percentage point, or how an em varies due to factors beyond your control such as window size and font rendering. Following is the example layout from the previous discussion of `inline-block`. Earlier, all the widths were specified in percentage values, but now there's a mixture of percentages, pixels, and ems:

```
body {
    width: 90%;
    margin: 0 5%;
    font-family:
       "Komika Hand", sans-serif;
}
header, section, aside, footer {
    margin: 1em;
    padding: 1em;
    outline: 4px dashed black;
    vertical-align: top;
}
section, aside {
    display: inline-block;
```

HEADING

I NEVER AM REALLY SATISFIED THAT I UNDERSTAND ANYTHING; BECAUSE, UNDERSTAND IT WELL AS I MAY, MY COMPREHENSION CAN ONLY BE AN INFINITESIMAL FRACTION OF ALL I WANT TO UNDERSTAND ABOUT THE MANY CONNECTIONS AND RELATIONS WHICH OCCUR TO ME, HOW THE MATTER IN QUESTION WAS FIRST THOUGHT OF OR ARRIVED AT, ETC, ETC.

SIDEBAR

FOOTER

```
    width: 54%;
}
aside {
    margin-right: 0;
    width: 25%;
}
```

You can see that the sidebar is poking out to the right of the header and the footer. The problem is worse than it appears because how much the sidebar pokes out depends on many factors. The following screenshots show the alignment of the sidebar with the footer at various browser window sizes (the gray bar has been added so you can more easily see the variation, and the sidebar and footer are shown next to each other for convenience).

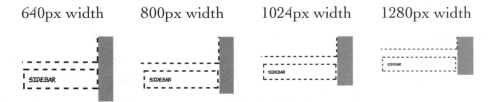

These issues are bound to occur when combining CSS lengths of different types. The number of pixels taken up by an em or a percentage will vary depending on font size and window size. On the other hand, it's rare that you'll want something like a border to be a different width depending on the width of the browser window. CSS3 provides the `calc` function to allow you to combine different units in a predictable way.

Take the earlier example CSS and, assuming everything else remains the same, you can change the widths to the following:

```
section, aside {
    width: calc(70% - 4.665em);
}
aside {
    width: calc(30% - 3.665em);
}
```

This produces a more reliable layout. And, as the following screenshots show, everything stays the same width at different screen widths.

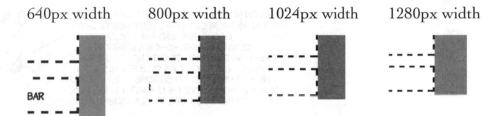

640px width   800px width   1024px width   1280px width

As always with `inline-block`, there's the issue of letter spacing. A certain amount of trial and error was involved in arriving at those 4.665em and 3.665em lengths. A more straightforward approach is to remove the letter spacing as a factor by setting it to a negative value.

```
body {
    letter-spacing: -0.5em;
}
header, section, article, aside,
footer {
    letter-spacing: normal;
}
section, aside {
    width: calc(70% - 4em);
}
aside {
    width: calc(30% - 4em);
}
```

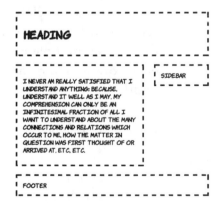

The negative letter spacing on the body allows saner width calculations, but then the letter spacing needs to be explicitly set on the child elements.

		Full	Partial
Browser support quick check: calc		-	19
		-	4.0
		9.0	-
		-	-
		-	5.2

EVEN WITH calc, IT'S DIFFICULT TO GET THINGS PERFECT FOR EVERY WIDTH WHEN USING PERCENTAGES BECAUSE OF ROUNDING ERRORS—ON A WINDOW 640 PIXELS WIDE, A BOX OF 30% WIDTH IN THIS LAYOUT WORKS OUT AS 172.8 PIXELS WIDE. THE BROWSER HAS TO CHOOSE WHETHER TO RENDER THAT AS 172 OR 173 ACTUAL PIXELS, AND YOU HAVE TO HOPE IT ALL WORKS OUT.

There's more to calc than simple addition and subtraction. calc makes it straightforward to do things that are hard with any other approach. Imagine that you have a set of elements of different widths that you want to display on multiple rows, but each row should be an identical width.

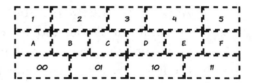

Here's the CSS to generate this screenshot:

```
div {
    float: left;
    margin: 0;
    padding: 1em 0;
    border: 4px dashed black;
}
.half_third {
    width: calc(50%/3 - 8px);
}
.half_half {
    width: calc(50%/2 - 8px);
```

```
}
.sixth {
    width: calc(100%/6 - 8px);
}
.quarters {
    width: calc(100%/4 - 8px);
}
```

And here's the HTML—assume it fits in a standard HTML5 document;
see ch08/calc-3.html for the full listing:

```
<div class="half_third">1</div>
<div class="half_half">2</div>
<div class="half_third">3</div>
<div class="half_half">4</div>
<div class="half_third">5</div>
<div class="sixth">A</div>
<div class="sixth">B</div>
<div class="sixth">C</div>
<div class="sixth">D</div>
<div class="sixth">E</div>
<div class="sixth">F</div>
<div class="quarters">00</div>
<div class="quarters">01</div>
<div class="quarters">10</div>
<div class="quarters">11</div>
```

Because table cells in a column share a width, this is extremely difficult
to do with a single table. And because of rounding errors, it can be difficult with any other approach unless you choose carefully for the overall width.

calc good	calc bad
ALLOWS PRECISE CONTROL OF LENGTHS SPECIFIED IN ANY COMBINATION	REQUIRES AN UNDERSTANDING OF HOW PADDING, MARGIN, AND BORDER COMBINE

USER FRIENDLY by J.D. "Illiad" Frazer

Controlling the box model

One of the more difficult aspects of layout in the late 1990s was the incompatible implementation of the CSS box model. Some browsers behaved as if the width and the height included the border, whereas the specification excluded the border and padding from width and height calculations.

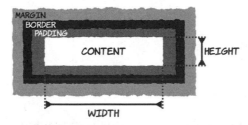

box-sizing: content-box;

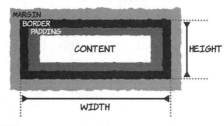

box-sizing: border-box;

Browser support quick check: box-sizing		Full	Partial
		10.0	1.0
		-	2.0
		8.0	-
		9.5	-
		5.1	3.1

IN SPITE OF IT BEING NONSTANDARD, MANY PEOPLE FELT THAT THE METHOD OF CALCULATING WIDTH THAT INCLUDED THE BORDER WAS MORE INTUITIVE. SO IN CSS3 YOU CAN SPECIFY THE SIZING CALCULATION YOU WANT WITH THE box-sizing PROPERTY. THE TWO ALTERNATIVES ARE SHOWN NEXT.

This CSS creates two boxes that are exactly the same size visually, despite differing in width and height by 50 pixels:

```
#one {
    box-sizing: content-box;
    width: 150px;
    height: 150px;
    border: 25px solid black;
}
#two {
    box-sizing: border-box;
    width: 200px;
    height: 200px;
    border: 25px solid black;
}
```

The markup required is

```
<div id="one"></div>
<div id="two"></div>
```

This feature isn't as obviously useful now that you have calc, but it might save you some effort if you want a set of elements to have the same size but different-width borders.

YOU'VE NOW LEARNED ABOUT ALL THE CURRENTLY VIABLE TECHNIQUES FOR LAYOUT WITH CSS. BUT EVEN WITH ALL THESE TOOLS, IT'S A CHALLENGE TO DESIGN A SINGLE LAYOUT THAT WORKS WELL ON POWERFUL DESKTOP PCS, PORTABLE TABLETS, AND MOBILE PHONES. MEDIA QUERIES ALLOW YOU TO TAILOR YOUR LAYOUTS TO THE CAPABILITIES OF THE DEVICE, AS YOU'LL LEARN IN THE NEXT SECTION.

Using media queries for flexible layout

CSS has long had the ability to apply different styles based on the output device, whether it's a PC screen, a handheld device, or a printer. For instance, a print stylesheet can be applied to an HTML document in several ways.

Linking from HTML	`<link rel="stylesheet" media="print" href="print.css">`
Embedding in HTML	`<style media="print"></style>`
Inline in CSS	`@media print { }`

Browser support quick check: CSS3 media queries		Full	Partial
		2.0	-
		3.5	-
		9.0	-
		9.5	-
		4.0	3.1

These are known as *media queries*. All three of the previous examples are constraining the styles they reference or include to only apply to print media. In CSS2 you could also restrict to screen, aural, braille, handheld, or speech, among others. The default, if you don't specify anything, is all—the styles will apply no matter what the output device is.

USER FRIENDLY by J.D. "Illiad" Frazer

Mobile browser support

CSS3 media queries are especially important for mobile browsers. All the current major smartphone browsers have support: the iOS and Android standard browsers; mobile Opera and Firefox; and IE in Windows Mobile 7.5.

Media queries avoid browser detection by letting the browser itself determine what support it has. If a new browser or device comes along that you hadn't anticipated, as long as you've used media queries, it should still select the most appropriate set of CSS rules. CSS3 dramatically extends the number of properties that can be used in media queries. In the following sections, you'll see some practical examples of media queries in use.

Resolution detection

The most common distinguishing features of different devices are screen resolution and window size. Most desktop users have a browser window at least 800 pixels wide, whereas most mobile browsers are less than 800 pixels wide. Media queries let you choose between the two situations. The basic syntax for creating a set of rules for a window 800 pixels wide is this:

```
@media screen and (max-width: 800px) { }
@media screen and (max-device-width: 800px) { }
```

Any CSS rules placed inside the squiggly brackets will only be applied if the conditions are met. The first rule selects based on the browser window size, and the second one selects based on display size—the browser window doesn't have to fill the entire width of the display for this rule to match. In this section, you'll create a layout that adapts to the size of the browser window. Here's what the layout looks like in a window 1024 pixels wide.

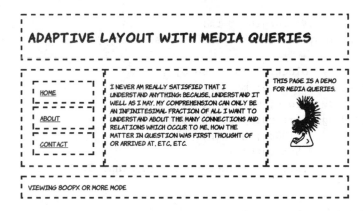

Here's the key markup (see the full listing in ch08/media-queries-adaptive.html):

```
<header>
    <h1>Adaptive Layout with Media Queries</h1>
</header>
<div>
    <nav>
        <ul>
```

```
            <li><a href="#">Home</a></li>
            <li><a href="#">About</a></li>
            <li><a href="#">contact</a></li>
        </ul>
    </nav>
    <article>
        <p>I never am really satisfied...</p>
    </article>
    <aside>
        This page is a demo for media queries.
        <img src="dust-puppy.svg">
    </aside>
</div>
<footer>
    <span id="msg480">Viewing 480px or less mode</span>
    <span id="msg800">Viewing 800px or less mode</span>
    <span id="msg801">Viewing 800px or more mode</span>
</footer>
```

The default three-column layout is for windows greater than 800 pixels wide:

```
body        { width: 90%; margin: 0 5%;
                font-family: "Komika Hand", sans-serif; }
header,
 footer    { display: block;  width: auto; }
nav ul     { list-style: none; margin: 0; padding: 0; }
nav a      { display: block; margin: 1em;
                padding: 1em; outline: 4px dashed black; }
img        { max-width: 100px; display: block;
                margin: 0.5em auto; }
div        { display: table; outline: none;  padding: 0; }
nav,
 article,
 aside     { display: table-cell; }
nav,
 aside     { width: 25%; }
article    { width: 50%; }
#msg480,
 #msg800 { display: none; }
```

If viewed in a window 800 pixels wide or narrower, the page switches to a two-column layout.

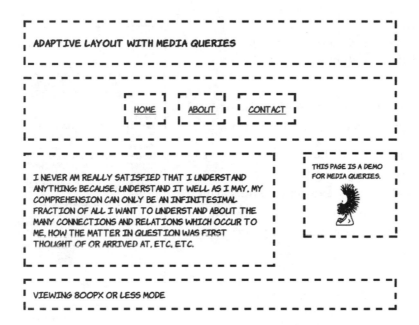

This layout is implemented with two sets of rules within media queries. The first provides a set of rules to be applied for any width less than 800 pixels, and the second is a set of rules that's applied only when the window is between 481 and 800 pixels wide. This approach saves repeating rules:

```
@media screen and (max-width: 800px) {
    div     { display: block; overflow: hidden; margin: 0; }
    nav     { display: block; width: auto; }
    nav ul  { display: table; border-collapse: collapse;
                margin: 0 auto; }
    nav li  { display: table-cell; }
}

@media screen and (max-width: 800px) and (min-width: 481px) {
    h1      { font-size: 110%; }
    article,
     aside  { display: block; }
    article { width: 60%; float: left; margin-right: 0; }
    aside   { width: 20%; font-size: 80%; float: right;
                margin: 1.2em; margin-left: 0; }
    img     { max-width: 60px; }
```

```
#msg480,
 #msg801 { display: none; }
 #msg800 { display: inherit; }
}
```

Finally, at a width of 480 pixels or less, the layout becomes single column.

The majority of the required rules for this layout were specified in the less-than-800 pixels example. These rules mostly adjust the size of elements to allow more content to appear on a mobile screen:

```
@media screen and (max-width: 480px) {
  h1      { font-size: 105%; }
  nav     { padding: 0; }
  nav a   { margin: 0; padding:
  0.25em 0.5em; }
  article,
   aside  { display: block; width: auto; }
  #msg800,
   #msg801 { display: none; }
  #msg480 { display: inherit; }
}
```

Following are screenshots of the same page on an Android phone in portrait mode (left) and landscape mode (right).

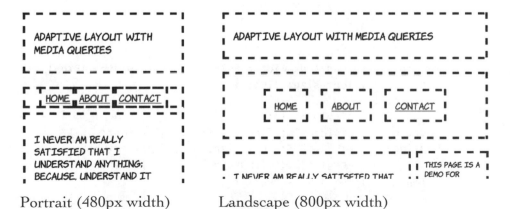

Portrait (480px width)   Landscape (800px width)

IN THIS EXAMPLE, THE DEFAULT LAYOUT IS A FULL-SIZED SCREEN DESKTOP EXPERIENCE. MEDIA QUERIES WERE USED TO ADAPT TO LOWER RESOLUTIONS. FOR PRACTICAL USES, IT'S OFTEN BETTER TO DO THINGS THE OTHER WAY AROUND— WHEN IE9 IS RELEASED ALL THE MAJOR DESKTOP BROWSERS WILL SUPPORT MEDIA QUERIES. BUT IE ON WINDOWS MOBILE 7 WON'T, AND NEITHER WILL BROWSERS ON OLDER FEATURE PHONES. IF YOU EXPECT LOTS OF THESE VISITORS, DESIGN FOR THE SMALL SCREEN AND USE MEDIA QUERIES TO ADAPT FOR LARGER DEVICES.

Changing layout based on orientation and aspect ratio

Maybe you want to do different things on a display that's 640 pixels wide and 480 pixels tall compared to one that is 640 pixels wide but 800 pixels tall—you want to know whether the aspect ratio is landscape or portrait for a given width. You can specify rules like this:

```
@media screen and (min-width: 640px and max-height: 480px) { }
@media screen and (min-width: 640px and min-height: 800px) { }
```

But this is a very fragile solution. For a start, you're missing windows that are 640 pixels wide but, perhaps thanks to a permanent toolbar, only 780 pixels tall. You could adjust to that particular case, but what if some innovative manufacturer came up with a 700 × 500 pixel device? In general, the idea behind media queries is for you to end up doing less work—not rewriting chunks of your stylesheet for every possible combination of width and height.

Fortunately, CSS3 provides an orientation media query for just this situation:

```
@media screen and (min-width: 640px and orientation: portrait) { }
@media screen and (min-width: 640px and orientation: landscape) { }
```

Orientation is a special case of aspect-ratio. The previous two rules are equivalent to these:

```
@media screen and (min-width: 640px and max-aspect-ratio: 1/1 ) { }
@media screen and (min-width: 640px and min-aspect-ratio: 1/1 ) { }
```

Using aspect-ratio, it's possible to distinguish between widescreen displays and traditional monitor sizes:

```
@media screen and (min-width: 640px and aspect-ratio: 16/9 ) { }
@media screen and (min-width: 640px and aspect-ratio: 4/3 ) { }
```

In this case you may want to select based on the monitor size rather than the window size:

```
@media screen and (min-width: 640px and device-aspect-ratio: 16/9 ) { }
@media screen and (min-width: 640px and device-aspect-ratio: 4/3 ) { }
```

`device-aspect-ratio:` always matches the monitor, regardless of the window size.

Additional device-detection features

Media queries can be used for more than just screen sizes. There are several other features for detection in the spec, and various browser vendors are introducing more as they add functionality to their browsers. Here are some of the more interesting ones:

- `color`—Select rules based on the number of bits available per color channel, where 8 bits is 255 levels per color. If you can remember the days of web-safe colors, this feature lets you work around the pixelation issues that web-safe colors avoided. Devices that have limited color support can be given a more constrained set of background colors.

- `resolution`—Select rules based on the dots per inch (dpi) of the display. A display with high dpi renders fonts more readably, so you can use a smaller font size.

- `touch-enabled`—This is currently a Mobile Firefox–only feature. Select rules based on whether the display is a touch input device, perhaps to give buttons and links more finger space.

- `device-pixel-ratio`—Currently a Mobile Safari–only feature. Select rules based on the zoom level, perhaps to provide a higher-resolution background image as the user zooms in so the image remains crisp and sharp.

Can you really make a mobile website with just CSS?

Is it possible to make your website deal with a full range of mobile devices and desktop PCs just by fiddling with CSS? As with most things, the answer is, "it depends."

(continued)

A *brochureware* website that is mostly static pages and doesn't expect much interaction from the user is almost certainly a good candidate for adaptation with media queries. Similarly, blogs or other text-heavy websites ought to be straightforward enough to make work on a wide range of devices. Mobile users, who are often paying for their connectivity by the megabyte, might appreciate not being forced to download huge video files, large graphics, and lots of ads; but if the site in question is relatively lightweight in this department it shouldn't be a problem. Also remember from chapter 4 that if you're using HTML5 to serve your video files, you have built-in functionality to serve lower-resolution and lower-quality files to mobile devices.

The more application-like a website is, the more likely it is that you won't be able to deliver the same content to all devices and end up with a usable experience for all users. In this situation, you should consider dynamically loading portions of your app with JavaScript after you've determined the capabilities of the device.

One last thing to bear in mind: studies have shown that many desktop users prefer to use the mobile versions of certain popular websites. The mobile versions are frequently simpler and more task focused—or, looked at another way, the desktop websites are too complex and confusing. Media queries and mobile websites don't absolve web authors from thinking about the needs of their users.

CSS3 PROMISES TO FINALLY EQUIP WEB AUTHORS WITH LAYOUT TOOLS WITH POWER SIMILAR TO THAT AVAILABLE IN NON-HTML FRAMEWORKS LIKE ADOBE FLEX, MICROSOFT SILVERLIGHT, AND JAVA SWING. IN THE NEXT SECTION, YOU'LL LEARN HOW POWERFUL CSS LAYOUT MAY BECOME IN THE NEXT FEW YEARS.

The future of CSS layout

CSS3 has several proposed standards currently under heavy development that could completely alter how layout on the web is done. In this section, you'll learn about these new approaches, all of which have at least experimental implementations available. They include flexible boxes, which are excellent for toolbars and menus; grid-align, which is great for traditional grid-based designs; and regions, exclusions, and positioned floats, which are good for multiple-column magazine-style layouts.

AT THE TIME OF WRITING NONE OF THE APPROACHES IN THIS SECTION ARE SUITABLE FOR USE ON A PUBLIC WEBSITE BECAUSE SUPPORT IS JUST TOO SPOTTY. YOU MAY BE ABLE TO MAKE USE OF THEM IN A TIGHTLY CONTROLLED ENVIRONMENT SUCH AS AN INTRANET, A WEB VIEW IN AN IOS OR ANDROID APP, OR A WINDOWS 8 METRO APP.

Using flexible boxes for nested layout

Flexible boxes, commonly referred to as *flexboxes*, are a layout approached developed in Firefox to be used for laying out various elements of the user interface. They're primarily aimed at creating menus and toolbars, particularly toolbars made up of nested elements. Currently Chrome, Firefox, IE10, and Safari have some support for flexboxes; you'll need to add the relevant prefix to get the listings in this section working.

This section first gives you a quick introduction to flexboxes using this simple markup fragment, and then looks at practical use cases and issues:

```
<div>
    <div>1</div>
    <div>2</div>
    <div>3</div>
    <div>4</div>
    <div>5</div>
</div>
```

To produce five equal-size boxes, set the parent element to display: box and set equal box-flex values on the child elements:

```
div {
    width: 90%;
    display: box;
}
div div {
    box-flex: 1;
}
```

Setting a larger `box-flex` value on certain elements causes them to take up an increasing proportion of the spare space:

```
div div:nth-child(2) {
    box-flex: 2;
}
div div:nth-child(4) {
    box-flex: 3;
}
```

Flexboxes allow elements to be displayed in a different order than their position in the markup:

```
div div {
    box-ordinal-group: 2;
}
div div:nth-child(5) {
    box-ordinal-group: 1;
}
```

Because the fifth child is set to be `ordinal-group: 1`, it appears before all the elements that are `ordinal-group: 2`.

		Full	Partial
Browser support quick check: flexbox	◉	-	2.0
	◉	-	2.0
	ℯ	-	10.0
	◎	-	-
	◉	-	3.1

Note that even though element 5 is now the first displayed, it's still the fifth element as far as the CSS is concerned. Element 2 and element 4 have larger `box-flex` values, even though they're now shown as the third and fifth elements.

Although flexboxes are horizontal by default, they can also be set to be vertical:

```
div {
    width: 5em;
    height: 600px;
    box-orient: vertical;
}
```

Note that in both horizontal and vertical cases, you need to specify a length in that direction in order to get the flex to appear. This is because the flex distributed among the elements comes from the left-over space after the intrinsic size of the elements is taken away. This can lead to some counter-intuitive results when the elements with flex don't have a well-defined intrinsic width.

This is easily demonstrated by adding some text—the cell will expand to contain it. The available space gets used up, so the flex can no longer be distributed.

For collections of elements that do have an intrinsic width, flexboxes offer an ability that can't be replicated by tables, `display: table`, floats, or `inline-block`: they can create flexible grids that can have a variable number of elements per row, as with `floats` and `inline-block`, but the individual elements flex so they exactly fill up each row, as with table rows and `display: table`. This is thanks to the `multiline` property. The following example has a grid of 60 cells, each containing a number.

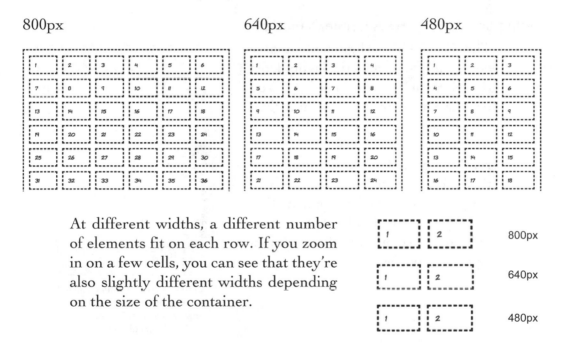

At different widths, a different number of elements fit on each row. If you zoom in on a few cells, you can see that they're also slightly different widths depending on the size of the container.

Following is a snippet of the markup (left) and the CSS (right) required for this layout. The key property is `box-lines`:

```
<ul>
    <li>1</li>
    <li>2</li>
    <li>3</li>
    <li>4</li>
    <li>...
        ...</li>
</ul>
```

```
ul {
    display: box;
    box-lines: multiple;
}
li {
    display: block;
    box-flex: 1;
    min-width: 3em;
}
```

Flexbox good	Flexbox bad
 CAN MANIPULATE LAYOUT ORDER WITH CSS. MULTILINE GRIDS THAT EXACTLY FILL THE AVAILABLE SPACE.	INTENDED FOR TOOLBARS, MENUS, AND SO ON RATHER THAN FULL PAGES. WEIRD THINGS HAPPEN WHEN CONTENT HAS NO FIXED INTRINSIC WIDTH. 

Using the CSS3 Grid Alignment module

The CSS3 Grid Alignment module completely separates the layout from the elements in your markup. You use CSS to define a grid and then assign elements to the grid using a row and column reference. Currently only IE10 has any support for this module, although the WebKit support is under development. Following is some simple markup that will be turned into the three-column layout shown here:

Browser support quick check: grid-align		Full	Partial
		-	19.0*
		-	-
		-	10.0
		-	-
		-	3.1

* Chrome needs a runtime flag to be set to enable the experimental support; see https://bugs.webkit.org/show_bug.cgi?id=60731 for details of progress.

```
<body>
 <header>Header</header>
 <aside class="b">Side bar</
aside>
 <article>I never am really
  satisfied... etc., etc.</
article>
 <aside class="d">Side bar</
aside>
 <footer>Footer</footer>
</body>
```

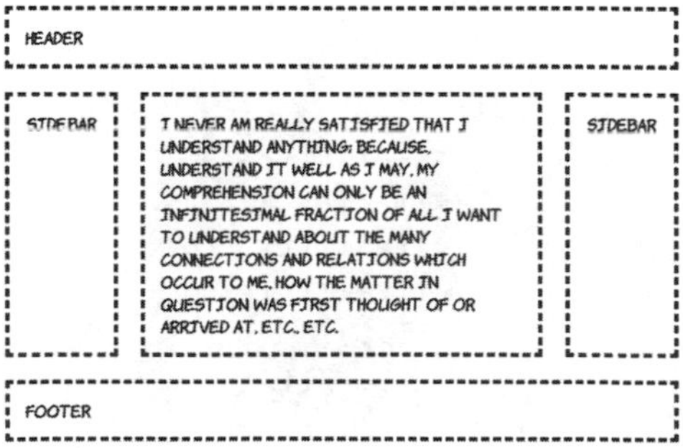

A grid is created by defining a set of rows and (or) columns. In this example, you'll go ahead and create three columns and three rows on the <body> element:

```
body {
    display: grid;
    grid-columns: auto 1fr auto;
    grid-rows: auto 1fr auto;
}
```

The first and last rows and columns will shrink to fit their content (auto), and the middle cell of each column will flex so the whole thing takes up all available space. These declarations create a conceptual grid into which to fit elements. All that remains is to assign the elements to the relevant spots of the grid:

```
header { grid-column: 1; grid-row: 1; grid-column-span: 3; }
aside.b { grid-column: 1; grid-row: 2; }
article { grid-column: 2; grid-row: 2; }
aside.d { grid-column: 3; grid-row: 2; }
footer { grid-column: 1; grid-row: 3; grid-column-span: 3; }
```

Note that unlike with display: table, it's possible to have elements spanning multiple slots in the layout. This means far less messing around with wrapper elements to control the styling.

As with template layouts, you can rearrange the content by modifying the CSS. Here the main content is moved into the top three slots:

```
header {
    grid-column: 1;
    grid-row: 2;
}
aside.b {
    grid-column: 2;
    grid-row: 2;
}
```

I NEVER AM REALLY SATISFIED THAT I UNDERSTAND ANYTHING; BECAUSE, UNDERSTAND IT WELL AS I MAY, MY COMPREHENSION CAN ONLY BE AN INFINITESIMAL FRACTION OF ALL I WANT TO UNDERSTAND ABOUT THE MANY CONNECTIONS AND RELATIONS WHICH OCCUR TO ME, HOW THE MATTER IN QUESTION WAS FIRST THOUGHT OF OR ARRIVED AT, ETC. ETC.

HEADER   SIDEBAR   FOOTER

SIDEBAR

```
article {
    grid-column: 1;
    grid-row: 1;
    grid-column-span: 3;
}
aside.d {
    grid-column: 1;
    grid-row: 3;
    grid-column-span: 3;
}
footer {
    grid-column: 3;
    grid-row: 2;
}
```

NOTE THAT EVEN THOUGH GRID-ALIGN GIVES YOU THE OPPORTUNITY TO COMPLETELY SEPARATE YOUR MARKUP FROM THE LAYOUT, THIS DOESN'T MEAN YOU SHOULD THROW YOUR CONTENT INTO THE HTML WILLY-NILLY. REMEMBER THAT MANY USERS OF YOUR CONTENT, SUCH AS SCREEN-READER USERS AND SEARCH ENGINES, DON'T CARE TOO MUCH ABOUT THE LAYOUT YOU'VE ACHIEVED WITH CSS—YOUR CONTENT SHOULD MAKE SENSE IN THE ORDER IT APPEARS IN YOUR MARKUP.

More complex layouts are possible if you nest elements. Adjust the body of your example page to contain the following markup; you'll then use a nested grid to lay out the content elements:

```
<header>Header</header>
<aside>Side bar 1</aside>
<div>
    <article>Content 1</article>
    <article>Content 2</article>
    <article>Content 3</article>
    <article>Content 4</article>
    <article>Content 5</article>
    <article>Content 6</article>
</div>
<aside>Side bar 2</aside>
<footer>Footer</footer>
```

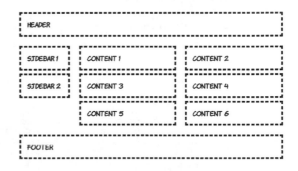

The relevant CSS (excluding some rules to add fonts, borders and padding) is shown next. The <body> element this time contains a two-column layout with four rows, but you also assign a two-column, three-row layout to the <div> element:

```
body {
    display: grid;
    grid-columns: auto 1fr;
    grid-rows: auto 1fr 1fr auto;
}
div {
    display: grid;
    grid-columns: 1fr 1fr;
    grid-rows: 1fr 1fr 1fr;
}
```

Now distribute the elements around the grid, making the <div> span two rows:

```
header { grid-column: 1; grid-row: 1; grid-column-span: 2; }
aside:nth-of-type(1) { grid-column: 1; grid-row: 2; }
aside:nth-of-type(2) { grid-column: 1; grid-row: 3; }
footer { grid-column: 1; grid-row: 4; grid-column-span: 2; }
div { grid-column: 2; grid-row: 2; grid-row-span: 2; }
```

Because the <article> elements are all children of the <div> element, the row and column references are for the grid defined on the <div>:

```
article { min-height: 2em; }
article:nth-child(1) { grid-column: 1; grid-row: 1; }
article:nth-child(2) { grid-column: 2; grid-row: 1; }
article:nth-child(3) { grid-column: 1; grid-row: 2; }
article:nth-child(4) { grid-column: 2; grid-row: 2; }
article:nth-child(5) { grid-column: 1; grid-row: 3; }
article:nth-child(6) { grid-column: 2; grid-row: 3; }
```

See the full listing in ch08/grid-align-3.html.

The ability of the grid-based layouts to rearrange content with only CSS makes them an ideal complement to media queries. You'll now adapt the previous example to make it respond to media queries. Here's what the layout will look like at lower screen resolutions (see the full listing in ch08/grid-align-4.html).

640px width   **480px width**

```
┌ ─ ─ ─ ─ ─ ─ ─ ─ ─ ─ ─ ─ ─ ─ ─ ┐     ┌ ─ ─ ─ ─ ─ ─ ─ ─ ─ ─ ─ ─ ─ ┐
│ HEADER                        │     │ HEADER                    │
└ ─ ─ ─ ─ ─ ─ ─ ─ ─ ─ ─ ─ ─ ─ ─ ┘     └ ─ ─ ─ ─ ─ ─ ─ ─ ─ ─ ─ ─ ─ ┘

┌ ─ ─ ─ ─ ─ ┐ ┌ ─ ─ ─ ─ ─ ─ ─ ─ ┐     ┌ ─ ─ ─ ─ ─ ─ ─ ─ ─ ─ ─ ─ ─ ┐
│ SIDEBAR 1 │ │ CONTENT 1       │     │ CONTENT 1                 │
└ ─ ─ ─ ─ ─ ┘ └ ─ ─ ─ ─ ─ ─ ─ ─ ┘     └ ─ ─ ─ ─ ─ ─ ─ ─ ─ ─ ─ ─ ─ ┘
┌ ─ ─ ─ ─ ─ ┐ ┌ ─ ─ ─ ─ ─ ─ ─ ─ ┐     ┌ ─ ─ ─ ─ ─ ─ ─ ─ ─ ─ ─ ─ ─ ┐
│ SIDEBAR 2 │ │ CONTENT 3       │     │ CONTENT 3                 │
└ ─ ─ ─ ─ ─ ┘ └ ─ ─ ─ ─ ─ ─ ─ ─ ┘     └ ─ ─ ─ ─ ─ ─ ─ ─ ─ ─ ─ ─ ─ ┘
              ┌ ─ ─ ─ ─ ─ ─ ─ ─ ┐     ┌ ─ ─ ─ ─ ─ ─ ─ ─ ─ ─ ─ ─ ─ ┐
              │ CONTENT 5       │     │ CONTENT 5                 │
              └ ─ ─ ─ ─ ─ ─ ─ ─ ┘     └ ─ ─ ─ ─ ─ ─ ─ ─ ─ ─ ─ ─ ─ ┘

              ┌ ─ ─ ─ ─ ─ ─ ─ ─ ┐     ┌ ─ ─ ─ ─ ─ ─ ─ ─ ─ ─ ─ ─ ─ ┐
              │ CONTENT 2       │     │ SIDEBAR 1                 │
              └ ─ ─ ─ ─ ─ ─ ─ ─ ┘     └ ─ ─ ─ ─ ─ ─ ─ ─ ─ ─ ─ ─ ─ ┘
              ┌ ─ ─ ─ ─ ─ ─ ─ ─ ┐     ┌ ─ ─ ─ ─ ─ ─ ─ ─ ─ ─ ─ ─ ─ ┐
              │ CONTENT 4       │     │ SIDEBAR 2                 │
              └ ─ ─ ─ ─ ─ ─ ─ ─ ┘     └ ─ ─ ─ ─ ─ ─ ─ ─ ─ ─ ─ ─ ─ ┘
              ┌ ─ ─ ─ ─ ─ ─ ─ ─ ┐     
              │ CONTENT 6       │     ┌ ─ ─ ─ ─ ─ ─ ─ ─ ─ ─ ─ ─ ─ ┐
              └ ─ ─ ─ ─ ─ ─ ─ ─ ┘     │ CONTENT 2                 │
                                      └ ─ ─ ─ ─ ─ ─ ─ ─ ─ ─ ─ ─ ─ ┘
┌ ─ ─ ─ ─ ─ ─ ─ ─ ─ ─ ─ ─ ─ ─ ─ ┐     ┌ ─ ─ ─ ─ ─ ─ ─ ─ ─ ─ ─ ─ ─ ┐
│ FOOTER                        │     │ CONTENT 4                 │
└ ─ ─ ─ ─ ─ ─ ─ ─ ─ ─ ─ ─ ─ ─ ─ ┘     └ ─ ─ ─ ─ ─ ─ ─ ─ ─ ─ ─ ─ ─ ┘
                                      ┌ ─ ─ ─ ─ ─ ─ ─ ─ ─ ─ ─ ─ ─ ┐
                                      │ CONTENT 6                 │
                                      └ ─ ─ ─ ─ ─ ─ ─ ─ ─ ─ ─ ─ ─ ┘

                                      ┌ ─ ─ ─ ─ ─ ─ ─ ─ ─ ─ ─ ─ ─ ┐
                                      │ FOOTER                    │
                                      └ ─ ─ ─ ─ ─ ─ ─ ─ ─ ─ ─ ─ ─ ┘
```

To start with, define the single-column, small-screen layout:

```
body {
    display: grid;
    grid-rows: auto;
    grid-columns: 1fr;
}
header { grid-row: 1; }
#sidebar { grid-row: 3; }
#content1 { grid-row: 2; }
#content2 { grid-row: 4; }
footer { grid-row: 5; }
```

For windows 600 pixels wide and greater, you'll switch to a two-column layout. Note that although the grid can be easily redefined on the body rule, the elements must be explicitly slotted into that grid:

```
@media screen and (min-width: 600px) {
    body {
        grid-columns: auto 1fr;
        grid-rows: auto 1fr 1fr auto;
    }
```

```
    header { grid-column: 1; grid-row: 1; grid-column-span: 2; }
    #sidebar { grid-column: 1; grid-row: 2; grid-rowspan: 2; }
    #content1 { grid-column: 2; grid-row: 2; }
    #content2 { grid-column: 2; grid-row: 3; }
    footer { grid-column: 1; grid-row: 4; grid-column-span: 2; }
}
```

This CSS defines a three-column grid for windows wider than 760 pixels. Again, the slot locations have to be explicitly set:

```
@media screen and (min-width: 760px) {
    body {
        grid-columns: auto 1fr 1fr;
        grid-rows: auto 1fr auto;
    }
    header { grid-column: 1; grid-row: 1; grid-column-span: 3; }
    #sidebar { grid-column: 1; grid-row: 2; }
    #content1 { grid-column: 2; grid-row: 2; }
    #content2 { grid-column: 3; grid-row: 2; }
    footer { grid-column: 1; grid-row: 3; grid-column-span: 3; }
}
```

GRIDS OFFER GREAT FLEXIBILITY IN LAYING OUT ELEMENTS ON THE PAGE AND SOLVE NEARLY ALL THE ISSUES DESIGNERS HAD WITH CSS LAYOUTS COMPARED TO TABLE-BASED LAYOUTS. BUT THE ELEMENTS BEING LAID OUT ARE STILL ESSENTIALLY SQUARE BOXES WITH A FIXED AMOUNT OF CONTENT. IN THE NEXT SECTION, YOU'LL LEARN ABOUT A PROPOSAL THAT LETS YOU FIT YOUR CONTENT INTO ANY SHAPE AND SPREAD IT ACROSS MULTIPLE ELEMENTS.

Controlling content flow with CSS3 Regions

In print-publishing tools such as Adobe InDesign, it's common to create several text boxes and then link them together so the content added to them automatically overflows from one box to the next. In this paradigm, text flows automatically from one region of the page to another and from one page to another — you don't need to calculate how much text will fit in each region. You specify some text and a collection of regions, and the application takes care of the rest.

Browser support quick check: regions		Full	Partial
	◎	-	19.0
	◉	-	-
	℮	-	10.0
	⦿	-	-
	◈	-	5.2

Adobe is a W3C member and has decided to give similar capabilities to web authors—this fulfills a dual goal of making web layout more powerful for web designers while making it easier for Adobe to generate content straight to the web from its print-publishing tools. To this end they have proposed the CSS3 Regions module. Adobe has helped implement support for their proposal in WebKit, and IE10 also has preliminary support. Here's an example page layout created with the new Regions module.

I NEVER AM REALLY SATISFIED THAT I UNDERSTAND ANYTHING; BECAUSE, UNDERSTAND IT WELL AS I MAY, MY COMPREHENSION CAN ONLY BE AN INFINITESIMAL FRACTION OF ALL I WANT TO UNDERSTAND ABOUT THE MANY CONNECTIONS AND RELATIONS WHICH OCCUR TO ME, HOW THE MATTER IN QUESTION WAS FIRST THOUGHT OF

IN ALMOST EVERY COMPUTATION A GREAT VARIETY OF ARRANGEMENTS FOR THE SUCCESSION OF THE PROCESSES IS POSSIBLE, AND VARIOUS CONSIDERATIONS MUST INFLUENCE THE SELECTIONS AMONGST THEM FOR THE PURPOSES OF A CALCULATING ENGINE.

ONE ESSENTIAL OBJECT IS TO CHOOSE THAT ARRANGEMENT WHICH SHALL TEND TO REDUCE TO A MINIMUM THE TIME NECESSARY FOR COMPLETING THE CALCULATION.

MANY PERSONS WHO ARE NOT CONVERSANT WITH MATHEMATICAL STUDIES IMAGINE THAT BECAUSE

The previous screenshot shows three text boxes. The diagram at right outlines each box explicitly. The content in the boxes flows between them without having to be assigned to one box or another as would normally be required on a web page.

The HTML contains four `<div>` elements. The `<div>` with `id` value source contains all the content: a set of four paragraphs.

```
<div id="source">
    <p>I never am really
        satisfied...</p>
    <p>In almost every
        computation...</p>
    <p>Many persons who...</p>
    <p>The Analytical Engine...</p>
```

This is followed by three empty `<div>` elements, all with a class of region. You'll flow the content into these three empty `<div>` elements.

```
</div>
<div id="region1" class="region">
</div>
<div id="region2" class="region">
</div>
<div id="region3" class="region">
</div>
<img src="00092.jpg" class="video">
<img src="dust-puppy.png"
    class="dp">
```

The magic happens in the CSS. First the source `<div>` is assigned to flow1. Then the declaration for elements with a class of region says to take the content for these elements from the flow that has just been defined.

The remainder of the CSS positions the region elements on the page as shown earlier. Check out ch08/regions-1.html file for the full code.

```
#source{
    flow-into: flow1;
    text-align:justify;
}
.region {
    flow-from: flow1;
}
```

Making complex shapes with CSS3 Exclusions and Shapes

The CSS3 Exclusions specification allows you to wrap content in and around complex shapes. This spec was also born out of Adobe's proposals; initially it was for shaping the regions now in the CSS3 Regions specification. The following layout can be achieved with a tweak to the

I NEVER AM REALLY SATISFIED THAT I UNDERSTAND ANYTHING BECAUSE, UNDERSTAND IT WELL AS I MAY, MY COMPREHENSION CAN ONLY BE AN INFINITESIMAL FRACTION OF ALL I WANT TO UNDERSTAND ABOUT THE MANY CONNECTIONS AND RELATIONS WHICH OCCUR TO ME, HOW THE MATTER IN QUESTION WAS FIRST THOUGHT OF OR ARRIVED AT, ETC, ETC.

IN ALMOST EVERY COMPUTATION A GREAT VARIETY OF ARRANGEMENTS FOR THE SUCCESSION OF THE PROCESSES IS POSSIBLE, AND VARIOUS CONSIDERATIONS MUST INFLUENCE THE SELECTIONS AMONGST THEM FOR THE PURPOSES OF A CALCULATING ENGINE. ONE ESSENTIAL OBJECT IS TO CHOOSE THAT ARRANGEMENT WHICH SHALL TEND TO REDUCE TO A MINIMUM THE TIME NECESSARY FOR COMPLETING THE CALCULATION.

MANY PERSONS WHO ARE NOT CONVERSANT WITH MATHEMATICAL STUDIES IMAGINE THAT BECAUSE THE BUSINESS OF BABBAGE'S ANALYTICAL ENGINE IS TO GIVE ITS RESULTS IN NUMERICAL NOTATION, THE NATURE OF ITS PROCESSES MUST CONSEQUENTLY BE ARITHMETICAL AND NUMERICAL, RATHER THAN ALGEBRAICAL AND ANALYTICAL. THIS IS AN ERROR. THE ENGINE CAN ARRANGE AND COMBINE ITS NUMERICAL QUANTITIES

EXACTLY AS IF THEY WERE LETTERS OR ANY OTHER GENERAL SYMBOLS: AND IN FACT IT MIGHT BRING OUT ITS RESULTS IN ALGEBRAICAL NOTATION WERE PROVISIONS MADE ACCORDINGLY.

THE ANALYTICAL ENGINE HAS NO PRETENSIONS WHATEVER TO ORIGINATE ANYTHING. IT CAN DO WHATEVER WE KNOW HOW TO ORDER IT TO PERFORM. IT CAN FOLLOW ANALYSIS, BUT IT HAS NO POWER OF ANTICIPATING ANY ANALYTICAL REVELATIONS OR TRUTHS. ITS PROVINCE IS TO ASSIST US IN MAKING AVAILABLE WHAT

CSS from the last example in the previous section. The key difference from the previous example is the addition of the `wrap-shape-mode` and `wrap-shape` properties:

```
.region {
  flow-from: flow1;
  wrap-shape-mode: content;
  wrap-shape: polygon(
        0px,160px 20px,232px 40px,262px
        60px,282px 80px,296px 100px,305px 120px,313px
        140px,316px 160px,320px 180px,316px 200px,313px
        220px,305px 240px,296px 260px,282px 280px,262px
        300px,232px 320px,160px 300px,90px 280px,52px
        260px,34px 240px,20px 220px,10px 200px,4px
        180px,1px 160px,0px 140px,1px 120px,4px
        100px,10px 80px,20px 60px,34px 40px,52px
        20px,90px 0px,160px
    );
}
#region1 {
  wrap-shape: polygon( 0px,320px 0px,0px 320px,320px 0px,320px );
}
#region3 {
  wrap-shape: polygon( 0px,320px 320px,0px 320px,320px 0px,320px );
}
```

The shapes don't have to contain content—they can also exclude it. This is what the CSS3 Exclusions module is concerned with. The syntax is exactly the same as for Regions, but instead of content flowing into the shapes, the content is flowed around them.

In this example, the content is displaying as normal inside the #source element. Then the shapes are absolutely positioned over that content. This is changed by using the around keyword instead of content:

`wrap-shape-mode: around;`

The Exclusions spec is still under heavy development, but it represents some useful additions to the web author's toolkit. *Positioned floats* are a concept created by the IE team at Microsoft; they first appeared in IE10 Platform Preview 2. They achieve results similar to the exclusions so they have been folded into the Exclusions spec. To demonstrate, let's use a simple page with five paragraphs:

```
<p>I never am really satisfied...</p>
<p>In almost every computation...</p>
<p>Many persons who are not...</p>
<p>The Analytical Engine has no pretensions...</p>
<p>The Analytical Engine weaves algebraic patterns...</p>
```

Making the last paragraph a positioned float is as simple as setting the both value for the wrap-flow property:

```
p:last-child {
    width: 200px;
    position: absolute;
    wrap-flow: both;
    top: 75px;
    left: 250px;
}
```

All the other text flows around the positioned float. Other possible values are start and end, which allow the text to flow only past the start or end of the object, leaving the other side empty, and minimum and maximum which allow flow only into narrowest or widest sides, respectively.

In the last example, the floated element looked a bit cramped. You can apply spacing to positioned floats with the `wrap-margin` property:

```css
p:last-child {
    width: 200px;
    position: absolute;
    wrap-flow: both;
    wrap-margin: 1em;
    top: 75px;
    left: 250px;
}
```

To demonstrate an alternative effect, let's arrange the other paragraphs into four columns:

```css
p { display: table-cell; }
```

You can see that the text still flows around the floated element, even though the four paragraphs are independently positioned.

Browser support for these new features is still fairly patchy, but they're worth exploring now so you can be prepared for the future.

Browser support

As discussed in the introduction, browser support for CSS layout has long been an issue. Everything in the CSS2 spec is now implemented in all major browsers: that includes everything discussed in the section "Underused CSS2 layout features." Support for the other features we've discussed is patchier, reflecting the experimental nature of the specifications. The following table shows the details.

	Chrome		Firefox		IE			Opera		Safari	
	12	14	4	6	8	9	10	11.5	12	5	5.1
inline-block	●	●	●	●	●	●	●	●	●	●	●
display: table	●	●	●	●	●	●	●	●	●	●	●
calc			○	○		●	●				
box-sizing	●	●	○	○		●	●	●	●	○	●
Media queries	●	●	●	●		●	●	●	●	●	●
Flexboxes	○	○	○	○			○			○	○
Multiline flexboxes							○				
Templates/grids							○				
Regions											
Exclusions							○				

Key:
- ● Complete or nearly complete support
- ○ Incomplete or alternative support
- Little or no support

inline-block in IE6 and IE7

Although IE didn't add support for inline-block until version 8, it's possible to achieve the same effect by taking advantage of some nonstandard behavior. IE has an internal concept called hasLayout that endows elements with special properties as far as the layout engine is concerned. For our current purposes, the only thing you need to know is that an element that is display: inline but also hasLayout will behave like an inline-block element in other browsers.

One of the simplest ways to trigger hasLayout is to use the IE-specific CSS extension zoom with a value of 1 (which makes no visible difference), coupled with the star hack:

```
display: inline-block;
*display: inline;
zoom: 1;
```

Most browsers will ignore the second two properties as invalid, whereas IE7 and earlier will ignore the first property but process the second two.

calc in Chrome and Firefox

Firefox requires the –moz– prefix for calc while Chrome requires –webkit–. For maximum support, you should specify four rules—one for browsers with no calc support, one for Firefox, and one for standards-compatible browsers (currently only IE):

```
width: 23%;
width: -moz-calc(100%/4 - 10px);
width: -webkit-calc(100%/4 - 10px);
width: calc(100%/4 - 10px);
```

This code sets the element width to 23% in browsers that have no support for calc and 100%/4–10px for any browser that does support it.

box-sizing in Firefox and Safari 5

Firefox and older versions of Safari require a –moz– prefix for box-sizing:

```
-moz-box-sizing: border-box;
-webkit-box-sizing: border-box;
box-sizing: border-box;
```

If you need to support IE8, because of the significant impact the box model can have on your layout, it's best to use either IE conditional comments or modernizr.js to provide alternative rules to that browser.

Flexboxes in Chrome, Firefox, IE, and Safari

Currently, prefixes are required in all browsers that support flexboxes. To get maximum support, you need to specify each property four times:

```
div {
    display: -moz-box;
    display: -webkit-box;
    display: -ms-box;
    display: box;
    -moz-box-orient: vertical;
    -webkit-box-orient: vertical;
    -ms-box-orient: vertical;
```

```
    box—orient: vertical;
}
div div {
    —moz—box—flex: 1;
    —webkit—box—flex: 1;
    —ms—box—flex: 1;
    box—flex: 1;
}
```

This code sets the parent `<div>` element to be a flexbox container and gives any child `<div>` elements the same amount of flex in all browsers that have support.

Media queries and old browsers

If a browser doesn't support media queries, then it won't apply any of the rules listed in a media query section. Any rules outside of a media query section will constitute the default state of your site, so you should always consider the sorts of devices the majority of your users will be browsing with. If your site is primarily for desktop users, then your default styles should be aimed at a desktop-style layout—around 1000 pixels wide and (most likely) using an older version of IE. If your site is more mobile focused, then it would be better to target a small screen by default and add media queries to improve the experience in modern desktop browsers.

Regions and exclusions

Although IE10 and Chrome both have some support for these modules, there are several limitations. In IE10 the source content for `flow—into` must be an `iframe`. In Chrome 17–20 you must explicitly enable support for regions in the `about:flags` page. Neither browser has much support for shaped exclusions, but IE10 does support rectangular exclusions.

Summary

In this chapter, you've learned about some of the murky past of CSS layout and how the situation has improved thanks to the gradual decline of old versions of IE, allowing the use of the full range of CSS2 layout tools. New features like `box—model`, `calc`, and media queries already have wide support and promise to improve the situation even further. Finally, you've glimpsed the bright future of CSS layout, thanks in no small part to the new versions of IE—flexboxes, templates, grids, and exclusions promise to make web page layout much easier and more flexible.

TO STAND OUT FROM THE CROWD, WHAT YOUR WEB PAGE NEEDS ISN'T AN ELEGANTLY CODED THREE-COLUMN LAYOUT—YOU WANT COLOR, MOVEMENT, AND INTERACTIVITY. IN THE NEXT CHAPTER, YOU'LL START TO LEARN ABOUT THE FLASHIER ASPECTS OF CSS3 AS WE LOOK AT COLORS, TRANSFORMATIONS, TRANSITIONS, AND ANIMATIONS.

Motion and color

This chapter covers

- *Making elements semitransparent with the* `opacity` *property*

- *Making colors semitransparent with RGBA*

- *A new, more intuitive way to specify color: HSL and HSLA*

- *Natural user interaction with transitions and animation*

In this chapter, we'll look at some of the snazzier aspects of CSS3—features that are much loved by graphic designers.

USER FRIENDLY by J.D. "Illiad" Frazer

IS ALREADY BEINK THREE WAYS TO SET COLOR IN CSS, WHY NEEDINK TWO NEW ONES? MONITOR IS BEINK RED GREEN BLUE, SENSIBLE KEEPINK CSS THE SAME

CSS ISN'T FOR MONITORS, IT'S FOR PEOPLE. DESIGNERS MORE OFTEN WANT COLORS WHICH DIFFER ONLY IN LIGHTNESS OR SATURATION

CRAZY DESIGNERS! WEB IS BEINK BETTER IN BLACK AND WHITE ANYWAY

Colors and opacity

In the beginning, the web was black and white, but these days there aren't many websites that don't make extensive use of color. It's unlikely the web will revert to black and white any time soon, so it's a good thing CSS3 includes several new features for colors. Later in this section, you'll learn about RGBA, HSL, and HSLA. First, though, let's investigate how CSS3 allows you to achieve another popular effect in modern web design: semitransparency with the opacity property.

Opacity

Opacity is a measure of what percentage of light is blocked by an object. In the case of HTML and CSS, the objects are elements on the page. They are, by default, fully opaque; no light is allowed through, so you can see nothing of the elements beneath (that is, earlier in the source code). If a paragraph has a blue background, it completely obscures any background on the element that contains the paragraph.

Browser support quick check: opacity		Standard	Prefixed
		1.0	-
		1.0	0.8
		9.0	-*
		9.0	-
		1.2	1.0

* IE has been able to do transformations with the nonstandard filter attribute since version 5.5.

Opacity can be used to de-emphasize page elements to let your user focus on a single important task. This is commonly seen on the web in the ubiquitous lightbox, shown in action here.

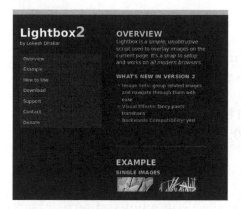

Before: The normal busy page. The user has lots of options.

After: The rest of the page is hidden behind a semitransparent layer so the user can concentrate on the picture.

IN THIS CHAPTER THE CSS EXAMPLES OMIT SIZING INFORMATION SO THAT YOU CAN FOCUS ON THE RULES FOR APPLYING OPACITY, COLOR, AND MOTION. IF YOU'RE RE-CREATING THE EXAMPLES FROM THE TEXT YOU'LL USUALLY NEED TO ADD THE FOLLOWING RULE TO REPLICATE THE SCREENSHOTS:

```
div {
    display: inline-block;
    margin: 0.5em;
    padding: 0.5em;
}
```

IN ADDITION TO THE ABOVE, SOME OF THE EXAMPLES USE A width: 12em; PROPERTY.

The opacity property is straightforward: you specify a value between 0 and 1. The fully opaque default is 1, and 0 is fully transparent:

```
div {
    background-color: #666;
    color: #ccc;
    border: 4px solid #ccc;
}
div:nth-child(1) { opacity: 1; }
div:nth-child(2) { opacity: 0.8; }
div:nth-child(3) { opacity: 0.6; }
div:nth-child(4) { opacity: 0.4; }
```

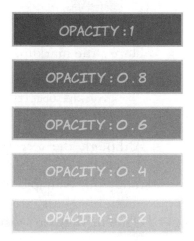

```
div:nth-child(5) { opacity: 0.2; }
div:nth-child(6) { opacity: 0; }
```

When all the elements are sitting against the same white background, the effect of decreasing opacity is the same as using lighter colors. The full code for this example is in ch09/opacity-1.html.

A common use of opacity is to make a continuous pattern or background image always be visible without clashing with the main content. Here the <h1> element lies on top of the <div> that contains it, but opacity is used to let the background of the <div> be partly visible through the <h1>:

```
body {
    background-color: #666;
}
div {
    background: url(example.png)
      no-repeat 50% 50%;
}
h1 {
    background-color: #fff;
    color: #000
    opacity: 0.75;
}
```

Here's the markup. You can see the full listing in ch09/opacity-4.html:

```
<body>
    <div><h1>Opacity is cool</h1></div>
</body>
```

Although the opacity property isn't inherited in the CSS sense, the opacity of the parent element affects that of its child elements. In the following example, on the right (listing ch09/opacity-2.html), all the child elements are invisible because they're contained within an element that isn't visible, regardless of their individual opacity values.

This is the same as setting an element to visibility: hidden—the element isn't visible, but it's still taking up space on the page. On the left (listing ch09/opacity-3.html), the outer element is fully visible, but transparent child elements don't cut holes in their opaque parents.

Descending opacity   **Ascending opacity**

```
div > div > div > div > div > div
  { opacity: 0; }
div > div > div > div > div
  { opacity: 0.2; }
div > div > div > div
  { opacity: 0.4; }
div > div > div { opacity: 0.6; }
div > div { opacity: 0.8; }
div { opacity: 1; }


<div><div><div><div><div><div>
                opacity : 0
              </div>
              opacity : 0 . 2
            </div>
            opacity : 0 . 4
          </div>
          opacity : 0 . 6
        </div>
        opacity : 0 . 8
      </div>
      opacity : 1
</div>
```

```
div > div > div > div > div > div
  { opacity: 1; }
div > div > div > div > div
  { opacity: 0.8; }
div > div > div > div
  { opacity: 0.6; }
div > div > div { opacity: 0.4; }
div > div { opacity: 0.2; }
div { opacity: 0; }


<div><div><div><div><div><div>
                opacity : 1
              </div>
              opacity : 0 . 8
            </div>
            opacity : 0 . 6
          </div>
          opacity : 0 . 4
        </div>
        opacity : 0 . 2
      </div>
      opacity : 0
</div>
```

MIRANDA'S ACRONYM CHEAT SHEET

WE TECHIES LOVE OUR ACRONYMS. LET ME
EXPLAIN THE COMMON ONES IN THIS CHAPTER:
RGB, RGBA, HSL, AND HSLA. THE SEVEN LETTERS
MEAN THE SAME THING IN ALL FOUR.

R = RED   HUE= **H**

G = GREEN   SATURATION = **S**

B = BLUE   LUMINOSITY = **L**

A =   ALPHA (OPACITY)   = **A**

RGBA

Sometimes you don't want to make an
entire element transparent or semitransparent. If you refer back to the
example from listing ch09/opacity-
4.html, the text and the background
are semitransparent.

If you want people be able to read large amounts of text like this, then
a semitransparent background would be better combined with fully
opaque text. Rather than make the entire element semitransparent,
CSS3 provides several ways of specifying color values that have a level
of transparency, the first of which is rgba(). You can use rgba() to make
just the background transparent. If you're used to the hexadecimal
shorthand for specifying colors, these two diagrams show how they're
related.

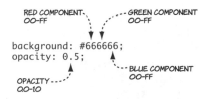

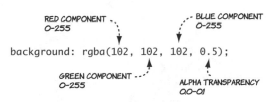

50% opacity element with a
dark gray background

Element with a background that is
both dark gray and 50% opacity

		Full	Partial
		2.0	-
		3.0	-
		9.0	-
		10.0	-
		3.1	-

Browser support quick check: rgba()

The primary benefit is that the opacity is now confined to the background—the rest of the element's contents and attributes can be full opacity.

The difference is even more pronounced for the nested element example, where previously setting the outer element to transparent made the entire set of elements disappear.

See the full code for this example in listing ch09/rgba-2.html.

With transparency confined to the background and not inherited, the text and borders remain visible on all the elements:

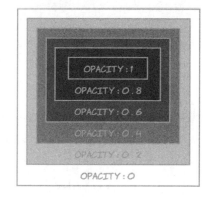

```
div > div > div > div > div > div {
  background-color:
    rgba(102,102,102, 1); }
div > div > div > div > div {
  background-color:
    rgba(102,102,102, 0.8); }
div > div > div > div {
  background-color:
    rgba(102,102,102, 0.6); }
div > div > div {
  background-color:
    rgba(102,102,102, 0.4); }
```

```
div > div {
  background-color:
    rgba(102,102,102, 0.2); }
div {
  background-color:
    rgba(102,102,102, 0); }
```

See listing ch09/rgba-3.html for the full code.

HSL and HSLA

You may have found yourself wanting a darker shade of a particular color as a contrasting element in one of your designs. This is easy to manage in simple cases with RGB—just make the numbers smaller, as in the next example.

For those of you reading this book on paper in black and white, the top pair of elements that follow are shades of gray, the middle pair are shades of blue, and the bottom pair are a sort of purple/pink combination:

		Full	Partial
Browser support quick check: hsl() and hsla()		2.0	-
		3.0	-
		9.0	-
		10.0	-
		3.1	-

```
.one {
  background-color:
    rgb(204,204,204);
  color: rgb(102,102,102);
}
.darkone {
  background-color:
    rgb(102,102,102);
  color: rgb(204,204,204);
}
.two {
  background-color: rgb(51,102,153);
  color: rgb(17,34,51);
}
.darktwo {
  background-color: rgb(17,34,51);
  color: rgb(51,102,153);
}
```

RGB(204 , 204 , 204)

RGB(102 , 102 , 102)

RGB(51 , 102 , 153)

RGB(17 , 34 , 51)

RGB(232 , 44 , 122)

RGB(83 , 9 , 40)

```
.three {
  background-color: rgb(232,44,122);
  color: rgb(83,9,40);
}
.darkthree {
  background-color: rgb(83,9,40);
  color: rgb(232,44,122);
}
```

Although in all three pairs the second color is a darker shade of the first color, it gets increasingly difficult to see the relationship in the pairs as the numbers become less regular.

NOTE THAT TO MAKE THE SAME COLOR DARKER, YOU HAVE TO ADJUST THREE VALUES. THE FACT THAT THESE PAIRS OF COLORS ARE RELATED PROBABLY WOULDN'T BE OBVIOUS IF YOU CAME ACROSS THEM ON DIFFERENT LINES OF A CSS FILE, UNLESS YOU'RE NATURALLY THE SORT OF PERSON WHO CAN'T LOOK AT A SET OF NUMBERS WITHOUT CALCULATING COMMON FACTORS IN YOUR HEAD.

HSL stands for *hue, saturation*, and *luminosity* in the same way that RGB stands for *red, green*, and *blue*. The basic color is provided by the hue, and the saturation determines the intensity of the color—lower saturation means more grey. The luminosity determines how light or dark the color is. Here's the same set of colors using HSL notation:

```
.one {
  background-color: hsl(0,0%,80%);
  color: hsl(0,0%,40%);
}
.darkone {
  background-color: hsl(0,0%,40%);
  color: hsl(0,0%,80%);
}
.two {
  background-color:
          hsl(210,50%,40%);
  color: hsl(210,50%,13.3%);
}
.darktwo {
  background-color:
          hsl(210,50%,13.3%);
color: hsl(210,50%,40%);
}
```

HSL(0 , 0% , 80%)

HSL(0 , 0% , 40%)

HSL(210 , 50% , 40%)

HSL(210 , 50% , 13.3%)

HSL(335, 80% , 54%)

HSL(335, 80% , 18%)

```
.three {
  background-color:
        hsl(335,80%,54%);
  color: hsl(335,80%,18%);
}
.darkthree {
  background-color:
        hsl(335,80%,18%);
  color: hsl(335,80%,54%);
}
```

In HSL, the luminosity of the color is controlled by one parameter. The relationship between the colors is therefore far more obvious from the code, because this is the only parameter that changes.

Here's what happens when you vary only the saturation. It's hard to make out the differences in a black-and-white book, so I'll describe them: the box at the top is light blue, and the one at the bottom is gray.

Open the example file to get a better look at the colors: ch09/colors-hsl-3.html.

If only the hue is varied, you get different colors with the same saturation and luminosity. The hue corresponds to a point on a color wheel, measured in degrees — 360 and 0 are the same hue. Using four evenly spaced points for this example yields a blue, two shades of green, and a red.

Unfortunately, because the colors have the same saturation and luminosity, they'll be even harder to tell apart in black and white. Open the example file to see for yourself: ch09/colors-hsl-4.html.

HSL(210 , 75% , 40%)

HSL(210 , 50% , 40%)

HSL(210 , 25% , 40%)

HSL(210 , 0% , 40%)

HSL(210 , 75% , 40%)

HSL(140 , 75% , 40%)

HSL(70 , 75% , 40%)

HSL(0 , 75% , 40%)

HSL has a semitransparent equivalent: HSLA. Like RGBA, it has a final parameter that specifies the percentage opacity:

```
.one {
  background-color:
    hsla(210,75%,40%,1);
  color: hsl(210,75%,13.3%);
}
.two {
  background-color:
    hsla(210,75%,40%,0.66);
  color: hsl(210,75%,13.3%);
}
.three {
  background-color:
    hsla(210,75%,40%,0.33);
  color: hsl(210,75%,13.3%);
}
.four {
  background-color:
    hsla(210,75%,40%,0);
  color: hsl(210,75%,13.3%);
}
```

CSS transforms

Browser support quick check: 2D transforms		Full	Partial
		-	7.0
		-	3.5
		-	9.0*
		-	10.5
		-	3.1

* IE has been able to do transformations with the nonstandard `filter` attribute since version 5.5.

COLORS AND TRANSPARENCY CAN ADD DEPTH AND INTEREST TO YOUR DESIGNS, BUT EVERYTHING IS STILL BASICALLY A COLLECTION OF RECTANGLES. IF YOU WANT ELEMENTS AT AN ANGLE, OR TEXT THAT RUNS VERTICALLY, THEN WITH CSS2 YOU HAVE TO RESORT TO IMAGES. IN THE NEXT SECTION, YOU'LL LEARN ABOUT CSS3 TRANSFORMS. THEY LET YOU ROTATE, SKEW, TRANSLATE, AND SCALE ELEMENTS TO CREATE AN INTERESTING VARIETY IN YOUR DESIGNS.

In chapter 3, you learned about transforms using the <canvas> element and SVG—these let you rotate, scale, and skew elements. Similar functionality is made available as part of CSS3. Because everything uses the same rendering engine (the browser), this shouldn't be too surprising. It's already implemented—the browser is just offering different ways to activate it. Transforms allow your designs to escape the rectangular world of standard web pages.

2D transforms

To demonstrate CSS 2D transforms, we'll use this simple page with three similar elements:

```
<body>
  <div>One</div>
  <div>Two</div>
  <div>Three</div>
</body>
```

Here's the basic CSS:

```
div {
    display: inline-block;
    padding: 1em;
    margin: 1em;
    background-color: #666;
    color: #fff;
}
```

This example picks out the second element and scales it to 150% of its initial size:

```
div:nth-child(2) {
    transform: scale(1.5);
}
```

ALL THE EXAMPLES IN THIS SECTION WILL NEED VENDOR PREFIXES APPLIED IF YOU WANT TO TRY THEM IN CURRENT BROWSERS. ADD -webkit-, -moz-, -o-, OR -ms- TO THE FRONT OF THE TRANSFORM PROPERTIES (NOT THE VALUES) FOR SUPPORT IN SAFARI/CHROME, FIREFOX, OPERA, AND IE9, RESPECTIVELY. SEE THE SECTION "BROWSER SUPPORT" AT THE END OF THIS CHAPTER FOR FURTHER DETAILS.

By default, transformed elements keep their center point in the same place. If you scale the third element to 250% of its original size, it partially covers the second element:

```
div:nth-child(3) {
    transform: scale(2.5);
}
```

The static point around which the transform is applied can be changed with the `transform-origin` property. Here we set the third element to expand from its left outward:

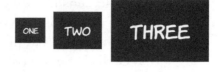

```
div:nth-child(3) {
    transform-origin: left;
    transform: scale(2.5);
}
```

You can also rotate elements:

```
div:nth-child(1) {
  transform: rotate(16.5deg);
}
div:nth-child(2) {
  transform: rotate(33deg);
}
div:nth-child(3) {
  transform: rotate(66deg);
}
```

When the elements are rotated around their centers, the visual spacing can look a little odd. In this example, `transform-origin` is set for each element to bring the elements closer together:

```
div:nth-child(1) div {
  transform-origin: bottom right;
  transform: rotate(16.5deg);
}
div:nth-child(2) div {
  transform-origin: top right;
  transform: rotate(33deg);
}
div:nth-child(3) div {
  transform-origin: top left;
  transform: rotate(66deg);
}
```

In this screenshot, the original positions of the elements have been drawn in so you can more easily see that each element is rotating around a different reference point.

The skew functions allow you to create perspective-like effects. Horizontal skewing is achieved with skewX and vertical with skewY:

```
div:nth-child(1) {
  transform: skewX(16.5deg);
}
div:nth-child(2) {
  transform: skewY(33deg);
}
div:nth-child(3) {
  transform:
   skewX(16.5deg) skewY(33deg);
}
```

It's also possible to move elements around on the page with translateX and translateY:

```
div:nth-child(1) {
  transform: translateX(50px);
}
div:nth-child(2) {
  transform: translateY(50px);
}
div:nth-child(3) {
  transform:
    translate(-50px, -50px);
}
```

NOTE THAT TRANSFORMING ELEMENTS DOESN'T AFFECT THE REST OF YOUR LAYOUT; EVERYTHING ELSE REMAINS IN THE PLACE IT WOULD BE IF THE THERE WAS NO TRANSFORM. TRANSFORMS CAN BE COMBINED TO CREATE INTERESTING EFFECTS. IN THE FOLLOWING EXAMPLE, THE THREE EXAMPLE ELEMENTS HAVE BEEN TRANSFORMED INTO A PSEUDO-3D CUBE USING SKEW, ROTATE, AND TRANSLATE.

For this trick, you need to add an extra <div> to the markup to preserve the direction of the content in the top face:

```
<div class="cube">
    <div>
        <div>One</div>
    </div>
    <div>Two</div>
    <div>Three</div>
</div>
```

The faces are then skewed by 30 or -30 degrees and positioned so the edges line up. Colors are set on each face individually to enhance the perception of depth.

See the blog post "3D Cube using 2D CSS transformation" by Paul Hayes for a full explanation of this technique: www.paulrhayes.com/2009-04/3d-cube-using-css-transformations/.

```
.cube div:nth-child(1) div,
.cube div:nth-child(2),
.cube div:nth-child(3) {
    padding: 10px;
    width: 180px;
    height: 180px;
}
.cube > div {
    position: absolute;
}
.cube div:nth-child(2) {
    transform: skewY(30deg);
    background-color: #444;
}
.cube div:nth-child(3) {
    transform: skewY(-30deg);
    background-color: #666;
    left: 200px;
}
.cube div:nth-child(1) div {
    transform:
        skewY(-30deg) scaleY(1.16);
    background-color: #888;
    font-size: 0.862em;
}
.cube div:nth-child(1) {
    transform: rotate(60deg);
    top: -158px;
    left: 100px;
}
```

3D transforms

Tricks with `transform`, `translate`, and `skew` are entertaining, but they aren't a substitute for real three-dimensional transformations. The example in the previous section is subtly off—it doesn't represent a proper perspective rendering of a cube and the sides don't quite line up. Fortunately, the CSS Working Group is working on a standard for transformations in three dimensions.

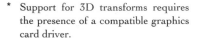

		Full	Partial
Browser support quick check: 3D transforms		-	12.0*
		-	10.0*
		-	10.0
		-	-
		-	4.0*

* Support for 3D transforms requires the presence of a compatible graphics card driver.

This time, because you're making an actual cube in a 3D space, you need six elements to form the sides:

```
<div class="cube">
    <div class="one"><p>One</p></div>
    <div class="two"><p>Two</p></div>
    <div class="three"><p>Three</p></div>
    <div class="four"><p>Four</p></div>
    <div class="five"><p>Five</p></div>
    <div class="six"><p>Six</p></div>
</section>
```

The first step in 3D transformations is to set a perspective. This defines the depth of the 3D space within which you'll be positioning the transformed elements:

```
body { perspective: 1000; }
```

Next, because you want all six sides of the cube to be transformed within the same 3D space, you set a transform-style value of preserve-3d on the parent element:

```
div.cube {
    transform-style: preserve-3d;
    position: relative;
}
```

To start with, all six sides will be stacked on top of each other with absolute positioning:

```
div.cube > div
    { position: absolute; color: #fff;
      width: 200px; height: 200px; }
```

Now the individual sides are transformed in 3D. Each side is rotated so it faces the correct way and then translated along the z-axis by 100 pixels (because the sides of the cube are 200 pixels deep). The z-axis is the third dimension available in the 3D space. Because the rotation occurs before the translation, each side is pushed away from the center of the cube in a different direction:

```
.one {
    transform: translateZ(100px);
    background: rgba(136,136,136,0.5);
}
.two {
    transform: rotateY(90deg) translateZ(100px);
    background: rgba(102,102,102,0.5);
}
.three {
    transform: rotateX(-180deg) translateZ(100px);
    background: rgba(68,68,68,0.5);
}
.four {
    transform: rotateY(-90deg) translateZ(100px);
    background: rgba(34,34,34,0.5);
}
.five {
    transform: rotateX(90deg) translateZ(100px);
    background: rgba(153,153,153,0.5);
}
```

```
.six {
    transform: rotateX(-90deg) translateZ(100px);
    background: rgba(34,34,34,0.5);
}
```

Finally, the whole cube is rotated in the z- and x-axes for artistic effect:

```
div.cube {
    transform: rotateZ(-45deg) rotateX(45deg);
}
```

WRAPPING YOUR WEB PAGE AROUND A CUBE WILL CERTAINLY BE MEMORABLE FOR VISITORS, BUT BE CAREFUL THAT YOU DON'T LET YOUR SNAZZY CSS GET IN THE WAY OF THEM ACCESSING YOUR CONTENT.

TRANSFORMS COME INTO THEIR OWN WHEN COMBINED WITH ANOTHER NEW CSS3 FEATURE: TRANSITIONS. YOU'LL LEARN ABOUT TRANSITIONS IN THE NEXT SECTION.

CSS transitions

A *transition* is a short animation between two element states, such as activating a drop-down menu or closing a pop-up message. Instead of having the elements immediately appear or disappear, the menu might slide down, and the pop-up message could fade out. Such effects improve usability by making interfaces more realistic and can be used to clarify relationships.

ONE OF THE KEY ATTRACTIONS OF THE JQUERY JAVASCRIPT LIBRARY FOR DESIGNERS IS THAT IT MAKES IT EASY TO CREATE THESE SMALL ANIMATIONS. CSS TRANSITIONS ARE INTENDED TO REMOVE THE NEED FOR JAVASCRIPT TO APPLY SMALL VISUAL EFFECTS, AND IN THIS SECTION YOU'LL LEARN ALL ABOUT THEM.

One simple way to apply transitions is with a dynamic pseudo-class like :hover. In the following sets of screenshots, three of the transformation examples from the previous section have been applied to the :hover state of a containing <div> with a transition lasting 10 seconds. Instead of flipping from one state to the other, the change happens gradually. If you look carefully, the fly-like speck on each screenshot is the mouse pointer.

Browser support quick check: CSS transitions		Full	Partial
		-	7.0
		-	4.0
		-	10.0
		-	10.5
		-	3.1

This example is from ch09/transforms-5.html with a 10-second transition.

This example is from ch09/transforms-6.html with a 10-second transition.

This example is from ch09/transforms-7.html with a 10-second transition:

The transition-duration property is the only thing required to create the animation:

```
div div {
    transition-duration: 10s;
}
```

Although all three elements have unique states when the parent element is hover, all three are transitioned according to the previous rule. Look at ch09/transitions-1.html to see for yourself.

```
div:hover div:nth-child(1) {
    transform-origin: bottom right;
    transform: rotate(16.5deg);
}
div:hover div:nth-child(2) {
    transform-origin: top right;
    transform: rotate(33deg);
}
div:hover div:nth-child(3) {
    transform-origin: top left;
    transform: rotate(66deg);
}
```

When transition-duration is set on the default state of the element (in this case, when it isn't hover), the same duration applies as the transition runs both forward and backward—as the element enters the hover state and leaves it, the transition will last 10 seconds as shown in the results of listing ch09/transitions-3.html.

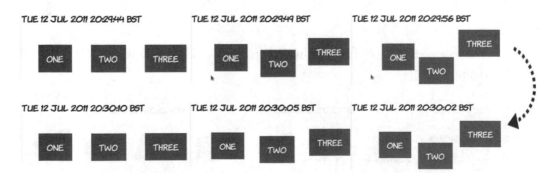

But you can put transition-duration on the hover state. In this case, it will only apply as the element enters the hover state. When the element leaves hover, it immediately snaps back to the starting position—a duration of zero.

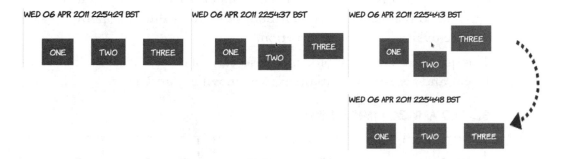

This is the critical bit of code from listing ch09/transitions-4.html:

```
div:hover div { transition-duration: 10s; }
```

You can also put transition-duration on both states. In the next example, the transition lasts 10 seconds as it enters the hover state and 5 seconds as it exits.

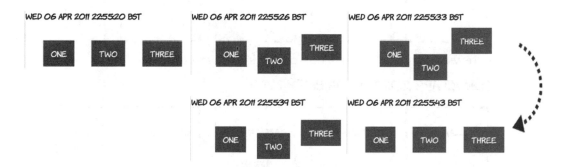

The duration for exiting the hover state is specified on the rule without the :hover:

```
div div { transition-duration: 5s; }
div:hover div { transition-duration: 10s; }
```

See the complete example in listing ch09/transitions-5.html.

Transition timing functions

By default, transitions happen at a constant rate, but you can adjust that with the transition-timing-function property. The default value is linear, but several other keywords are available: ease-in-out, ease-in, ease-out, and ease. The difference is much easier to see than it is to explain, so the next four screenshots show the values in operation side by side over a 20-second transition.

The quickest out of the blocks is ease-out, followed by ease. Both ease-in-out and ease-in are initially slower-moving than linear.

SUN 10 APR 2011 11:45:01 BST

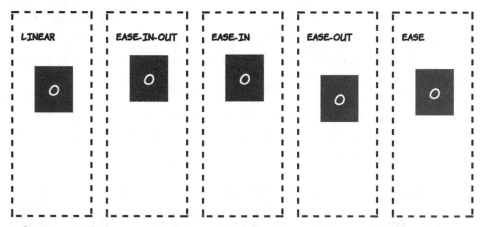

A few seconds later, ease has overtaken ease-out.

SUN 10 APR 2011 11:45:04 BST

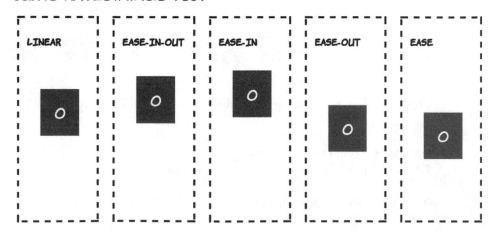

As you go past the halfway point, `ease-in-out` has accelerated and is ahead of `linear`.

SUN 10 APR 2011 11:45:09 BST

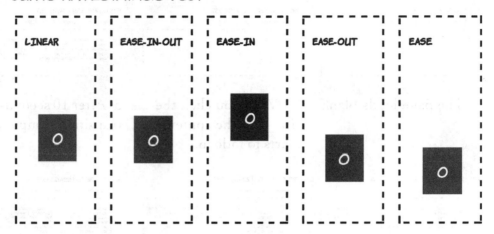

Toward the end of the transition, `ease-in` is starting to catch up with the rest; remember, all five transitions take 20 seconds to complete.

SUN 10 APR 2011 11:45:15 BST

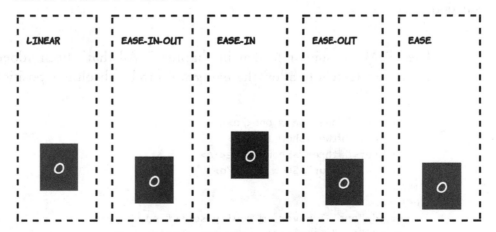

The non-`linear` transition timings often appear more natural—things tend to accelerate and decelerate rather than suddenly start and stop moving.

You're also not limited to effects on hover; any other dynamic pseudo-class will work just as well. With a slight modification, the :target example from chapter 7 can be made to fade smoothly in and out.

1. The page loads blank.

2. When you click the first link, the content starts to fade in.

3. After 10 seconds, the transition completes.

4. Clicking the second link starts two transitions. The current text starts to fade out...

5. ...as the new page starts to fade in.

6. After 10 seconds, the new content has replaced the old.

The HTML is similar to that in chapter 7. All that's been added is a <section> element to allow the paragraphs to be absolutely positioned:

```
<menu>
    <a href="#one">Show one</a>
    <a href="#two">Show two</a>
    <a href="#three">Show three</a>
    <a href="#four">Show four</a>
</menu>
<section>
    <p id="one">I never am really satisfied...</p>
    <p id="two">In almost every computation...</p>
    <p id="three">Many persons who are not conversant...</p>
    <p id="four">The Analytical Engine has no pretensions...</p>
</section>
```

The paragraphs then fade in and out over 10 seconds. The fade-in uses the timing function ease-in (start slow and finish fast), and the fade-out uses ease-out so the disappearing paragraph begins to fade out as quickly as possible, giving immediate feedback to the user:

```
section { position: relative; }
p {
    opacity: 0;
    position: absolute;
    transition-duration: 10s;
    transition-timing-function: ease-out;
}
p:target {
    opacity: 1;
    transition-timing-function: ease-in;
}
```

See the full source code in ch09/transitions-6.html.

Transition property

So far, the examples have implicitly chosen which properties they will apply to by only listing the changed ones in the transition state. Every property has therefore been subject to the same duration and timing function. But it's possible to apply multiple transitions to the same element, with each one affecting a different property.

In this section, you'll take advantage of the fact that all the transition properties accept multiple properties in a comma-separated list. You can declare two transition durations, one of 10 seconds and one of 20, like this:

```
transition-duration: 10s, 20s;
```

Then, if you declare transition-property like this

```
transition-property: top, transform;
```

the transition of the top property will take 10 seconds, and the transition of the transform property will take 20 seconds. The next example compares two elements with the same transition duration but different transition properties.

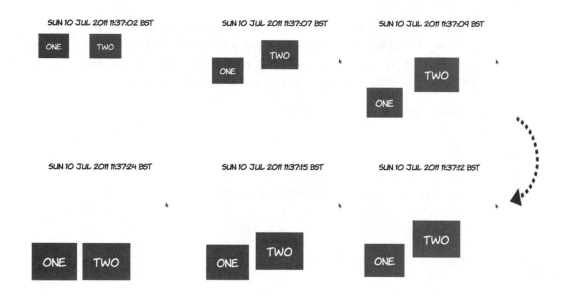

As you can see, element one drops quickly and expands slowly, whereas element two expands quickly and drops slowly. The markup is two <div> elements inside a <section> with this CSS applied to it:

```
section div {
    position: absolute;
    top: 0px;
    transition-duration: 10s, 20s;
    transition-property: top, transform;
}
section div:nth-child(2) {
    left: 200px;
    transition-property: transform, top;
}
section:hover div {
    top: 280px;
    transform: scale(1.5);
}
```

Transition delay

You don't have to start a transition immediately after whatever action initiated it. The transition-delay property allows you to specify a wait before a transition starts. In the following screenshots, element two doesn't begin transitioning until five seconds after element one started, and element three's transition begins a further five seconds after that.

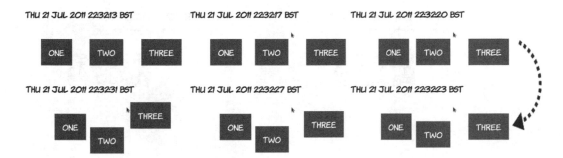

The code, from listing ch09/transition-delay-1.html, is identical to that from ch09/transitions-3.html except for these two rules:

```
div div:nth-child(2) { transition-delay: 5s; }
div div:nth-child(3) { transition-delay: 10s; }
```

The most common use for transition-delay is to chain a number of transitions together. If you want an element to first move and then enlarge, you specify two transitions like this:

```
div {
    transition-duration: 10s, 10s;
    transition-delay: 0, 10s;
    transition-property:  top, transform;
}
```

The element will first transition the top value and then transition the transform. You can see a full example in the code file ch09/transition-delay-2.html. With transition-delay, it's possible to create multiple-step animations, providing that at each step a different property is transitioned. For a more complete approach to animation with CSS, see the later section "CSS Animation."

Triggering transitions with JavaScript

After a transition is defined on an element, any change in the computed style will trigger the animation. This doesn't have to be due to a

dynamic pseudo-class taking effect; you can also change the styles with
JavaScript.

Clicking the Change Left button starts an animation.

Over 10 seconds, the element moves
to the left.

Similarly, clicking Change Top
starts another animation.

Over 10 seconds, the element moves
down from the top of the page.

Here's the HTML for the page:

```
<menu>
    <button onclick="clickme('changeleft')">Change left</button>
    <button onclick="clickme('changetop')">Change top</button>
    <button onclick="clickme('changecolor')">Change color</button>
    <button onclick="reset()">Reset</button>
</menu>
<div id="animateme">Animate Me</div>
```

The CSS defines the animation and three classes that adjust the relevant properties:

```
#animateme {
    background-color: #666;
    position: absolute;
    color: #fff;
    left: 100px;
    top: 100px;
    transition-duration: 10s;
}
.changeleft { left: 250px !important; }
.changetop { top: 300px !important; }
.changecolor { background-color: #ff00ff !important; }
```

Note that you must use !important because otherwise the ID selector would take precedence. Finally, here's the JavaScript function to apply the styles to the element when the buttons are clicked:

```
function clickme(classname) {
    var el = document.getElementById('animateme');
    el.className += " " + classname;
}
```

And here's a reset function to clear the styles:

```
function reset() {
    var el = document.getElementById('animateme');
    el.setAttribute("style","");
}
```

IF YOU KNOW EXACTLY WHERE THE ELEMENT NEEDS TO GO, THEN ADDING PREDEFINED CLASSES IS FINE. BUT IF YOU WANT TO ANIMATE AN ELEMENT BASED ON THE RESULT OF A CALCULATION OR USER INPUT, YOU CAN SET THE STYLE PROPERTIES OF THE ELEMENT DIRECTLY. THE NEXT EXAMPLE DEMONSTRATES THIS APPROACH.

This example switches to Opera so you can take advantage of the color input type.

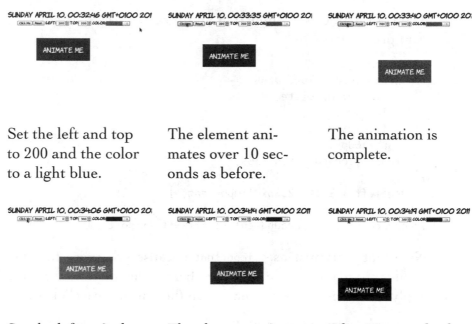

Set the left and top to 200 and the color to a light blue.

The element animates over 10 seconds as before.

The animation is complete.

Set the left to 0, the top to 300, and the color to black.

The element animates from its current position.

After 10 seconds, the new properties are in effect.

```
<menu>
    <button onclick="clickme()">Click Me</button>
    <button onclick="reset()">Reset</button>
    <label for="myleft">left</label>:
        <input id="myleft" type="number" value="100">
    <label for="mytop">top</label>:
        <input id="mytop" type="number" value="100">
    <label for="mycolor">color</label>:
        <input id="mycolor" type="color" value="#666666">
</menu>
<div id="animateme">Animate Me</div>
function clickme() {
    var el = document.getElementById('animateme');
    var left =  document.getElementById('myleft').value;
    var top =  document.getElementById('mytop').value;
    var color =  document.getElementById('mycolor').value;
    el.setAttribute("style","left: " + left + "px; top: " + top +
        "px; background-color: " + color + ";");
}
```

SOMETIMES YOU MAY WANT MORE THAN THE SIMPLE LINEAR MOVEMENT BETWEEN A SET OF PROPERTIES THAT A TRANSITION ALLOWS. FOR EXAMPLE, YOU MAY WANT AN ELEMENT TO BOUNCE OR CYCLE THROUGH SEVERAL STATES. THE NEXT SECTION SHOWS YOU HOW TO CREATE THESE KINDS OF ANIMATIONS.

CSS Animation

CSS Animations are a way of chaining multiple transitions together on the same property to be performed one after the other. Transitions are always linear—a single transition can move an element from one location to another, but it can't move it to a third location after that. Although you can chain transitions together using transition-delay, this technique quickly becomes unwieldy for more than a few steps, and you can still transition only one property at a time. You could, of course, perform a whole sequence of transitions with JavaScript, but that would defeat the purpose of transitions—a declarative solution for simple animations.

Browser support quick check: CSS Animation		Full	Partial
	(Chrome)	-	4.0
	(Firefox)	-	5.0
	(IE)	10	
	(Opera)	-	12
	(Safari)	-	4.0

This first example makes an element bounce up and down.

SUN 10 JUL 2011 15:54:34 BST   SUN 10 JUL 2011 15:54:38 BST   SUN 10 JUL 2011 15:54:42 BST

ANIMATE ME   ANIMATE ME   ANIMATE ME

To declare an animation, use the @keyframes directive. The first word after the directive is the name of the animation, followed by a list of keyframes in braces. Keyframes are defined by the keywords `from` or `to`, or a percentage value:

```
@keyframes bounce {
    from { top: 50px; }
    25% { top: 350px; }
    50% { top: 50px; }
    75% { top: 350px; }
    to { top: 50px; }
}
```

For each keyframe, you provide a semicolon-separated list of CSS properties, just as in a normal CSS rule. For best effect, these should be properties that can be transitioned; then the browser can take care of the intermediate animation. The previous keyframes set the top of the element to be alternately 50 and then 350 pixels.

To apply the animation to an element, use the `animation-name` property:

```
#animateme {
    position: absolute;
    left: 100px;
    top: 50px;
    animation-duration: 20s;
    animation-name: bounce;
    animation-iteration-count: infinite;
}
```

This rule also sets an `animation-duration`—this works the same way as `transition-duration`. The animation will run for 20 seconds, so you can calculate that the element will have a value of 350 pixels for `top` after 5 seconds: there are four steps after the `from` state, and 5 is 25% of 20 seconds. You can also specify `animation-iteration-count`—this can be a fixed value such as 3 or, as here, `infinite`, so the element can bounce up and down forever (or until you get annoyed enough by the bouncing that you close the tab). See the full source code in ch09/animations-1.html.

In the next example, two properties are animated simultaneously—the element still bounces up and down, but it also gets bigger as it reaches the bottom of the bounce.

As mentioned earlier, a keyframe is just like a regular CSS rule: you can list as many properties as you need (although like transitions, not all properties are animatable). For this example, all that's been added to the previous one is a scale transform; see the full source code in ch09/animations-2.html:

```
@keyframes bounce {
    from { top: 50px; transform: scale(1); }
    25% { top: 350px; transform: scale(1.25); }
    50% { top: 50px; transform: scale(1); }
    75% { top: 350px; transform: scale(1.25); }
    to  { top: 50px; transform: scale(1); }
}
```

Just like transitions, multiple animations can be applied simultaneously. Next, you see the element doing the same up-and-down bounce animation as before, but now it's also sliding left to right.

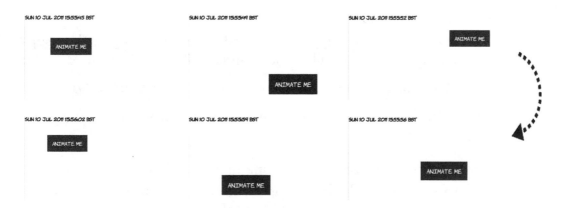

NOW YOU'VE LEARNED HOW IT ALL WORKS: HOW MUCH OF IT CAN YOU USE RIGHT NOW? YOU'LL LEARN ABOUT BROWSER SUPPORT IN THE NEXT SECTION.

See the complete example in listing ch09/animations-3.html.

Browser support

	12	14	4	6	8	9	10	11.1	11.5	5	5.1
Opacity	●	●	●	●	○	●	●	●	●	●	●
RGBA	●	●	●	●		●	●	●	●	●	●
HSL/HSLA	●	●	●	●		●	●	●	●	●	●
2D transforms	○	○	○	○		○	○	○	○	○	○
3D transforms	○	○					○			○	○
Transitions	○	○	○	○		○	○	○	○	○	○
Animation	○	○		○			○			○	○

Key:

- ● Complete or nearly complete support
- ○ Incomplete or alternative support

  Little or no support

Opacity in IE8 and earlier

Although IE8 doesn't support the CSS3 opacity property, it does support setting opacity through its nonstandard filter mechanism:

```
-ms-filter:"progid:DXImageTransform.Microsoft.Alpha(Opacity=50)";
```

This CSS will make the element it's applied to have an opacity value of 0.5.

Transforms, transitions, and animations in current browsers

All current browsers that have support for transforms, transitions, and animations require a vendor prefix to make things work. For transforms and

transitions, this is the normal level of pain for using experimental CSS—
each property has to be listed five times. Here's a section of code from ch09/
transition-delay-2.html:

```
-moz-transition-duration: 10s, 10s;
-webkit-transition-duration: 10s, 10s;
-o-transition-duration: 10s, 10s;
-ms-transition-duration: 10s, 10s;
transition-duration: 10s, 10s;
-moz-transition-delay: 0s, 10s;
-webkit-transition-delay: 0, 10s;
-o-transition-delay: 0, 10s;
-ms-transition-delay: 0, 10s;
transition-delay: 0, 10s;
-moz-transition-property: top, -moz-transform;
-webkit-transition-property: top, -webkit-transform;
-o-transition-property: top, -o-transform;
-ms-transition-property: top, -ms-transform;
transition-property: top, transform;
```

For animations, it's more of a pain. Even if you're only animating standard properties, you must specify the keyframes for every browser you
want to target, not including the standard declaration:

```
@-moz-keyframes bounce {
    from { top: 50px; }
    25% { top: 350px; }
    50% { top: 50px; }
    75% { top: 350px; }
    to { top: 50px; }
}
@-webkit-keyframes bounce {
    from { top: 50px; }
    25% { top: 350px; }
    50% { top: 50px; }
    75% { top: 350px; }
    to { top: 50px; }
}
@-o-keyframes bounce {
    from { top: 50px; }
    25% { top: 350px; }
    50% { top: 50px; }
    75% { top: 350px; }
```

```
    to { top: 50px; }
}
@-ms-keyframes bounce {
    from { top: 50px; }
    25% { top: 350px; }
    50% { top: 50px; }
    75% { top: 350px; }
    to { top: 50px; }
}
```

Then the element itself needs all the `animation-*` properties for each browser:

```
#animateme {
    -moz-animation-duration: 20s;
    -moz-animation-name: bounce;
    -moz-animation-iteration-count: infinite;
    -webkit-animation-duration: 20s;
    -webkit-animation-name: bounce;
    -webkit-animation-iteration-count: infinite;
    -o-animation-duration: 20s;
    -o-animation-name: bounce;
    -o-animation-iteration-count: infinite;
    -ms-animation-duration: 20s;
    -ms-animation-name: bounce;
    -ms-animation-iteration-count: infinite;
}
```

Of course, you should add the standard properties to this listing as well. This will get really fun when the animation properties are standardized, but you want to use them to animate prefixed properties. For example, it's not yet clear if gradients and animations will be standardized at the same time (or even if gradients will be animatable) but if animations get standardized first in browsers, you could end up writing code like this:

```
@keyframes swipe {
    from {
        -moz-linear-gradient(to right, #fff, #f00)
        -webkit-linear-gradient(left, #fff, #f00)
        -o-linear-gradient(to right, #fff, #f00)
        -ms-linear-gradient(to right, #fff, #f00)
        -linear-gradient(to right, #fff, #f00)
```

```
    }
    50% {
        -moz-linear-gradient(to right, #f00, #fff, #f00)
        -webkit-linear-gradient(left, #f00, #fff, #f00)
        -o-linear-gradient(to right, #f00, #fff, #f00)
        -ms-linear-gradient(to right, #f00, #fff, #f00)
        -linear-gradient(to right, #f00, #fff, #f00)
    }
    to {
        -moz-linear-gradient(to right, #f00, #fff)
        -webkit-linear-gradient(left, #f00, #fff)
        -o-linear-gradient(to right, #f00, #fff)
        -ms-linear-gradient(to right, #f00, #fff)
        -linear-gradient(to right, #f00, #fff)
    }
}
```

THIS IS A POSSIBLE WORST-CASE SCENARIO; NO NEED TO START
PANICKING JUST YET. IT'S TO ILLUSTRATE THAT ANIMATIONS
NECESSARILY MULTIPLY THE BROWSER PREFIX PROBLEM.

Using modernizr.js and jQuery for animation in older browsers

CSS Animations are intended to replace those implemented in libraries like jQuery. Using modernizr.js, it's easy to detect whether a browser supports CSS Animations and, if it doesn't, to supply equivalent jQuery animations instead. The following code is taken from ch09/animations-modernizr.html; it's based on the earlier example ch09/animations-1.html:

```
function bounce(el) {
  $(el).animate({top: '350px'}, 5000)        ◀──    JQUERY EQUIVALENT
       .animate({top: '50px'}, 5000)                TO BOUNCE
       .animate({top: '350px'}, 5000)
       .animate({top: '50px'}, 5000);
}
$(document).ready( function() {
  if(!Modernizr.cssanimations) {              ◀──    TRUE IF ANIMATION
    var refreshId;                                   IS SUPPORTED
      $(function() {
```

```
$('#wrapper').hover(function() {
  bounce($('#animateme'));
    refreshId = setInterval(function(){
        bounce($('#animateme')) }, 20000);
      }, function(){
        clearInterval(refreshId);
        $('#animateme').stop(true,false)
                        .animate({top: '50px'},500);
    });
  });
  }
})
```

HOVER() EQUIVALENT
TO :HOVER

Summary

You're now fully prepared to produce Web 2.0–style designs with layers of semitransparent elements thanks to opacity and rgba(). You're also fully equipped to create sets of complementary colors in your head thanks to hsl() and hsla(). Transforms and transitions create lots of possibilities for making user interfaces smoother and more professional.

IN THE NEXT CHAPTER, YOU'LL LEARN ABOUT EVEN MORE CSS3 EYE CANDY. WE'LL COVER THE NEW FEATURES IN CSS3 FOR BACKGROUNDS AND BORDERS, INCLUDING THE EXTREMELY POPULAR ROUNDED CORNERS AND DROP SHADOWS.

Borders and backgrounds with CSS3

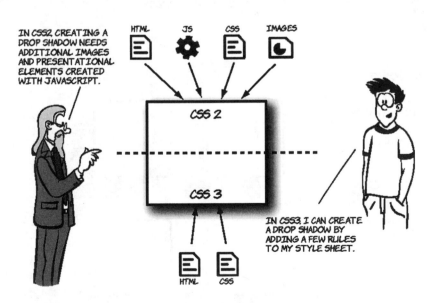

CSS3 makes the traditional background image approaches more flexible and provides declarative options for drop shadows, rounded corners, and gradients. Solutions that have involved images, JavaScript, and extra markup can be replaced with simple HTML and CSS.

Drop shadows with CSS3

The pseudo-3D effect provided by drop shadows is a popular design approach. In the past, designers have gone to great lengths to add this visual effect, but CSS3 saves a lot of time and resources by having the functionality built in.

CSS3 defines two types of shadow: box and text. They use a similar syntax:

```
text-shadow: rgb(0,0,0) 3px 3px 3px;
box-shadow: rgb(0,0,0) 3px 3px 3px;
```

A basic shadow, in either case, is defined by four values:

```
<color> <offset-x> <offset-y> <blur-radius>
```

THE NEXT SECTION LOOKS AT WHAT EACH OF THE FOUR VALUES USED TO DEFINE A SHADOW DOES.

Box shadows

color is any valid CSS color value, such as #6699cc, rgb(102,153,204), or rgba(102,153,204,255).

offset-x is a CSS length, such as 3px or 0.5em. Negative values are allowed.

offset-y is also a CSS length; negative values are allowed.

blur-radius is also a CSS length. Negative values aren't allowed, but this value is optional.

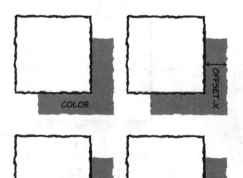

		Standard	Prefixed
Browser support quick check: box-shadow		10.0	5.0
		4.0	3.5
		9.0	-
		10.5	-
		5.0	3.0

SIMPLE BOX SHADOWS

Without the optional `blur-radius`, a box shadow isn't much different from a border. Here's an example that only sets an `offset-x`:

```
box-shadow:
 rgb(0,0,0) 12px 0px;
```

And here's a plain `offset-y`:

```
box-shadow:
 rgb(0,0,0) 0px 12px;
```

Adding a `blur-radius` by itself creates a more shadow-like effect, even without any offsets:

```
box-shadow:
 rgb(0,0,0) 0px 0px 12px;
```

By combining the `blur-radius` with the offsets, you can set the apparent light source:

```
box-shadow:
  rgb(0,0,0) 0px 12px 12px;
```

COMPLEX BOX SHADOWS

For complex effects, you can add multiple shadows in a comma-separated list; they can all use different colors and directions. The following example has a red/orange shadow down and to the right and a purple shadow up and to the left. Whether this is a good idea is up to you!

PSYCHEDELIC!

```
box-shadow:rgb(255,0,0) 3px 3px 3px,
           rgb(255,102,0) 6px 6px 6px,
           rgb(255,204,0) 9px 9px 9px,
           rgb(255,0,204) -3px -3px 6px;
```

The full `box-shadow` definition includes two additional, optional elements:

<inset> <color> <offset-x> <offset-y> <blur-radius> **<spread-radius>**

`inset`, if present, puts the shadow inside the element instead of outside.

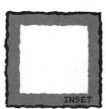

INSET

SPREAD-RADIUS

`spread-radius` is a CSS length; it causes the shadow to grow (positive values) or shrink (negative values) relative to the size of the element.

Here the shadow grows by six pixels on every side:

```
box-shadow: rgb(0,0,0)
 0px 0px 12px 6px;
```

This creates a shadow that extends evenly all around the element.

This example shows a `spread-radius` combined with an `offset-y`:

```
box-shadow: rgb(0,0,0)
 0px 12px 12px 12px;
```

Using inset, you can achieve bevel-like effects:

```
box-shadow: inset rgb(0,0,0)
 0px 0px 12px 6px;
```

Or you can make an element appear to drop into the page, in this case by using the `:hover` pseudo-class:

```
div:hover {
 box-shadow:
  inset rgb(0,0,0)
  3px 3px 5px;
}
```

Text shadows

Text shadows work exactly the same as box shadows. They're defined by the same four values:

```
<color> <offset-x> <offset-y> <blur-radius>
```

We won't look at these values again; instead, let's look at some examples.

Browser support quick check: text-shadow		Standard	Prefixed
	Chrome	4.0	-
	Firefox	3.5	-
	IE	-	5.5*
	Opera	10.0	-
	Safari	2.0	-

* IE can create text-shadow effects using its proprietary `filter` property, but only on elements that have a transparent background.

Here's a simple `offset-x`:

```
text-shadow:
 rgb(51,51,51) 6px 0px;
```

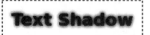

And here's an `offset-y`:

```
text-shadow:
 rgb(51,51,51) 0px 6px;
```

As with box shadows, things become more interesting when you invoke `blur-radius`:

```
text-shadow:
 rgb(51,51,51) 0px 0px 6px;
```

And combining that with an offset can create a 3D feel to match your box shadows:

```
text-shadow:
  rgb(51,51,51) 0px 6px 6px;
```

Multiple shadows work as well:

```
text-shadow:
  rgb(51,0,0) 6px 0px,
  rgb(0,0,51) 0px 6px;
```

But be careful, because it's easy to create completely unreadable text:

```
text-shadow:
  rgb(51,0,0) 6px 0px 3px,
  rgb(0,0,51) 0px 6px 3px;
```

In most cases, you'll want to keep your text shadows small and subtle.

You can use negative values for `offset-x` and `offset-y`. Doing so allows for some interesting pseudo-3D effects if you set the text color to be the same as the background color:

```
color: rgb(255,255,255);
text-shadow:
  rgb(51,51,51) -1px -1px;
```

AFTER DROP SHADOWS, THE EFFECT MOST BELOVED OF GRAPHIC DESIGNERS IN THE LAST DECADE IS ROUNDED CORNERS. FOR A LONG TIME WEB AUTHORS HAVE BEEN USING A NUMBER OF APPROACHES (OR HACKS) TO CREATE BOXES WITH ROUNDED CORNERS. THEY'RE SUCH A USEFUL EFFECT THAT CSS3 PROVIDES A WAY TO MAKE THEM WITHOUT ANY OF THESE HACKS.

Easy rounded corners

Perhaps even more common than the drop shadow in modern web design is the rounded corner. Even otherwise simple website designs often use rounded corners for visual effect.

THE LENGTHS WEB AUTHORS HAVE TO GO TO GET THE ROUNDED CORNER LOOK IN CSS2 IS EXTRAORDINARY—ONE POPULAR METHOD INVOLVES ADDING HUNDREDS OF ELEMENTS TO A PAGE JUST TO GET ROUNDED CORNERS ON A SINGLE ELEMENT; WE'LL LOOK AT THAT IN THIS SECTION.

Browser support quick check: border-radius

	Standard	Prefixed
Chrome	7.0	5.0
Firefox	4.0	3.5
Internet Explorer	9.0	-
Opera	10.5	-
Safari	5.0	3.0

Many of the rounded corners you see on the web aren't strictly necessary. An engineer at Yahoo! once created a version of the company's home page without any rounded corners and discovered that it reduced the amount of data a user had to download by more than 50%. When he showed the two different versions of the page to designers, they didn't spot the difference.

CurvyCorners is a JavaScript library for creating rounded corners on elements. Let's see how it compares to the new CSS3 techniques for creating rounded corners.

OK, I'M GOING TO CREATE AN ELEMENT WITH ROUNDED CORNERS USING THE CURVY CORNERS JAVASCRIPT LIBRARY.

MEANWHILE, I'LL CREATE AN IDENTICAL-LOOKING ELEMENT USING CSS3.

SO FAR THE RESULT DOESN'T LOOK ANY DIFFERENT, WHICHEVER APPROACH YOU TAKE.

I AGREE. LET'S COMPARE THE CODE WE HAD TO WRITE TO GET THE ROUNDED CORNER EFFECT.

```html
<style>
#myBox {
    background-color: #999;
    border: 6px solid #000;
}
</style>
<script
 src="curvycorners.js"></script>
<script>
  addEvent(window,
    'load', initCorners);
  function initCorners() {
    var settings = {
      tl: { radius: 40 },
      tr: { radius: 40 },
      bl: { radius: 40 },
      br: { radius: 40 },
      antiAlias: true
    }
</script>
```

```html
<style>
#myBox {
    background-color: #999;
    border: 6px solid #000;
    border-radius: 40px;
}
</style>
```

IT'S STARTING TO LOOK LIKE THE CSS APPROACH IS THE WINNER. EVEN THOUGH THE CURVYCORNERS CODE ISN'T COMPLEX,

THERE'S TWICE AS MUCH OF IT. BUT I THINK YOU'VE CHEATED—TO GET THE WIDEST BROWSER SUPPORT, YOU NEED TO ADD BROWSER-SPECIFIC RULES TO YOUR CODE.

THAT'S TRUE. THERE WOULD BE FOUR EXTRA LINES IN MY CSS IF THIS WAS PRODUCTION CODE. I THINK I'D STILL BE WINNING, THOUGH!

THIS ISN'T A COMPETITION, AJ. WE'RE COLLABO RATING TO TRY TO FIND THE BEST APPROACH! LET'S LOOK AT THE CLIENT-SIDE MARKUP FOR EACH.

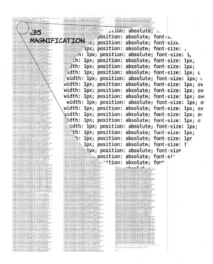

ER, OK THERE'S A LITTLE EXTRA MARKUP INVOLVED WITH CURVYCORNERS, BUT IT'S NOT LIKE I HAD TO WRITE ALL THAT HTML MYSELF. ALTHOUGH IT WAS A BIT OF A PAIN HAVING TO ATTACH A SCRIPT, IT WASN'T THAT MUCH EFFORT ON MY PART.

STILL, THERE'LL BE A PERFORMANCE IMPACT ON THE BROWSER WHEN SCROLLING OR RESIZING, DUE TO HAVING THOUSANDS OF EXTRA ELEMENTS IN THE DOM.

WITH THE CSS3 APPROACH, THE BROWSER TAKES CARE OF IT ALL IN THE BACKGROUND AND MAY EVEN HAND OFF THE PROCESSING TO GRAPHICS HARDWARE RATHER THAN RENDER SHADOWS ITSELF.

ON THE OTHER HAND, THE CURVYCORNERS APPROACH WILL WORK ON NEARLY EVERY BROWSER OUT THERE, INCLUDING OLD VERSIONS OF INTERNET EXPLORER.

CSS3 ISN'T SUPPORTED IN EVERY BROWSER YET, AND WEB AUTHORS WILL BE DEALING WITH OLD VERSIONS OF SOME BROWSERS FOR YEARS.

THAT'S TRUE, BUT YOU CAN EASILY DETECT SUPPORT FOR BORDER-RADIUS WITH JAVASCRIPT AND ONLY RUN THE CURVYCORNERS SCRIPT ON BROWSERS WITHOUT SUPPORT.

BROWSERS THAT SUPPORT BORDER-RADIUS WILL GET FASTER AND LIGHTER WEIGHT PAGES. EVERYONE ELSE WON'T SEE ANYTHING AMISS.

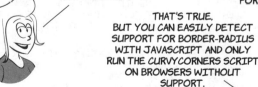

In addition to the single-value form you saw in the previous example, you can also use different values for each corner of an element.

Like the `border`, `padding`, and `margin` properties, the `border-radius` property can accept up to four values. They apply starting from the upper-left corner and proceed clockwise around the element:

```
border-radius: 40px 160px 80px 120px;
```

LATER IN THIS CHAPTER, YOU'LL LEARN ABOUT SEVERAL FEATURES IN CSS3 THAT PROVIDE NATIVE SUPPORT FOR EFFECTS WEB AUTHORS HAVE PREVIOUSLY TRIED TO ACHIEVE WITH BACKGROUND IMAGES. THERE ARE ALSO NEW FEATURES FOR BACKGROUND IMAGES THEMSELVES. WE'LL LOOK AT THESE IN THE NEXT SECTION.

New features for background images

CSS3 offers four new features for the venerable background image: sizing; multiple backgrounds on a single element; positioning relative to the border, padding, or content; and clipping according to the border, padding, or content. In this section, you'll learn about each of these new features.

Background size

	Standard	Prefixed
Chrome	7.0	5.0
Firefox	4.0	3.6
Internet Explorer	9.0	-
Opera	10.5	10.10
Safari	5.0	3.0

Browser support quick check: background-size

Background images are intended to be used purely for decoration, whereas images placed in HTML are supposed to mean something—this is the same separation-of-concerns principal that's been discussed in several previous chapters. But images placed in the markup have certain practical advantages that can discourage web authors from doing the right thing.

ONE OF THE ADVANTAGES OF IMAGES IN MARKUP IS THAT IT'S EASY TO MAKE AN INLINE IMAGE SCALE ACCORDING TO THE SIZE OF ITS CONTAINER: SET THE WIDTH OF THE IMAGE TO BE 100%. BUT IN CSS2 BACKGROUNDS, THERE'S NO WAY TO MAKE THE IMAGE BE ANYTHING OTHER THAN ITS INNATE SIZE. THE FOLLOWING EXAMPLE SHOWS THIS ISSUE.

In this example, an image has been set as a decorative background to a header:

```
h1 {
    background-image:
      url('head-banner.png');
    background-repeat: no-repeat;
    padding-top: 1.85em;
}
```

Top padding has been set to allow room for the background image, and the image itself is sized to match the width of the heading.

If the heading was to change at all, the background image might look a little incongruous. If you translate "Columbia Internet" into French, for example, suddenly you have an image with some text sticking out underneath. The visual relationship is lost.

The new background-size property allows the image to be stretched in proportion to the dimensions of the element:

```
h1 {
    background-image:
      url('head-banner.png');
    background-repeat: no-repeat;
    background-size: 100% 1.85em;
    padding-top: 1.85em;
```

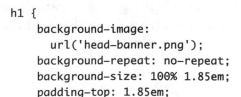

```
    display: inline-block;
}
```

The h1 is set to be inline-block so its
width shrink-wraps its content. Then
the background image is set to be a fixed
height and full width. You can see that
the image becomes distorted as the
width of the element forces it to stretch.
For this reason, this approach is suitable
only to allow for small changes in
expected element width.

If the text will stay the same but will
appear in different font sizes, it's possible to avoid the aspect-ratio issue. If you
know how wide the text will be, specify
the width and height in proportion to
the aspect ratio:

```
h1 {
    background-image:
      url('head-banner.png');
    background-repeat: no-repeat;
    padding-top: 2.18em;
    display: inline-block;
    background-size: 11.1em 2.18em;
}
section:nth-of-type(1) h1 {
    font-size: 200%;
}
section:nth-of-type(2) h1 {
    font-size: 250%;
}
section:nth-of-type(3) h1 {
    font-size: 300%;
}
```

The ability to size backgrounds aligns well with vector graphics. In
chapter 3, you learned that SVG graphics, because they're vectors, are

smooth and sharp no matter how much you stretch them, whereas bitmap graphics become blocky and blurry. Following are two examples, one using a bitmap PNG format and the other SVG. The SVG image is much sharper.

```
div {
    background-image:
url('aj.png');
    background-repeat: no-repeat;
    background-size: 50% 100%;
    padding-left: 50%;
    display: inline-block;
}
```

```
div {
    background-image:
url('aj.svg');
    background-repeat: no-repeat;
    background-size: 50% 100%;
    padding-left: 50%;
    display: inline-block;
}
```

ALTHOUGH SVG WORKS WELL WITH BACKGROUND SIZING, IT'S A BAD FIT FOR PHOTOGRAPHIC-TYPE IMAGES. YOU MAY WANT TO SET A SINGLE PICTURE BEHIND YOUR CONTENT, SIMILAR TO THE EFFECT ACHIEVED BY SETTING A DESKTOP BACKGROUND ON YOUR COMPUTER. IN THIS CASE, THE DETAIL OF THE IMAGE ISN'T AS IMPORTANT, SO DISTORTION IS LESS OF AN ISSUE.

This example shows the main content with a semitransparent background overlaid on a background image set to fill the entire box. Here's the markup:

```
<section>
  <div>
    <p>In almost every...</p>
```

```
    </div>
</section>
```

And here's the CSS:

```
section {
    margin: 1em;
    padding: 5%;
    outline: 4px dashed black;
    background: url('10years.jpg') top /
100% no-repeat;
    display: inline-block;
    min-height: 342px;
    min-width: 300px;
}
div {
    background-color:
rgba(255,255,255,0.66);
}
```

Unlike the previous examples, it uses the shorthand syntax. The size appears with the position separated by a slash: `top / 100%`.

NOTE THAT ALTHOUGH SEVERAL BROWSERS HAVE IMPLEMENTED background-size, ONLY OPERA HAS IMPLEMENTED THE SHORTHAND SYNTAX. FOR OTHER BROWSERS, YOU'LL HAVE TO STICK WITH A SEPARATE background-size DECLARATION.

SCALING ISN'T THE ONLY NEW BACKGROUND FEATURE ADDED IN CSS3. YOU CAN ALSO ATTACH MULTIPLE BACKGROUNDS TO A SINGLE ELEMENT. IN THE PREVIOUS EXAMPLE, AN ELEMENT WAS ADDED TO THE MARKUP WHOSE ONLY ROLE WAS TO ADD A BACKGROUND TO THE TEXT. IN THE NEXT SECTION, YOU'LL SEE HOW CSS3 ALLOWS YOU TO DO THIS WITHOUT ADDITIONAL MARKUP FOR STYLING.

Multiple backgrounds

In CSS2, you're only allowed one background image per element, but there are many situations in which you might want more than one image:

- A header has a background image spanning the width of the page as well as a company logo.

- A decorative pull-quote box has opening and closing quotes on either side.
- Beveled buttons or tabs have images for the left and right sides.
- A rough-edged paper scroll effect needs a repeating image down both sides.

Often, web authors use CSS tricks to size a child element to match its container so their background images can overlap (this is known as the *sliding doors* technique). But they frequently have to introduce an extra element to support the styling, or even add a decorative image inline in the markup.

Browser support quick check: multiple backgrounds		Standard	Prefixed
		7.0	-
		3.6	-
		9.0	-
		10.5	-
		3.0	-

ALL THESE APPROACHES END UP ADDING PURELY PRESENTATIONAL MARKUP TO THE PAGE OR, DEPENDING ON THE ELEMENTS, BEING COMBINED IN A PARTICULAR WAY. ALTHOUGH THIS USUALLY ISN'T A MAJOR ISSUE IN THESE ISOLATED INSTANCES, IT INDICATES A LACK OF POWER IN THE PRESENTATION LANGUAGE, CSS. THIS LACK OF POWER IS ADDRESSED IN CSS3, AS YOU'LL SEE IN THE EXAMPLES THAT FOLLOW.

Let's revisit the last example from the previous section, except this time without the additional `<div>` element for wrapping the content:

```
<section>
  <p>In almost every...</p>
</section>
```

Despite losing the extra element, the page looks the same, because two

backgrounds are applied to the
`<section>` element:

```
section {
    margin: 1em;
    padding: 5%;
    outline: 4px dashed black;
    background:
      url('trans-66.png')
        50% 50% no-repeat,
      url('10years.jpg') no-repeat;
    background-size: 90% 90%,
                     100%;
    display: inline-block;
}
```

Adding multiple background images
is a matter of listing them in the background property, along with any relevant attributes, separated by
commas:

```
background: top right
  url('pitr-head.png') no-repeat,
 bottom right
  url('aj-head.png') no-repeat,
 top left
  url('mike-head.png') no-repeat,
 bottom left
  url('sid-head.png') no-repeat;
```

See the full example in ch10/back-
grounds-5.html.

All the other background properties also allow a comma-separated list,
so you could write the previous example as follows:

```
background-image: url('pitr-head.png'), url('pitr-head.png'),
                  url('mike-head.png'), url('sid-head.png');
background-position: top right, bottom right,
                     top left, bottom left;
background-repeat: no-repeat, no-repeat,
                   no-repeat, no-repeat;
```

The background image you list first will be the closest to the viewer. If you put all the images in the same place, you can see that the first image covers the rest:

```
background: center
  url('pitr-head.png') no-repeat,
 center
  url('aj-head.png') no-repeat,
 center
  url('mike-head.png') no-repeat,
 center
  url('sid-head.png') no-repeat;
```

See the full example in ch10/backgrounds-6.html.

You can use this behavior to your advantage to create interesting effects. This examples use a semitransparent PNG image in between each of the other background images to create a progressive fade:

```
background: top right
  url('pitr-head.png') no-repeat,
 url('trans-66.png'),
 bottom right
  url('aj-head.png') no-repeat,
 url('trans-66.png'),
 top left
  url('mike-head.png') no-repeat,
 url('trans-66.png'),
 bottom left
  url('sid-head.png') no-repeat;
```

See the full example in ch10/backgrounds-7.html.

Background origin and clipping

CSS2 has no control over what part of an element the background applies to. Because CSS2 doesn't allow background sizing, most authors haven't encountered this limitation; but CSS3 introduces two new properties to give web authors fine-grained control: `background-origin` and `background-clip`.

THIS SECTION REQUIRES AN UNDERSTANDING OF THE CSS BOX MODEL TO GET THE MOST OUT OF IT. IF YOU AREN'T SURE, PLEASE REFER TO THE DISCUSSION IN APPENDIX C OR THE DIAGRAMS IN CHAPTER 8 BEFORE PROCEEDING.

The default for `background-origin` is `padding-box`. This means the background applies to the area containing the padding but not to the area containing the border:

```
section {
    margin: 1em;
    padding: 1em;
    border: 1em dashed black;
    background-origin: padding-box;
}
```

Remember, this example image is scaled to fill its container and set to not repeat.

Setting the origin to `border-box` means the background now extends out under the border:

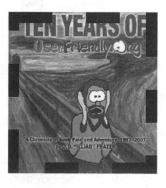

```
section {
    margin: 1em;
    padding: 1em;
    border: 1em dashed black;
    background-origin: border-box;
}
```

Finally, content-box limits the background to the content area, inside the padding:

```
section {
    margin: 1em;
    padding: 1em;
    border: 1em dashed black;
    background-origin: content-box;
}
```

The default value for background-clip is border-box:

```
section {
    margin: 1em;
    padding: 1em;
    border: 1em dashed black;
    background-clip: border-box;
}
```

Remember that the example is scaled and set to not repeat.

When applied to backgrounds that don't repeat, this is indistinguishable from padding-box, because of the default value of background-origin:

```
section {
    margin: 1em;
    padding: 1em;
    border: 1em dashed black;
    background-clip: padding-box;
}
```

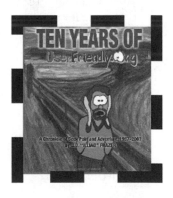

But if the background is allowed to repeat, the difference becomes apparent. A setting of padding-box clips the image inside the border, but for border-box you can see the repeating image under the border:

```
section {
    background-clip: border-box;
    background-repeat: repeat;
}
```

Finally, content-box clips the background to the content area:

```
section {
    margin: 1em;
    padding: 1em;
    border: 1em dashed black;
    background-clip: content-box;
}
```

Note that even though the background is clipped, the image is still sized to the pad-ding-box.

SCALING BACKGROUNDS UNIFORMLY MAY NOT ALWAYS PRODUCE THE EFFECT YOU WANT. ALTHOUGH THE SLIDING DOORS TECHNIQUE PROVIDES A WORKAROUND, THERE'S A MORE STRAIGHTFORWARD CSS3 APPROACH TO ACHIEVE THE SAME EFFECT: border-image. LET'S LOOK AT THAT NEXT.

Selective background scaling with border images

When you're trying to create flexible layouts, you often want a back-ground that looks the same for most of its length, but with a certain num-ber of pixels at either end that are slightly different. This is especially true when you want to create a rounded element with a beveled effect.

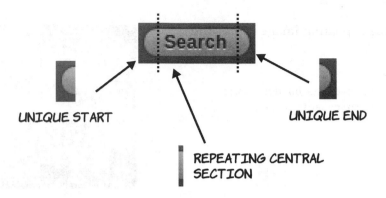

UNIQUE START

UNIQUE END

REPEATING CENTRAL
SECTION

Here are some examples:

Rounded corners on a beveled
background from bbc.co.uk

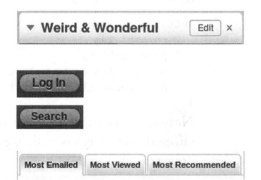

Buttons with rounded corners
and shading on wordpress.com

Tabs with rounded corners and
shading on yahoo.com

The border-image property allows you to slice up an image and apply
transformations selectively to each slice. It's simpler than it sounds, as
you'll see after a few examples.

THE ABILITY TO ADD AN IMAGE TO A BORDER IS ONE OF THE MORE POWERFUL
FEATURES OF CSS3; UNFORTUNATELY IT'S ALSO ONE OF THE LEAST INTUITIVE.
DESPITE BEING SUPPORTED BY FIREFOX SINCE VERSION 3.0 IT'S SEEN FAR
LESS UPTAKE THAN SEVERAL OTHER FEATURES IN THIS CHAPTER.

Basic border-image

To start with, let's use the following example image. It's 240 pixels
square, and it contains five smaller images, each of which is approximately 80 pixels square.

		Standard	Prefixed
Browser support quick check: border–image		4.0	-
		3.5	-
		-	-
		10.5	-
		3.0	-

Let's start with the simplest possible example and apply the border image to an element 720 pixels wide and 400 pixels high:

```
height: 400px;
width: 720px;
border-width: 80px;
border-style: solid;
border-image: url('border1.png') 80;
```

As you can see, the center disappears.

If you want to retain the center of the image, use the fill keyword:

```
height: 400px;
width: 720px;
border-width: 80px;
border-style: solid;
border-image:
 url('border1.png') 80 fill;
```

The center of the image is stretched to fill the space, but the corners stay where they are.

This diagram shows what's going on. The `border-image` value of 80 specifies a pixel length, which the browser uses to slice the image into nine sections, each of which is 80 pixels square.

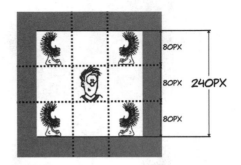

The four corner sections aren't adjusted: they remain in the corners of the elements. The center segment expands to fill the remaining space.

Stretching and repeating border-image sections

 IN THE PREVIOUS EXAMPLE, THE MIDDLE SEGMENTS ON THE SIDES ARE ALSO STRETCHED, BUT YOU CAN'T SEE THAT BECAUSE THEY'RE SOLID WHITE. TO ILLUSTRATE, LET'S LOOK AT AN EXAMPLE WITH A DIFFERENT IMAGE.

Let's apply the same rules with this new image:

```
height: 400px;
width: 720px;
border-width: 80px;
border-style: solid;
border-image: url('border2.png') 80;
```

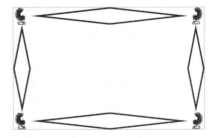

Now the stretching of the middle segments on the sides is more apparent.

The pattern fits neatly inside the middle segments, each 80 pixels square. As you saw before, the corners stay the same but the middle segments are stretched. This is because when you omit the third parameter to border-image, you get the default. The previous example is equivalent to this:

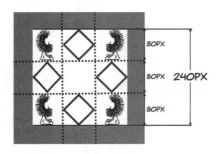

```
border-image:
 url('border2.png') 80 stretch;
```

You can use two other keywords instead of stretch. The first is repeat:

```
height: 400px;
width: 720px;
border-width: 80px;
border-style: solid;
border-image:
 url('border2.png') 80 repeat;
```

The image in the middle segment is repeated across the available width and height.

The second is round:

```
border-image:
 url('border2.png') 80 round;
```

It looks like there's no difference between repeat and round, but that's due to a careful choice of element size to demonstrate the technique. If the size of the element is reduced slightly, the difference is apparent. Look at the following two screenshots of the same two rules applied to a 680 × 360-pixel element.

 repeat RETAINS THE WIDTH OF THE CENTER SEGMENT— IF IT DOESN'T FIT ACROSS THE WIDTH OF THE BOX, THEN PARTS OF THE SEGMENT ARE CUT OFF.

round ADJUSTS THE WIDTH OF THE CENTER SEGMENT TO FIT A WHOLE NUMBER OF TIMES ACROSS THE WIDTH.

 WHEN YOU HAVE A MIDDLE SEGMENT THAT MAKES A REPEATED PATTERN, round WILL USUALLY BE WHAT YOU WANT. IF THE MIDDLE SEGMENT IS A SOLID COLOR OR GRADIENT, LIKE A BEVELED EDGE, USE repeat TO AVOID ANY DISTORTION FROM THE BROWSER ADJUSTING THE IMAGE.

You may be curious about what happens to the middle segment when you use repeat or round. This screenshot shows that the middle behaves in the same way as the middle segments on the border:

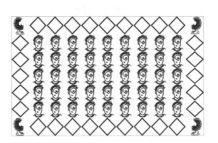

```
border-image:
 url('border3.png') 80 fill round;
```

If you ever need to create internet bank notes, this may be the way to go.

You can also use different approaches on the horizontal and vertical borders:

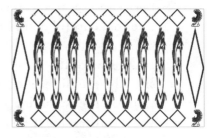

```
border-image:
 url('border3.png')
 80 fill round stretch
```

The first keyword applies to the horizontal borders, and the second to the vertical borders.

Using border-image to create common effects

NOW YOU KNOW ENOUGH TO IMPLEMENT ALL THREE EXAMPLES FROM THE BEGINNING OF THIS SECTION. LET'S TAKE A SINGLE, FIXED-SIZE IMAGE AND USE IT TO MAKE ELEMENTS THAT ADAPT IN SIZE TO THEIR CONTENTS YET RETAIN A SHARP IMAGE AT THE EDGES FOR ROUNDED-CORNER AND BEVEL EFFECTS.

First, let's make some buttons and tabs. Here's a generic image to provide the background for both.

Using this image, you can easily create buttons like these.

The code for the border image on each of these buttons is

```
border-width: 45px;
border-style: solid;
border-image: url('border4-bevel.png') 45 fill repeat;
```

Each button's text size is set individually, and each has a different amount of text. Notice that the buttons aren't even the same shape as the original image, but it has been adapted seamlessly.

Now let's use the same image to create some tabs.

To achieve tabs, you have to adjust one line of CSS from the previous example. Set the bottom border width to 0:

```
border-width: 45px 45px 0px 45px;
border-style: solid;
border-image: url('border4-bevel.png') 45 fill repeat;
```

The border image, as with the buttons, adapts to the size of the content.

You've already seen the direct support for box shadows in CSS3, but they can also be achieved with `border-image`. If you combine this CSS with the image on the right, you can achieve the results that follow:

```
border-image:
 url('drop-shadow.png') 70 repeat;
```

You're not likely to use this technique often, but on occasion you may want more precise control over a shadow than `box-shadow` allows.

Drop shadow 1	The Second drop shadow	Shadow Three

`border-image` IS HARD TO OVERRIDE SELECTIVELY. IF YOU WANT TO SCALE AN IMAGE ACROSS A BACKGROUND WITH THE BUILT-IN CSS SUPPORT (IF AVAILABLE) AND `border-image` IF NOT, YOU'LL NEED TO USE SOMETHING LIKE MODERNIZR.JS.

Creating gradients with CSS

Gradients—smooth transitions from one color to another—have always been popular with designers. In CSS2, the only way to implement a gradient is to create it as an image in a graphics program and attach it as a background to the element. This has problems and limitations, several of which you're already familiar with:

- Images don't always scale well, which can create problems when you use an image as a background for content that's intended to scale.

- If you decide to change your color scheme slightly, you may have to regenerate all your gradient images.

- Every different gradient you want to use means an extra download from the server, increasing page-load times for users and your bandwidth requirements.

- If the element color will change in response to user interaction—for example, a menu item on mouse-over—you need to make twice as many images, doubling all the problems just mentioned.

		Standard	Prefixed
Browser support quick check: gradients		-	3.0
		-	3.6
		-	10.0*
		-	11.10
		-	4.0

* IE has been able to do simple gradients with the nonstandard `filter` attribute since version 5.5.

CSS GRADIENTS ARE ALLOWED ANYWHERE YOU CURRENTLY CAN SPECIFY AN IMAGE. AT THIS TIME, BROWSERS ONLY HAVE SUPPORT FOR USING THEM AS BACKGROUNDS, SO THE EXAMPLES CONCENTRATE ON THAT.

In this section you'll use a snippet of HTML like this:

```
<div id="gradient"> 
</div>
```

You'll also need some basic CSS like this:

```
#gradient {
    outline: 1px solid #999;
    min-height: 400px;
    max-width: 400px;
    background: none;
}
```

The CSS snippets shown next should be inserted in place of the `back-ground: none;` property to achieve the screenshots shown in a supporting browser. See the section "Browser support" for details of prefixes required to access experimental support.

A simple gradient is easy—specify the direction and two colors. The browser calculates a gradient across the entire background, treating the first color as the starting color and the second as the end color:

```
background: linear-gradient(
 to bottom, #000, #fff
);
```

In addition to up and down, gradients can go from one side to another:

```
background: linear-gradient(
 to right, #000, #fff
);
```

Maybe you want something other than up and down or left and right. You can combine the two to get diagonal gradients:

```
background: linear-gradient(
 to bottom left, #000, #fff
);
```

The direction can also be specified in degrees. The above rule is equivalent to this:

```
background: linear-gradient(
 315deg, #000, #fff
);
```

If you add more colors, the browser treats them as equally spaced color stops and calculates the gradient accordingly:

```
background: linear-gradient(
 to bottom, #000, #fff, #000, #fff
);
```

Finally, if you don't want the color stops to be evenly spaced, you can give percentage values for each color stop:

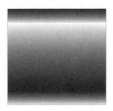

```
background: linear-gradient(
  to bottom,
  #000,
  #fff 15%,
  #000 85%,
  #fff
);
```

LINEAR GRADIENTS ARE ALL VERY WELL, BUT SOMETIMES YOU WANT A MORE CIRCULAR EFFECT—FOR EXAMPLE, A SPOT HIGHLIGHT ON A GLASSY BUTTON. CSS3 LETS YOU CREATE RADIAL GRADIENTS; WE'LL LOOK AT THEM NOW.

Radial gradients are as simple as linear gradients. You supply a start color and an end color:

```
background: radial-gradient(
  #000, #fff
);
```

The gradient starts at the center and extends to the boundary of whatever element it's applied to.

You can achieve more interesting effects by positioning the center of the gradient:

```
background: radial-gradient(
  at top, #000, #fff
);
```

The at keyword is used to specify the center point.

The gradient center can be positioned anywhere:

```
background: radial-gradient(
  at 25% 25%, #000, #fff
);
```

Using the `contain` keyword means the gradient stops when it touches the edges of the containing element:

```
background: radial-gradient(
 at 25% 25%, contain, #000, #fff
);
```

As with linear gradients, a radial gradient can have any number of color stops:

```
background: radial-gradient(
 at 25% 25%, #000, #fff, #000, #fff
);
```

BECAUSE GRADIENTS REPLACE BACKGROUND IMAGES, YOU CAN USE THE SAME BACKGROUND PROPERTIES ON THEM AS YOU USE FOR BACKGROUND IMAGES. YOU CAN USE THIS TO YOUR ADVANTAGE TO PRODUCE SOME USEFUL EFFECTS, AS YOU'LL SEE NEXT.

If you want your gradient to only cover part of the background, you can use the `background-size` property:

```
background: linear-gradient(
 top, #000, #fff
) no-repeat;
background-size: 100% 50%;
```

This might be most useful when you want to put a gradient in a fixed part of the background rather than scale it across the whole thing.

You can also size a radial gradient, although the effect isn't as pleasing:

```
background: radial-gradient(
 at 25% 25%, #000, #fff
) no-repeat;
background-size: 100% 50%;
```

This does let you see another property of radial gradients: by default they're ellipsoid rather than circular. You haven't noticed until now because you've been applying them to square elements.

You can make the gradient circular using the circle keyword:

```
background: radial-gradient(
 circle at 25% 25%, #000, #fff
) no-repeat;
background-size: 100% 50%;
```

NOTE THAT THE SPECIFICATION ALLOWS YOU TO SPECIFY A SIZE FOR THE GRADIENT WITHIN THE GRADIENT ITSELF. ONE OF THE REASONS THE to AND at KEYWORDS WERE ADDED WAS TO ALLOW LENGTHS FOR SIZING TO BE ADDED UNAMBIGUOUSLY ALONGSIDE THE POSITION. HOWEVER, AS YET NO BROWSER SUPPORTS THIS SYNTAX, SO CURRENTLY IT'S MORE RELIABLE TO USE background-size.

It's also possible to layer multiple gradients if you use RGBA colors. Here's a radial gradient over a linear gradient to create a highlight effect:

```
background: radial-gradient(
 circle at 25% 25%,
 rgba(255,255,255,0.75),
 rgba(255,255,255,0)
) no-repeat,
linear-gradient(
 to bottom, #000, #fff
) no-repeat;
```

There's no reason your gradient can't have the same starting and ending colors. This example modifies the final example from "Multiple back-grounds" to use a gradient instead of loading an extra image from the server:

```
background: top right
  url('pitr-head.png') no-repeat,
```

```
linear-gradient(top,
 rgba(255,255,255,0.5),
 rgba(255,255,255,0.5)),
bottom right
 url('aj-head.png') no-repeat,
linear-gradient(
 top,rgba(255,255,255,0.5),
 rgba(255,255,255,0.5)),
top left
 url('mike-head.png') no-repeat,
linear-gradient(top,
 rgba(255,255,255,0.5),
 rgba(255,255,255,0.5)),
bottom left
 url('sid-head-bg.png') no-repeat;
```

This replaces the image used in the multiple-background example in listing ch10/backgrounds-7.html.

NOW YOU'VE SEEN ALL THE NEW FEATURES. LET'S TAKE A DETAILED LOOK AT CURRENT BROWSER SUPPORT.

USER FRIENDLY by J.D. "Iliad" Frazer

Browser support

Browser support for CSS3 border, background, and gradient features is pretty good—all the major browsers have some support, or will soon have support, for everything but border-image in currently released versions. A lot of vendor extensions are involved, and IE8 and earlier take quite a bit of work, as we'll look at next.

	12	14	4	6	8	9	10	11.1	11.5	5	5.1
text-shadow	●	●	●	●	○	○	○	●	●	●	●
box-shadow	●	●	●	●	○	●	●	●	●	○	●
border-image	○	○	○	○				○	○	○	○
border-radius	●	●	●	●		●	●	●	●	●	●
Multiple backgrounds	●	●	●	●		●	●	●	●	●	●
background-size	●	●	●	●		●	●	●	●	●	●
Gradients	○	○	○	○			●	○	○	○	○

Key:
- ● Complete or nearly complete support
- ○ Incomplete or alternative support
-    Little or no support

Cross-browser drop shadows

Chrome (before 10), Safari (before 5.1), and Firefox (before 4.0) use a vendor extension for box and text shadows; the vendor extension is the same for both. Neither of the WebKit browsers initially supported inset but current versions do; spread-radius support was added in Chrome 8 and Safari 5 but didn't work reliably until Chrome 10 and Safari 5.1. Opera and Microsoft were confident enough in the stability of the spec to skip the vendor extension stage and implement the box-shadow rule directly.

To support all browsers, you'll need to issue multiple declarations like this:

```
-moz-box-shadow: rgb(0,0,0) 3px 3px 3px 9px;
-webkit-box-shadow: rgb(0,0,0) 3px 3px 3px, rgb(0,0,0) 3px 3px 9px;
box-shadow: rgb(0,0,0) 3px 3px 3px 9px;
```

Note that, because the old WebKit-based browsers don't support `spread-radius`, an extra shadow has been added in an effort to simulate the effect. Text shadows are supported, using the standard syntax in Safari 1.1 and Chrome 2.0, but support for multiple shadows was only added in the 4.0 versions.

Cross-browser CSS3 gradients

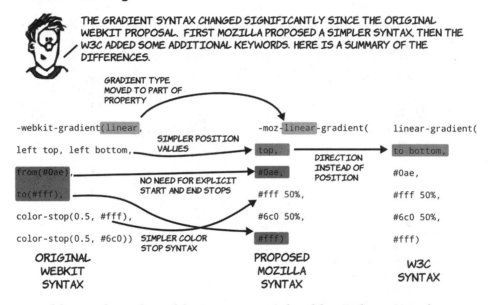

For older WebKit-based browsers, you should use the original syntax. Use the Mozilla syntax in older Firefox and newer versions of Safari and Chrome. Newer Firefox as well as Opera 12 and the IE10 preview support the standard syntax, Firefox and Opera with a vendor prefix. To support all browsers that support CSS gradients, your cross-browser code should look something like this:

```css
background: #6c0;
background: -webkit-gradient(linear, left top, left bottom,
            from(#00abeb), to(#fff),
            color-stop(0.5, #fff),
            color-stop(0.5, #66cc00));
background: -webkit-linear-gradient(
            top, #0ae, #fff 50%, #6c0 50%, #fff);
background: -moz-linear-gradient(
```

FALLBACK FOR BROWSERS WITH NO SUPPORT

LEGACY WEBKIT SUPPORT

WEBKIT SUPPORT

LEGACY FIREFOX SUPPORT

```
                          top, #0ae, #fff 50%, #6c0 50%, #fff);
background: -moz-linear-gradient(
                          to bottom, #0ae, #fff 50%, #6c0 50%, #fff);
background: -o-linear-gradient(
                          to bottom, #0ae, #fff 50%, #6c0 50%, #fff);
background: linear-gradient(
                          to bottom,#0ae,#fff 50%,#6c0 50%,#fff);
```

FIREFOX SUPPORT

OPERA SUPPORT

SUPPORT FOR CURRENT DRAFT IMPLEMENTATIONS (AT THE TIME OF WRITING, JUST IE10)

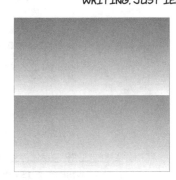

This will produce a two-tone gradient like the following in all browsers that support CSS3 gradients.

You can see this example in ch10/gradient-15.html. Browsers that don't support gradients display a green background; everything else shows the gradient.

Cross-browser backgrounds and border-image

border-image has changed significantly since it was first introduced. All the original implementations follow the shorthand property from the September 2008 Working Draft. Following that draft, significant changes were made that added specific properties for each component, such as border-image-source, border-image-slice, and the fill keyword. Before, border-image was like a subproperty of border; now it's a stand-alone property with subproperties of its own.

It's likely that vendors will move toward the new syntax when the spec reaches the Proposed Recommendation status. In the meantime, you can use it in a cross-browser way while still being compatible with the current spec:

```
-moz-border-image: url('border1.png') 80;
```

LEGACY FIREFOX SUPPORT

```
-webkit-border-image: url('border1.png') 80;
```

LEGACY WEBKIT SUPPORT

```
-o-border-image: url('border1.png') 80;
```

LEGACY OPERA SUPPORT

```
border-image: url('border1.png') 80;
```

SUPPORT FOR 2008 DRAFT IMPLEMENTATIONS

```
border-image: url('border1.png') 80 fill;
```

SUPPORT FOR CURRENT DRAFT IMPLEMENTATIONS

To get border-image to work in current browsers, you need to first specify the vendor-specific properties for Firefox and Safari/Chrome. Next, give the September 2008 version of the property for Opera, and finally the current version of the property with the fill keyword. This will ensure that future browsers that fully implement the property will render identically to current browsers, which treat fill as being the default and ignore the fill keyword.

 UNFORTUNATELY, IF YOU DON'T WANT THE BEHAVIOR FROM THE 2008 SPEC THAT TREATS fill AS THE DEFAULT, THERE'S NO WAY TO OVERRIDE IT IN CSS IN OLDER BROWSERS. THE EASIEST WAY TO ACHIEVE THIS IS TO USE AN IMAGE THAT'S BLANK OR TRANSPARENT IN THE CENTRAL AREA.

Supporting old versions of Internet Explorer

Internet Explorer was the first browser to implement a method for specifying drop shadows in CSS, way back in the version 5.5 release. Microsoft implemented a method of calling an ActiveX control and applying it to an element that can be used either from CSS or Java-Script. ActiveX has a pretty bad reputation in web developer circles that may partly explain why these techniques weren't seriously explored until recently. There are two filters for shadows in IE8: Drop-Shadow and Shadow.

DropShadow can accept a color value with alpha transparency(make sure all this code goes on a single line in your CSS):

```
-ms-filter: "progid:
➥ DXImageTransform.Microsoft.DropShadow
➥ (color=#ff000000, offX=4, offY=4)"
```

The color parameter here uses four hexadecimal pairs. The last three pairs are equivalent to the way you specify black in CSS: #000000. The first hex pair is a value between 0 and 255 for opacity: FF is fully opaque.

Shadow fades the color to transparent, like box-shadow, but you must specify an opaque color:

```
-ms-filter: "progid:
➥ DXImageTransform.Microsoft.Shadow(
➥ color=#000000, direction=135,
➥ strength=4)"
```

The main difference between the two is that Shadow applies a gradient to the edges, whereas DropShadow is a constant color. The listing for this example is in ch10/shadow-ie-1.html.

THE EXAMPLE HAS A BACKGROUND COLOR ON THE ELEMENT TO WHICH THE SHADOW APPLIES SO IT WILL APPLY TO THE ENTIRE ELEMENT RATHER THAN JUST THE TEXT. IF YOU WANT A SHADOW ON THE TEXT, YOU NEED TO LEAVE THE BACKGROUND TRANSPARENT. AS YOU MAY GUESS, THIS MAKES APPLYING A SHADOW TO BOTH THE TEXT AND THE BOX A BIT MORE INTERESTING.

There's also an IE filter for gradients. Here are two examples; the full code is in ch10/gradient-ie-1.html (the lines have been broken so they fit on the page; in your CSS make sure they appear on a single line):

```
-ms-filter: "progid:DXImageTransform.Microsoft.gradient(
    GradientType=1, startColorstr=#CC1C5B9B, endColorstr=#F56CBFFF)";
```

```
-ms-filter: "progid:DXImageTransform.Microsoft.gradient(
➥ GradientType=0, startColorstr=#88FFFFFF, endColorstr=#00FFFFFF)";
```

Compared to CSS gradients, they're very limited. You can specify only start and end colors; no additional color stops are available, and they can only be vertical or horizontal.

Note that if you want to use semitransparent colors in the gradient, you should also set the background color back to transparent in the rule:

```
background: transparent;
-ms-filter: "progid:DXImageTransform.Microsoft.gradient(
➥ GradientType=0, startColorstr=#88FFFFFF, endColorstr=#00FFFFFF)";
```

Otherwise both the background color and the gradient will apply, and you'll see the gray background through the gradient. The -ms-filter property doesn't override an existing background property.

 IE9 HAS FULL SUPPORT FOR THE CSS STANDARDS FOR BOX SHADOWS AND ROUNDED CORNERS. IE10 PREVIEW RELEASES HAVE INCLUDED SUPPORT FOR CSS3 GRADIENTS. USE CONDITIONAL COMMENTS TO PROVIDE A SPECIFIC STYLESHEET TO IE8 AND EARLIER IF YOU WANT TO SUPPORT ALL VERSIONS, OR INVESTIGATE A SOLUTION LIKE CSS3 PIE.

CSS3 PIE for easy IE support

CSS3 PIE takes advantage of another proprietary IE CSS extension—behaviors—to make older versions of IE support standard CSS3 syntax. A *behavior* is a script file that executes as the CSS is being applied to an element. Although there are some performance and security concerns, behaviors offer a convenient way to add CSS3 support in IE8 and earlier. This element with rounded corners, a gradient, and a drop shadow was created by applying a mostly standard CSS rule.

The screenshot was taken in IE8. Here's the CSS (see the page in full in ch10/css-pie.html):

```
div {
    border: 1px solid #999;
    border-radius: 10px;
    box-shadow: rgb(0,0,0) 3px 3px 3px 3px;
    -pie-background: linear-gradient(top, #000, #fff);
    behavior: url(../libs/PIE/PIE.htc);
}
```

There are two nonstandard properties here. Behavior is the proprietary IE property that allows all the magic to happen; it contains the URL of the file that implements the behaviors. -pie-background is required because, unlike border-radius and box-shadow, IE8 already understands the background property and will discard any values that it considers invalid.

Summary

In this chapter, you've learned about features of CSS3 for creating drop shadows, rounded corners, background effects, and gradients. Most of these effects could be accomplished visually with CSS2, but that would involve creating images and various bits of additional markup to apply them to elements. The CSS3 approach removes the need for extra markup and additional requests to the server and is easily adaptable to the content—you don't need to re-create your background image just because you decide to make an element 20 pixels wider.

CSS3 ISN'T JUST FOR VISUAL EFFECTS AND BACKGROUND IMAGES; IT ALSO INCLUDES SEVERAL NEW FEATURES FOR THE FORMATTING AND DISPLAY OF TEXT. IN THE NEXT CHAPTER YOU'LL LEARN ABOUT USING CUSTOM FONTS, AUTOMATICALLY FORMATTING TEXT INTO COLUMNS, AND ADVANCED FONT CONTROL FEATURES.

11

Text and fonts

This chapter covers

- Adding custom fonts to your pages with `@font-face`
- Detailed control of font rendering with `font-feature-settings`
- Improving readability with CSS columns
- Controlling text wrapping and overflow

Despite being designed from the start as a way to share text documents, the web has traditionally had poor typography. In this chapter, you'll learn how all that is changing as CSS3 brings in many new features for control of fonts and text.

Basic web fonts

Typography, the art of setting and arranging type, is a big part of design; a particular typeface is often as much a part of a company's image as its logo or corporate color scheme. But in CSS2, there's basically no way to specify a font that will be used by all users across all browsers and operating systems.

Typography on the web has always been limited because of its client-server design—the font has to be on the client machine, where the rendering is done, and not on the server. This is what leads to standard font-family declarations like this:

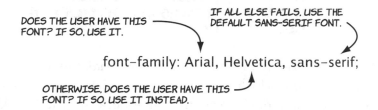

```
font-family: Arial, Helvetica, sans-serif;
```

DOES THE USER HAVE THIS FONT? IF SO, USE IT.

IF ALL ELSE FAILS, USE THE DEFAULT SANS-SERIF FONT.

OTHERWISE, DOES THE USER HAVE THIS FONT? IF SO, USE IT INSTEAD.

The idea is that Arial (a Microsoft font), Helvetica (the standard Apple font), and sans-serif will all look relatively similar—but is that true? Instead of specifying a set of fallbacks, let's compare what each font by itself looks like in some different browsers. Here's the standard CSS rule split into three:

```
h1 { font-size: 32px; font-weight: bold; }
div:nth-child(1) { font-family: Arial; }
div:nth-child(2) { font-family: Helvetica; }
div:nth-child(3) { font-family: sans-serif; }
```

To see the results, let's use this simple bit of markup repeated three times:

```
<div><h1>Hello! HTML5 and CSS3</h1></div>
```

Here's what the three elements look like in Firefox on my laptop. As you can see, there's quite a variation in both size and thickness.

Hello! HTML5 and CSS3 **Hello! HTML5 and CSS3** **Hello! HTML5 and CSS3**

But that's not the only interesting thing going on. Here's the same page in Chrome on my laptop. All the fonts look the same!

Hello!   **Hello!**   **Hello!**
HTML5 and   **HTML5 and**   **HTML5 and**
CSS3   **CSS3**   **CSS3**

To add to the confusion, I'll now reveal that my Linux laptop has neither the Arial nor the Helvetica font installed, which is more obvious in this screenshot of the same page in Opera.

Hello!   **Hello!**   **Hello!**
HTML5 and   **HTML5 and**   **HTML5 and**
CSS3   **CSS3**   **CSS3**

Opera falls back to Bitstream Vera Sans for Arial but renders the browser default font—which is serif rather than sans-serif—for Helvetica. Chrome renders all three the same because it falls back to Bitstream Vera Sans for Arial and Helvetica and also uses it for the default sans. Firefox tries to use a font similar to the requested one, so it replaces Arial with Liberation Sans and Helvetica with Nimbus Sans L, and it uses Bitstream Vera Sans for the default sans font. You can try it on your own system with listing ch11/font-comparitor.html. This shows that web authors have almost no control over what fonts end up being used in their pages. As you can imagine, that drives some designers nuts! It's one reason you've seen so many bad hacks over the years that replace text with images or Flash movies. But there's now a practical standards-based alternative: @font-face.

Gaining control of fonts with the @font-face rule

The @font-face rule allows you to specify a font to be downloaded with the web page in the same way as markup, images, and script. Here's a basic declaration to download the Liberation Sans Bold font:

```
@font-face {
    font-family: "Liberation Sans Bold";
    src: url(LiberationSans-Bold.ttf) format("truetype");
}
```

		Standard	Prefixed
Browser support quick check: @font-face		4.0	-
		3.5	-
		4.0	-
		10.0	-
		3.1	-

THIS EXAMPLE HAS TWO PROPERTIES; font-family AND src. font-family IS A NAME; ANY NAME WILL DO, ALTHOUGH IT WILL MAKE YOUR LIFE EASIER IF IT'S REPRESENTATIVE OF THE ACTUAL FONT NAME. src SPECIFIES A URL TO THE FONT FILE AND A FILE FORMAT.

Here are the declarations for the other two fonts in the earlier example:

```
@font-face {
    font-family: "Nimbus Sans L Bold";
    src: url(NimbusSanL-Bold.ttf) format("truetype");
}
@font-face {
    font-family: "Bitstream Vera Sans Bold";
    src: url(VeraBd.ttf) format("truetype");
}
```

Now that the downloadable fonts have been defined, you can reference them in CSS rules like any other font:

```
h1 { font-size: 32px; font-weight: normal; }
div:nth-child(1) { font-family: "Liberation Sans Bold"; }
div:nth-child(2) { font-family: "Nimbus Sans L Bold"; }
div:nth-child(3) { font-family: "Bitstream Vera Sans Bold"; }
```

These rules lead to consistent results cross-browser (except, of course, Internet Explorer 8 and earlier). Try it for yourself with listing ch11/font-face-1.html.

Hello! HTML5 and CSS3   **Hello! HTML5 and CSS3**   **Hello! HTML5 and CSS3**

Hello!
HTML5 and
CSS3

Hello!
HTML5 and
CSS3

Hello!
HTML5 and
CSS3

Hello!
HTML5 and
CSS3

Hello!
HTML5 and
CSS3

Hello!
HTML5 and
CSS3

 A SUBTLE DIFFERENCE YOU MAY HAVE NOTED IS THAT THE ORIGINAL EXAMPLE USED A font-weight OF bold, BUT THE SECOND EXAMPLE USED A font-weight OF normal. THIS IS BECAUSE THE @font-face RULES EXPLICITLY SPECIFIED THE BOLD VERSIONS OF THE FONTS, BUT IT'S POSSIBLE TO HANDLE THAT DIRECTLY WITH font-face.

The browser has two options when bold text is needed: it can either use a bold version of the font if one is available or scale up the normal font to make it look bold.

Let's start with some normal text using the Yanone Kaffeesatz font:

Hello! HTML5 and CSS3

```
<p>Hello! HTML5 and CSS3</p>
```

Here's the CSS:

```
@font-face {
    font-family: "Yanone Kaffeesatz";
    src: url(YanoneKaffeesatz-Regular.otf) format("opentype");
}
p {
    font-size: 32px;
    font-family: "Yanone Kaffeesatz";
}
```

Now add a couple of elements that will render as bold:

Hello! HTML5 and CSS3

```
<p>Hello! <strong>HTML5</strong> and
<strong>CSS3</strong></p>
```

The browser doesn't have a bold version of Kaffeesatz, so it adjusts the normal font to be thicker and wider.

Add another `@font-face` declaration. Notice that it uses the same `font-family` name, but it has a different URL and specifies a `font-weight`:

Hello! HTML5 and CSS3

```
@font-face {
    font-family:
     "Yanone Kaffeesatz";
    src:
     url(YanoneKaffeesatz-Bold.otf)
     format("opentype");
    font-weight: bold;
}
```

The browser is now using the bold version of the Yanone Kaffeesatz font for the bold text. This is more compact and more cleanly rendered than the standard version of the font automatically adjusted to be bold. The same approach also works for italics, but using `font-style` instead of `font-weight`. Unfortunately Kaffeesatz doesn't have an italic variant, so this example uses the thin variant:

```
@font-face {
    font-family: "Yanone Kaffeesatz";
    src: url(YanoneKaffeesatz-Thin.otf) format("opentype");
    font-style: italic;
}
```

With a minor adjustment to the HTML you can see three different fonts, all from the same family, in one paragraph:

```
<p>Hello!
  <strong>HTML5</strong> and
  <em>CSS3</em></p>
```

Hello! HTML5 and CSS3

Font formats: EOT, TTF/OTF, and WOFF

The @font-face rule was originally introduced in an early draft of the CSS2 spec, but it was dropped back in 1998, mostly because of the lack of fonts with licenses that allowed web distribution.

TO OVERCOME THE RESISTANCE OF THE FOUNDRIES, THE BROWSER MANUFACTURERS DEVELOPED THEIR OWN FONT FORMATS SPECIFICALLY FOR THE WEB: NETSCAPE CAME UP WITH THE PORTABLE FONT RESOURCE FORMAT (PFR), NOW AS DEAD AS THE NETSCAPE BROWSER; AND MICROSOFT CREATED EMBEDDED OPENTYPE (EOT), WHICH IS STILL SUPPORTED IN IE TODAY. NEITHER WAS SUCCESSFUL; FEW FONTS WERE EVER MADE AVAILABLE IN EITHER FORMAT.

Since 1998, several things have changed:

- Bandwidth has increased to the point that including a 100–300 KB font file in your page seems less of a big deal.
- Font foundries now have the example of the music industry to learn from.
- The rise of open source operating systems has led to the creation of several free but professional fonts funded by companies such as Red Hat, Canonical, and Google.
- Tools have improved to the point that it's now feasible for professional font designers to produce free fonts in their spare time.

In June 1998, Safari 3.1 was released with support for downloading TrueType/OpenType fonts (TTF/OTF) with @font-face in its desktop incarnation and SVG Web fonts, a format tied to the SVG specification, on mobile devices. Firefox added support with the release of 3.5 in June 2009, and a brave new world of web typography was born.

Although several smaller font foundries jumped on the bandwagon and started making their fonts available with web-friendly licenses, the major ones still weren't keen to get involved. They wanted a font file format that couldn't be used as a desktop font. The answer is the new W3C Web Open Font Format (WOFF), which is being developed collaboratively between browsers, vendors, font foundries, and the W3C.

Browser support for downloadable fonts

The previous section mentioned several different font file formats, among them EOT, TTF/OTF, WOFF, and SVG. The following table shows which of them are supported in various browsers today.

Browser	Support from	Support of
	4	TTF, OTF, and SVG
	3.5	TTF and OTF only
	3.6	WOFF support added
	4.0	Embedded Open Type (EOT) only
	9.0	WOFF support added
	10.0	TTF, OTF, and SVG
	11.1	WOFF support added
(desktop)	3.1	TTF, OTF, and SVG
	5.1	WOFF support added
(iOS)	3.1	SVG
	4.2	TTF and OTF support added

For widest support across browsers, you need to provide your font in four different formats—assuming you can find fonts available in all four formats, or with a liberal enough license that you can convert the font between formats yourself. In addition, you have to worry about various bugs in different browsers' support of @font-face (see the browser support section at the end of the chapter for details).

THE PRACTICAL ASPECTS OF SUPPORTING FONTS CROSS-BROWSER AND CROSS-DEVICE GIVE YOU PLENTY TO WORRY ABOUT. FORTUNATELY, SEVERAL SERVICES HAVE ARISEN ONLINE TO DO THAT THINKING FOR YOU; THE NEXT SECTION WILL LOOK AT THEM.

Making your life easier with font services

Rather than search through many different web sites to find the exact fonts you want, and then purchase them from several different websites and figure out how to set up your server to deliver them correctly to clients and integrate everything into your CSS, it's much easier to get someone else to do that for you. Many online services have appeared in recent years to simplify getting the fonts you want on your website. These can be broken down into three broad categories:

- *Font converters and packagers*—These services convert fonts you already have into the formats supported by browsers and provide you with CSS to incorporate them into your site. You have to deal with the server-setup side of things yourself.
- *Free font services*—The font services deliver the fonts directly from their own servers, and all you need to do is link to a CSS file provided by the service. Being free, these services only include freely downloadable and open source fonts.
- *Paid font services*—These services are just like free ones except that, because you're paying license fees, the range of fonts available is vastly improved.

This section walks through one example of each type of service listed, from choosing fonts to getting them on your web page.

Downloadable kits: FontSquirrel

FontSquirrel (www.fontsquirrel.com) is an online tool for building packages of font files. These packages contain everything you need to use the fonts on your own website. Here's how to use FontSquirrel:

1 Go to the website home page and click the @font-face Kits link in the main menu.

2 You'll be taken to a page that lists hundreds of fonts available for download. Scroll down to the Serif section, and find the Gentium Pro font. Click View Font to see the details.

3 On the details page, you can see what each character looks like and try out text of your own. Go to the @font-face Kit tab to select which font file types you want to use: TTF, EOT, WOFF, and SVG.

4 On this page you can also select a subset of the characters—so you only download the English characters if you won't be using any

other languages, keeping the file size down.

Click the Download @font-face Kit button to download a zip file of everything you'll need.

5 Look in the zip file you've downloaded. It contains the following:

Each font in the formats you selected

A style-sheet file that you can include directly in your pages

A web page demonstrating the font

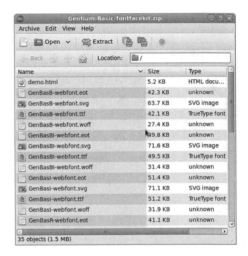

Here's a rule from the included stylesheet.css file:

```
@font-face {
    font-family: 'GentiumBasicRegular';
    src: url('GenBasR-webfont.eot');
    src: url('GenBasR-webfont.eot?iefix') format('eot'),
        url('GenBasR-webfont.woff') format('woff'),
        url('GenBasR-webfont.ttf') format('truetype'),
        url('GenBasR-webfont.svg#webfontLblSsz10') format('svg');
    font-weight: normal;
    font-style: normal;
}
```

6 And here's a rule from the HTML file, demonstrating how it should be used:

```
p.style1 {
  font: 18px/27px
```

```
      'GentiumBasicRegular',
      Arial,
      sans-serif;
}
```

Font-face Demo for the Gentium Basic Font

Gentium Basic Regular - Lorem ipsum dolor sit amet, consectetur adipisicing elit, sed do eiusmod tempor incididunt ut labore et dolore magna aliqua. Ut enim ad minim veniam, quis nostrud exercitation ullamco laboris nisi ut aliquip ex ea commodo consequat. Duis aute irure dolor in reprehenderit in voluptate velit esse cillum dolore eu fugiat nulla pariatur. Excepteur sint occaecat cupidatat non proident, sunt in culpa qui officia deserunt mollit anim id est laborum.

Gentium Basic Italic - Lorem ipsum dolor sit amet, consectetur adipisicing elit, sed do eiusmod tempor incididunt ut labore et dolore magna aliqua. Ut enim ad minim veniam, quis nostrud exercitation ullamco laboris nisi ut aliquip ex ea commodo consequat. Duis aute irure dolor in reprehenderit in voluptate velit esse cillum dolore eu fugiat nulla pariatur. Excepteur sint occaecat cupidatat non proident, sunt in culpa qui officia deserunt mollit anim id est laborum.

You can see the file in ch11/Gentium-Basic-fontfacekit/demo.html.

Free font services: Google Web Fonts

Downloading a kit with everything you need takes a lot of the work out of things, but you still have to deal with serving the files yourself. This means you have to make sure your server is configured correctly for the font files. In addition, the users downloading the fonts will be using up your bandwidth. Wouldn't it be nice if someone else took care of the server-side stuff for you? Well, Google is offering to do it for free!

1 The Google Web Fonts service is available at www.google.com/ webfonts. Click the Start Choosing Fonts button to begin.

2 Like many Google services, the interface is search based. Search for a font called Crimson Text by typing in the Search box.

3 The See All Styles link lets you see all the different weights and styles available. Click the Quick Use link alongside that.

4 You can select which font variants you want to include (weights of bold and/or italics). To the right of the selection is a large graphic indicator that estimates the impact of the fonts you've chosen on page load time.

5 Instead of a download, you're offered two snippets of code to copy and paste. Scroll down the page to find them.

The first bit of code is a `<link>` element to include in your document head. The second is an example CSS rule making use of the font. The exact code is as follows:

```
<link
  href='http://
fonts.googleapis.com/
css?family=Crimson+Text:400,700'
  rel='stylesheet' type='text/
css'>
font-family: 'Crimson Text',
serif;
```

6 Include these two snippets in your page, adjusting the CSS rule as necessary, and you're good to go.

1. Choose the styles you want:

⊟ Crimson Text

☑ Normal 400

☐ *Normal 400 italic*

☐ **Semi-Bold 600**

☐ *Semi-Bold 600 italic*

☑ **Bold 700**

☐ *Bold 700 italic*

4. Integrate the fonts into your CSS:

The Google Web Fonts API will generate the necessary browser-specific CSS to use the fonts. All you need to do is add the font name to your CSS styles. For example:

```
font-family: 'Crimson Text', serif;
```

Hello! HTML5 and CSS3

Many persons who are not conversant with mathematical studies imagine that because the business of [Babbage's Analytical Engine] is to give its results in numerical notation, the nature of its processes must consequently be arithmetical and numerical, rather than algebraical and analytical. This is an error. The engine can arrange and combine its numerical quantities exactly as if they were letters or any other general symbols; and in fact it might bring out its results in algebraical notation, were provisions made accordingly.

See the full example listing in ch11/fontservices-google.html.

Subscription font services: Fontdeck

The Google service is straightforward and available at an excellent price—nothing—but this strength is also a weakness. Google can only offer free fonts for download through its service. If the fonts you want to use aren't available, you'll have to look into one of the subscription services; several such services are now available.

1   This example looks at Fontdeck (http://fontdeck.com/) because it allows you to try the fonts for free and I already have an account.

2   You need to provide an email address to register, and then you set up a website. This is as simple as typing in a name and one or more domain names.

The first 20 distinct IP addresses to access your website will be allowed to download any fonts you choose free of charge, so you can use Fontdeck to test fonts and even demonstrate them to clients without financial outlay.

3   After you've set up a website, you need to choose some fonts. These are arranged by category—serif, sans-serif, and so on—or you can search by font name or tag. For this example, look for Monosten, which is under Slab Serif > Monospaced. Either browse to the font or search for it.

4 On the page for Monosten, look for the A (regular) and C (bold) variants and click the Add to Website link alongside them.

5 You should see a banner at the top of the page with a link that says Grab the Code for This Font—go ahead and click it.

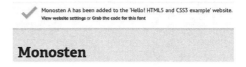

6 You're presented with a page that has code you can copy and paste into your pages. The code I got is shown next; I changed the CSS slightly to apply to the body and level-one headings.

```
<link rel="stylesheet" href="http://f.fontdeck.com/s/css/
 9tuWCgd+qpLZNXRFuo1XneWWjNE/www.dotrob.com/8881.css"
 type="text/css" />
<style>
body {
    font-family:"Monosten A", Courier, monospace;
    font-size-adjust:0.5;
    font-weight:normal;
    font-style:normal;
```

```
    }
    h1 {
        font-family:"Monosten C", Courier, monospace;
        font-size-adjust:0.5;
        font-weight:bold;
        font-style:normal;
    }
    </style>
```

7 Here's my example page in action using the previous code. See the full listing in ch11/fontservices-fontdeck.html. You'll need to edit the example file to insert your own style sheet link to Fontdeck; otherwise you won't be able to download the fonts.

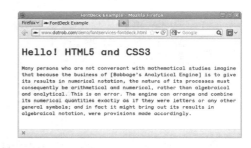

Advanced web typography

Even with a working @font-face directive, control over fonts on the web is still far behind what you might see in a typical desktop-publishing program or design package. CSS3 goes beyond letting web developers control which fonts appear on their web pages: it also offers features for controlling the details of how those fonts are rendered.

font-size-adjust

As you saw earlier, one of the issues with fonts on the web is that, should the primary font be unusable for some reason, the fallback font may have different size characteristics. Fonts that are nominally of the same size can have visible differences in weight; this is the case because the measure of a font depends on the height of the letters including any

Browser support quick check: font-size-adjust		Standard	Prefixed
		-	-
		3.0	-
		-	-
		-	-
		-	-

potential ascenders and descenders, whereas the visual size of the font is more dependent on the x-height—the size of the lowercase characters.

The font size in all three examples in the section "Basic web fonts" was set to 32 pixels. But as you can see in this magnified view of the Nimbus Sans L letter *M*, the characters are only about 24 pixels tall.

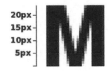

Following is a diagram showing how the various font size metrics are related.

The `font-size-adjust` property allows you to specify a ratio between the x-height and the size of your first-choice font. If the browser has to use one of the fallback fonts, it will automatically adjust the size so the x-height remains consistent.

You don't have to work out the x-height exactly; you can discover an appropriate value through trial and error instead. If you provide a "wrong" value for `font-size-adjust`, the font will be noticeably smaller.

Following is an example that shows the difference that specifying `font-size-adjust` can make. To begin, let's look at what happens without that property:

```
p {
    font-size: 32px;
    padding: 0.5em;
    font-family: "Yanone Kaffeesatz", sans-serif;
}
```

If the font is available, then everything is fine.

Hello! HTML5 and CSS3

But if the font isn't available for some reason, the fallback font takes up considerably more space.

Hello! HTML5 and CSS3

Now let's add a `font-size-adjust` property:

```
p {
    font-size: 32px;
    padding: 0.5em;
    font-family: "Yanone Kaffeesatz", sans-serif;
    font-size-adjust:0.5;
}
```

Again, everything is fine if the font is available.

Hello! HTML5 and CSS3

But this time, if the font isn't available, the fallback font takes up a similar height.

Hello! HTML5 and CSS3

Note that `font-size-adjust` only impacts the x-height—the width is still different. The property's main advantage is that it preserves the vertical rhythm of your blocks of text.

Advanced font control

This section looks at some of the advanced features offered by modern fonts and how they can be controlled from CSS. We'll start with *ligatures*: the replacement of sequences of separate characters with a single, joined *glyph* (the typographical term for the elements of a font) and then explore some features available for numbers before finishing with fancy text options known as *contextual swashes*.

Browser support quick check: font features

		Standard	Prefixed
	(Chrome)	-	16*
	(Firefox)	-	4.0
	(Internet Explorer)	-	10
	(Opera)	-	-
	(Safari)	-	-

* (Win/Linux only)

ALL OF THESE FEATURES ARE ATTRIBUTES OF THE FONT BEING USED. CSS DOESN'T CREATE ADDITIONAL GLYPHS—THEY HAVE TO BE PRESENT IN THE FONT—BUT IT LETS YOU CONTROL WHEN THEY'RE USED.

Glyphs and ligatures

Glyph is the typographical term for the graphical elements that make up a font. It differs from a *letter*—any individual letter can be represented by any one of a number of glyphs in a font depending on the context in which it's placed. A common example in old English was the long *ſ* and short *s* forms that were used at the start and end of words, respectively—both represented the letter *s* but use a different glyph.

A *ligature* is a glyph that replaces a sequence of letters. In traditional English printing, this was generally used to increase legibility or to work around limitations of ink or lead type. But in some scripts, the particular ligature used can affect the meaning.

Ligatures are a feature of the font being used. Each font has a replacement table that maps certain sequences of characters in the text to single glyph.

Following are some example ligatures from the Calluna Regular font.

No ligatures   ff fi fl   ffi ffl

Ligatures   ff fi fl   ffi ffl

Currently, Firefox and Safari render ligatures automatically, if they're available in the font, above a certain font size. CSS3 gives you complete control over them through the font-feature-settings property. The property requires a single value: a quoted string containing a comma-separated list of font settings. To turn on ligatures, you use this CSS:

```
font-feature-settings: "liga";
```

All the features have a four-character code. If the value is present, it means the feature is enabled. It's also possible to add a value to each feature:

```
font-feature-settings: "liga" 1;
```

A value of 1 or on means the feature is enabled, and 0 or off means the feature is disabled. The complete list of possible features is available in the OpenType specification: www.microsoft.com/typography/otspec/ featurelist.htm.In addition to the regular ligatures, a font may also have a set of more decorative discretionary ligatures. These aren't enabled by default but can be enabled through `font-feature-settings`. Here's another example from the Calluna Regular font.

Normal ligatures

it qu st ct

Discretionary ligatures

it qu st ct

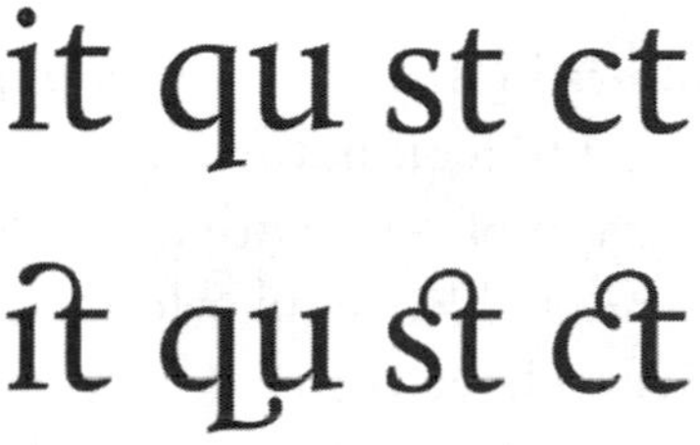

As you can see, the discretionary ligatures are a lot more decorative. You would normally only enable them for headings or other small sections of text with a decorative as well as informative role. The CSS for the second line in the previous example is this:

```
font-feature-settings: "liga" 1, "dlig";
```

It's also possible to select only the additional ligatures:

```
font-feature-settings: "liga" 0, "dlig";
```

Letters aren't the only thing that can be represented by more than one glyph in a font, and you may have good reason for wanting different glyphs in different situations. This screenshot shows four numbers in the Calluna font with the default rendering. Can you quickly tell which one of the four is the largest value?

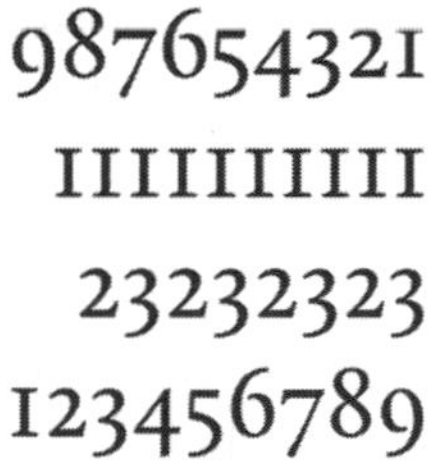

987654321
IIIIIIIII
23232323
123456789

The problem with the normal rendering of numbers is that, like the rest of the text, they're proportionally spaced. This is fine for numbers in text but not so good for quick visual comparison in tables. The Calluna font has several

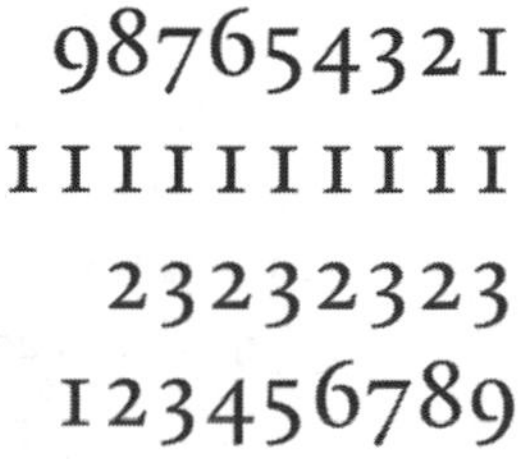

987654321
I I I I I I I I I
23232323
123456789

different sets of numerals, and in this case the tabular set is more useful:

```
font-feature-settings: "tnum";
```

Now you can see immediately that the largest value number is the second one.

987654321
1111111111
23232323
123456789

The numbers in the previous examples are designed to look natural when used in a paragraph of text, with ascenders and descenders like regular letters. You may prefer to have the numbers be a more consistent height; these are known as *lining numerals*:

```
font-feature-settings: "lnum";
```

The default that's being overridden here is Old Style Numerals, which can be selected with the short code "onum".

Calluna allows you to combine the tabular and lining properties:

```
font-feature-settings:
  "tnum", "lnum";
```

987654321
1111111111
23232323
123456789

Calluna also has a special set of ligatures for fractions:

```
font-feature-settings: "frac";
```

The column on the left is the normal rendering of the text; the fractions are typed with a slash as in 1/2. The column on the right has fractions turned on; the three letters have been replaced with a single glyph representing the fraction.

1 1/2   1 ½
2 1/3   2 ⅓
3 1/4   3 ¼
4 3/5   4 ⅗

It's often difficult to distinguish an uppercase letter *O* from a zero. In fonts used in things like text editors, the zero will have a slash through it to make it more distinctive. Calluna has both a regular and a slashed zero. The slashed zero can be enabled with the zero feature:

```
font-feature-settings: "zero";
```

OOOOO
O0O0O0

Historical forms can give an authentic old look to your text. For instance, in days of yore, the current form for *s* was only used at the end of words. It was normal to use a long *s* at the start and in the middle of words. You can enable the long *s* in Calluna with the hist feature:

```
font-feature-settings: "hist";
```

succession
fucceffion

Fonts can also contain stylistic alternates — usually more decorative versions of certain characters. Calluna has just one set of stylistic alternates, which contains only two glyphs. Turn on stylistic alternates by setting salt to on:

```
font-feature-settings: "salt";
```

& OO   & ∞

The Calluna font used so far for the examples doesn't have much in the way of historical forms or stylistic alternatives. Let's switch to the MEgalopolis Extra font, which has plenty of both.

Here's a sample paragraph with no special typographic formatting. The code follows.

THE ANALYTICAL ENGINE HAS NO PRETENSIONS WHATEVER to originate anything. It can do whatever we know how to order it to perform.

I again rely on Ada Lovelace for the quote:

```
<p>The Analytical Engine has no pretensions whatever to
originate anything.
It can do whatever we know how to order it to perform.</p>
```

Here's the CSS to apply the font:

```
@font-face {
    font-family: megalopolis;
    src: url(MEgalopolisExtra.woff) format("woff"),
         url(MEgalopolisExtra.otf) format("opentype");
}
p {
    font-family: megalopolis, sans-serif;
}
p::first-line {
    font-variant: small-caps;
}
```

You can see the additional ligatures in effect on the small-caps combinations *ca*, *re*, and *at*.

Additional ligatures

THE ANALYTICL ENGINE HAS NO PRETENSIONS WHATEVER TO originate anything. It can do whatever we know how to order it to perform.

Additional ligatures plus default stylistic alternatives

THE ANALYTICL ENGINE HAS NO PRETENSIONS WHATEVER TO originate anything. It can do whatever we know how to order it to perform.

The default stylistic alternatives adds a more curvy *s* but also a more traditional *y*. The property for the second example is as follows:

```
font-feature-settings: "salt","dlig";
```

MEgalopolis has six other style sets, which can be turned on with `ss01` to `ss06`. Here are a couple of examples. If you're following along at home, I suggest you try `ss06` for yourself:

"ss01"

THE ANALYTICL ENGINE HAS NO PRETENSIONS WHATEVER TO originate anything. It can do whatever we know how to order it to perform.

"ss05"   THE ANALYTICL ENGINE HAS NO PRETENSIONS WHATEVER TO
                                originate anything. It can do whatever
                                we know how to order it to perform.

BROWSER SUPPORT

Recent versions of the major browsers support some parts of CSS3
advanced font control features using vendor-specific extensions. The
following example shows a complete code listing that enables standard
and discretionary ligatures cross-browser:

```
-moz-font-feature-settings: "liga", "dlig";
-moz-font-feature-settings: "liga=1, dlig=1";
-ms-font-feature-settings: "liga", "dlig";
-webkit-font-feature-settings: "liga", "dlig";
font-feature-settings: "liga", "dlig";
```

NOTE THAT FIREFOX SUPPORTED AN OLDER VERSION OF THE SPEC FROM
VERSION 4 ONWARDS. IT SUPPORTS THE CURRENT SYNTAX FROM VERSION 14
ONWARDS. IN ORDER TO SUPPORT BOTH OLD AND NEW FIREFOX, YOU MUST PUT
THE OLD SYNTAX SECOND. NEWER VERSIONS WILL IGNORE THE OLD SYNTAX,
BUT THE OLD VERSIONS WILL ATTEMPT TO APPLY THE NEW SYNTAX AND FAIL.

THE `font-feature-settings` PROPERTY IS INTENDED TO BE
USED ONLY FOR LOW-LEVEL CONTROL. THE FINAL STANDARD WILL
INCLUDE MORE READABLE VERSIONS FOR ALL THE MOST COMMON
OPTIONS. THE FOLLOWING TABLE INDICATES HOW THE PREVIOUS
EXAMPLES MAP ONTO THE PROPERTIES CURRENTLY IN THE SPEC.

`font-feature-settings`	Standard CSS3 properties and values
`font-feature-settings:` ` "liga";`	`font-variant-ligatures:` ` common-ligatures;`

`font-feature-settings:`
` "liga" 0,`
` dlig";`
	`font-variant-ligatures:`
	` no-common-ligatures`
	` additional-ligatures;`

`font-feature-settings:` ` "tnum";`	`font-variant-numeric:` ` tabular-nums;`

`font-feature-settings:`
` "tnum",`
` "lnum";`
	`font-variant-numeric:`
	` tabular-nums`
	` lining-nums;`

(continued)

font-feature-settings	Standard CSS3 properties and values

font-feature-settings:
  "frac";
	font-variant-numeric:
	  diagonal-fractions;

font-feature-settings:
  "hist";
	font-variant-alternates:
	  historical-forms;

font-feature-settings:
  "ss01";
	font-variant-alternates:
	  styleset(1);

Text columns

Browser support quick check: CSS columns		Standard	Prefixed
	(Chrome)	-	1.0
	(Firefox)	-	1.5
	(Internet Explorer)	10.0	-
	(Opera)	11.10	-
	(Safari)	-	3.0

Columns in printed media, such as newspapers and magazines, make text easier to read by keeping the line length to an optimal 10–15 words. With CSS2, the only way to create columns of text is to split the content among multiple elements and then position them on the page. This causes issues when updating the content, because you have to make sure it remains balanced, and when reading it, because nothing in the markup indicates that the two elements share a common text source. CSS3 adds the ability to render any element across multiple columns, solving both issues. You'll learn how in this section.

Column count and width

Here's a simple page with a couple of paragraphs of text:

```
<body>
    <p>I never am really
        satisfied...</p>
    <p>In almost every
        computation...</p>
</body>
```

I NEVER AM REALLY SATISFIED THAT I UNDERSTAND ANYTHING; BECAUSE, UNDERSTAND IT WELL AS I MAY, MY COMPREHENSION CAN ONLY BE AN INFINITESIMAL FRACTION OF ALL I WANT TO UNDERSTAND ABOUT THE MANY CONNECTIONS AND RELATIONS WHICH OCCUR TO ME, HOW THE MATTER IN QUESTION WAS FIRST THOUGHT OF OR ARRIVED AT, ETC, ETC.

IN ALMOST EVERY COMPUTATION A GREAT VARIETY OF ARRANGEMENTS FOR THE SUCCESSION OF THE PROCESSES IS POSSIBLE, AND VARIOUS CONSIDERATIONS MUST INFLUENCE THE SELECTIONS AMONGST THEM FOR THE PURPOSES OF A CALCULATING ENGINE. ONE ESSENTIAL OBJECT IS TO CHOOSE THAT ARRANGEMENT WHICH SHALL TEND TO REDUCE TO A MINIMUM THE TIME NECESSARY FOR COMPLETING THE CALCULATION.

Turning that into two columns of text is straightforward:

```
body {
    column-count: 2;
}
```

The text flows naturally into two columns with no markup changes, as you can see in the screenshot.

> I NEVER AM REALLY SATISFIED THAT I UNDERSTAND ANYTHING; BECAUSE, UNDERSTAND IT WELL AS I MAY, MY COMPREHENSION CAN ONLY BE AN INFINITESIMAL FRACTION OF ALL I WANT TO UNDERSTAND ABOUT THE MANY CONNECTIONS AND RELATIONS WHICH OCCUR TO ME, HOW THE MATTER IN QUESTION WAS FIRST THOUGHT OF OR ARRIVED AT, ETC, ETC.
>
> IN ALMOST EVERY COMPUTATION A GREAT VARIETY OF ARRANGEMENTS FOR THE SUCCESSION OF THE PROCESSES IS POSSIBLE, AND VARIOUS CONSIDERATIONS MUST INFLUENCE THE SELECTIONS AMONGST THEM FOR THE PURPOSES OF A CALCULATING ENGINE. ONE ESSENTIAL OBJECT IS TO CHOOSE THAT ARRANGEMENT WHICH SHALL TEND TO REDUCE TO A MINIMUM THE TIME NECESSARY FOR COMPLETING THE CALCULATION.

An alternative approach is to specify a column width:

```
body {
    column-width: 260px;
}
```

With a window 640 pixels wide, as in this example, and taking into account page margins and padding, this has a result that's identical to the previous rule.

> I NEVER AM REALLY SATISFIED THAT I UNDERSTAND ANYTHING; BECAUSE, UNDERSTAND IT WELL AS I MAY, MY COMPREHENSION CAN ONLY BE AN INFINITESIMAL FRACTION OF ALL I WANT TO UNDERSTAND ABOUT THE MANY CONNECTIONS AND RELATIONS WHICH OCCUR TO ME, HOW THE MATTER IN QUESTION WAS FIRST THOUGHT OF OR ARRIVED AT, ETC, ETC.
>
> IN ALMOST EVERY COMPUTATION A GREAT VARIETY OF ARRANGEMENTS FOR THE SUCCESSION OF THE PROCESSES IS POSSIBLE, AND VARIOUS CONSIDERATIONS MUST INFLUENCE THE SELECTIONS AMONGST THEM FOR THE PURPOSES OF A CALCULATING ENGINE. ONE ESSENTIAL OBJECT IS TO CHOOSE THAT ARRANGEMENT WHICH SHALL TEND TO REDUCE TO A MINIMUM THE TIME NECESSARY FOR COMPLETING THE CALCULATION.

The difference between the two becomes obvious if the browser window is wider. Here are the same two pages at 1024-pixel width.

> I NEVER AM REALLY SATISFIED THAT I UNDERSTAND ANYTHING; BECAUSE, UNDERSTAND IT WELL AS I MAY, MY COMPREHENSION CAN ONLY BE AN INFINITESIMAL FRACTION OF ALL I WANT TO UNDERSTAND ABOUT THE MANY CONNECTIONS AND RELATIONS WHICH OCCUR TO ME, HOW THE MATTER IN QUESTION WAS FIRST THOUGHT OF OR ARRIVED AT, ETC, ETC.
>
> IN ALMOST EVERY COMPUTATION A GREAT VARIETY OF ARRANGEMENTS FOR THE SUCCESSION OF THE PROCESSES IS POSSIBLE, AND VARIOUS CONSIDERATIONS MUST INFLUENCE THE SELECTIONS AMONGST THEM FOR THE PURPOSES OF A CALCULATING ENGINE. ONE ESSENTIAL OBJECT IS TO CHOOSE THAT ARRANGEMENT WHICH SHALL TEND TO REDUCE TO A MINIMUM THE TIME NECESSARY FOR COMPLETING THE CALCULATION.

`column-count: 2 at 1024px width`

> I NEVER AM REALLY SATISFIED THAT I UNDERSTAND ANYTHING; BECAUSE, UNDERSTAND IT WELL AS I MAY, MY COMPREHENSION CAN ONLY BE AN INFINITESIMAL FRACTION OF ALL I WANT TO UNDERSTAND ABOUT THE MANY CONNECTIONS AND RELATIONS WHICH OCCUR TO ME, HOW THE MATTER IN QUESTION WAS FIRST THOUGHT OF OR ARRIVED AT, ETC, ETC.
>
> IN ALMOST EVERY COMPUTATION A GREAT VARIETY OF ARRANGEMENTS FOR THE SUCCESSION OF THE PROCESSES IS POSSIBLE, AND VARIOUS CONSIDERATIONS MUST INFLUENCE THE SELECTIONS AMONGST THEM FOR THE PURPOSES OF A CALCULATING ENGINE. ONE ESSENTIAL OBJECT IS TO CHOOSE THAT ARRANGEMENT WHICH SHALL TEND TO REDUCE TO A MINIMUM THE TIME NECESSARY FOR COMPLETING THE CALCULATION.

`column-width: 260px at 1024px width`

NOTE THAT NONE OF THE COLUMNS SHOWN IS EXACTLY 260 PIXELS WIDE. THE COLUMNS WILL ADJUST THEIR WIDTH SO THEY USE THE ENTIRE HORIZONTAL SPACE AVAILABLE. IF YOU WANT COLUMNS OF AN EXACT WIDTH, YOU SHOULD PUT THEM IN AN APPROPRIATELY SIZED CONTAINER ELEMENT.

Column spans

You don't always want everything to fit neatly into columns. You may sometimes want an individual element to span multiple columns. For example, in newspapers it's common for photographs to span multiple columns of text.

Inserting an element in the text doesn't produce useful results:

```
<p>I never am really satisfied that
I understand anything; because,
 understand it well as I may, <img
src="uf012314.gif">my comprehension
can
...</p>
```

The image is 720 pixels wide, and the columns are 260 pixels wide. The result is that the image sticks out from its column and lies underneath the text of the next column.

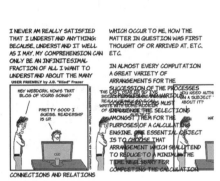

One useful approach is to limit the width of any images. When columns are in use, a width of 100% applies to the width of the column rather than the width of the page:

```
img {
    max-width: 100%;
}
```

But for pictures that are far wider than they are high, the result may be that the image is too small. We need a way for an element to take up 100% of the page width and have the text columns flow around it. This is what column-span is for.

In the current CSS3 Multi-column spec, the `column-span` property can take one of two values: 1 or `all`. The default is 1: elements span a single column. A value of `all` makes the element span every column:

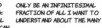

```
img {
    max-width: 100%;
    column-span: all;
}
```

Gaps and rules

The `column-gap` property allows you to control the spacing between columns:

```
body {
    column-width: 200px;
    column-gap: 100px;
}
```

Three properties control the column rule. This example shows all three of them:

```
body {
    column-width: 200px;
    column-gap: 100px;
    column-rule-style: solid;
    column-rule-color: #999;
    column-rule-width: 20px;
}
```

Note that these are analogous to the border properties.

Rather than specify the three properties individually, you can use a shorthand version to set all three at once:

```
body {
    column-width: 200px;
    column-gap: 100px;
    column-rule: 4px dashed #333;
}
```

I NEVER AM REALLY SATISFIED THAT I UNDERSTAND ANYTHING; BECAUSE, UNDERSTAND IT WELL AS I MAY, MY COMPREHENSION CAN ONLY BE AN INFINITESIMAL FRACTION OF ALL I WANT TO UNDERSTAND ABOUT THE MANY CONNECTIONS AND RELATIONS WHICH OCCUR TO ME, HOW THE MATTER IN QUESTION WAS FIRST THOUGHT OF OR ARRIVED AT. ETC. ETC.

IN ALMOST EVERY

COMPUTATION A GREAT VARIETY OF ARRANGEMENTS FOR THE SUCCESSION OF THE PROCESSES IS POSSIBLE, AND VARIOUS CONSIDERATIONS MUST INFLUENCE THE SELECTIONS AMONGST THEM FOR THE PURPOSES OF A CALCULATING ENGINE. ONE ESSENTIAL OBJECT IS TO CHOOSE THAT ARRANGEMENT WHICH SHALL TEND TO REDUCE TO A MINIMUM THE TIME NECESSARY FOR COMPLETING THE CALCULATION.

NOTE THAT THE COLUMN RULE SITS WITHIN THE COLUMN GAP—INCREASING OR DECREASING THE WIDTH OF THE COLUMN RULE DOESN'T MOVE THE COLUMNS FARTHER APART OR CLOSER TOGETHER. YOU CAN EVEN HAVE THE COLUMN RULE EXTEND UNDERNEATH THE COLUMNS, AS IN THE FOLLOWING EXAMPLE.

In this example, the column rule is wider than the column gap:

```
body {
    column-width: 200px;
    column-gap: 100px;
    column-rule: 300px ridge
#ccc;
}
```

I NEVER AM REALLY SATISFIED THAT I UNDERSTAND ANYTHING; BECAUSE, UNDERSTAND IT WELL AS I MAY, MY COMPREHENSION CAN ONLY BE AN INFINITESIMAL FRACTION OF ALL I WANT TO UNDERSTAND ABOUT THE MANY CONNECTIONS AND RELATIONS WHICH OCCUR TO ME, HOW THE MATTER IN QUESTION WAS FIRST THOUGHT OF OR ARRIVED AT. ETC. ETC.

IN ALMOST EVERY

COMPUTATION A GREAT VARIETY OF ARRANGEMENTS FOR THE SUCCESSION OF THE PROCESSES IS POSSIBLE, AND VARIOUS CONSIDERATIONS MUST INFLUENCE THE SELECTIONS AMONGST THEM FOR THE PURPOSES OF A CALCULATING ENGINE. ONE ESSENTIAL OBJECT IS TO CHOOSE THAT ARRANGEMENT WHICH SHALL TEND TO REDUCE TO A MINIMUM THE TIME NECESSARY FOR COMPLETING THE CALCULATION.

Wrapping and overflow

Text wrapping has traditionally been something that, as a web author, you had to let the browser take care of. In situations where you'd like more control, CSS3 offers a couple of new properties: word-wrap and text-overflow. This section looks at each in turn.

Word wrap

CSS3 provides a word-wrap property that controls whether line breaks are allowed in the middle of words. Normally, text wrapping only occurs at spaces and punctuation. If a word is too long to fit inside the containing element without the opportunity for a break, then the element expands to contain it.

For regular paragraphs of text, this isn't usually a problem. But it can be an issue for headings and URLs, particularly if they're in constrained-width containers such as sidebars or text columns. Imagine that you have a word-of-the-day feature in your site's sidebar. The sidebar has a width of 15em, which is normally plenty of room; but one day the word is a long one:

		Standard	Prefixed
Browser support quick check: word-wrap		1.0	-
		3.5	-
		5.5	-
		10.50	-
		1.0	-

```
<div>
    <h1>Floccinaucinihilipilification</h1>
    <p>The act or habit of describing or regarding
        something as unimportant.</p>
</div>
```

Even though the width of the element is constrained, the length of the word forces the entire container to be wider:

```
div { width: 15em; }
```

Note that the paragraph is still constrained by the width set.

Here's where you can use the word-wrap property. Setting a value of break-word allows wrapping to occur within the long word:

```
div { width: 15em; }
h1 { word-wrap: break-word; }
```

FLOCCINAUCINIHILIPILIFICATION

THE ACT OR HABIT OF
DESCRIBING OR REGARDING
SOMETHING AS
UNIMPORTANT.

FLOCCINAUCI
NIHILIPILIFI
CATION

THE ACT OR HABIT OF
DESCRIBING OR REGARDING
SOMETHING AS
UNIMPORTANT.

Text overflow

It may be that you want to keep the word on one line, so `break-word` isn't appropriate. A normal way to do this in CSS2 is to set the element to `overflow: hidden`.h1 {
`overflow: hidden; }`

This works, but it doesn't look tidy. The word is cut off part way through a letter.

The `text-overflow` property lets you make things look neater:

```
h1 {
    overflow: hidden;
    text-overflow: ellipsis;
}
```

Now the word ends at a letter, and an ellipsis gives a visual indication that the word has been truncated. This property is particularly useful if you're dealing with user-generated content that appears in constrained areas—for example, a Twitter feed in a sidebar.

FLOCCINAUCIN

THE ACT OR HABIT OF DESCRIBING OR REGARDING SOMETHING AS UNIMPORTANT.

FLOCCINAUC...

THE ACT OR HABIT OF DESCRIBING OR REGARDING SOMETHING AS UNIMPORTANT.

Browser support quick check: text-overflow		Standard	Prefixed
		1.0	-
		7.0	-
		6.0	-
		11.0	9.0
		1.3	-

Browser support

Support for downloadable fonts and WOFF is now available in all major browsers, but so far, the more advanced font-control features are available only in Firefox. In terms of other text features, the other browsers take the lead.

	12	14	4	6	8	9	10	11.1	11.5	5	5.1
@font-face	●	●	●	●	○	●	●	●	●	●	●
WOFF	●	●	●	●		●	●	●	●		●
font-size-adjust			●	●							
Font features			○	○			○				
CSS columns	○	○	○	○			●	●	●	○	○
Column span	○	○					○		●		○
word-wrap	●	●	●	●	●	●	●	●	●	●	●
text-overflow	●	●			●	●	●	●	●	●	●

Key:
- ● Complete or nearly complete support
- ○ Incomplete or alternative support
- Little or no support

Summary

Text has always been a fundamental component of web content, but until recently control of typography has been somewhat limited. In this chapter, you've seen how @font-face can finally provide beautiful (while still accessible) text on the web, and how web font services can make it easier to get those fonts onto your web pages. You've also had a tour through the desktop-publishing-like font control capabilities CSS3 will give us in the future through `font-feature-settings`. And, continuing the publishing theme, you've seen the new features for controlling columns of text. Finally, you saw some CSS3 features for controlling text wrapping and overflow, which are useful when you're fitting content into text columns and other narrow containers.

THAT'S THE END OF THE BOOK, BUT HOPEFULLY JUST THE START OF YOUR JOURNEY WITH HTML5 AND CSS3. BOTH STANDARDS ARE EVOLVING AT A FASTER RATE THAN EVER BEFORE, OPENING NEW POSSIBILITIES FOR WEB AUTHORS EVERY MONTH. IT'S AN EXCITING TIME TO BE INVOLVED WITH THE WEB; ALL OF US HERE AT COLUMBIA INTERNET (AND OUR FRIENDS AT MANNING PUBLICATIONS) HOPE YOU CAN TAKE THE KNOWLEDGE YOU'VE GAINED FROM THIS BOOK AND GO OUT AND MAKE A BETTER WEB!

Appendix A

A history of web standards

In this appendix, you'll get a brief overview of how the web was invented and its subsequent development. You'll also learn how standards are made by the W3C, why the Web Hypertext Application Technology Working Group (WHATWG) was formed, and the aims behind HTML5. To conclude, we'll take a brief look at the process behind the other major standard that's covered in this book: CSS3. None of this information is necessary to use web standards but, like many other human endeavors, web standards are a product of their history as much as they are rational technical documents. An appreciation of the history will help you understand why the standards are the way they are.

A short history of the web

In the following sections, you'll learn about the history of the web, from its beginnings as an easy way to share physics papers to its current incarnation as the repository of all the world's knowledge and possible replacement for traditional operating systems. You'll also learn about the World Wide Web Consortium (W3C) and its role in providing the standards on which the entire web relies. You'll see how web developers have pushed the boundaries of what's possible with HTML4 and CSS2 to create the need for new standards, and you'll learn about how many of the common issues that today's web developers encounter can be solved easily in HTML5 and CSS3.

In the beginning

In 1989, Tim Berners-Lee was thinking about the difficulties scientists at CERN encountered when sharing their papers and research results. Each had tools for writing papers and other documentation on their own computers, but CERN was mostly populated by researchers visiting from the universities that employed them. They brought their own computers with them, so there was a wide variety of different computers, each with unique documents. If you wanted a document from a fellow researcher's computer, then it was likely you'd either need to learn to use a different computer or program than you were used to, or you'd need to transform the output of your colleague's software to make it compatible with your own. Berners-Lee had written several of these

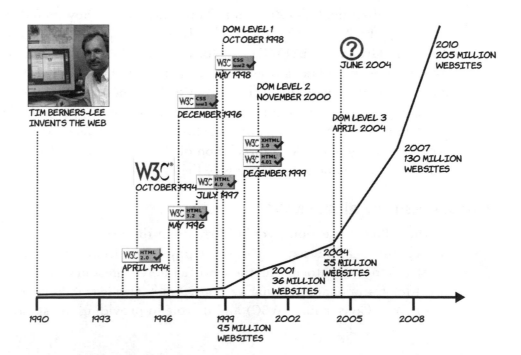

TIM BERNERS-LEE
INVENTS THE WEB

DOM LEVEL 1
OCTOBER 1998

W3C CSS level2
MAY 1998

DOM LEVEL 2
NOVEMBER 2000

W3C CSS level1
DECEMBER 1996

JUNE 2004

2010
205 MILLION
WEBSITES

DOM LEVEL 3
APRIL 2004

W3C XHTML 1.0
W3C HTML 4.01
DECEMBER 1999

2007
130 MILLION
WEBSITES

W3C®
OCTOBER 1994

W3C HTML 4.0
JULY 1997

W3C HTML 3.2
MAY 1996

2004
55 MILLION
WEBSITES

W3C HTML 2.0
APRIL 1994

2001
36 MILLION
WEBSITES

1990   1993   1996   1999   2002   2005   2008

9.5 MILLION
WEBSITES

conversion utilities but realized that, instead of a succession of small utilities, he would be better off solving the general problem. He believed a hypertext system would be ideal, but systems at the time were too complex and difficult to author for. He set about designing a simple hypertext system based on Standard Generalized Markup Language (SGML) for a distributed client-server architecture.

This culminated in the release, on Christmas Day 1990, of the World-WideWeb browser and server. It allowed each individual to publish their documents in a standard format that anyone else could then read across the network using the browser. The browser didn't need to be a particular bit of software; anyone was free to implement a viewer. The HTML document format was plain text interspersed with special tags marked by angle brackets, such as <p> for paragraph or <li> for list item, to mark the purpose of the text. These documents could be easily created on any type of computer.

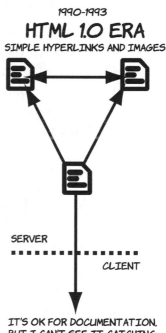

1990-1993
HTML 1.0 ERA
SIMPLE HYPERLINKS AND IMAGES

SERVER
CLIENT

IT'S OK FOR DOCUMENTATION. BUT I CAN'T SEE IT CATCHING ON FOR ANYTHING ELSE.

The idea quickly caught on in the academic world, and several more browsers appeared: libwww, Mosaic, Midas, Erwise, ViolaWWW, and Arena, among others. The authors of the various web browsers collaborated on the www-talk mailing list, discussing implementation strategies and arguing about new features. Implementation usually won out over theory—when Marc Andreessen proposed the <img> tag, it was felt by many to be the worst of several proposals put forward. But Andreessen was the first person to implement his proposal, so that was the tag everyone used in their pages, and it's the tag we still use today.

The primacy of features over standardization threatened to destroy the ideals on which the web was founded before it even really got started—the situation was heading back toward the original state of affairs— documents compatible with only a single client application.

In an effort to stem the tide, Tim Berners-Lee and Dave Raggett produced a draft document in April 1993, "Hypertext Markup Language, Ver 1.0," and submitted it to the Internet Engineering Task Force (IETF).

The IETF was the standards body that controlled most of the standards relevant to the internet: TCP/IP for network communication; DNS for name resolution, so you can type in an easy-to-remember address like yahoo.com instead of 67.195.160.76; and SMTP for email, among many others. The published standards were known as Requests for Comments (RFCs), reflecting the consensual attitude that marked the growth of the internet over the previous two decades.

The HTML 1.0 draft was overtaken by the rapid development of browsers. In the time it took to move through the standards process, the state of the art in web browsers moved on significantly. But the web was becoming increasingly popular, so the need for some sort of standard was even more acute: HTML 1.0 was soon to be replaced by HTML 2.0.

Browser wars

The first commercially successful web browser was Netscape Navigator. Version 1.0 was released on December 15, 1994 and quickly captured huge market share. It was based on the Mosaic code originally developed by Marc Andreessen.

Also in 1994, the World Wide Web Consortium (W3C) was founded by Tim Berners-Lee. The goal of the W3C was to encourage the adoption of standards across the internet industry, but initially the HTML standard efforts remained focused within the IETF.

In August 1995 Microsoft launched Internet Explorer, also based on the Mosaic code. It was not very competitive with Navigator in features and was quickly superseded by version 2.0 in November 1995.

The same year also saw the launch of Yahoo.com (March 1995), Amazon.com (July 1995), and eBay.com (September 1995), along with many other shorter-lived web brands—or, as they soon became known, dot-coms. The internet boom was ready to happen, and both Netscape and Microsoft wanted to be in position to take advantage of it.

The first official standard for HTML (HTML 2.0) was published in April 1994 with revisions in July 1994 and February 1995; it was finally accepted as a standard by the IETF in September 1995. The goal of the document was to describe common browser capabilities as of June 1994, so it reflected most of the functionality available in the browsers released that year.

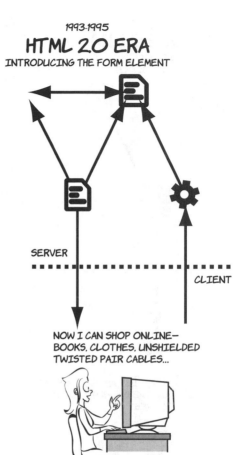

By the time versions 3.0 of IE and Navigator were released in August 1996, IE was much closer in terms of features, and the browser wars were on. In an effort to grab market share, both vendors rushed to implement new features with little regard for compatibility. Initially this wasn't a problem, because Netscape had as much as 80% of the market; but as IE gained ground, thanks to improved features and an aggressive marketing campaign, developers had to contend with two browsers with similar features but very different implementations.

1995-1997
HTML 3.2 ERA
CLIENT-SIDE INTERACTIVITY WITH JAVASCRIPT

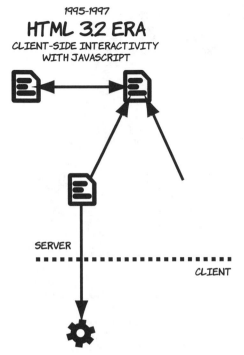

SERVER

CLIENT

HMM, ANNOYING ANIMATIONS AND LAYOUT TABLES, NOT SURE THIS IS PROGRESS.

The W3C attempted to stem the tide by publishing a draft standard, HTML3. It wasn't compatible with either of the major browsers, so it struggled to gain traction. A short-term compromise was reached in HTML 3.2. This more closely reflected the functionality of contemporary browsers. Many of the features proposed for HTML3 were carried forward to the spec for HTML4.

1997-2010
HTML 4.0 ERA
CLIENT-SIDE INTERACTIVITY WITH JAVASCRIPT

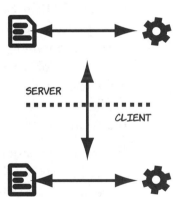

SERVER

CLIENT

I CAN DO EVERYTHING ON THE WEB. NO NEED FOR DESKTOP APPS!

> ## W3C standards process in 1998
>
> In May 1998, the W3C formalized its standards process with the publication of the document "World Wide Web Consortium Process." It listed three stages a standard had to go through:
>
> - *Working Draft (WD)*—The proposed standard may go through several drafts. Once the standard has stabilized, the editor issues a Last Call for comments, and then the standard can move on to the next stage.
> - *Proposed Recommendation (PR)*—The Proposed Recommendation stage lasts at least four weeks. A PR is voted on by W3C members. After the vote, the standard is either returned to the Working Draft stage or, perhaps with modifications, advances to be a full recommendation.
> - *W3C Recommendation (R)*—A Recommendation indicates that consensus has been reached among W3C Members and the specification is appropriate for widespread use. After the standard has become a Recommendation, only minor revisions are allowed to correct minor errors or clarify issues.

From web pages to web applications

As you've just seen, HTML was originally designed for sharing documents. The only interactive elements in HTML 1.0 were the hyperlinks between documents. HTML 2.0 introduced forms, which allowed users to send information back to the server. Shortly after that, Netscape introduced JavaScript that enabled web pages to respond to user actions without going back to the server at all. In this section, you'll see how the addition of client-side interactivity turned out to be a game-changing move for the web.

Although the early versions of JavaScript were limited, it caught the imagination of web developers. It was initially developed by Netscape, but was copied by Microsoft and soon became standardized under the umbrella of Ecma International as ECMAScript in 1997 (these days, though, nearly everyone still refers to it as *JavaScript*).

JavaScript can update browser content through the Document Object Model (DOM). The DOM represented the HTML document as a tree of objects, so you'll frequently hear it referred to as a *DOM tree*. With the release of Netscape Navigator (now Communicator) 4.0 and IE 4.0, the DOM became a complete interface, and developers were able to produce highly interactive web pages. This became known as Dynamic HTML (DHTML).

Unfortunately, the DOMs implemented in Navigator and IE were very different—far more incompatible than the implementations of Java-Script in each browser. This meant that coding DHTML in a cross-browser—compatible manner was something of a challenge; developers had to produce two versions of their application code, one for IE and one for Navigator. The extra code made it more likely that developers would make mistakes. Sites that made heavy use of DHTML tended to be unreliable and slow in at least one, if not both, major browsers. As a result, DHTML and JavaScript gained a bad reputation. On the other hand, JavaScript was often the only way to work around the incompatibilities between browsers. This is a purpose for which JavaScript is still used extensively today. The W3C stepped in with the DOM Level 1 standard in late 1998, and Microsoft provided partial support for it in IE5. Netscape planned to add support in its version 5.0; but as Netscape struggled to compete with the far greater resources of Microsoft, that plan never saw the light of day. When Microsoft released versions 5.5 and 6.0 of IE, version 6.0 claimed "full DOM Level 1 support," although inconsistencies in the standard meant that not everyone agreed. Meanwhile, Netscape faded into the background, was bought out by AOL, and eventually gave up on browser development. The code for Navigator was donated to the world as open source and eventually was reborn as Firefox.

W3C standards process in 1999

In November 1999, an update to the "World Wide Web Consortium Process" document added an additional stage to the process: the Candidate Recommendation. This recognized the need for implementation feedback prior to the standard being published as a Recommendation:

* *Working Draft (WD)*—The initial publication of the standard, used to gather public feedback. A standard typically has several Working Drafts before advancing to the next stage.
* *Candidate Recommendation (CR)*—After the specification has stabilized, it becomes a CR. At this point, browser vendors are expected to begin implementing

(continued)

the standard in order to provide feedback about its practicality. It isn't unusual for a standard to revert to a WD several times after becoming a CR.

◉ *Proposed Recommendation (PR)*—After some practical implementation experience has been gained, preferably at least two independent and interoperable implementations, the standard can advance to the PR status. This is an opportunity for final review within the W3C. The standard is either approved by the Advisory Committee and advances to a full Recommendation, or it returns to WD status for further work.

◉ *W3C Recommendation (R)*—As before, when published as a Recommendation, the standard is ready for widespread deployment.

After the frantic pace of releases in the second half of the 1990s, things slowed down for HTML. The DOM Level 2 spec was published in late 2000, followed by DOM Level 3 in 2004. CSS saw a major revision to 2.1 in February 2004, but it didn't see full support in IE until the version 8 release in March 2009.

Microsoft, no longer under much pressure to advance IE other than to add features that would be useful within the company's own products, drastically reduced the resources devoted to its development. One of the few features added in this period was the XMLHTTP ActiveX control (equivalent to a plug-in) as a standard component of IE5. The XMLHTTP object allowed JavaScript to make an asynchronous request back to the server to get new data without the user loading a new page. This feature was required for Microsoft's new web-based client for the Exchange 2000 email server.

The stage was now set for the boom, from 1998 to 2000, and bust, from then until 2002, of the dot-com bubble. The web exploded, both in popular awareness and size, taking advantage of all the features of HTML4 and, somewhat later, CSS2. Where features were lacking in the standards, developers used JavaScript or third-party plug-ins, such as Macromedia's (now Adobe's) Flash, to fill in the gaps.

Still, many people thought the future of the web was not with HTML and CSS. This quote from a *Dr. Dobbs* article in 2002 is typical: "Even today, HTML offers scant control over design essentials like typography and screen layout, and does little to accommodate complex interactions between browsers and servers. Making a trip to the server after each mouse click is a fairly inefficient way to deliver information. As Web development increasingly focuses on applications, markup's limitations are becoming more and more apparent."

Two events heralded a new approach to web applications. First, the Firefox browser, which is the open source descendant of Netscape Navigator, added its equivalent to IE's XMLHTTP: the `XmlHttpRequest` (XHR) object. Second, Google launched a web-based email application that took advantage of this feature: Gmail.

Gmail was unlike contemporary websites: after the interface was loaded, the page was hardly ever reloaded. Whenever the user clicked a link, instead of visiting a new page, some JavaScript intercepted it, sent an XHR request to the server, and then updated the already-loaded page when the request returned. Gmail worked in both IE and Firefox, and it was fast to use, comparable to desktop email clients such as Microsoft Outlook.

Although it was far from the first web application to use XHR or similar techniques, Gmail captured the imagination of web developers worldwide and led to a spurt in XHR-based web applications and renewed interest in JavaScript. The approach was soon given the acronym AJAX (for Asynchronous JavaScript and XML), which helped to distance it from the tawdry reputation of DHTML despite being mostly the same thing. Although the web had long been touted as a platform for applications, the AJAX trend looked like it had a chance of making that possibility a reality.

The competing standards

You may have wondered what the W3C has been doing in the decade since HTML 4.01 was released. It has, of course, been working on plenty of standards other than HTML, but it's also working on a replacement for HTML4. The W3C decided that the future of HTML lay in XML. XML is superficially similar to HTML—documents, tags, and elements all exist in XML, but it has two major differences:

- *XML parsing is much stricter than HTML.* A few mistakes in an HTML document will, in many cases, not even be noticed; the browser will correct the errors as best it can and carry on. A single error in an XML document causes the parsing to fail and an error message to be displayed. The stricter approach allows browsers to be more efficient, which is particularly useful on mobile and low-power devices.

- *XML is extensible.* If you want to add new elements to your XML page, you can do so. You describe those elements in a separate file and link to it from your document. Your new elements are then just as valid as any specified by the W3C.

The first step was to redefine HTML 4.01 as an XML standard. XHTML 1.0 became a Candidate Recommendation in October 2000. It contained no new elements or features; all the valid elements were identical to those in HTML 4.01. The only changes came from it now being a dialect of XML. The plan was to extend XHTML in a modular fashion by plugging in new XML dialects. Some of the better-known XML dialects the W3C expected to be plugged in to XHTML were Scalable Vector Graphics (SVG), which became a CR in August 2000; and MathML, an XML language for describing equations, which became a CR in April 1998. The modular approach allowed different technologies to be worked on at different paces.

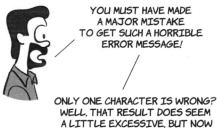

The drive toward XML meant that HTML was largely sidelined. The focus was on building compound documents out of various XML dialects. This included the HTML-like XHTML and the previously mentioned SVG, MathML, but also XForms, RDF (Resource Description Framework), and any number of other proposals. It was envisaged that you might write web applications without using any XHTML at all.

In 2004, at the W3C Workshop on Web Applications and Compound Documents, Opera and Mozilla, concerned that the standards process might become increasingly irrelevant to the web as it existed in the real world, put forward a position paper outlining an alternative approach. This paper outlined seven "Design Principles for Web Application Technologies" and, in the context of these, proposed answers to the questions the workshop had set out to answer.

The document was voted down by the rest of the attendees, who wanted to stick with the current XML, rather than HTML, -based approach. Two days later, the Web Hypertext Application Technology Working Group (WHATWG) was formed.

Step forward WHATWG

The WHATWG set out to define the next HTML standard according to the seven principles set out in Opera's and Mozilla's document. They underpin the entire approach taken by the WHATWG during the development of HTML5, so let's look at them now:

○ *"Backwards compatibility, clear migration path"*—In 2004, IE6 was the browser of choice for 80% of web users. The WHATWG felt that there was little point in specifying new HTML functionality unless it could at least be emulated in IE6 with JavaScript. If a plug-in was required to emulate the new features in IE6, then the chances were it would never see large uptake among web developers.

○ *"Well-defined error handling"*—A major point of incompatibility in contemporary browsers was not what happened when the page author got everything correct, but what happened when they made a mistake. The next standard should specify error handling and error recovery.

○ *"Users should not be exposed to authoring errors"*—This addressed a major difference of opinion with the XML-based approach at the W3C. WHATWG wanted browsers to recover from errors gracefully and, where recovery was possible, not display an error message to the user—just like HTML.

- *"Practical use"*—New features should be added based on use cases. Ideally, these should be based on real issues developers experience in working around the limits of existing standards.
- *"Scripting is here to stay"*—JavaScript had become something of a second-class citizen in XHTML. Although the WHATWG preferred a declarative markup approach, especially for the initial application state, it recognized that scripting will always have a significant role.
- *"Device-specific profiling should be avoided"*—The W3C produced a cut-down version of the XHTML spec for mobile devices. The WHATWG felt that authors shouldn't have to produce different versions of their markup for different devices.
- *"Open process"*—Although the W3C has open mailing lists, it also has private ones. WHATWG activity is conducted entirely under public scrutiny.

This isn't to say the principles of the WHATWG were entirely orthogonal to those being followed by the W3C's XML-focused working groups, but there was a significant difference in approach. The W3C continued to work on XHTML2 while the WHATWG worked on HTML5. XHTML2 had the backing of the recognized standards body, but it primarily appealed to people who wanted to use other XML-based technologies. HTML5 garnered far more popular support with its "evolution rather than revolution" approach and its exhaustive documenting of browser behavior.

In addition to the seven principles, the HTML5 spec took the step of combining the separate HTML and DOM specs by the W3C. Experience had shown that trying to maintain them as two specifications led to inconsistencies and incompatibilities. In the HTML5 spec, the DOM became the basis of correct parsing—two implementations would be interoperable if they produced the same DOM tree from an HTML document.

Eventually the W3C realized that it risked being made irrelevant by real-world events. In March 2007, it relaunched the HTML Working Group. Mozilla, Apple, and Opera proposed that the WHATWG HTML5 specs be taken as the starting point of this new group's work, and the rest of the working group agreed. At this point, XHTML2 was put on hold and everyone was able to agree that the future of the web would be HTML5.

CSS2 evolves into CSS3

While all this was going on in the world of markup, work was continuing on CSS at the W3C in the form of CSS Level 3, or CSS3 for short. CSS3 also tried to correct a number of past mistakes in drafting specifications, starting with fixing CSS2.

The CSS2 specification had been through the 1998 standards process and thus had no implementation feedback before being published as a Recommendation. As vendors tried to implement it, a number of issues were found that made it impossible, or impractical, to achieve compliance with the standard.

CSS 2.1 set out to rectify those mistakes and provide a solid, implementable base on which to build CSS3. The work to set CSS 2.1 right has taken more than eight years, but was finally completed in June 2011. But the timing of this was unfortunate. IE6 was released in August 2001, a few years after the CSS2 publication but a year before the first draft of CSS 2.1. This is significant because IE6 is the browser that won the first round of the browser wars. It achieved 83% market share by 2004 as Netscape collapsed. With no competition, Microsoft wound up IE development; the web would be stuck on IE6 for many years. In comparison to the two-year-or-less gap between most previous IE releases, it would be nearly five years before IE7 appeared. Even though IE6 had good support for CSS2 compared to other browsers available in 2001, it soon fell behind standards.

CSS3 is modular; it's split into sections such as Backgrounds and Borders, Values and Units, and Text Layout. This means that instead of waiting years for a huge, monolithic standard to be finalized, as has happened with CSS 2.1, less controversial and more useful sections can be prioritized and pushed through the standards process more quickly. In the meantime, until a particular module is ready, the corresponding section of the CSS 2.1 spec is regarded as the current standard.

HEY! IT SEEMS LIKE HALF OF CSS3 IS REALLY CSS 2.1

WHAT'S TAKING SO LONG?

BUT EVEN IE8 SUPPORTS CSS 2.1!

AH! BECAUSE IT'S NO GOOD JUST SAYING YOU MEET THE STANDARD; YOU NEED TO BE ABLE TO PROVE IT!

IT'S ALL THE WORK OF THE SAME GROUP AT THE W3C. CSS2 HAD TO BE FIXED BEFORE THEY COULD MOVE FORWARD.

CSS2 BECAME A STANDARD UNDER THE OLD PROCESS. NOW TWO FULLY INTEROPERABLE IMPLEMENTATIONS ARE NEEDED.

THE W3C HAD TO WAIT FOR A LIBRARY OF TEST CASES; WE NEED TO BE ABLE TO TEST WHETHER BROWSERS MEET THE STANDARD.

EXACTLY. THE CSS 2.1 SPECIFICATION FINALLY BECAME A W3C RECOMMENDATION IN JUNE 2011.

NOW THAT THE HISTORY LESSON IS OUT OF THE WAY, THE REST OF THE APPENDIXES ARE TARGETED AT TAKING A COMPLETE NOVICE AT WEB DEVELOPMENT AND GIVING THEM ENOUGH KNOWLEDGE TO APPRECIATE THE REST OF THIS BOOK. THEY ALSO CONSTITUTE A USEFUL REFRESHER COURSE FOR MORE EXPERIENCED WEB AUTHORS. FIRST YOU'LL LEARN ABOUT HTML ITSELF.

Appendix B

HTML basics

I f you've never created a web page before picking up this book, this appendix will bring you up to speed on the fundamentals of Hypertext Markup Language (HTML) so you can fully enjoy the rest of the book. It covers these areas:

- Basic HTML syntax: what it's made up of
- Common HTML elements for text, metadata, links, and images
- What makes a particular text file an HTML document
- How to learn by example with View Source

This short appendix will be a whirlwind introduction. To get you up to speed as quickly as possible it's opinionated about issues that are fundamentally a matter of style or preference. I won't waste your time showing you several slightly different ways of doing the same thing; I'll concentrate on the things you need to know to understand the HTML in this book.

The components of hypertext

HTML is a language for describing hypertext documents. Hypertext documents are made up of headings, paragraphs, bulleted lists, and, importantly, links to other hypertext documents; it's the links that constitute the *hyper* part of hypertext. In this section, we'll look at things from the bottom up, starting with how an HTML document indicates the existence of a paragraph or a heading before combining everything to make a document. The following diagram shows the concepts that make up HTML, from simple components on the left to complete documents on the right.

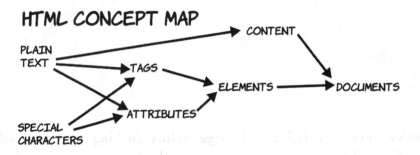

Tags, elements, and attributes

A *tag* is a bit of text that acts as a point demarcation. To create a tag, HTML gives certain characters special meaning: the angle brackets < and >.

Putting characters within angle brackets creates a tag. You can see in this diagram that there are two tags, <h1> and </h1>: a start tag and an end tag. An end tag always matches a start tag, except that it has a slash after the opening angle bracket.

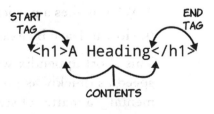

The combination of a start tag and an end tag defines an *element*. Everything between the two tags is referred to as the *contents* of the element.

Start tags can also have attributes: a name optionally followed by a value. An attribute is used to select between different options of element function or to provide extra information about what the element describes.

AN ATTRIBUTE

```
<p class="special">
  A special paragraph
</p>
```

Some elements need to have at least one attribute to be any use; for instance, a `<link>` element has an attribute that contains the address of the HTML page it links to. Some attributes are specific to certain elements, and others can be applied to any element. The two most common attributes you'll see are `id`, to assign a unique identifier to an element, and `class`, to assign a space-separated list of classes (think of them as categories or tags). You'll see these two attributes a lot in appendix C when you learn about CSS.

Elements can contain text, but they can also contain other elements. In this example we would say, "The `<p>` element contains the `<em>` element."

```
<p>
  A paragraph
  <em>with emphasis</em>
</p>
```
PARENT ELEMENT

CHILD ELEMENT

Any element that contains other elements is said to be the *parent* of those other elements; those are in turn its *children* — the idea is that the elements form a tree structure, like a family tree.

The `<p>` element has two children: the text "A paragraph" and an `<em>` element. The `<em>` element has one child: the text it contains.

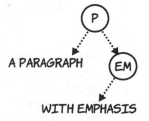

HTML documents

An HTML *document* is a tree of elements descending from an `<html>` element and its two children: `<head>` for metadata (literally, "data about data") and other nonvisible elements, and `<body>` for the page content.

A minimal HTML document can be created out of the earlier fragment by adding these three necessary elements and a title:

```html
<html>
<head>
    <title>Minimal document</title>
</head>
<body>
    <p>A paragraph
    <em>with emphasis</em></p>
</body>
</html>
```

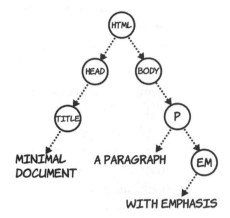

You can create an HTML document yourself by opening a text editor, copying this code into it, and saving it as a file with the extension .html. After you've done that, double-clicking the file will open it in your browser.

As you see more complex documents with many more elements, bear in mind that ultimately the browser turns them into a tree like this. When you're applying CSS or doing scripting, it's common to think in terms of nodes in this tree rather than elements in the document.

Markup, parsing, and rendering

The activity of taking plain text (the content) and turning it into an HTML document is called *marking up*: adding markup to the plain text to indicate which bits of it are headings, paragraphs, bulleted lists, and links. Note that after a text document has been marked up into HTML, it's still also a text document. You can open it in Notepad or any other text editor, and it's treated like any other plain text. Only when the text document is loaded into a browser does it become a hypertext document. When a string of text like "<p>A paragraph</p>" is described as "a paragraph element," that's shorthand for "this string of text, when read by the right piece of software under the right conditions, will create within that software an entity that is a paragraph element." The process of taking the text file containing the markup and turning it into the tree-like representation of an HTML document is called *parsing*. The process of taking that tree and showing it to the user is called *rendering*.

Now that you've got the general idea, the next section will go into more detail about common elements for marking up text content.

Elements for text

This section looks at HTML elements for marking up text—which, for many web pages, is the majority of the content. Nearly every element can contain text, but several are specifically dedicated to the task. The most common of these is the paragraph element, `<p></p>`, of which you've already seen several examples, but there are many others for headings, unordered lists, ordered lists, line breaks, horizontal rules, and more.

Headings and paragraphs

Paragraphs and headings work in concert to create the bulk of the text content of a document and its implicit structure. HTML has six heading elements, which are numbered 1 through 6: `<h1>`, `<h2>`, `<h3>`, `<h4>`, `<h5>`, and `<h6>`. The most significant is `<h1>`, which is usually the document title; the sections should begin with `<h2>` elements and the subsections with `<h3>`, and so on:

```
<html>
<head>
    <title>
        Headings and
        implicit structure
    </title>
</head>
<body>
    <h1>The main heading</h1>
    <p>Main introduction</p>
    <h2>First section</h2>
    <p>Section introduction</p>
    <h3>Subsection heading 1.1</h3>
    <p>Subsection 1.1</p>
    <h2>Second section</h2>
    <p>Section introduction</p>
    <h3>Subsection heading 2.1</h3>
    <p>Subsection 2.1</p>
    <h4>Sub-subsection</h4>
```

The main heading

Main introduction

First section

Section introduction

Subsection heading 1.1

Subsection 1.1

Second section

Section introduction

Subsection heading 2.1

Subsection 2.1

Sub-subsection

Subsection 2.1.1

```
<p>Subsection 2.1.1</p>
</body>
</html>
```

As you can see, the headings get smaller as they decrease in importance.

Both headings and paragraphs automatically break the flow of text at the position of their end tag. Although the previous markup shows the elements on separate lines to match the screenshot, this isn't necessary. The markup could be all on a single line, and it wouldn't change the results in the browser—all whitespace characters (see sidebar) are collapsed to a single space.

> ### Whitespace
>
> *Whitespace* is a collective term for any sort of spacing character. To understand it fully, we need to take a step back and consider what a text file really is. A text file is a long list of characters, some of which are special *control characters* to indicate line feeds, carriage returns, and tab stops. Think of an old-style teletype or line printer with a print head: these characters are instructions telling the print head to do something other than print a character but that does take up space.
>
> On modern computers, these characters control the layout you see in a text editor; you see several lines of text, but only because the text contains several carriage returns and line feeds. For HTML purposes, many of the control characters are considered whitespace. The full list of these characters is as follows: space, tab, form feed, zero-width space, carriage return, line feed, and combined carriage return and line feed.

Here's an example with longer paragraphs. The markup is wrapped at 70 characters, ignoring the position of the tags. The tags are shown in bold so they're easier to spot:

```
<h1>A quote from Ada Lovelace</h1><p>The Analytical Engine has no
pretensions whatever to originate anything. It can do whatever we
know how to order it to perform. It can follow analysis, but it has
no power of anticipating any analytical revelations or truths. Its
province is to assist us in making available what we are already
acquainted with.</p><p>The Analytical Engine weaves algebraic
patterns, just as the Jacquard loom weaves flowers and leaves.</p>
```

Viewing this markup in the browser reveals that the line breaks go wherever the elements and the size of the window dictate:

A quote from Ada Lovelace

The Analytical Engine has no pretensions whatever to originate anything. It can do whatever we know how to order it to perform. It can follow analysis, but it has no power of anticipating any analytical revelations or truths. Its province is to assist us in making available what we are already acquainted with.

The Analytical Engine weaves algebraic patterns, just as the Jacquard loom weaves flowers and leaves.

A quote from Ada Lovelace

The Analytical Engine has no pretensions whatever to originate anything. It can do whatever we know how to order it to perform. It can follow analysis, but it has no power of anticipating any analytical revelations or truths. Its province is to assist us in making available what we are already acquainted with.

The Analytical Engine weaves algebraic patterns, just as the Jacquard loom weaves flowers and leaves.

If there's a situation where a paragraph requires a line break, such as an address or a verse of poetry, you can use the <br> element:

```
<p>The Analytical Engine
 weaves algebraic<br>patterns,
 just as the<br>Jacquard loom
 weaves<br>flowers
 and<br>leaves.</p>
```

The Analytical Engine weaves algebraic patterns, just as the Jacquard loom weaves flowers and leaves.

The <br> element is unique among those covered so far because it consists of a single tag. It can have no children. The <br> element and others like it are known as *self-closing elements*. They're sometimes written with a closing slash like this: <br/>.

Line breaks aren't for layout

A common beginner's mistake is to use line-break elements or empty paragraph tags to increase vertical spacing between two other elements. There's no need to do this in HTML: spacing between elements can be entirely controlled with Cascading Style Sheets (CSS, covered in appendix C).

HTML is for describing content, not presentation. You'll benefit in the long run if you avoid using meaningless, empty elements for layout.

HTML's ability to ignore spacing and line breaks and reflow text to fit the available space is usually an advantage: text flows automatically into the space available to it in the browser window, mobile device, or web-enabled refrigerator on which it happens to be displayed. But sometimes the original text formatting is significant: for example, program listings or command-prompt output. For preformatted text like this, HTML has the `<pre>` element:

```
<pre>The Analytical Engine weaves
 algebraic patterns, just
 as the Jacquard loom
 weaves flowers and
 leaves.</pre>
```

```
The Analytical Engine weaves
 algebraic patterns, just
 as the Jacquard loom
 weaves flowers and
 leaves.
```

Notice that the leading space on each line is faithfully reproduced in the browser output.

Lists

Another common textual feature is lists. Bullet points can make a memorable way to highlight key facts. Some documents are nothing but lists—you may have sat through terrible presentations that were built on the philosophy that bulleted lists were an appropriate way to show paragraphs of text that should be read out loud.

This section will introduce the two most common HTML lists:

- Unordered
- Ordered

Each consists of a parent element and one or more child elements. Unordered and ordered lists differ only in the parent element.

- List item
- List item
- List item

1. List item
2. List item
3. List item

```
<ul>
    <li>List item</li>
    <li>List item</li>
    <li>List item</li>
</ul>
```

```
<ol>
    <li>List item</li>
    <li>List item</li>
    <li>List item</li>
</ol>
```

An unordered list, the traditional bulleted list of PowerPoint legend, is made up of a `<ul>` element and a collection of `<li>` child list items, and an ordered list is made up of a `<ol>` element and a collection of child `<li>` items. The list items can themselves include more list elements with their own list items, resulting in a nested list.

- List item
- List item
  - Nested item
  - Nested item
- List item

1. List item
2. List item
   1. Nested item
   2. Nested item
3. List item

```
<ul>
    <li>List item</li>
    <li>List item
        <ul>
            <li>Nested item</li>
            <li>Nested item</li>
        </ul>
    </li>
    <li>List item</li>
</ul>
```

```
<ol>
    <li>List item</li>
    <li>List item
        <ol>
            <li>Nested item</li>
            <li>Nested item</li>
        </ol>
    </li>
    <li>List item</li>
</ol>
```

It's perfectly acceptable to nest ordered lists within unordered lists and unordered lists within ordered lists.

- List item
- List item
  1. Nested item
  2. Nested item
- List item

1. List item
2. List item
   - Nested item
   - Nested item
3. List item

```
<ul>
    <li>List item</li>
    <li>List item
        <ol>
            <li>Nested item</li>
            <li>Nested item</li>
        </ol>
    </li>
    <li>List item</li>
</ul>
```

```
<ol>
    <li>List item</li>
    <li>List item
        <ul>
            <li>Nested item</li>
            <li>Nested item</li>
        </ul>
    </li>
    <li>List item</li>
</ol>
```

Lists are commonly used to mark up navigation: a *list of links*. Nested lists are a good match for the sections and subsections of a website. In the next section, we'll look at some elements intended to be used inside the major structural elements we've covered.

Emphasis and typography

Some words and phrases are so important in the context of their paragraph that they need to be given special emphasis. HTML provides two elements for this: <em> for emphasis and <strong> for strong emphasis.

```
<p>The Analytical Engine has no
pretensions whatever to
<em>originate</em> anything. It
can do whatever we know how to
order it to perform. It can
follow analysis, but it has
<strong>no power of anticipating
any analytical revelations or
truths</strong>. Its province is
to assist us in making available
what we are already acquainted
with.</p>
```

The Analytical Engine has no pretensions whatever to *originate* anything. It can do whatever we know how to order it to perform. It can follow analysis, but it has **no power of anticipating any analytical revelations or truths**. Its province is to assist us in making available what we are already acquainted with.

<em> and <strong> are *inline elements*, intended to appear within a line of text, whereas <p>, <h1>, and <ul> are *block elements*, intended to create a new line of text. See the sidebar "Block and inline elements" for further details.

Block and inline elements

Visible HTML elements can be split into two broad categories: block and inline. A block element naturally takes up the full width available to it; consecutive block elements naturally start below the previous block element. Block elements include paragraphs, all the headings, and all the list elements you've seen.

Inline elements fit exactly to their content and sit naturally on the line of text in which they're situated. Inline elements include <strong> and <em> (covered here) and others such as <b>, <i>, and <abbr>.

The key thing to remember at this point is that block elements can't appear in an HTML document as the children of inline elements.

The important consequence is that <em> and <strong> are always descendants of a block-level element like <p>. Block-level elements should never be children of inline elements, but inline elements can be children of other inline elements.

```
<p>A paragraph with
    <em>emphasis</em>
</p>
```
✓

```
<em>
    <p>A paragraph with emphasis</p>
</em>
```
✗

```
<p>A paragraph with
    <em>
        <strong>strong</strong>
        emphasis
    </em>
</p>
```
✓

There are several other inline elements, but we don't have room to go into them. The final section of this appendix lists resources where you can look them up yourself; in the meantime, remember the rule discussed here.

Neutral elements: <div> and <span>

```
<div class="person">
    <p class="full_name">
        <span class="first_name">
            Rob
        </span>
        <span class="surname">
            Crowther
        </span>
    </p>
    <p class="hometown">
        London
    </p>
</div>
```

Rob Crowther

London

Not everything can be marked up semantically as a paragraph or as emphasized text. Sometimes an element is needed to group other elements, or to allow other information to be attached to a part of the document. For these situations, HTML provides the two elements `<div>` and `<span>`.

A `<div>` is a block-level element, and a `<span>` is an inline element. By themselves, these elements are intentionally semantically neutral; they don't "mean" anything—or, looked at another way, they can mean whatever you want them to mean, with the judicious use of id and class attributes, as in the previous examples. These elements are useful when you're applying CSS and creating layouts (more about this in appendix C).

In this section, you've seen a variety of elements for text: paragraphs, lists, emphasis, and neutral elements. The web would be a dull place if this was all web pages were capable of. In the next section, you'll learn about the elements that make the web interesting: links, images, and other embedded resources.

Links and embedded resources

Text is all very well, but to make text into hypertext you need to add links. This section looks at links between documents and links within documents. It then covers other ways of linking external elements to HTML documents, both images and more general-purpose objects. To finish, it looks at `<iframe>` elements, which give you a way to embed an entire web page inside another one.

Links and anchors

In HTML content, links that are supposed to be interacted with use the anchor element, `<a>`. A link ought to go somewhere, so the target location is given in the href (hypertext reference) attribute of the `<a>` element. Three categories of link can be used in the href attribute. The first is a full URL:

```
<p>Use
  <a href="http://www.google.com/">
    the Google
  </a>.
</p>
```

Use <u>the Google</u>.

This is normally used to link to a different website. It works equally well for linking to pages on the current site, but the extra characters required for a full URL are unnecessary, as the next example shows.

```
<p>Go to
  <a href="pages/links-3.html">
    another page
  </a>.
</p>
```

Go to <u>another page</u>.

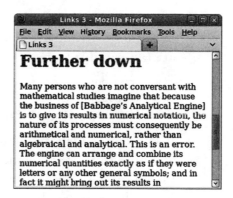

It's common to annotate long documents in this fashion. Applying an ID to each of the headings allows a table of contents to be built up, letting a reader quickly access the relevant section. For example, on Wikipedia, each article has a table of contents made up of links you can click to take you to the relevant part of the article.

Images and other objects

Images are embedded in HTML with the `<img>` element. The basic syntax is extremely simple; just the element itself and a single attribute are required:

```
<img src="dust-puppy.svg">
```

In this case, the image is much larger than the available browser window, so only the upper-left part of it appears on the screen.

A less obvious problem is that if the image is unavailable for some reason, perhaps due to a failure on the server, or because the user is browsing without images, or because the author misspelled the image name, then there will be no evidence that the image is there at all.

You can correct both these issues with a couple of common attributes, `width` (and/or `height`) and `alt` (alternative text):

```
<img src="dust-puppy.svg"
 width="252px" height="356px"
 alt="An image of Dust Puppy">
```

It's recommended that you always add an `alt` attribute to an `<img>` element. In cases where the image is purely decorative or is described textually in some other way, it's permissible to set the `alt` attribute to an empty string: `alt=""`.

Usually you can do without `width` and `height` attributes, either because the image is sized appropriately to start with or because the size of the image is controlled with CSS (see appendix C). This lets you determine how big the image should be depending on what device is used to access the page. The main benefit of providing dimensions is that browsers know how much space to allocate when laying out the page, which improves performance. Notice that the image element is self closing—it isn't allowed to have any descendants. The only widely supported possibility of providing fallback content should the image be unavailable is the alt attribute. If the image doesn't load or isn't in a format supported by the browser, then the user sees the alternative text. This isn't something you're likely to have noticed unless you tried viewing the previous example in IE8, in which case you saw something like the image at right.

Many people have long considered this a failing of the `<img>` element. Images appeared in the HTML spec because the most popular browser had support for them, and with the current syntax. Of course, it was the most popular browser because, in part, it was the first one that allowed the viewing of images without launching a separate application. Several features common to the early alternative proposals to the `<img>` element have ended up as features in the `<object>` element, a general-purpose element for embedding content in your page.

The `<object>` element can link to an arbitrary file. The only additional requirement is that you specify the file type:

```
<object
  data="dust-puppy.svg"
  type="image/svg+xml"
  width="252px" height="356px">
    An image of Dust Puppy
</object>
```

In browsers that support SVG images, the visible result is no different than including the image with the `<img>` element.

But in browsers that don't support SVG, such as IE8 shown in the screenshot here, the content of the `<object>` element is shown instead. Unlike `<img>`, `<object>` can have as many descendants as you need. The descendants are known as the *fallback content*.

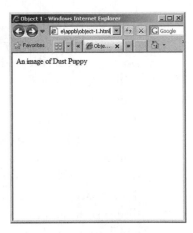

In this case, an obvious option is to make the fallback content another image, except this time one that IE8 does support:

```
<object
  data="dust-puppy.svg"
  type="image/svg+xml"
  width="252px" height="356px">
    <img
      src="dust-puppy.png"
      width="252px"
      height="356px">
</object>
```

IE8 users will miss out on some of the advanced possibilities enabled by SVG, such as perfect scaling to any resolution, but they'll still see appropriate content.

If you have no plans to take advantage of the additional capabilities of SVG, you're better off sticking to a standard image format in an `<img>` element. But outside of simple examples in books, the `<object>` element also allows the extension of the browser with plug-ins. A *plug-in* is an external program with support for a particular file type or technology. It registers the types of files it can support with the browser and, when the browser comes across an object element specifying one of these file types, it hands the data over to the plug-in and lets it control what is displayed in the element. This is how the popular Flash plug-in works; it's the basis for popular sound and video sites like YouTube and last.fm.

Why href and src and data?

It may seem like the href, src, and data attributes do the same job for different elements. Why didn't HTML standardize on one or the other? Usually href indicates somewhere a user can go, and src indicates something a browser should fetch, but it's mostly historical accident whether an element uses one or the other. It may seem that the <object> element has a data attribute just to force you to remember a third alternative, but the reasons are mostly historical. Back when the web was young, some browsers implemented new elements with href and some with src. The elements that survived to become the first HTML specification kept their attributes so as not to break backward compatibility.

Inline frames

Another common way of embedding content in your web page is the inline frame, known as the <iframe> element. This lets you create an embedded browser window inside the one the page is rendering in:

```
<p>Here is another page:</p>
<iframe
  src="http://www.userfriendly.org/"
  width="320" height="240">
</iframe>
```

The <iframe> is given dimensions and an entire other web page has been loaded into it. The page can be one from the same site as the parent page, specially designed to fit within the bounds of the <iframe>. This is an easy way to allow parts of the page to be updated without reloading the whole thing.

The <iframe> element is used a lot for embedding advertising, displaying videos, and Facebook applications.

Nonvisible elements

Some HTML elements aren't intended to be visible in the page. These usually appear in the head section of the markup, although they can appear anywhere. You've seen at least one example already: the `<title>` element, which is usually visible only in the title bar or tab of the browser, or in search results. Three other elements are commonly seen in the head section:

- `<link>` *elements* — Reference external resources such as style sheets
- `<script>` *elements* — Specify code to be run in the browser
- `<meta>` *elements* — Provide key-value pairs of metadata

Style sheets and scripting are covered in the next two appendixes, but the `<meta>` element isn't too important. Just remember when you come across one that it isn't expected to be displayed.

In the previous sections, there have been a few statements along the lines of, "You can't put a paragraph element inside a heading element" and, "Inline elements should only contain other inline elements, not block elements." But what do those statements really mean? The next section considers these issues.

Parsing and validation

What will happen to you and your web pages if you ignore the advice given in the previous sections? If you nest a `<div>` inside a `<span>` and

SIR! THIS IS THE MARKUP POLICE. CLOSE THE
TEXT EDITOR AND STEP AWAY FROM THE
KEYBOARD!

put it on a website, will the whole thing come crashing down around your ears? Will you be arrested for crimes against markup?

Well, no.

The less trusting among you may have created a document with a paragraph inside a heading and noted that the document loaded into the browser just fine, so it may seem as though you can do what I've been saying you can't. This is an aspect of a wider debate — is an HTML document what some bloke says it is, or is it anything that works in the browser? This is a complex issue, and I don't have room here to go into every part of it. This section aims to equip you with a basic understanding of the terms involved and highlight some of the consequences of not following "the rules."

Is this an HTML document?

There are different ways that markup can be invalid. In this section, we'll look at several examples of invalid HTML, see what a browser does with them, and then use the examples to introduce the concepts and terminology involved. To start with, here's the valid document from earlier:

```
<html>
<head>
    <title>Minimal document</title>
</head>
<body class="simple">
    <p>A paragraph
    <em>with emphasis</em></p>
</body>
</html>
```

A paragraph *with emphasis*

A valid document contains only elements listed in the HTML specification, and those elements contain each other in ways described in the specification; there's a single `<html>` element with two children, `<head>` and `<body>`; inline elements like `<em>` are contained within block elements like `<p>`; and so on.

The document can be made invalid in a number of ways. One is to use elements that don't exist in the HTML specification. This invalid document replaces all the regular tag names with shortened versions:

```
<ht>
<he>
    <t>Minimal document</t>
</he>
<bo c="simple">
    <p>A paragraph
    <em>with emphasis</em></p>
</bo>
</ht>
```

Minimal document

A paragraph *with emphasis*

The browser copes well with this; the main difference is that the title is now visible, because the browser has no idea what a <t> element is.

In this document, the closing angle bracket has been left off the end of each line:

```
<html
<head
    <title>Minimal document</title
</head
<body class="simple"
    <p>A paragraph
    <em>with emphasis</em></p
</body
</html
```

Minimal documentA paragraph *with emphasis*

Again the browser copes fairly well. The <title> element is lost because now it's in position to be an attribute of the <head> element; but the content is all visible, and the one complete element, <em>, is displayed properly. This demonstrates that web browsers are resilient to badly constructed HTML markup, but these two documents are broken in significantly different ways. To highlight this, let's force the browser to attempt to render these documents as XML, which is a much stricter standard, instead of HTML. To do so, you can change the file extension from .html to .xhtml. The two documents then create very different results:

Invalid document 1

> This XML file does not appear to have any style information associated with it. The document tree is shown below.

```
-<ht>
  -<he>
     <t>Minimal document</t>
   </he>
  -<bo c="simple">
    -<p>
       A paragraph
       <em>with emphasis</em>
     </p>
   </bo>
 </ht>
```

Invalid document 2

> **XML Parsing Error:**
> **not well-formed**
> **Location: malformed.xhtml**
> **Line Number 3, Column 1:**
>
> <head
> ^

The first document, even though it has only one valid HTML element, is structured in a valid way, so the browser still parses it into a tree structure. Although this document isn't valid HTML, it's *well formed*: the elements, tags, and attributes follow the basic rules of markup. The second document doesn't follow these basic rules, so as well as being invalid, it's also not well formed.

There are more subtle ways to make the markup invalid. Consider the following markup fragment:

```
<p><strong>A slightly <em>odd</strong> looking sentence</em></p>
```

This is invalid because the <em> and <strong> elements aren't nested correctly. The <em> element starts before the <strong> element end tag, but the <em> element end tag is outside the <strong> element. Either the two elements should be entirely separate, or one should be contained within the other. In keeping with the resiliency demonstrated previously, most browsers manage to render this fragment similarly.

Firefox	Chrome	Opera	IE

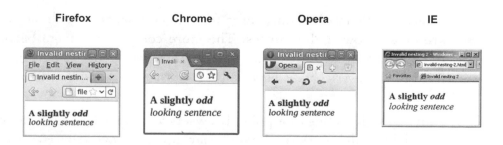

You may be thinking that browsers seem to handle the markup whether it's invalid or not, so why should you bother with writing valid markup? The next section answers that question.

Validation and why you should bother

If browsers can cope just fine with invalid and even not-well-formed markup—and not only that, different browsers manage to do a similar job of rendering that invalid markup—why should you bother writing valid markup in the first place? There are at least three good reasons, as this section summarizes.

First, even though things look the same when they're this simple, differences probably exist underneath. The earlier sidebar "Markup, parsing, and rendering" distinguished between the markup in the text file, the parsing of that markup into an internal structure by the browser, and the final rendering of that internal structure on the screen. In the screenshots at the end of the previous section, you saw the final result of the invalid markup for this fragment:

```
<p><strong>A slightly <em>odd</strong> looking sentence</em></p>
```

Although it looked the same in all four browsers, here are the internal trees they built.

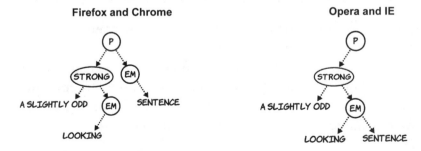

This example involves only three (or four) elements, and already there are cross-browser differences. The more complex the page becomes, the more likely invalid markup is to cause an oddity in rendering that's hard to discover. This is especially true when CSS and JavaScript are involved.

Moving on from this first point, browsers and other web tools are optimized for valid markup. Invalid markup is always dealt with as an exception; this means browsers have to do extra work to parse and render it, which ultimately means invalid pages are slower to render. Also, unless the particular structure of the invalid markup causes a browser or tool to crash, bugs in the parsing and rendering of invalid markup are less likely to be fixed than are those for valid markup. Subtle differences in parsing and rendering between browsers will eventually lead to hard-to-discover cross-browser issues in web pages.

Finally, especially when you're learning, it's likely that you'll at some point ask for help with something that isn't working the way you expect. In most online communities that specialize in markup, the first thing you'll be asked to do is fix any invalid markup, or at least explain its existence. This is true for several reasons:

- As discussed in the previous point, invalid markup often leads to subtle issues.
- Error-checking tools are far more useful if they're pointing out one major error in your markup rather than the major error buried in hundreds of minor ones.
- If you haven't bothered to write valid markup, many members of these online communities will view you as not worth their time and effort to help.

To summarize, the three reasons why you should write valid markup are as follows:

1 Invalid markup leads to subtle differences in parsing and rendering.
2 Browsers and development tools are optimized for valid markup.
3 It's easier to get help with valid markup.

Or, looked at from the perspective of why *not* to write *invalid* markup, these three reasons can be rephrased:

1 You make things harder for yourself.
2 You make things harder for your tools.
3 You make it harder for others to help you.

You want to write valid markup, but how do you tell if your markup is valid? In the final section, you'll learn about tools you can use to check your markup for errors as well as tools that will help you examine the results of your markup in the browser. With these tools, you'll be well equipped to learn more for yourself.

Learning more

In this chapter, you've learned enough to get you started with HTML. The best way to build on this foundation is to try things for yourself and see what happens. This section shows you some tools for doing this and resources for learning more.

Web tools

After you've written some markup, how can you tell if it's correct? You've seen in this appendix that even when things look OK in the browser, there can be hidden problems that will eventually trip you up. Here are a couple of online tools that can help.

The first tool is from the World Wide Web Consortium (W3C—the body that defines many web standards): http://validator.w3.org.

This service checks that your markup is well formed and follows the rules described previously, such as no block-level elements as descendants of inline elements. You should try to fix any errors reported.

The validator will check that your markup is technically correct, but it doesn't concern itself with matters of best practice. For this, you need a *linter* like HTML Lint: http://lint.brihten.com/html/.

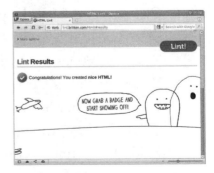

Errors reported by a linter are more concerned with matters of style than a validator, so it's reasonable in some situations to ignore any advice given if you know what you're doing. But while you're still learning, it's all likely to be good advice.

Browser tools

In addition to websites to help you write markup, all major web browsers come with built-in tools for analyzing what's going on with your markup. These differ in the details but all work in broadly the same fashion. In this section the screenshots come from Opera but instructions are given for all major browsers.

The easiest way to activate the tools in Opera, Chrome, and Safari is to right-click the area of the page you're interested in and select Inspect Element.

In Firefox, look for the Web Developer menu option, and select Inspect. You can activate IE's tools by pressing the F12 key or by selecting Developer Tools from the Tools menu.

The tools open with a tree view of the markup, similar to the tree diagrams in the opening sections of this appendix. Use this to highlight elements you're interested in and check that the tree structure the browser has built corresponds to what you intended.

Resources and where to go for help

This appendix has been a high-speed introduction to HTML. If your head is still spinning, here are some alternative resources that take things at a slightly slower pace:

- *HTML Dog HTML Beginner Tutorial*—www.htmldog.com/guides/htmlbeginner/
- *W3C Web Standards Curriculum*—www.w3.org/wiki/Web_Standards_Curriculum

When you're building pages of your own, you'll run into issues that aren't described in introductory material. When you have questions, these are good resources:

- *Web Standards Group mailing list*—http://webstandardsgroup.org/mail/
- *WebDesign-L mailing list*—www.webdesign-l.com/
- *Doctype Q&A website*—http://doctype.com/

YOU SHOULD NOW KNOW ENOUGH ABOUT MARKUP TO GET STARTED CREATING YOUR OWN WEB PAGES. BUT EVEN WITH THE ODD IMAGE, THEY'LL BE A BIT DULL. YOU CAN ADD VISUAL EXCITEMENT TO YOUR WEB PAGES WITH CSS, WHICH YOU'LL LEARN ABOUT IN THE NEXT APPENDIX.

Appendix C

CSS basics

If you've just read appendix B, you're probably wondering how those rather dull textual examples end up looking like the beautiful web pages you see every day. The answer isn't some secret extra markup you didn't learn about yet, but Cascading Style Sheets (CSS). This appendix will introduce the main features of CSS, including

- The basic syntax of CSS
- Using CSS selectors to apply styles only to certain elements
- The most common properties and values
- Using CSS for layout

Rules, selectors, properties, and values

A CSS style sheet is made up of *rules*. Here are three example CSS rules.

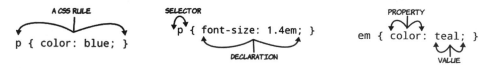

A CSS rule is made up of a selector and a semicolon-separated list of declarations inside brackets. Each declaration has a property and a value separated by a colon. If an element in an associated HTML document matches a selector in the style sheet, then the declarations will be applied to that element.

To help you get the idea, here's a full example page with a style sheet. The style sheet is in the head section of the document in a <style> element. There are three rules in the style sheet: a rule for the <body> element, a rule for the <p> element, and a rule for the <em> element:

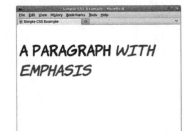

```
<!DOCTYPE html>
<html>
<head>
 <title>Simple CSS Example</title>
  <style>
  body {
    font-family: "Komika
Hand";
    font-size: 250%;
   }
  p {
    color: blue;
    font-size: 1.4em;
  }
  em {
    color: teal;
  }
  </style>
</head>
<body>
  <p>A paragraph
    <em>with emphasis</em>
  </p>
</body>
</html>
```

If a second paragraph is added, it has the same style as the first paragraph because they both match the rule:

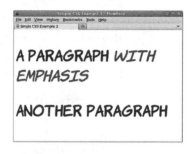

```
<body>
  <p>A paragraph
    <em>with emphasis</em>
  </p>
  <p>Another paragraph</p>
</body>
```

These are called *type selectors* because they match any element of the stated type.

In the previous example, the style rules are included directly in the HTML inside a `<style>` element. This is just one way of applying CSS to your web pages; the next section will summarize the alternatives.

Adding a style sheet to your HTML

There are four ways to include CSS in HTML. At the lowest level, you can apply it directly to individual elements with the `style` attribute. This is known as an *inline style*:

```
<p style="color: red;">Another paragraph</p>
```

This rule makes just this one paragraph have red text, but it has no effect on any other paragraphs in your document. The limited impact of the `style` attribute means it's the least efficient way of applying CSS; it's usually only seen on elements unique within a site, when people are creating copy-and-paste widgets, or to work around a localized cross-browser issue.

Slightly more useful is the `<style>` element used earlier. The `<style>` element should appear in the `<head>` element of the HTML document, although all popular browsers will use the styles if they're added to the body instead. Rules in a `<style>` element apply to everything in that page:

```
<style> p { color: red; } </style>
```

The main benefit of this approach over inline styles is that you can control the styles of multiple elements from a single rule, but they still only affect the page on which they're placed. On a multiple-page site, the rules would have to be included on every page, so it's far more common to put all the CSS in a separate file and then link to it from each page. This `<link>` element references an external style sheet:

```
<link href="styles.css" rel="style sheet">
```

> **Whitespace in CSS**
>
> The `<style>` element example is a more compact representation than used previously: everything is on a single line instead of broken out into individual lines. It doesn't matter to the browser how the CSS is spaced—whitespace is ignored just as with HTML, but most human readers find it easier to read if the styles are broken up across multiple lines.

Like the `<style>` element, the link should appear in the head of the document. The file styles.css would then contain the CSS:

```
p { color: red; }
```

This same CSS file can be used with every page on the site that links to it. Most browsers download style.css only once and then reuse it, saving bandwidth and page-rendering speed.

The final way to include CSS is to link from within existing CSS. This requires that some CSS has already been included, via a link or a `<style>` element:

```
<style> @import url('styles.css'); </style>
```

In this example, the style sheet is imported from a `<style>` element in the head section of the document.

Inheritance

One of the key properties of CSS is that styles are inherited down the document tree. In the simple example in the previous section, it's already possible to see this feature in action. The `font-family` property is specified only for the `<body>` element, but the elements in the document are displayed with the Komika Hand font from that rule. This is because all the other elements are children of the `<body>` element, so they inherit the `font-family` property.

font-family isn't the only property that's inherited. Here are the rules for the <p> and <em> elements:

```
p { color: blue; font-size: 1.4em; }
em { color: teal; }
```

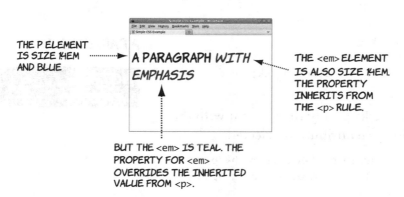

THE P ELEMENT
IS SIZE 1.4EM
AND BLUE

A PARAGRAPH *WITH*
EMPHASIS

THE <em> ELEMENT
IS ALSO SIZE 1.4EM.
THE PROPERTY
INHERITS FROM
THE <p> RULE.

BUT THE <em> IS TEAL. THE
PROPERTY FOR <em>
OVERRIDES THE INHERITED
VALUE FROM <p>.

Inheritance means you don't have to write style rules for every element in the document. Setting a font or a color on the <body> element usually means that all text in the document will be that font and color. To style specific elements, you need to learn how to write selectors; these will be covered in the next section.

Selecting elements to style

You learned in the previous section that a CSS rule consists of a selector and a declaration. The declaration is the set of visual effects to be applied, and the selector determines what elements will be styled by the declaration. You saw some selectors in the previous section; they were examples of type selectors, where the selector consists of the element name and selects a type of element. But there are many other CSS selectors as well. In this section, you'll learn about ID and class selectors; using combinators to join selectors together for greater specificity; using pseudo-classes to select elements in particular states; and using media queries to target devices such as printers or cell phones.

ID selectors

An ID selector chooses an element based on the id attribute. This attribute should have a unique value in any given document, so an ID selector will only ever apply to a single element and its descendants. An ID selector consists of a hash character followed by the id. In the following example, an element matching the ID selector will reverse the normal colors: white text on a black background instead of black text on white.

```
#myelement {
    color: white;
    background-color: black;
}
```

In the markup, only the element with the matching id attribute is selected:

```
<p id="yourelement">A paragraph</p>
<p id="myelement">Another paragraph</p>
```

By themselves, ID selectors aren't very useful. You certainly wouldn't want to add an ID to every element you needed to style. They're normally used to pick out particular landmarks on a page. For a more general-purpose approach, it's much better to use the class selector discussed in the next section.

Class selectors

The class selector chooses elements based on the class attribute. Unlike the id attribute, values in the class attribute don't have to be unique throughout the document, so rules based on class selectors usually apply to a selection of elements in a document. A class selector consists of a period (.) followed by the class name and selects any element with the value myclass in the class attribute:

```
.myclass {
    color: white;
    background-color: black;
}
```

In this example, only one of the paragraphs has the myclass class:

```
<p class="myclass">A paragraph</p>
<p class="yourclass">Another paragraph</p>
```

The main benefit of a class selector over the ID selector is that multiple elements can have the same class. Here, a third paragraph is added:

```
<p class="myclass">A paragraph</p>
<p class="yourclass">Another paragraph</p>
<p class="myclass">One more paragraph</p>
```

It's also possible to apply multiple classes to a single element. In the next example, the middle paragraph has two classes applied:

```
<p class="myclass">A paragraph</p>
<p class="yourclass myclass">Another
paragraph</p>
<p class="yourclass">One more paragraph</p>
```

The `.myclass` selector selects all the elements that have `myclass` as one of the values in the `class` attribute.

Although the previous examples use paragraph elements, it isn't necessary for all elements with a particular class to be of the same type. This allows you to use the semantically correct element for a given bit of content but style related items uniformly. In the source code for this appendix, you'll find two additional examples of the class selector that demonstrate this: class-selectors-4.html and class-selectors-5.html.

Now that you have a basic grasp of simple selectors, the next section will look at ways of combining them with combinators to make more complex selectors.

Combinators

Combinators allow simple selectors, like the element, ID, and class selectors in the previous sections, to be combined into more complex rules. This makes it easy to apply one style to `<link>` elements in the main content but different styles to links in the navigation or the page footer.

The most common combinator in CSS is the *descendant combinator*: a space between two simple selectors. For the selector to match the rightmost element, that element must be a descendant of the previous element. This is easier to understand with an example. Consider this fragment of HTML:

```
<h1>A <em>heading</em></h1>
<p>A paragraph <em>with emphasis</em></p>
```

Now look at these two style rules, both of which select <em> elements:

```
em { color: teal; }
p em { color: darkgreen; }
```

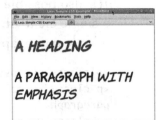

The second rule selects only those <em> elements that appear as children of a <p> element. In this example, the first <em> (a child of the <h1> element) is teal, but the second <em> (a child of the <p> element) is dark green. The second rule is more specific than the first one, so it will be preferred whenever both apply.

More on this in the next section. In the meantime, you need to learn about the child combinator.

The *child combinator* is a greater-than bracket: >. It allows you to select elements that are direct children of a parent. Because you can already select according to ancestor elements, you might be wondering why you also need a child combinator, so let's look at an example. Here's a simple HTML document:

```
<header>
  <h1>Header</h1>
</header>
<article>
  <h1>Article</h1>
  <p>Paragraph 1</p>
  <p>Paragraph 2</p>
  <footer>Article footer</footer>
</article>
<footer>
  Body footer
</footer>
```

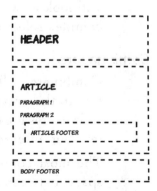

It has a header, an article, and a footer, but note that the `<article>` element also has its own footer. This lets you see the difference between the descendant and child combinators.

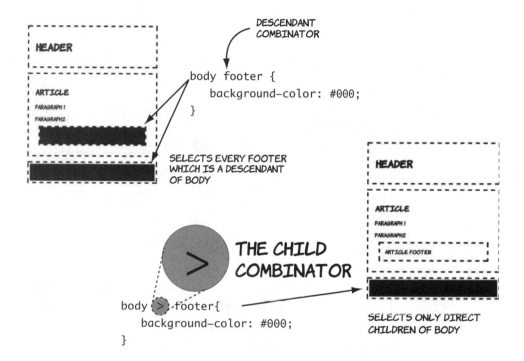

The child combinator is useful when you have nesting and the same element appears multiple times at different depths: for example, a menu made up from unordered lists where each item is itself an unordered list. With the child combinator, it's easy to apply different styles to the top-level and lower-level items.

Cascading and specificity

The *cascading* part of Cascading Style Sheets refers to the rules that determine which of a set of competing rules apply to an element. This is important because multiple rules can have a definition that applies to the same property of the same element.

In case this isn't making much sense to you, let's look at an example. Here's a basic style sheet:

```
p {
    color: white;
    background-color: black;
}
```

Let's link to it from the head of a document that also includes a `<style>` element:

```
<head>
    <title>CSS Cascade 1</title>
    <link href="style-1.css" rel="stylesheet">
    <style>
    p {
        color: black;
        background-color: white;
    }
    </style>
</head>
```

Notice that both the linked style sheet and the `<style>` element include a declaration for the color of paragraph elements. Which one should the browser use? The situation can be complicated further by adding a style attribute to a `<p>` element:

```
<p>A paragraph</p>
<p style="color: silver; background-color: gray;">
    Another paragraph
</p>
```

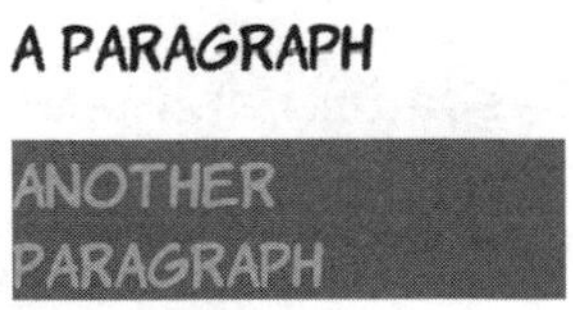

As the screenshot shows, the browser chooses the inline style on the element that has one, rather than either of the styles in the head or the linked style sheet. Inline styles always override linked style sheets and styles in the head; other rules are usually used in reverse order to which they're encountered. Try moving the `<link>` element after the

A PARAGRAPH

ANOTHER
PARAGRAPH

`<style>` element in this example, and you'll see that the rule in that file is then applied.

But there is a complication. The last rule encountered is used only because the previous rules used the same selector. If the selector in the linked style sheet is changed, then this rule will win:

```
body p {
    color: white;
    background-color: black;
}
```

This rule wins because it has a higher specificity. The specificity is based on the selectors used in the rule. You can use this straightforward process to calculate the specificity of any selector.

Step	Action	#myelement em	.myclass em	body p em
1	Count the number of ID selectors in the rule, and make a note of this value as *a*.	*a* = 1	*a* = 0	*a* = 0
2	Count the number of class selectors in the rule, and make a note of this value as *b*.	*b* = 0	*b* = 1	*b* = 0
3	Count the number of type selectors in the rule, and make a note of this value as *c*.	*c* = 1	*c* = 1	*c* = 3
4	Combine *a*, *b*, and *c* into a number where each letter represents a digit. The highest number is the most specific.	101	011	003

Any rule with an ID selector is more specific than any rule with just a class selector, which in turn is always more specific than any rule made up of only type selectors. But within each group the number of selectors for each type is the significant factor.

Pseudo-classes

One of the original uses for JavaScript when it was introduced by Netscape back in 1995 was for *rollover effects*: changing a background image when the mouse pointer enters or leaves an element. Rather than require an entire scripting language for a simple visual effect like this, the ability to select elements based on user activity has been built into CSS with pseudo-classes.

This example is a page with a paragraph element:

```
<p>Hover me</p>
```

By default, the paragraph is black text on a white background.

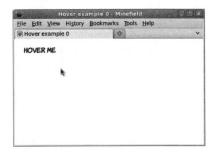

The notation for a pseudo-class is a colon followed by a keyword. For rollover effects, the keyword is hover:

```
p:hover { background-color: #000; }
```

This rule sets the background of the element to black when the mouse pointer hovers over the element.

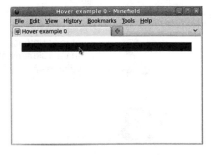

IT'S ALSO POSSIBLE TO USE PSEUDO-CLASSES WITH COMBINATORS, DEFINING RULES FOR CHILDREN OF AN ELEMENT DEPENDING ON ITS DYNAMIC STATE. SEVERAL INTERESTING EFFECTS ARE POSSIBLE ONLY WHEN YOU DO THIS. LET'S LOOK AT A SIMPLE EXAMPLE.

This snippet of markup might be part of a content management system. The idea is that the buttons allow the user to enable edit mode or delete the element:

```
<article>
    <header>
        <h1>Article</h1>
        <menu>
            <button>Edit</button><button>Delete</button>
        </menu>
    </header>
</article>
```

Most of the time, the menu needs to be hidden so the user can see the end result more clearly. The menu is therefore hidden with this CSS:

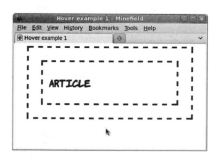

```
header menu {
  display: none;
}
```

You'll learn more about the display property in the next section.

With the menu hidden, there's no point adding the hover pseudo-class to that—the mouse pointer will never be able to hover over an element that isn't there. But the <header> element is visible, so here's a rule that makes the <menu> element visible when the mouse pointer is hovering over the <header> element:

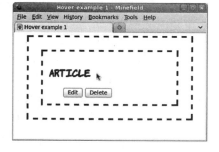

```
header:hover menu {
  display: inline;
}
```

This bit of CSS is the basis of most pop-up and drop-down menus on the web. The only requirement is that the element to be shown is a descendant of the element that will be hovered over. It lets you present extra information only when the user indicates they're interested in it by putting the mouse pointer in that location.

NOTE THAT THE hover PSEUDO-CLASS ASSUMES USERS ARE ACCESSING THE PAGE WITH A DESKTOP BROWSER AND USING A MOUSE. FOR MANY POTENTIAL USERS, THIS ISN'T TRUE, INCLUDING PEOPLE WITH DISABILITIES AND USERS OF MOBILE OR TABLET DEVICES.

You should now have a good grasp of the basic syntax involved in CSS and how to write selectors to pick out the required elements for styling. All that's left to learn is the properties and values needed to create styles.

Properties and values

The interesting parts of CSS are the properties and values that cause the visible effects seen on the web page. The sheer variety of properties and values is such that entire books have been written about them. This section covers the most common values used in styling web pages.

Colors and lengths

The most common values in CSS are colors and lengths. A number of different properties accept either colors or lengths, or both, as values. This section gives a brief overview of them; then, in the following section, you'll learn about properties where they can be used.

The previous sections have included several examples of color values. Mostly the examples have used color keywords such as black and red, because it's obvious what these mean even to people who don't know CSS, but there are several other ways to describe colors in CSS. These approaches are more flexible because they provide separate values for the amount of red, green, and blue that makes up the color. The following table shows the same colors expressed four different ways.

Name	#rrggbb	#rgb	rgb(r,g,b)
Black	#000000	#000	rgb(0,0,0)
Blue	#0000ff	#00f	rgb(0,0,255)
Red	#ff0000	#f00	rgb(255,0,0)
Yellow	#ffff00	#ff0	rgb(255,255,0)
Green	#008000	–	rgb(0,128,0)
Teal	#008080	–	rgb(0,128,128)
Silver	#c0c0c0	–	rgb(192.192,192)
Gray	#808080	–	rgb(128,128,128)
White	#ffffff	#fff	rgb(255,255,255)

The middle two columns use hexadecimal notation. These are numbers in base 16: after getting to 9, the next number is A, then B, and so on, up to F. The hexadecimal value FF is equivalent to 255 in decimal. If the two numerals for each of the red, green, and blue values are the same, then you can use the shorthand notation in the third column.

Color has its own property. The following example sets the foreground (text) color of an element and its descendants to blue:

```
color: #00f;
```

Lengths are less complicated than colors: they consist of a number followed by a unit. The most common units are shown in the next table.

Unit	Measures by	Description
px	Pixels	Length in pixel units. The actual size is determined by monitor resolution.
pt	Points	A measure from typography, equivalent to 1/72 of an inch.
cm	Centimeters	Absolute length in centimeters. If you're not in a metric country, you can also use in for inches.
em	Ems	Size of the capital *M* in the current font.
%	Percentage	Length as a proportion of the size of the element's parent.

The next section looks at some common properties where these values are used.

Borders and backgrounds

Two of the most common things to style are borders and backgrounds. Each is controlled by several different CSS properties, and each has a shorthand notation that lets you set all the properties in a single line. This section looks at both of them, starting with borders.

A border has a width, a type, and a color. All three can be set separately using the properties border-width (a length), border-style (a special property for borders), and border-color (a color, unsurprisingly):

```
.one {
    border-width: 5px;
    border-style: solid;
    border-color: #999;
}
.two {
    border-width: 0.75em;
    border-style: dashed;
    border-color: #000;
}
```

The CSS above assumes that some elements with appropriate classes are defined:

```
<div class="one"></div>
<div class="two"></div>
<div class="three"></div>
<div class="four"></div>
```

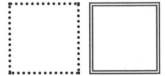

The shorthand notation uses the border property. All that's required is for the same three values to be listed with a space between:

```
.three {
    border: 5pt dotted #333;
}
.four {
    border: 0.25cm double #666;
}
```

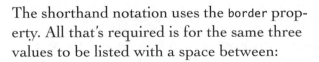

Having both separate and shorthand properties is useful when you need to style a collection of elements similarly. For instance, if a page has a pop-up alert message that changes the border color according to the importance of the image, you can set the general style in one rule and override the border color with specific classes. If you later decide to create a thicker border on all message boxes, then only the general style needs to be updated rather than each rule for every level of importance.

Backgrounds are slightly more complicated than borders because they allow the use of images, and these images can be positioned.

Property	Example values	Description
background-color	red, #f00, rgb(255,0,0)	Any valid color.
background-image	url(background.png)	A link to an image.
background-repeat	repeat, no-repeat, repeat-x, repeat-y	Should the background image tile across the background, or only appear once?
background-position	top left, 100px 200px, 50% 50%	Where should the first background image be placed?
background-attachment	scroll, fixed	Should the background scroll with the page or remain fixed behind the page?

As with borders, background properties can be combined into a single property. The following example places a single copy of background.png in the center of the element with the rest of the background red:

```
background: url(background.png) 50% 50% no-repeat fixed #f00;
```

Now that you've learned the basics of visual styling, it's time to move on to layout. To understand CSS layout, you first need to know how CSS describes the dimensions of elements using the box model.

The box model

The CSS box model defines the dimensions of elements as they're laid out on the page. In order to do page layout with CSS, as covered in the next section, it's important to know how elements are sized.

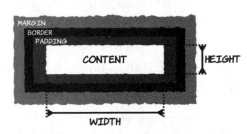

Elements have a width and height, padding, a border, and a margin. The diagram at left shows how they fit together.

The element's width is either defined explicitly or determined automatically by the browser based on the content and display mode. Between the content and the border is the padding; then you have the border (discussed in the previous section), and finally the margin, which is the space between this element and the next one.

The padding, border, and margin have associated collections of properties in CSS. The width of each side can be applied separately, or you can use shorthand syntax. In the previous section, you saw the `border-width: 5px;` shorthand. This could also be written in either of these two ways:

```
border-width: 5px 5px 5px 5px;
```

```
border-top-width: 5px;
border-right-width: 5px;
border-bottom-width: 5px;
border-left-width: 5px;
```

There are equivalent properties for the padding and margin:

```
padding-width: 5px 5px 5px 5px;
```

```
padding-top-width: 5px;
padding-right-width: 5px;
padding-bottom-width: 5px;
padding-left-width: 5px;
```

```
margin-width: 5px 5px 5px 5px;
```

```
margin-top-width: 5px;
margin-right-width: 5px;
margin-bottom-width: 5px;
margin-left-width: 5px;
```

The shorthand property lets you specify one to four lengths. The next diagram shows a practical example:

```
padding: 20px 30px;
border-width: 10px;
margin: 20px 30px 40px 20px;
```

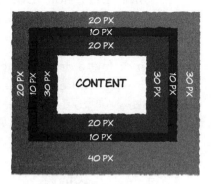

If just one length is given, all four top, left, bottom, and right are set to that width. Two lengths set the top and bottom widths to the first value and the left and right to the second value. If three lengths are given, the first and last values set the top and bottom, and both left and right are set to the second value. Finally, four values are applied in the order top, right, bottom, left.

Quirks mode and Standards mode

In the late 1990s, there was a lot of confusion about the correct way to implement CSS. This was particularly apparent in the way different browsers treated the box model. By the time understanding of the spec stabilized, several browsers were using incorrect approaches. Worse, many websites had been created that depended on the incorrect approach; when the designer is trying to make everything line up exactly, a difference of a few pixels in width is very visible.

As new browsers were released, they wanted to implement the correct behavior, but they didn't want to break the web by making all websites follow the new rule. To solve the problem, vendors created two rendering modes in their new browsers:

- *Standards mode*—The browser displays according to the current standards, as far as they're understood and can be implemented by the vendor.

- *Quirks mode*—The browser displays according to the incorrect rules implemented by previous versions of that browser.

There's only one standard, so the way different browsers implement Standards mode has (sometimes slowly) converged on the correct implementation. But there are as many different ways to implement Quirks mode as there are old versions of browsers, so pages that render in Quirks mode can vary wildly even among modern browsers.

In order to decide whether to use Quirks mode or Standards mode, the browser takes various hints from the HTML. This also varies from browser to browser; but, broadly, documents that follow the standards—which have correct markup according to the HTML4 or XHTML1 specs—use Standards mode. Pages that don't follow the standards, or claim to be following earlier versions of HTML, use Quirks mode.

Generally this has worked pretty well. Web authors creating new pages and paying attention to their markup have their pages rendered as they expect, and old pages or pages created by unskilled authors are rendered as expected (by users who have the same browser as the designer, at least).

The situation has added complexity to the task of improving from an unskilled to a skilled web author. Some errors in your markup won't trigger Quirks mode, but other errors of apparently similar complexity will. Authors may make small changes in their code only to have unexpectedly large changes in the end results. This inconsistency can be frustrating and is one of the main reasons cross-browser web authoring has gained a reputation for being confusing and capricious.

Right now, you need to understand that if you're seeing markedly different results for the same page across several modern browsers, it's likely you've accidentally triggered Quirks mode through an error in markup. The solution is usually to run your markup through one of the online validators and correct any errors reported.

Display modes: inline, block, and none

Appendix B discussed the difference between block and inline elements. In addition to being a way to categorize HTML elements, these also assume a default visual presentation. Inline elements sit in the flow of text, whereas block elements cause line breaks before and after. This visual presentation can also be controlled by CSS through the display property by setting the value to either inline or block.

A simple example will illustrate the key differences. Here are three <div> elements:

```
<div>1</div> <div>2</div> <div>3</div>
```

The following styles show the elements' position and shape:

```
div {
    width: 2.5em;
    height: 2.5em;
    margin: 0.5em;
    padding: 0.5em;
    border: 5px dashed black;
}
```

Setting the display property to block causes all three elements to sit on a line by themselves, each with the width, height, padding, and margin specified:

```
div { display: block; }
```

Of course, a <div> element is display: block by default, so explicitly stating it in CSS isn't necessary.

Setting the <div> elements to display: inline has a drastic effect:

```
div { display: inline; }
```

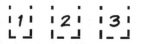

Not only are the elements now sitting on the same line, but they're considerably smaller. This is because the width and height properties don't apply to inline elements, so each <div> is now the size of its content plus the margin specified.

Other values are allowed for the display property. Several are covered in chapter 8, but one you've seen used in this appendix is none. In the section on pseudo-classes, it was used to hide elements until the user hovered over a particular area on the screen.

Now that you've learned about the box model and display modes, you have all the prerequisite knowledge required for page layout.

Positioning and layout

In the last 10 years, most CSS layouts have been built around floated elements, commonly referred to as *floats*. A floated element is one that's outside of the normal flow of text, like a cutout. The text flows around these floated elements as long as there's room, as illustrated by the following diagram.

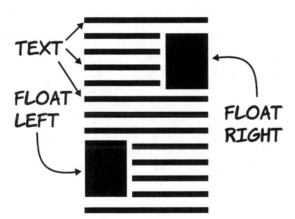

Originally, floated elements were intended to be pictures, tables, and figures sitting in single columns of text, but people soon figured out that floats could be used to lay out entire pages.

Floats rely on two CSS properties: float and clear. The float property determines which side the element floats to, whereas the clear property determines how the element behaves with respect to other floated elements. Values for float are left, right, and none; values for clear are left, right, both, and none.

If two consecutive elements are floated the same way and not cleared, then as long as there's available width, they sit alongside each other. But if the second has clear set, it drops below the first element.

Let's create this simple layout with CSS floats. The sidebar is floated left, the main content is floated right, and the footer is set to clear both of them.

Widths are set on the sidebar and the main content to ensure that there's room for them to sit side by side.

The markup and CSS for this layout follow. Some additional CSS is used, but not shown, to add borders, margin, and padding to the elements. Copy the code from the earlier examples if you're following along:

```html
<div id="header">
  <img src="dust-puppy.svg">
  <h1>Heading</h1>
</div>
<div id="main">
  <p>I never am really
   satisfied...</p>
</div>
<div id="sidebar">
  Side bar
</div>
<div id="footer">
  <div id="nav">
    <a href="/l1">Link 1</a>
    <a href="/l2">Link 2</a>
  </div>
  <div id="smallprint">Credits</div>
</div>
```

```css
#header img {
    float: right;
}
#header h1 {
    margin-right: 150px;
}
#main {
    float: right;
    width: 60%;
}
#sidebar {
    float: left;
    width: 25%;
}
#footer {
    clear: both;
}
#footer > div {
    display: inline;
}
```

Note that the `<footer>` element needs to have `clear` set even though it's not floated. Nonfloated elements must also be cleared if they appear below any floated elements; otherwise the floated elements will overlap them. In this case, the footer would appear directly below the previous nonfloated element, the header.

There's plenty more to CSS layout than this simple example can demonstrate, but you now know the basics. As you see more complex layouts and advanced approaches, you should be able to use the knowledge you've gained here to work out what's going on.

NOW YOU'RE UP TO SPEED WITH CSS, IT'S TIME TO MOVE ON TO THE THIRD KEY WEB DEVELOPMENT TECHNOLOGY: JAVASCRIPT. WHEREAS HTML AND CSS ARE NATURALLY FIXED AFTER THEY'RE CREATED AT THE SERVER, JAVASCRIPT ALLOWS YOU TO MANIPULATE WEB PAGES IN THE BROWSER ITSELF. THE NEXT APPENDIX WILL GET YOU STARTED CREATING THESE "DYNAMIC" WEB PAGES.

Appendix D

JavaScript

The main focus of this book is HTML5 and CSS3, but to take full advantage of many of the features of these two technologies you'll end up using JavaScript quite a lot. The APIs in HTML5 are accessible through JavaScript, and the techniques you've seen for detecting HTML5 and CSS3 support depend on JavaScript.

The goal of this appendix isn't to teach you to be a great JavaScript programmer even if you've never programmed before, but to teach you enough syntax that you can recognize what the examples in the book are trying to do and enough practical knowledge that you can experiment on your own to learn more.

Setting up an interactive console

In this appendix, you'll learn by doing. To do that, you need a way to type JavaScript code into your browser and immediately see the results. Most modern browsers come with a built-in facility for this as part of their developer tools.

Chrome (and Safari)

Chrome and Safari are both based on the WebKit browsing engine, so apart from some stylistic differences, their developer tools are identical.

Access the developer tools by right-clicking any element on the page and selecting the Inspect Element option.

A panel opens at the bottom of the browser window like the one shown here.

Look for the Console button in the toolbar across the top of the panel, and click it.

You should see a command prompt > and a cursor. You can type in JavaScript and see it executed immediately.

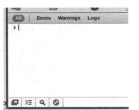

Here are the key features of the Chrome console. All the examples in this appendix should work in Chrome.

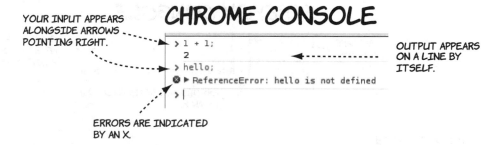

YOUR INPUT APPEARS ALONGSIDE ARROWS POINTING RIGHT.

OUTPUT APPEARS ON A LINE BY ITSELF.

ERRORS ARE INDICATED BY AN X.

Firefox

Thanks to its extensible nature, Firefox has long relied on add-ons to fill the developer tool gap, notably Firebug (discussed in a moment). Newer versions of Firefox (since version 8) have developer tools built in.

Access these tools from the main menu under Web Developer. For now, either select Web Console or press Ctrl+Shift+K.

The console monitors four things by default: network requests (Net), CSS, JavaScript (JS), and console logging (Web Developer or Logging in newer versions). You can turn them on and off individually by clicking the buttons along the top of the console. In this appendix, you may find it helpful to turn off everything except JavaScript and console logging.

The next figure shows the key details of the Firefox console. Most of the screenshots in the following sections were taken using Firefox.

FIREFOX CONSOLE

YOUR INPUT APPEARS ALONGSIDE ARROWS POINTING LEFT.

```
10:07:37.961  ◄ 1 + 1;
10:07:37.968  ▶ 2
10:07:44.79   ◄ hello;
10:07:44.802  ✗ ReferenceError: hello is not defined
```

OUTPUT APPEARS AFTER AN ARROW POINTING RIGHT.

ERRORS ARE INDICATED BY AN X.

Other browsers

Several other browsers ought to work equally well. Here's how you get to the console in them:

- *Internet Explorer* — Press F12, or look for developer tools in the Page menu.
- *Opera* — Right-click the page, and choose Inspect Element from the context menu.
- *Firefox with Firebug* — Press F12, or right-click and select Inspect with Firebug from the context menu.

NOW THAT YOU KNOW HOW TO EXECUTE JAVASCRIPT IN YOUR BROWSER OF CHOICE, IT'S TIME TO START LEARNING SOME JAVASCRIPT. YOU'LL BEGIN WITH ARITHMETIC AND STORING THE RESULTS. OVER A FEW SHORT PAGES, THESE SIMPLE OPERATIONS WILL BUILD UP TO PROGRAMS THAT CAN DO USEFUL THINGS IN YOUR WEB PAGES.

Arithmetic and variables

A computer program is based on math. It boils down to a sequence of mathematical operations on a collection of numbers. If you've always been bad at math, don't let this frighten you: programming—the act of composing a program—has as much in common with writing a story as it does with solving math problems (albeit a story written with unusually strict grammar and far more punctuation then you're used to). Think of it as an obscure subgenre of science fiction. But the simplest programs that can be written are basic mathematical statements, so we'll start with them. Open the JavaScript console in your preferred web browser, and follow along with the examples.

Arithmetic

In this section, you'll learn how basic arithmetic operations are represented in JavaScript. The examples are all shown in the Firefox Web Console, but you should see the same results in any other browser.

Basic addition, subtraction, multiplication, and division are written in much the same way as they were in your high school book. The asterisk (*) is used to indicate multiplication and the forward slash (/) division. Expressions and their values are shown in the console output. Try typing a few expressions and pressing Enter.

```
X  ■Net ∨ ■CSS ∨ ■JS ∨
20:44:38.573  ◂ 2 + 2;
20:44:38.577  ▸ 4
20:44:41.998  ◂ 2 - 2;
20:44:42.002  ▸ 0
20:44:54.307  ◂ 2 * 2;
20:44:54.311  ▸ 4
20:45:00.795  ◂ 2 / 2;
20:45:00.799  ▸ 1
>
```

Programmers refer to numbers as *operands* and symbols as *operators*. The entire combination is called an *expression*. A sequence of expressions terminated by a semicolon is a *statement*. The following diagram should help you get the vocabulary straight.

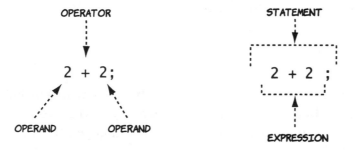

Any number of operands and operators can be chained together, but they're not evaluated left to right. Some operators are more important than others and are always evaluated first.

In the first example, the multiplication is performed before the addition, so the result is 8. The terminology is that multiplication has a *higher precedence* than addition.

```
CSS ▾   JS ▾   Web
◄ 2 * 2 + 2 * 2;
► 8
◄ ((2 * 2) + 2) * 2;
► 12
```

To explicitly control the order of evaluation, you can use parentheses to group operations. The second example shows a forced left-to-right evaluation.

In addition to adding numbers, the + operator can add text together. Text values in a JavaScript program are referred to as *strings*. Strings are always demarcated by either double or single quotes—it doesn't matter which as long they're used in pairs, as the first two examples show.

```
CSS ▾   JS ▾   Logging ▾
◄ "Hello!" + ' HTML5' + " and" + " CSS3";
► "Hello! HTML5 and CSS3"
◄ 'Hello!' + " HTML5" + " and" + ' CSS3';
► "Hello! HTML5 and CSS3"
◄ "Hello!" + " HTML" + 5 + " and" + " CSS" + 3;
► "Hello! HTML5 and CSS3"
◄ "HTML5" * "CSS3";
► NaN
```

Strings and numbers can be added to each other in certain circumstances, although using any of the other arithmetic operators with strings leads to a not-a-number (NaN) result.

If the string is also a number, it can be used with normal arithmetic operations, but the results won't always be what you expect. JavaScript makes up its own mind about whether you mean arithmetic or string addition.

In the first two examples, string addition is used rather than numeric, because addition can be performed on both numbers and strings and one of the operands is a string.

The multiplication operation can only be used with numbers, so the strings are converted automatically to numbers.

```
◄ "2" + "2";
► "22"
◄ "2" + 2;
► "22"
◄ "2" * 2;
► 4
◄ "2" * "2";
► 4
```

THE AUTOMATIC CONVERSION OF NUMBERS TO STRINGS CAN LEAD TO SOME UNEXPECTED AND UNWANTED BEHAVIOR, OR *BUGS* IN PROGRAMMER PARLANCE, IN YOUR JAVASCRIPT PROGRAMS. IN THE SECTION "BRANCHING AND LOOPING," YOU'LL LEARN HOW TO FORCE YOUR OPERAND TO BE A NUMBER.

Comparisons

Comparisons are operators that produce a true or false value, otherwise known as a *Boolean* value. Comparison operators are crucial when it comes to branching and looping (see "Branching and looping"). There are general-purpose comparison operators as well as several operators that are intended for Boolean values. The three main Boolean operators are as follows:

&&	AND	Returns true if both operands are true
||	OR	Returns true if either operand is true
!	NOT	Returns true if its operand is false

```
◄ true && false;
► false
◄ true || false;
► true
◄ !true;
► false
◄ !false;
► true
```

Experiment with these operators in the console until you're comfortable with these meanings.

You can compare two values for equality with these operators:

```
◄ true != false;
► true
◄ true == !false;
► true
◄ !(true == false);
► true
◄ !(true && false);
► true
◄ !(true || false);
► false
```

==   EQUAL   Returns true if both operands are the same

!=   NOT EQUAL   Returns true if the operands are different

Note that if you begin comparing things of different types, you may get unexpected results.

Because JavaScript helpfully converts types for you, the equality operators aren't always reliable.

```
◄ "HTML" == "HTML";
► true
◄ 2 == 2;
► true
◄ 2 == "2";
► true
◄ 2 === "2";
► false
```

===   IDENTICAL   Returns true if the operands are the same type and have the same value

Again, if you compare things of different types, you may get unexpected results. In the example here, 2 == "2" (comparing an integer with a string) evaluates to true, since JavaScript converts the integer 2 to a string "2" before comparison. But 2 === "2" evaluates to false because an integer is not a string.

You can check whether something is smaller or larger than another thing:

```
◄ 1 < 2;
► true
◄ 1 > 2;
► false
◄ "HTML" < "CSS";
► false
◄ "HTML" < "SVG";
► true
```

<	LESS THAN	Returns true if the first value is less than the second value
>	GREATER THAN	Returns true if the first value is greater than the second value

When you compare strings with < and >, JavaScript takes the numeric value of the characters and compares them. This means *H* is greater than *C*, but *H* is less than *c*, because lowercase letters are all larger than uppercase letters for comparison purposes. As with the arithmetic operations you saw earlier, bugs can occur if you're expecting to compare numbers but in reality are comparing strings. JavaScript doesn't complain in either case.

```
◄ "H" < "C";
► false
◄ "H" < "c";
► true
```

You can also compare smaller and larger and equal to:

```
◄ 2 < 2;
► false
◄ 2 <= 2;
► true
◄ 2 >= 2;
► true
```

<=	LESS THAN OR EQUAL TO	Returns true if the first value is less than or equal to the second value
>=	GREATER THAN OR EQUAL TO	Returns true if the first value is greater than or equal to the second value

Now you can perform arithmetic and comparisons, but what can you do with them? Comparisons are used extensively in branching and looping, which we'll examine in the section "Branching and looping," but if you compare the same fixed values in your program you'll see the same results every time. You need to store variable factors in the program so you can provide different results according to different starting conditions: you need variables.

Variables

A variable is a place to store the result of a calculation. If you remember any of your high school algebra, the concept of a variable ought to be somewhat familiar. You may remember algebra problems something like this:

```
5 = 2 + x
```

In math, working out the variable's value results in the answer. In this case, it's clear that x = 3. But in JavaScript, you express it like this:

```
var x = 5 - 2;
```

This code is saying "Create a storage space called x; calculate the result of 5 – 2; store the result in the storage space called x. The var keyword allocates a variable."

After you've stored a value in a variable, you can use it in another calculation, as shown here. First a value is assigned to x and then to y, and then the variables x and y are used in a calculation that assigns a value to z.

```
◄ var x = 5 - 2;
► undefined
◄ var y = 2 + 2;
► undefined
◄ var z = x * y;
► undefined
◄ console.log(z);
  12
► undefined
```

The console.log(z) statement is an example of calling a method on an object. For now, you don't need to know what that means (you'll learn more in the section "Functions and objects"); just be aware that it prints out the current value of whatever variable you put in the brackets.

Unlike in algebra, you have to define all the variables that appear on the right side of the equals sign before you use them. The sequence of operations here shows what happens if you don't.

```
◄ var a = b + c;
✗ ReferenceError: b is not defined
◄ var b = 3;
▶ undefined
◄ var a = b + c;
✗ ReferenceError: c is not defined
◄ var c = 4;
▶ undefined
◄ var a = b + c;
▶ undefined
◄ console.log(a);
  7
▶ undefined
```

When JavaScript can't understand your code or is unable to execute it, an error occurs. Usually this immediately stops the execution of whatever program is running. You can see in this example that the error that c isn't defined wasn't discovered until b was defined, because the initial error stopped execution.

After you create a variable, you can assign it a new value at any time. When you use the variable in a calculation that assigns a new value to itself, remember that the assignment operator sets the new value, and that always happens last—the value isn't updated until the end of the calculation.

```
◄ var a = 2;
▶ undefined
◄ a = a * a * a;
▶ 8
◄ a = "HTML5";
▶ "HTML5"
◄ a = a * a * a;
▶ NaN
```

If you put a number in a variable, nothing stops you from adding a string to it. But as with previous situations where JavaScript is equally happy with a string or a number, this can lead to confusing errors.

YOU'VE GAINED SOME FAMILIARITY WITH VARIABLES, BUT YOU SHOULD KNOW ABOUT A FEW MORE OPERATORS. THESE OPERATORS DON'T HAVE ANY ANALOGUE IN ARITHMETIC; THEY'RE ONLY USEFUL WHEN YOU HAVE VALUES STORED IN A VARIABLE.

Special operators for variables

Two operators that won't be familiar to you from school arithmetic are the *post-increment* (++) and *post-decrement* (--) operators. They increase and decrease, respectively, the value of a number by one. *Post* means they perform the change *after* the value has been used in an expression.

Study the sequence of operations in this screenshot. Notice that the values assigned to a and b are those of i before the increment or decrement.

```
◄ var i = 0;
► undefined
◄ console.log(i);
  0
► undefined
◄ var a = i++;
► undefined
◄ console.log(a);
  0
► undefined
◄ console.log(i);
  1
► undefined
◄ var b = i--;
► undefined
◄ console.log(b);
  1
► undefined
◄ console.log(i);
  0
► undefined
```

You also need to know about the += operator and its relatives.

The need to store the result of an expression into a variable when it's one of the operands is so common that a shortcut is built into JavaScript. Instead of writing

```
a = a + b;
```

you can write

```
a += b;
```

This works for the other arithmetic operators, as you can see in the screenshot.

```
◄ var a=2,b=3;
► undefined
◄ a += b;
► 5
◄ a -= b;
► 2
◄ a *= a;
► 4
◄ a /= a;
► 1
◄ var s = 'H';
► undefined
◄ s += 'el';
► "Hel"
◄ s += 'lo';
► "Hello"
```

In this section, you've learned how to do calculations and comparisons and store the results in variables. That is fundamental to writing programs but not very useful by itself.

IN PROGRAMMING, WE CALL CHOOSING BETWEEN DIFFERENT ACTIONS *BRANCHING* AND REPEATING ACTIONS *LOOPING*. YOU'LL LEARN ABOUT THEM IN THE NEXT SECTION.

You need to be able to take different actions depending on the results, or perform actions repeatedly to make it worth your while to write a program in the first place.

Branching and looping

If your program did some calculations and always produced the same output, there wouldn't be a point to it. A program can't do much unless it can make decisions based on the variables being passed into it. When a program executes one block of code rather than another based on the value of a variable, that's what we call *branching*. *Looping* is a related concept: executing a block of code multiple times. In this section, you'll step back from the console for a few pages and learn about the various branching and looping concepts in JavaScript so that in the following sections you can see how they're used.

A *BLOCK OF CODE* IS ONE OR MORE STATEMENTS CONTAINED WITHIN BRACES LIKE THESE: { }.

The term *branching*, unsurprisingly, comes from an analogy to a tree branch. Imagine you're walking along the branch of a tree: eventually you come to a point where it divides into two. You can choose to go up one branch or the other one. That's all branching is in programming—choosing to go one way or another. The simplest branching construct is the if statement.

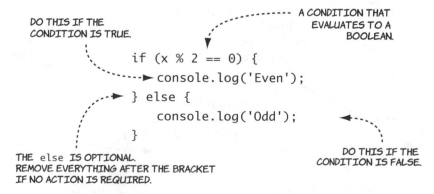

DO THIS IF THE CONDITION IS TRUE.

A CONDITION THAT EVALUATES TO A BOOLEAN.

```
if (x % 2 == 0) {
    console.log('Even');
} else {
    console.log('Odd');
}
```

THE else IS OPTIONAL. REMOVE EVERYTHING AFTER THE BRACKET IF NO ACTION IS REQUIRED.

DO THIS IF THE CONDITION IS FALSE.

If you need to check for more than one condition, you can nest the `if...else` statements.

THE FIRST CONDITION
IS THE SAME AS BEFORE.

```javascript
if (y % 2 == 0) {
    console.log('Even');
} else if (y % 3 == 0) {
    console.log('Divisible by 3');
} else {
    console.log('Not a multiple');
}
```

IF THE CONDITION
IS FALSE, CHECK
ANOTHER CONDITION.

An alternative to `if...then...else` is the `switch` statement. It lets you choose from a long list of alternatives based on the value of a variable. It doesn't allow the flexibility of `if...then...else` in comparison operations but does offer a more easily comprehensible way of presenting multiple choices.

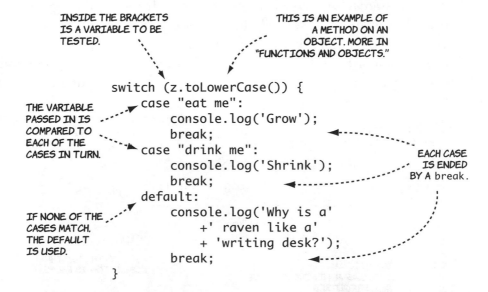

INSIDE THE BRACKETS
IS A VARIABLE TO BE
TESTED.

THIS IS AN EXAMPLE OF
A METHOD ON AN
OBJECT. MORE IN
"FUNCTIONS AND OBJECTS."

THE VARIABLE
PASSED IN IS
COMPARED TO
EACH OF THE
CASES IN TURN.

EACH CASE
IS ENDED
BY A break.

IF NONE OF THE
CASES MATCH,
THE DEFAULT
IS USED.

```javascript
switch (z.toLowerCase()) {
    case "eat me":
        console.log('Grow');
        break;
    case "drink me":
        console.log('Shrink');
        break;
    default:
        console.log('Why is a'
            +' raven like a'
            + 'writing desk?');
        break;
}
```

That's all you need to know about branching, so on to looping. Looping lets you repeat an operation multiple times. The most common loop is for.

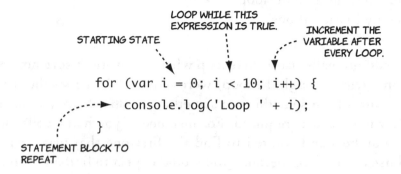

This screenshot shows the output in the console from the for loop. It logs 10 lines, counting up from 0 to 9. This is the normal programmer way of counting 10 things, starting at 0, so get used to it!

It's also normal to use the loop index variable, i in this case, to modify the code's behavior on each iteration through the loop.

An alternative to the for loop is the while loop. As you can see from the following diagram, it has all the same features as the for loop, but the arrangement is slightly different.

This screenshot shows the output in the console from the `while` loop. Incrementing by two each time through the loop means only five iterations.

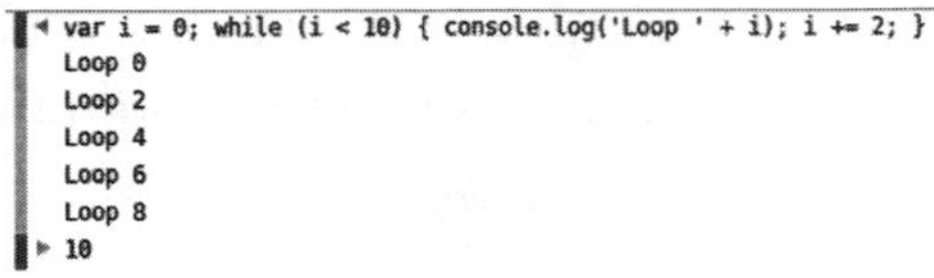

```
◄ var i = 0; while (i < 10) { console.log('Loop ' + i); i += 2; }
  Loop 0
  Loop 2
  Loop 4
  Loop 6
  Loop 8
► 10
```

You would normally use a `while` loop when you weren't sure how many iterations (trips through the loop) were required. Whereas the `for` loop always counts from something to something, a `while` loop does as many or as few iterations as required. For instance, if you had a collection of 10,000 numbers and wanted to find the first one that was even, you would use a `while` loop because you would expect to find an even number in the first few you looked at.

There's a variation on the `while` loop called the `do...while` loop. As you can see in the next diagram, it's similar to the `while` loop; the main difference is that the test to see whether the loop should continue is at the end.

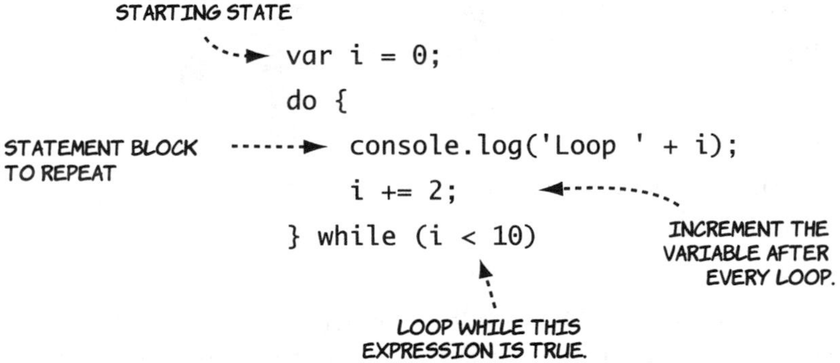

STARTING STATE

```
    ····► var i = 0;
          do {
STATEMENT BLOCK ······►  console.log('Loop ' + i);
TO REPEAT
          i += 2;       ◄········
        } while (i < 10)        INCREMENT THE
                                 VARIABLE AFTER
                                 EVERY LOOP.

            LOOP WHILE THIS
            EXPRESSION IS TRUE.
```

The previous `do...while` loop produces exactly the same output as the earlier `while` loop. For a large number of iterations, this will always be true. The main difference comes when the `while` loop may not be executed at all.

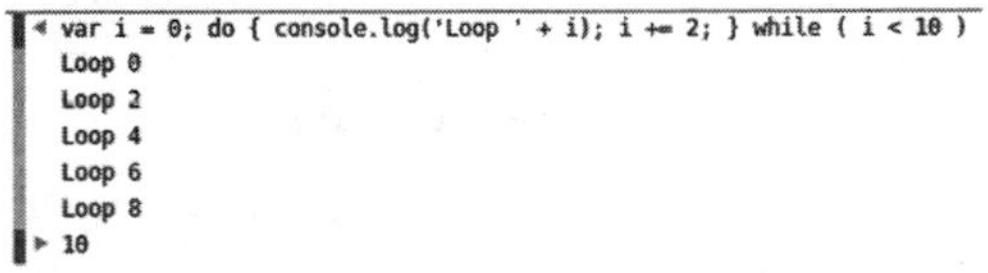

```
◄ var i = 0; do { console.log('Loop ' + i); i += 2; } while ( i < 10 )
  Loop 0
  Loop 2
  Loop 4
  Loop 6
  Loop 8
► 10
```

Following on the left is a `while` loop; on the right is a `do...while` loop with the same code block and test expression. You can see from the console output that the `while` loop doesn't execute its code block because the test expression is `false`. But the `do...while` loop does execute its code block, because the test expression isn't checked until the end of the loop.

```
while (false) {
    console.log('Loop');
}
```

```
do {
    console.log('Loop');
} while (false)
```

```
◄ while (false) { console.log('Loop'); }
► undefined
```

```
◄ do  { console.log('Loop'); } while (false)
Loop
► undefined
```

The loop never executes if the condition expression evaluates to `false`.

The loop always executes at least once.

YOU NOW KNOW ABOUT ALL THE LOOP TYPES IN JAVASCRIPT BUT ONE. THE FINAL LOOP TYPE IS `for...in`, BUT IT'S ONLY USEFUL WITH OBJECTS. YOU'LL LEARN ABOUT OBJECTS IN THE NEXT SECTION.

Functions and objects

So far, we've covered basic arithmetic operations and comparisons, variables in which to store results of those operations, and structures that allow you to control program flow based on variables and comparisons. Next you need to learn how to structure those components into complete programs. This is where functions and objects come in.

Functions

A function takes input, transforms it in some way, and produces output. Here's an example.

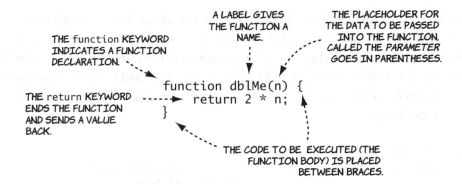

THE function KEYWORD INDICATES A FUNCTION DECLARATION.

A LABEL GIVES THE FUNCTION A NAME.

THE PLACEHOLDER FOR THE DATA TO BE PASSED INTO THE FUNCTION, CALLED THE PARAMETER GOES IN PARENTHESES.

THE return KEYWORD ENDS THE FUNCTION AND SENDS A VALUE BACK.

```
function dblMe(n) {
    return 2 * n;
}
```

THE CODE TO BE EXECUTED (THE FUNCTION BODY) IS PLACED BETWEEN BRACES.

This function is short enough that you can experiment with it in the console. To run the code in the function (or *call* the function, as a developer would say), you use the function name followed by parentheses containing the argument you want to pass. The argument is assigned to the parameter within the function body.

```
9  ◄ function dblMe(n) { return 2 * n; }
2  ► undefined
2  ◄ dblMe(2);
7  ► 4
0  ◄ dblMe(3);
4  ► 6
```

It's worth explaining that again: the *parameter* is the placeholder in the function definition. The *argument* is the value passed into the function when it's called. In practice, people ignore this subtle distinction and use the two terms interchangeably; we'll try to keep them straight, but don't worry about the difference too much.

Real functions generally contain more complex logic, but the examples here are short so it's feasible for you to type them into the console. Here's a slightly more complex example.

```
5  ◄ function evenMe(n) { if (n % 2 == 1) { return n + 1; } else { return n; } }
0  ► undefined
4  ◄ evenMe(2);
9  ► 2
5  ◄ evenMe(3);
0  ► 4
```

When you write your own functions, it's more common to put each operation on a single line, like this:

```
function evenMe(n) {
    if (n % 2 == 1) {
        return n + 1;
    } else {
        return n;
    }
}
```

But JavaScript, like HTML, doesn't care about whitespace; that just makes it easier for humans to read. It works no matter how many lines it takes up, but for the console you need to get everything onto one line. Functions can take more than one argument.

```
9  ◄ function baseMe(n,a) { while (n % a != 0) { n++; }; return n; }
4  ► undefined
7  ◄ baseMe(3,3);
1  ► 3
4  ◄ baseMe(4,3);
9  ► 6
7  ◄ baseMe(5,3);
4  ► 6
```

Here's the previous function written in a more conventional style to make it easier to read. The function rounds the argument n up to the next multiple of a:

```
function baseMe(n,a) {
    while (n % a != 0) {
        n++;
    };
    return n;
}
```

Precedence, which you saw in the simple arithmetic examples earlier, also applies with functions. This is important when you want to pass the result of one function as an argument to another.

Functions are evaluated from the inside out. This probably seems intuitive; but to confuse the situation, it's possible to pass functions as arguments to other functions.

```
1  ◄ dblMe(evenMe(3));
6  ► 8
8  ◄ evenMe(dblMe(3));
3  ► 6
```

Here's a simple function that expects a function as a parameter:

```
function applyMe(f,n)
   {return f(n);}
```

To pass the function as an argument, you specify the function name without adding parentheses.

```
8  ◄ function applyMe(f,n) { return f(n); }
2  ► undefined
1  ◄ applyMe(dblMe,3);
5  ► 6
3  ◄ applyMe(evenMe,3);
8  ► 4
```

Passing functions as arguments is a common pattern in calling HTML5 APIs. It's also common to declare simple, single-use functions directly. This is called an *inline function*: it's declared and then thrown away. You can use it only within the function it's being passed to, not elsewhere in your program, because there's no label to refer to it.

```
1  ◄ applyMe(function (n) { return n * 3; }, 3);
6  ► 9
```

That's all you need to know about functions—time to move on to objects.

Objects

Functions let you group your code into convenient units that can then be called in your program, but you'll also want to group data and functions together. In JavaScript you do this with objects. In loose terms, an object is a collection of stuff. The stuff can be variables, functions, and other objects. JavaScript has several built-in objects, HTML provides another set of objects, and the browser still more. You can also create your own objects; let's start with that.

The simplest way to create an object is with an *object literal*. An empty object is a pair of braces. The object can contain variables and functions, but when they're part of an object they're referred to as properties and methods.

```
2  ◄ var myObject = {};
7  ► undefined
6  ◄ console.log(myObject);
1    [object Object]
7  ► undefined
```

In JavaScript, you can access a property or method on an object by using a period (.) followed by a label. You can create properties and methods by assigning a value, as shown here.

```
2  ◄ myObject.myProperty = 2;
6  ► 2
3  ◄ myObject.myMethod = function(n) { return n * 3; }
2  ► (function (n) {return n * 3;})
5  ◄ myObject.myMethod(myObject.myProperty);
4  ► 6
```

This is the same code in an easier-to-read format:

```
var myObject = {};
myObject.myProperty = 2;
myObject.myMethod = function(n) {
        return n * 3;
}
```

You can then call the method, passing in the property like this:

```
myObject.myMethod(myObject.myProperty);
```

Now that you have an object to play with, it's time to learn about the final type of loop: for...in. The following screenshot of the console shows a for...in loop in action on the myObject object just created.

```
◄ for (var prop in myObject) { console.log(prop + ':' + myObject[prop]) }
  myProperty:2
  myMethod:function (n) {
      return n * 3;
  }
► undefined
```

For...in loops through the properties and methods of an object. The variable prop is set to the label associated with the property or method. You'll see it used most often in scripts that check to see if a browser supports certain HTML5 features. Note that the syntax myObject ['myProperty'] is an alternative way of accessing the myProperty method. This alternative approach is handy for use inside for...in loops.

Before we finish with objects, it's important to know that variables that refer to objects behave slightly differently than variables that refer to normal values like numbers. To see the difference, let's do a little experiment in the console.

1 Create a variable a, and give it the value 2.

2 Create a variable b, and give it the value of a.

3 Set the variable b to have a value of 4 instead.

```
var a = 2;
 undefined
var b = a;
 undefined
b = 4;
 4
console.log(a);
 2
 undefined
```

Notice that after you do this, the value of a is unchanged. Setting b to have a value of a doesn't create any sort of relationship between them. The value contained in a is copied into b.

Now try a similar sequence of operations with two variables that refer to objects. Notice that after assigning myObject as the value of myOtherObject, changing the value of myOtherObject .myProperty also changes the value of myObject.myProperty. This is because assigning the object to another variable creates two variables that refer to the *same object*.

```
var myObject = {};
 undefined
myObject.myProperty = 2;
 2
var myOtherObject = myObject;
 undefined
myOtherObject.myProperty = 4;
 4
console.log(myObject.myProperty);
 4
 undefined
```

There are several other features of objects, as well as a few different ways to create them, but you won't need to know them for this book. Just bear in mind that whenever you see periods, you're almost always looking at objects with properties and methods.

YOU NOW KNOW ENOUGH TO START PUTTING JAVASCRIPT TO THE USE IT WAS INTENDED FOR—MANIPULATING WEB PAGES. BUT TO DO THAT, YOU NEED TO UNDERSTAND HOW TO LINK JAVASCRIPT TO A WEB PAGE.

How JavaScript fits into HTML

The point of learning JavaScript is using it in browsers to do things with web pages. In this section, you'll learn how to get your JavaScript into HTML. You can do this three primary ways: inline in a <script> element, linked in a separate file, and inline in an event handler. Let's look at each in turn.

Inline <script> element

The most straightforward way to add JavaScript to your web page is to include it inside a <script> element. Here's a simple example:

```
<!DOCTYPE html>
<html>
<head>
    <title>Inline script</title>
</head>
<body>
    <script>
        window.alert("Inline script!");
    </script>
</body>
</html>
```

If you create a web page using this code and load it in your browser, you should see something like the following screenshot (if you're using IE, you may need to click the warning bar to allow JavaScript in a local file).

After the previous section, you should have noticed that window is an object and alert is a method. This is built-in functionality provided by the browser.

JavaScript linked in a file

In the same way that CSS can be kept in a separate file so it can be used in more than one web page, so can JavaScript. When you load the page in your browser, it looks much the same as the previous example.

For this you need two files. The first is an HTML page:

```
<!DOCTYPE html>
<html>
<head>
    <title>Linked script</title>
</head>
```

```
<body>
    <script src="myscript.js"></script>
</body>
</html>
```

Then you need a file called myscript.js containing this line of code:

```
window.alert('Linked script!');
```

Inline event handlers

The final way to include JavaScript in a page is through an inline event handler. *Events* are things that can happen in a page, such as a user clicking a button. You'll learn more about them in the section "Events"; for now, you just need to know that you can create a handler for a click event by adding an `onclick` attribute to an element. This is what the page looks like.

When you click the button, the alert pops up. Here's the code:

```
<!DOCTYPE html>
<html>
<head>
    <title>Inline event handler</title>
</head>
<body>
    <button onclick="window.alert('Inline event!');">
        Click me
    </button>
</body>
</html>
```

You should notice two things about this code. First, no `<script>` elements were required: the JavaScript is directly in the markup. Second, the quotes around the argument to alert are single quotes, unlike the double quotes used in the previous example. In JavaScript, you can use either single or double quotes—it doesn't make any difference as long as you start and end a given string with the same type of quote. But double quotes are used in the HTML for the attribute value, so using double quotes in the JavaScript would make the HTML invalid.

ALL THREE APPROACHES FOR INCLUDING JAVASCRIPT IN A WEB PAGE THAT YOU'VE SEEN IN THIS SECTION USE THE DOCUMENT OBJECT MODEL (DOM) TO CAUSE THINGS TO HAPPEN WITHIN THE PAGE. THE NEXT SECTION LOOKS AT THE DOM MORE CLOSELY.

The DOM

The Document Object Model (usually referred to as the DOM) is the way you access a web page through JavaScript. As the name implies, it's based on an object called window. You already used the alert method of the window object in the previous section. The window object contains properties and methods provided by the browser, the most important of which is the document object. The document object contains properties and methods provided by the web page. To experiment with the document object, create a simple web page:

```
<!DOCTYPE html>
<html>
<head>
    <meta charset="utf-8">
    <title>DOM Example</title>
</head>
<body>
    <div id="first">
        <h1>First div</h1>
        <p>Paragraph in
            first div</p>
    </div>
    <div id="second">
        <h1>Second div</h1>
    </div>
</body>
</html>
```

Open the console, and type in this code:

```
document.getElementById('first');
```

```
5  ◄ document.getElementById('first');
4  ► [object HTMLDivElement]
```

As you can see, the getElementById method returns an object. This object also has methods and properties that you can call:

```
var d =

document.getElementById('first');
console.log(d.innerHTML);
```

```
5  ◄ var d = document.getElementById('first');
2  ► undefined
2  ◄ console.log(d.innerHTML);
5
         <h1>First div</h1>
         <p>Paragraph in first div</p>

2  ► undefined
```

The elements inside the <div> can also be accessed through methods and properties of the element. This code grabs the first child of the <div>:

```
var h = d.children[0]
```

```
5  ◄ var d = document.getElementById('first');
1  ► undefined
9  ◄ var h = d.children[0];
2  ► undefined
8  ◄ console.log(h);
1    [object XrayWrapper [object
     HTMLHeadingElement]]
5  ► undefined
```

The DOM isn't just a way to access the document. You can also use it to modify the page. Here's a quick example.

Here's the code in more detail:

CREATE A
PARAGRAPH
ELEMENT.

```
var d = document.getElementById('second');
var p = document.createElement('p');
var t = document.createTextNode(
    'Paragraph in the second div');
p.appendChild(t);
d.appendChild(p);
```

CREATE A
TEXT NODE.

ADD THE TEXT NODE
TO THE PARAGRAPH.

ADD THE
PARAGRAPH TO
THE <div>.

THE DOM IS A HUGE SUBJECT, BUT THIS INTRODUCTION HAS GIVEN YOU AN IDEA
ABOUT WHAT IT DOES AS A FOUNDATION FOR LEARNING MORE. CHECK THE FINAL
SECTION OF THIS APPENDIX FOR ADDITIONAL RESOURCES. IT'S TIME TO COMPLETE
YOUR UNDERSTANDING OF JAVASCRIPT WITH A QUICK TOUR OF EVENTS.

Events

You saw an event handler in "How JavaScript fits into HTML"—in that case, an inline event handler. A *handler* is a function that's called when an event happens (when the event *fires*). In this section, you'll see how to deal with events in an external JavaScript file. When you're attaching handlers from an external JavaScript file, you need to use the DOM.

Use the simple page you created for exploring the DOM in the previous section, but add a reference to an external JavaScript file:

```html
<!DOCTYPE html>
<html>
<head>
    <meta charset="utf-8">
    <title>DOM Example</title>
    <script src="events.js"></script>
</head>
<body>
    <div id="first">
        <h1>First div</h1>
        <p>Paragraph in first div</p>
```

```
    </div>
    <div id="second">
        <h1>Second div</h1>
    </div>
</body>
</html>
```

Of course, you also need to create the JavaScript file. Start with this code in it:

```
var d = document.getElementById('first');
console.log(d.innerHTML);
```

If you load the page now, you'll see this in the console.

```
01:56:56.201  × d is null                                        events.js:2
```

This happens because at the point where the JavaScript executes, no element has the ID first. The JavaScript is executed as soon as it's referenced, in the <head> element. You need the JavaScript to await execution until after the document is loaded. Fortunately, there's an event for just such a scenario.

NOTE THAT EVENT-HANDLING CODE WORKS VERY DIFFERENTLY IN OLDER VERSIONS OF IE. WE DON'T HAVE ROOM TO GO INTO THE DETAILS HERE; CHECK THE "FURTHER READING" SECTION FOR MORE ON THE DIFFERENCES.

Wrap the code you want to run in a function:

```
function go() {
    var d = document
        .getElementById('first');
    console.log(d.innerHTML);
}
```

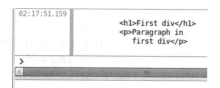

Then use the addEventListener method to attach your function as a handler for the window's load event:

```
window.addEventListener('load', go);
```

You can see in the console that the code now runs as expected. Notice that a function is being passed as an argument, as discussed earlier.

Now let's extend this example to add a button element and then add a click handler to the element. The following screenshots show the page before and after clicking the button.

This is the code to put in the events.js file:

```javascript
function add_element() {
    var d = document.getElementById('second');
    var p = document.createElement('p');
    var t = document.createTextNode('Paragraph in the second div');
    p.appendChild(t);
    d.appendChild(p);
}
function go() {
    var b = document.createElement('button');
    var t = document.createTextNode('Click me');
    b.appendChild(t);
    b.addEventListener('click', add_element);
    var d = document.getElementById('second');
    d.appendChild(b);
}
window.addEventListener('load', go);
```

CALLED ON BUTTON CLICK

SAME CODE YOU USED TO MODIFY THE DOCUMENT EARLIER

CREATES BUTTON AND ADDS EVENT LISTENER

LISTENS TO LOAD EVENT

The final thing you need to be aware of is event *bubbling*. When an event occurs, such as a click event, it *bubbles* up the document tree. This means the click event is fired from the element where the event occurred all the way up to the document root. This example attaches to the document a click handler that determines what type of element was clicked.

Returning to the example, edit events.js one more time:

```
function click_handler(event) {
    var el = event.target;
    switch (el.nodeName) {
        case "DIV":
            window.alert('Div');
            break;
        case "H1":
            window.alert('Heading');
            break;
        case "P":
            window.alert('Paragraph');
            break;
    }
}
function go() {
    document.addEventListener('click', click_handler);
}
window.addEventListener('load', go);
```

TARGET PROPERTY ❷

❶ EVENT OBJECT AS PARAMETER

❸ NODENAME PROPERTY

❹ HANDLES CLICK EVENTS

Any function added as an event handler receives the event object as a parameter ❶. The target property of the event object ❷ is the element where the event originated. The element object has a nodeName property ❸ that tells you the type of element clicked. You attach click_handler to the document to handle all click events ❹.

The main benefit of this approach is that it reduces the number of event listeners required. This can reduce memory and processing requirements for large and complex pages. You'll see it used frequently in large-scale web applications.

YOUR RAPID INTRODUCTION TO JAVASCRIPT IS NOW COMPLETE. DON'T WORRY IF YOU'RE STILL CONFUSED—IT'S UNLIKELY THAT YOU'LL PICK IT ALL UP IN A FEW PAGES. AT LEAST NOTHING YOU SEE IN THE REST OF THE BOOK SHOULD BE UNFAMILIAR TO YOU. FEEL FREE TO REFER BACK HERE ANY TIME. IF YOU WANT TO GO INTO JAVASCRIPT IN MORE DEPTH, CHECK OUT THE RESOURCES IN THE NEXT SECTION.

Further reading

For a detailed discussion of the differences between event handling in IE and all the other browsers, refer to quirksmode.org: www .quirksmode.org/js/introevents.html.

For a complete reference of all the methods and properties of the DOM, check out the Mozilla Developer Network: https://developer .mozilla.org/en/DOM/.

For an alternative introduction to JavaScript, try "Thau's JavaScript Tutorial": www.webmonkey.com/2010/02/javascript_tutorial/.

THAT CONCLUDES THE APPENDIXES FOR HELLO! HTML5 AND CSS3. AFTER READING THEM YOU SHOULD HAVE AN UNDERSTANDING OF HOW THE WEB WAS BUILT AND HOW WE ARRIVED AT THE CURRENT STANDARDS AS WELL AS A WORKING KNOWLEDGE OF THE TECHNOLOGIES WHICH MAKE UP MODERN WEB PAGES: HTML, CSS, AND JAVASCRIPT. WELCOME TO THE WORLD OF WEB DEVELOPMENT, I HOPE YOU ENJOY IT!

Index

RELATED MANNING TITLES

HTML5 in Action
by Robert Crowther, Joe Lennon, and Ash Blue

ISBN: 978-1-617290-49-7
375 pages, $39.99
December 2012

jQuery in Action, Second Edition
by Bear Bibeault and Yehuda Katz

ISBN: 978-1-935182-32-0
488 pages, $44.99
June 2010

Sass and Compass in Action
by Wynn Netherland, Nathan Weizenbaum,
    Chris Eppstein, and Brandon Mathis

ISBN: 978-1-617290-14-5
300 pages, $44.99
December 2012

Hello! iOS Development
by Lou Franco and Eitan Mendelowitz

ISBN: 978-1-935182-98-6
300 pages, $29.99
February 2013

For ordering information go to www.manning.com